How to
Talk
American

Also by Jim Crotty

With Michael Lane:
Mad Monks on the Road
Monk's Guide to New York CD-ROM
Monk, the Mobile Magazine

With Colleen Cotter, Eagle/Walking Turtle,
and Albert J. Schutz:
The USA Phrasebook

How to Talk American

A Guide to Our Native Tongues

Jim "the Mad Monk" Crotty

A Mariner Original
Houghton Mifflin Company
Boston • New York
1997

For information about permission to reproduce selections from this book,
write to Permissions, Houghton Mifflin Company, 215 Park Avenue South,
New York, New York 10003.

Book design: Lisa Diercks. Set in Journal Text from Emigre.

Library of Congress Cataloging-in-Publication Data
Crotty, Jim.
    How to talk American : a guide to our native tongues / Jim "the Mad Monk"
Crotty.
    p.   cm.
    ISBN 0-395-78032-2
    1. English language—Dialects—United States. 2. English language—Spoken
English—United States. 3. Figures of speech. 4. Americanisms.   I. Title.
PE2841.C76 1997
427'.973—dc21   97-19794
                                                                          CIP

Printed in the United States of America
QUM 10 9 8 7 6 5 4 3 2 1

*I always wanted to write a book my mom
would be proud of.*

Well, Mom, here it is (sort of).

*And to Michael "Monk" Lane, for putting out big time
in all areas—from proofing, researching,
and transcribing to faxing, Fedexing,
and, above all, believing.*

Sir, you are one of the world's great rainbow brothers.

Acknowledgments

S PECIAL ALL-AROUND THANKS GO OUT TO TOM JAWETZ, Ben Sternberg, John Kennedy, and Ray Misra for their able and thorough research assistance. And to my incredibly supportive, patient, and generous editor, "Mahnie" Patterson Cochran, my heroic and gracious manuscript editor, Luise Erdmann, and my brilliant designer, Lisa Diercks. For specific entries, I want to thank Rusty Logan from the Little Rock Free Press, "Arkana" columnist Richard Allin, and the folks at August House Publishing for some humorous Bubbaspeak (portions adapted from their classic, *A Field Guide to Southern Speech*), Amy Green for insight into the Beltway, Urban "Did Someone Say Klang?" Hutchins and Chris "Geech" Dorr for a wildly entertaining look at Maine, the newly married John Love (aka John Kennedy, which in Gaelic means "uglyshaped head"—absolutely not true for John, as Cinnamon can attest) and his buddy Sum-One for the graffer's mind-set, Don Francis and the "Unsinkable" Marty Brown for their generous helpings of Portland vernacular, Dominic "Doc" Boswell (aka "the Park Guy") for military jargon, Lex, the Cosmic-Psychic, for some incredibly inaccurate predictions, JJ, Kill, and the gang at the Habit (my hands-down favorite cybercafé in the universe, 21st and Clinton in P-town), Her Highness Ellen "from Eugene" Klowden for gutter punks, Roger C. Thompson, one of the Kentucky Brush Brothers, and his lady, Marlene, for a taste of the Bluegrass State, Mr. Bribach back there in Kansas, Rick "Clearly Under the Code" Crotty for some sports slang, Des, Paul, Dick, and Irene Crotty for Iowa and "Dakota" (with brilliant help from Hawkeye expatriate David Immel), Paul Young and Kevin Allman for some amazing Los Angelese, recycling madwoman Marcia "Sasha" Dolphin for some "pretty okay" and "altogether not bad" help with Minnesota, Gareth Branwyn, Jonathan Steur, et al., for help in assembling the finest selection of cyberspeech in the known universe (portions copyright © 1993, 4 Wired Ventures, Ltd., all rights reserved), John Clarke for diner slang, Al "Thrift On" Hoff and Rick Sebak for Pittsburgh, Aon and Kenny, Brad Pease and Bruce Roberts for some excellent "dish" terms, Kyle MacDonald, Jahnava Heller (who wants to thank Al Carter for the word "cobbin'" and who stole one of my computers—I want it back, Heller!) and Darcy Nelson for their totally awesome insiders' view of skateboarding, Trevor "Sparkle Factor" Cralle for the freshest terms from the world of surfing (the mother of all dude vernacular), Hunter Mann of Highway Cinema and Steven "Dragonslayer" Lane for insight into truckers, and, of course, Heidi "Cobbler to the Stars" Snellman for the "bitchin'" Docs, Gus "the Premier" Van Sant for trying to get me a "real job," Chris "the Man" Monlux for being, well, the Man, Thomas "Aquinas" Dalzell for generous access to the House of Slang, for guiding me into the secret order of slangsmiths, and for being a truly high brother in all ways, Paul Dickson for emergency ver-

nacular care, and the deity of all deities (move over, Bob Dobbs), the guiding face of this journey, Scott Thomason, for the red Subaru Monkmobile.

The path of American vernacular is wide, large, and well paved. Since there are already excellent books on Pidgeon, Preppie, and Politically Correct, I left out mention of these and other essential examples of modern American speech.

Hopefully in this guide you will find many words you do not find anywhere else. Finally, in every issue of *Monk, the Mobile Magazine*, I write a "How to Talk" column, showcasing the vernacular of the region we are featuring. If you would like to subscribe to *Monk* and receive these quarterly slices of Americana, send $10 for four episodes, $18 for eight episodes, or $100 for a lifetime after lifetime of episodes to *Monk*, 175 Fifth Avenue, Suite 2322, New York, New York 10010. To subscribe by phone, call 212-465-3231. Of course, I'm always looking for new and bodacious American vernacular. So please drop me a line if you get your hands on any. Or e-mail me at Monkmag@aol.com.

As a Tribute to Leona Helmsley, I want to thank "the Little People" Who Made This Book Possible

Donny Akers

Steve Albini

Kurt Anderson

Jeff "Book of Virtues" Bennett, Andrew "Pancho" Villa,
and the ESPN Research Department

Nils Bernstein

Jack Boulware

Glenda Bradshaw

Josh Brann

Marla Chiasson Brown

Steve Conroy

Carolyn Crotty

Julia "Give Us Bread, but Give Us" Rose Dalzell

J. Dawg

John "Choppy Market" Dolphin

Doty Drahota

John Exworthy

Becky Fabick-Rank

Jake Foster "Freeze"

Elizabeth and Lou Gibbens

Susan Green

Lynnel Herrera

Susan Hoffman

Mark Kates

→

David Loftus

Gale Mayron and Astri Kingstone of Bowery Productions

Greg "the Big Hairy Man" McMickle

Jay Peterson

Bobby Pittelkow

Anthony Rhodes

Clarissa Richardson

Duncan "Numkin Pies" Sylvester

Laurie Taylor

Kym Trippsmith

Hank Trotter

Heather Wakefield

Walter Heber Wheeler IV (aka "Quad")

Writer's Preemptive Strike

IF THERE IS ONE FAULT IN THE AMERICAN DEMOCRATIC experiment, it is the insistence on making all speech recognizable to all, regardless of age, class, and educational background. Because of this tendency, I launch this salvo to all reviewers: because you or a few of your friends have not heard of a word defined here does not mean it doesn't exist. Take my word for it, every term in this book is used by more than a few members of any subculture. Yes, there are some very obscure entries, but their inclusion only adds to the flair, not to any confusion. It's the mind-set of people who seek out terms they've heard before (and check to see if I included them too) that is at the heart of the growing monoculture sweeping this country. If anything, this book is a forceful assault on that disturbing trend.

Contents

ILLUSTRATION CREDITS

FRONT MATTER

Author: <u>Monk</u> magazine

Author and mom: Bev Crotty Collection

Scott Thomason: Pete Stone

ALASKA

Mrs. Frances Kokochurak making Eskimo ice cream: Eskimo
Heritage Program

Eskimo golf: Tom Barto/Nome Visitor Center

Man with salmon: Anchorage Convention and Visitors Bureau

Anchorage skyline: Anchorage Convention and Visitors Bureau

BLACK RAP CULTURE

"Bad Habits" cartoon of "wigger": Norman Dog

Sir Mix-a-Lot: BBored@oz.net

BOSTON

Celtics logo: Boston Celtics

Governor Weld with author: Rose Marston

The Pru: Richard Mitchell

Walden Pond sign: Jim Crotty

CAR CULTURE

White Cadillac: Jim Crotty

Beaded car: Harrod Blank

Pop-top trailer: John Deming

Monkmobile: <u>Monk</u> magazine

CHICAGO

"Greetings from Chicago" postcard: Bev Crotty Collection

Orange juice squeezer building: Bahai House of Worship

Jane Byrne: City of Chicago

Richard J. Daley: City of Chicago

CRIME

Cop: Suzanne Plunkett

Cartoon of judge: John Callahan

Patty Hearst: Susan G. Ehmer, <u>San Francisco Chronicle</u>

CYBERSPEECH
Hacker: Michael Lane

DEADHEADS
Jerry Garcia: Jay Blakesberg

DETROIT
Detroit skyline: Vito Palmisano
Tire: Ken Brown

DINERS
Diner interior: Coffee Cup Publishing
Elephant: John Clarke
Man sitting on stool: Coffee Cup Publishing

DISNEY
Disney dollar: Walt Disney Company
Epcot Center: Walt Disney Company
Disney characters: Walt Disney Company

DRUGS
Captain Jack postcard: Ken Brown

ECOBABBLE
Environmental racism: Sam Kittner
Environmental wacko: Jim Crotty
Cartoon of environmentalist: John Callahan

FILM AND TV
<u>Casablanca</u>: Los Angeles CVB
Drive-in: Jonathan Thomas Bokenkamp
Mann's Chinese Theater: Los Angeles CVB/Michele and Tom
    Grimm
Ginger Rogers and Katharine Hepburn: Los Angeles CVB

FLORIDA
Gator crossing: Michael Lane
Conch: Florida Department of Tourism
Flamingo: Michael Lane
Fat tourists: Robert Lost

GAMBLING
Roulette postcard: Anthony Bondi Collection

GAYS
Drag diva Paige Turner: Jim Crotty
"Silence = Death": ACT-UP
Trannie: Jim Crotty

GRAFFITI
Wall of graffiti: Marissa Roth
Graffer at work: Michael Lane

HOOPS
Woman and man with basketball: NCAA Photos
Stomach and ball: Jim Crotty
Player dunking: NCAA Photos

LAS VEGAS
Liberace (p. 155): The Liberace Museum
Casino sign: <u>Monk</u> magazine
Tower of Bobel: Stratosphere Casino

LOS ANGELES
"Camp O.J.": Jim Crotty
L.A. skyline: Los Angeles CVB/ Michele and Tom Grimm
John Wayne statue: Jim Crotty
Hollywood sign: Los Angeles CVB/ Michele and Tom Grimm

LOVE
Kissing statue: Jim Crotty

MAINE
Boat in water: Michael Lane
Lobster sign: Jim Crotty
Shack with buoys: Jim Crotty
Maineiac: Michael Lane

THE MIDWEST
Author in drag with pitchfork: Doris Bouma
People and tractor: Beverly Crotty
Cartoon of weather conversation: Bob Boze Bell, <u>Westword</u>
Cartoon of Midwesterners at funeral: Bob Boze Bell, <u>Westword</u>

Bob Devaney: Bev Crotty Collection
Mrs. B: Omaha World Herald

MINNESOTA
Paul Bunyan statue: Ken Brown

THE MOUNTAIN STATES
Hunter S. Thompson: Chris Buck
Potato on tractor: Ken Brown

THE MUSIC BIZ
Bodysurfing: Charles Peterson
Kurt Cobain and Courtney Love: Michael Lane

NEW YORK CITY
Manhattan: New York Convention and Visitors Bureau
Donald Trump: Jay Manis
MTA signs: Jim Crotty
Social x-ray: Jim Crotty
Man washing windshield: Jim Crotty

ODDS AND ENDS
Dashboard publishing: Linda Bleck
Monk magazine cover: Monk magazine
Trekkers: Jim Crotty

PITTSBURGH
Aerial view of Pittsburgh: Courtesy of WQED
Primanti sandwich: Rick Sebak
Tunnels: County of Allegheny Division of Photography

PORTLAND, OREGON
Waterfront: Portland, Oregon, Visitors Association/Larry Geddes
Tom Peterson: Jim Crotty
RIP OCA: Monk magazine
Nike sign: Jim Crotty
Skateboarders: Michael Lane
Windsurfer: Michael Lane

PSYCHOBABBLE
Swami Beyondananda/David Frankel
"Going Beyond a Shadow of a Doubt" cartoon: Andrew Lehman

RAINBOW NATION
Man holding flowers: Heather Wakefield

SAN FRANCISCO
Bonnie Baker road race entrants: Jim Crotty

"Breeders": Atlantic City Convention Center

Cyclists: Chris Carlson

Herb Caen billboard: Jim Crotty

Louis and Jane: <u>Wired</u> magazine

The Twins: Florence McCall

SANTA FE
Cartoon of Indian weaving bar code: Jerome Milord

Adobe buildings: <u>Monk</u> magazine

SEATTLE
Dick's Burger Joint: Michael Lane

Bob's Java Jive: Michael Lane

Kurt Cobain making latte: Shot in the Dark Photography/<u>Monk</u>
   magazine

Space Needle: Michael Andel/In Your Face Photography

THE SOUTH
Bullfrog: Gerard Quinn

Welcome to Arkansas sign: Michael Lane

Hawg: James Neff

Rocking chairs: Jim Crotty

Visiting: Jim Crotty

SPORTS
Gashouse Gang: Baseball Hall of Fame Library

SURFING
Skate rats: Jim Crotty

Surfer: Scott Winer

TRUCKERS
Wheel and road: Martin Jehnichen

<u>Willie Shaw Express</u> letterhead: Steven Lane

12 STEPS
Cartoon of codependent auto parts: Andrew Lehman

WALL STREET
Author and FedEx driver: Michael Lane

WASHINGTON, D.C.
Donkey: Ken Brown
Jefferson Memorial: Washington Convention Assocation
Jerry Brown: Jim Crotty
Ronald Reagan: Jim Crotty

CONCLUSION
Earth from afar: NASA

Introduction

DO WORDS MAKE OUR REALITY? OR DOES REALITY make our words? Frankly, my dears, this book doesn't give a damn.

How to Talk American puts aside in a nice academic corner all those debates about how words originate, what is the American tongue, and, by extension, whether English should remain our official language and instead shows, free of ax-grinding polemic, how we in America talk.

It is a wily beast, this American language thing, inventive and fast-changing and as varied as the melting pot of our nation. And it is indubitably us—at times passionate, at times clinically cold, at times rich, at times frighteningly bland, at times clear, at times completely obtuse. You can't teach this stuff. You have to live it. This book is my gift to all Americans who yearn to know it.

How to Talk American is the definitive look at how we really talk in this country, and I mean *really* talk, and how we have created a language—God save the mother tongue!—that is the communication currency of the world. What's happening next in worldwide vernacular? It's right here between these covers, dude.

I wrote this book while going through a painful yet strangely humorous breakup with a tall, blond, and black-booted German woman named Elke, who was every bit my match in style, upbringing, aesthetic appreciation, and pigheadedness, but there was one gap we could never quite bridge, and that, of course, was language. I would make a subtle innuendo and it would be missed entirely. A sly commentary would be taken literally. She even misheard Shakespeare as "love alters when it alteration finds." Of course, the correct quotation is "love does *not* alter when it alteration finds," and, quite ironically, she lived out the first interpretation quite literally. Rightly so, I might add.

For I am beset with a few alterations from the norm. Living on the road for twelve years does that to a man. You keep talking about stability but haven't the faintest clue what it actually entails. You live the life of adrenaline, of a quick-change artist, not that of a placid and patient gardener.

There is one salient advantage to this existence—I've seen and heard a lot. I have caught the nuances of America's hilariously eccentric, and amazingly wide, linguistic heritage. Other, better-trained authors can go on at great and fascinating length about the character of various expressions as they cut across linguistic bioregions, or they can trace etymology over centuries or make a cogent if a tad bit PC defense of various kinds of "street" slang. I am not interested in nor am I up to that task. What I offer is a snapshot of a place, occupation, and culture. I don't look exclusively for dialects or accents (though they are here too). Rather, I look for colorful words and expressions, insider terms, the overall rhetoric (both spoken and unspoken). If nothing else, this book should clearly reveal how different kinds of Americans think by noting the way they talk.

Undergirding this enterprise is a deep love of this country. I am as annoyed as the best of us with the degradation of our discourse by the far right and far left. But I am more annoyed at the small ways we try to censor one another on a daily basis. For example, a checkout woman at a health food store in Portland once gave me a spirited argument against calling her "gal" and went on to denounce "ma'am," "girl," and "babe," all of which, if used to denigrate, might rightly be rejected by any American, male or female. But here, I thought, is where my German friend might have gotten it right. When men and women jokingly called her "chick," Elke laughed at the deliberate and gentle humor in the utterance. She wasn't "oppressed" but tickled and intrigued. As a foreigner, she had "beginner's mind" toward the nuances of the American tongue. Don't get me wrong. I do not defend the demeaning speech of those using the same words with no humorous, creative, or loving intent, but I do believe we need to lighten up and see even these words in context. As the Buddha said, a true bodhisatt-va knows when to break the vows. By extension, a true speaker of "American" knows when it is kosher to use so-called "out words."

Dancing with words, both familiar and verboten, is enlivening. It gets the synapses working. And, ultimately, it empowers us all to dance more, swing more, love more, laugh more, roll with it more.

We are a vibrant and creative people, continually on the make, continually making it new. Our language should reflect that pioneering and playful spirit.

How to Talk American

Alaska

"To many, TV's <u>Northern Exposure</u> is what they envision as an Alaskan town: quaint eccentrics, wise native people, and moose. What they did not show you was that the quaint eccentrics are often neo-Nazis, lotsa natives are bitter alcoholics, and that moose routinely kick people to death."
—KEITH BEARDEN

"Alaska has only three seasons: winter, breakup, and road construction. Some people think even that's bragging, that the state has only two: mosquitoes and no mosquitoes."
—MIKE DOOGAN

AMERICANS HAVE ABSOLUTELY NO IDEA OF THE mythical hold this one state has on the imagination of other people in the world. I learned this firsthand from my girlfriend Elke's father, Dr. Hans Ditschuneit, of Ulm, Germany. On my first night in the *Vaterland*, I was introduced to the good doctor, whom my rather strong and steady girlfriend held in great awe. Dr. D. was not a large man, certainly not the rotund Helmut Kohl meets Sergeant Schultze stereotype we routinely use to characterize Germans in America. Closer to Colonel Clink in build, but far less goofy.

On meeting me, Dr. Ditschuneit went right to work showing off his prized possessions, his computer, his computerized weather tracking system. But what struck me was the giant polar bear hide on the living room floor and the dozens of buck antlers lining the walls.

"I can see you like to hunt," I offered cautiously.

"Have you ever been to Al-ah-skah?" he asked with a penetrating glint in his eyes.

"No," I said.

His eyes grew more intense, his voiced dropped several octaves, and then his face beamed with delirious, carnivorous glee as he whispered in a hushed voice, as if confiding some manly confidence, "Al-ah-skah, it is my favorite place in zee *WORLD!*"

I learned that one of the highlights of the good doctor's life was his fabled trip to the bush country of Alaska. There, alone with one other German and a guide, he was a man among beasts. Living out *The Call of the Wild*. Indeed, at that moment, as the doctor regaled me with his exploits, I too felt the gusto men feel on encountering this vast expanse of snow, ice, and tundra. And, above all, I felt the red-blooded exhilaration of the hunt.

This is the myth of Alaska—America's "last great frontier."

The truth of modern Alaska is slightly different, a truth not readily apparent to gung-ho Germans in search of wild game. For, though it has always been a refuge for the wild in nature, and an end-of-the-road destination for the wildest in human beings, unbeknownst to the good doctor (and to most Americans, for that matter), Alaska is becoming positively crass and commercial. There are still plenty of those gnarly men of the wilds, but just as common are espresso bars, Fairbanks condos, girls in spandex and high heels, and guys wearing Motley Crue T-shirts.

Alaska has been tamed, and it will get even tamer if the oil people have any say in the matter. Which is why today's Alaska is a battleground between the forces of profit and the forces of nature. The vernacular of the area clearly reflects this struggle.

Alaska: the name itself is vernacular, since it is probably a distortion of the Aleutian word *alyeska,* "the great land." Others claim it is the Aleutian word for "mainland," to distinguish Alaska from the Aleutian Islands to the south.

Alaska divorce: murdering one's spouse. Aka "Spenard [a suburb of Anchorage] divorce."

Alcan: the fabled Alaska-Canada Highway, aka "the Alaska Highway," the state's sole land link with North America. Originally used as a military supply route during World War II, it is now undergoing many improvements, which will make the journey far easier on your back, car, and intestines. Caveat: if you want to get anal about it, the Alcan specifically refers to the section that runs from Dawson Creek, British Columbia, to Delta Junction, Alaska.

ANWR (pron. "*ann*-wahr"): the Arctic National Wildlife Refuge. A very remote part of the state that is a fierce battleground between environmentalists and "the forces of darkness" (i.e., developers).

Arctic haze: industrial pollution that has migrated over to Alaska courtesy of our friends the Russians.

banya: Russian for a steam bathhouse, once regularly used in rural Alaska before the arrival of running water.

barn door: a huge halibut, usually in excess of at least 100 pounds. Aka "soaker."

bear paws: big round snowshoes worn while doing outdoor work.

Black Friday: the "Good Friday Earthquake" of March 28, 1964, whose epicenter was in Prince William Sound. At 9.2 on the Richter scale, it is considered the strongest in U.S. history.

blue ticket: one-way airplane ticket out of Alaska. Used in the past as a way to export criminals and other undesirables.

breakup: the snow is melting, the snow is melting! Never mind the stench.

breakup boots: rubber slip-on boots used to slosh around in the puddles that follow "breakup." Aka "Juneau sneakers."

bugdope: any idiot that goes far in summer without bug repellent.

bunny boots: large white insulated rubber boots originally used by the armed forces to guard against frostbite. When worn by the Baroness Von Elke Ditschuneit, they are known as "Honey Bunny boots." Though the Toronto company that made them went bankrupt, Alaskans save and still wear them. Aka "Korean boots" (referring to where they were first worn, during the Korean War), "vapor boots," or "Mickey Mouse boots."

the bush: Alaska's version of the Australian Outback, a vast roadless expanse that makes up most of the state. Accessible only by bush plane.

bush caucus: a contingent of Native Alaskans who work to preserve their rights in the state legislature.

the bush tuxedo: slacks and a jacket made of wool whipcord (the ideal fabric for Alaska because it is both tough and presentable—made by Seattle's Filson Company since the Gold Rush). The quintessential attire of the hardy Alaskan.

cheechako: a newcomer to Alaska. A greenhorn.

chickens: halibut smaller than 20 pounds or so. Example: "How was it out there?" "Oh, lots of chickens. One guy had one that looked like a barn door when it came to the surface, but it got off before we could get it into the boat."

Cicely: mythical town popularized by the TV series *Northern Exposure*. The show was actually filmed in Roslyn, Washington, much to the chagrin of the Alaska Division of Tourism. Want to see an angry Alaskan? Ask for directions to Cicely.

combat fishing: shoulder-to-shoulder, pole-to-pole fishing on Alaska's most popular waters.

"the congressman for all Alaska, except most of us": Don Young, Alaska's sole representative in Congress. When he was elected, the marijuana initiative on the ballot got more votes than he did.

Denali: traditional Athabaskan Indian name for Mount McKinley. Aka "the Mountain." "McKinley" was first used in 1876 by a miner who wanted to honor the 25th president for his support of a gold standard.

dog mushing: sled dog racing, Alaska's state sport.

dog salmon: chum, one of the least desirable types of salmon. It ends up either at the cannery or as fish bait. Chum doesn't taste bad, but the doglike appearance of the male at spawning and its customary use in feeding canines have given it this undeserved appellation.

ear weight: an event at the annual Eskimo Olympics in Fairbanks that determines how far one can carry a 16-pound weight attached to one's ear by a string. A more gruesome alternative is the "ear pull," where two contestants play tug-of-war with a string connecting their ears. Those crazy Alaskans!

Eskimo doughnut: a deep-fried biscuit, Inupiat Eskimo style. Basically a mixture of seal oil, flour, and water, baked or fried in seal oil. Aka "mukparuks."

Eskimo ice cream: this mixture of berries, snow, sugar, and whipped seal oil is not likely to make it into Baskin-Robbins any time soon. When trying this at home, use Crisco in lieu of seal oil.

Eskimo potato: a long white root vegetable popular with Native Alaskans and mice. The former end up stealing their share from the latter.

fish burners: nickname for sled dogs because they are often fed a steady diet of dried fish.

freezeup: that time in late October, early November, when the dog's water dish freezes up. Winter has arrived. Come spring you have "breakup."

frost heaves: bumps, dips, and twists in the road caused by the melting and contracting of the permafrost.

gee!: a directive to a dogsled team to turn right.

gee-haw: the lead dog in a dogsled team.

gussuk: the Eskimo word for whitey. Said to derive from the Russian Cossack.

haw!: a directive to a dogsled team to turn left.

honey bucket: a rural Alaskan commode in villages with no plumbing. Though the term is not unique to Alaska, these days it is where you are most likely to find one.

hooch: vile, poorly distilled booze. From the Alaskan word *hoochinoo*. Now applied to liquor in general.

ice pool: a yearly gambling game dear to Alaskans that asks you to bet when the river at a particular location will "break up" or "go out" come spring. The exact time is determined by a connection from a stake or tripod in the middle of a river channel to the bank, which stops a clock when the ice has moved a certain distance. Aka "ice classic" (as in the Nemana Ice Classic).

ice worms: 1-inch yellow, white, brown, or black worms that flourish inside glaciers.

Iditarod: the annual sled dog race, a thoroughly exhausting endurance event that covers the grueling 1,049 miles between Anchorage, Knik, and Nome.

igloo: not common to Alaska but rather to the Canadian Eskimo, who built structures out of snow and ice. The Alaskan Eskimo preferred dwellings of whalebone, driftwood, and sod (aka a "sod igloo").

Inuit: the people. The North American Eskimos' name for themselves. Asian Eskimos are known as Yuit.

jacks: young, not fully grown king salmon.

kings, reds, pinks, dogs, silvers: the five main types of salmon that play a major role in Alaska's economy, both for sport and commercial fishing. Alternatively known as Chinooks,

Sockeyes, Humpys, Chums, and Cohos respectively. Example: "How did you guys do?" "Oh, we got a couple reds, but we couldn't hook into any kings." Caveat: sockeyes got their nickname because they turn bright red during freshwater spawning. Trivia: pinks account for nearly half the annual salmon catch.

lowbush moose: a snowshoe rabbit. What a hunter says he "bagged" when he doesn't return with a real moose.

lower 48: the continental U.S. Example: "The cost of living is a lot higher in Alaska than in the lower 48." Aka "Outside" or "the lower 49."

moose droppings: now this is perverse. People in Alaska collect this stuff and fashion it into jewelry. There's even an annual Moose Dropping Festival in the town of Talkitna. One year, some misguided animal rights activists showed up, thinking moose were going to be dropped from helicopters, much to the enjoyment of festival organizers and participants.

mukluk: traditional Alaskan footwear made from the skins of either caribou, moose, or oogruk seal. From the Yupik word for "bearded seal," the skin of which was used widely for the soles of boots. Now applies to all similar high boots, even those made with canvas, rubber, or felt.

"Mukluk Telegraph": a radio program for rural Alaskans that delivers local news, including weddings and births, in lieu of telephones and regular mail delivery. Example: "To John in Elam, from Lucy in Nome: 'Meet me on the snow machine trail around six o'clock.'"

muktuk: the outer skin layers of a whale, eaten by Eskimos as a delicacy.

mush!: what a dogsled team commander utters to get the dogs moving. It literally means "to travel by dog sled."

musher: the commander of a dogsled team.

Native: one of the indigenous peoples of Alaska, including Eskimo, Aleut, or one of several tribes of Indians (Haida, Tsimpshian, Tlingit, or Athabaskan). One always spells indigenous Natives with a big *N* to distinguish them from those simply born in the state, which would be native with a small *n*. Aka "Alaska Native."

native Alaskan: "nonaboriginal Alaskan." In other words, whitey.

old believer: older members of a very specific sect of the Russian Orthodox Church, who carry on many traditional beliefs and customs. A good number speak only Russian. Found primarily in villages around Homer.

oosik: the penis bone of the walrus, a clublike mass that is the source of many jokes. Sold as a souvenir.

Outside: specifically, it's the evil, fanatical, "continental U.S.," but usually refers to simply going out of state. "He went Outside for a couple of weeks, but he'll be back come winter." Or, "More and more things are becoming like Outside. Much of Alaskan culture and customs, neighborliness and frontier hospitality, is disappearing" (Ginny Alexander, *Fairbanks Daily News-Miner*). Ironically, "Outside" is the place of origin for most Alaskans today.

Outsiders: residents of the lower 48. Ironically, in traditional Aleut culture, there is a term for "the Outside man," an evil spirit who lives outdoors and forever attempts to enter the houses of his relatives to do them harm.

the panhandle: the part of Alaska that extends down toward the lower 48 along the side of Canada. Where Juneau, the capital, is located. Also known as "southeast."

permanent fund: a yearly $1,000 flat cash dividend paid to every legitimate resident of the state. Generated by a 1982 amendment to the state constitution, which sets aside a portion of state oil and gas revenues for investment.

Pet Four: the National Petroleum Reserve, a 37,000-square-mile landmass that runs from the mouth of the Colville River to Icy Cape. Formerly known as U.S. Petroleum Reserve No. 4.

pilot crackers: big round dry crackers that are a staple in the bush. Aka "pilot bread."

plug-ins: electrical outlets reserved for car engine block heaters. You will often find this uniquely Alaskan innovation attached to a parking meter. Absolutely essential to keep your car running on some of Alaska's bitter cold winter days.

poochki: extremely tall wild celery.

posy-sniffer: a pejorative word for an environmentalist.

pukers: tourists. Stems from the fact that tourists often get sea-sick when they go out on fishing charter boats or other seagoing craft. Example: "Man, look at all those pukers, that campground is just packed."

quaq (pron. "*coe*-ock"): walrus meat or fish that is frozen and eaten raw, usually accompanied by seal oil. Alaska's version of sushi.

Seward's Day: a state holiday on the last Monday in March, commemorating the 1867 U.S. purchase of Alaska from Russia (aka "Seward's Folly" and later "Seward's Icebox") for roughly $7.2 million.

Sleeping Lady: Mount Susitna, which overlooks the city of Anchorage from Cook Inlet.

the Slope: the north slope of the Brooks Mountain Range. Aka "the Arctic Slope." Also refers to the northern part of Alaska in general, including the coastal plain, where there is a large oil industry, especially around Prudhoe Bay. Also a synonym for Prudhoe Bay itself, site of the largest oil find in the northern hemisphere.

socked in: unable to travel due to bad weather.

sourdough: an old-timer in Alaska, especially one who has spent a lot of time out in the bush. From the gold prospectors' custom of keeping a sourdough starter for making bread, biscuits, and the like.

the spill: though there have been many oil spills in recent Alaskan history, there is only one that really sticks in the craw—the *Exxon Valdez* spill of 1989.

spillionaires: people who made an exorbitant sum of money working on "the spill" either by leasing fishing boats for cleanup work or doing other highly paid work, such as consulting Exxon on the preparation of its defense. Aka "Exxon whore."

spotter: a pilot who uses his aircraft to isolate or "spot" schools of herring for commercial fishermen.

squaw man: a pejorative term for a white man married to a Native Alaskan woman. A "creole" is a Russian man married to a Native woman. Used only in written form today.

stink heads: an Eskimo version of aged cheese. You bury fish heads in the tundra until they stink, then dig them up to eat. Tasty. Word of warning: don't drink and eat fish heads. Gives ya the runs. Other fermented foods include "stink *eggs*" and "stink oil."

Baked Alaskan,
or How to Talk Homer

Since I was unable to make forays deep into the heart of America's last great frontier, I solicited the help of a native Alaskan, Josh Brann. Here's his look at the fascinating vernacular of his hometown of Homer.

I have been reawakened to the world of Homer slang. It's crazy. A good portion is based on the word "chud," which is a synonym for "drunk" or "stoned," usually "stoned." From that comes "chudification," "chudified," "chudweiser," and "chudev" (a variation on "whatev," short for "whatever," used basically in any way all the time). And anything else you can think up with "chud" is probably acceptable too. Then there's "darry," which is sort of like "that sucks" but not used quite the same way. Example: "I got pulled over last night, man." "Darry, dude." Apparently "darry" was originally a variation on "sorry" and can be used similarly.

There is also the word "lations." Homer is kind of a pot town, and "lations" is a synonym for "pot." But you can also use it abbreviated as "laish" (phonetic) as a synonym for "stoned," as in "Let's get laish." On the same subject, the term "'ode it" is the same as "load it," referring to loading a "bowl" of pot.

Further vocab are "fall" and "pull," which are antonyms. "Fall" is short for "fallthrough" and "pull" is short for "pullthrough," referring to whether something happened or not. You can also add an *s* to the end if you use the full version. Example: "Did you guys go to that party?" "No, it was fallthroughs, but we pulled and found a buyer." You can also add "age" to the end of any word—such as "chudage" or "laishage."

Then there's "stressing," "stressed," "stresscase," "stresshard," "stressage," and "getting stressed." That's getting in trouble or being nervous. If somebody gets on your case, they are stressing you. "My brother got stressed by a couple of guys the other night. He was driving fast around a corner, and a couple of older teenage guys pulled him over, came over, opened the car door, started yelling in his face, and threatened to beat him up if he didn't drive more safely."

$\rightarrow$

And don't forget "peaked" (pron. "peak-ed"), which is a real word meaning to have a sickly appearance. This is also used a lot to describe being drunk or stoned, particularly being hung over, but it can refer to anything unpleasant. For example, "That rotten halibut carcass smells peaked." You also have "beatings," "beatdowns," and "meltdown-from-the-beltdowns," which I think are all pretty self-explanatory.

One very important word is "lube." It's used like "hook up." Example: "They were lubing in the back seat of his truck." There are also the variations: "lubing," "lubey," "lubage," "lubified," "lubification," etc. "They were gettin' lubey." "I opened the door to the bedroom and there was some serious lubage going on."

One of my favorites, the word "probably," has kind of died out, but it is still used on occasion, especially if something is very unlikely to happen. It is said very sarcastically, and it is always shortened to "probly." "Man, I think I can pull a C+ if I don't fail this test." "Probly that, dude, not gonna happen."

"Blar" is an adjective used to describe any person or thing in an extreme state. Example: "He's blar, he's so drunk he doesn't know what's going on." Or, "When I woke up in the morning I was blar." The s-on-the-end rule can apply to just about any word. Example: "He's lassouts hard." (He's passed out.) "Hard" is an affirmation, used to express gratitude or enthusiasm. Example: "Our buyer was pullthroughs. Hard!"

The expression "Whaaaaaaaa?!?!" comes from "Whadd-ya???" which comes from "What???" This is used if someone is doing or saying something stupid. It's kind of an insult. Or if someone is insulting you, you can say it to them to make their insults seem stupid. For example, my brother's friend Jeff was getting stressed by another guy, and finally he just said to him, "Whaaaa?!?!?!" Then the other guy stressed him hard, he was like, "Did you give me the Whaaaaa?!?!?! Did you give me the Whaaaaa?!?!?!!!!!" I think it all originally comes from the phrase "What're you thinkin'?!?!"

A "laxer" is a cigarette and is often used in the phrases "Tax me a laxer" (Give me a cigarette) and "I'm going to tax a laxer" (I'm going to smoke a cigarette). There is also a →

sundogs: mirror images of suns that appear on either side of the sun in winter due to the reflection of sunlight off airborne ice crystals.

swing dog: the dog directly behind the lead dog in a dogsled team.

termination dust: snowfall. Signals the end of summer, though Alaskans don't really take snow seriously until it no longer melts.

toe-pinching: trapping.

tundra: the vast, treeless, flat expanse that covers most of Alaska. "Alpine tundra" is above the treeline. "Arctic tundra" is low-lying. Aka "the bush."

up the road a ways: anywhere along the highway, up to a couple hundred miles away.

Valdez (pron. "val-*deez*"): the most famous and ideologically loaded word out of Alaska in recent memory. Officially a town of 3,000 along the south-central coast; more important, the shorter version of the oil tanker *Exxon Valdez,* which spilled its cargo into Prince William Sound Harbor back in 1989, the worst oil spill in U.S. history. Caveat: the *Exxon Valdez* crashed on a Good Friday. Ironically, the Black Friday earthquake also occurred on a Good Friday.

the valley: the Matanuska Valley, just north of Anchorage. Good farmland, the home of record-size produce, the Alaska milk industry, and "MTF."

---

current belief going around that if you light someone's cigarette, you'll have seven years of good sex with them.

The important thing to remember is that you can use any of these words in any way as long as your meaning is clear, and even that isn't really necessary. The basic idea is to not use your brain and not think before you speak.

So, as you see, Homer slang can be lots of fun if you work at it: "Hey, did you go to that party last night?" "No, that was fall, but I saw my old girlfriend with some guy going to go get lubey." "Darry, man, I thought you were on that?" "Probly that, dude, I'm goin' for Allison Trimble" (a real person). "Aw, you'll never pullthrough on her. Matt" (her boyfriend) "will stress you hard and you'll get beatdowns, plus she's peaked anyway." "Yeah, tax me a laxer." "Do you have any lations, let's go get chud."

WEIO: the annual World Eskimo Indian Olympics in Fairbanks. It features all manner of fascinating yet painful games, including the "ear pull" and the "knuckle hop" (aka "seal crawl").

wheel dog: the dog harnessed just in front of the sled in the traditional dogsled team.

white socks: a pesky form of biting black fly that is absolutely hellacious come summer. Its feet appear to be white, hence the name.

whiteout: a blizzard.

williwaws: sudden gusts of wind.

Yupik: the Eskimos of southwestern and western Alaska and the language they speak. Economy still based on hunting and fishing. Territory runs from Bristol Bay to Norton Sound.

Black Rap Culture
Aka "Hooked On Ebonics"

"DO YOU LOVE BLACK PEOPLE?" I CAN'T HEAR YOU. I said, "DO . . . YOU . . . LOVE . . . BLACK . . . PEOPLE?" "YES, WE LOVE BLACK PEOPLE!"

You better, because no single ethnic group has had a more profound impact on American slang in the 20th century than African Americans. From jive to swing to the Beats to rock and beyond, black speech is invariably hipster speech. And by logical extension the speech of the young, the most innovative slangsters in any generation.

The 1990s are no exception, as the lingo of rap and hip-hop becomes the dominant slang of teens and twentysomethings with attitude. Here's the speech of your average young black American and what is, or soon will be, the speech of your 12-year-old white, black, brown, or Asian son.

ace boon coon: best buddy. Aka "ace."

answer: one rapper's reply to another's song. Example: Common Sense's answer to Ice Cube in the song "I Used to Love H.E.R."

ax: ask.

B.C.: Before Crack. A very important demarcation in black culture.

bad: good. "Bad" is perhaps the longest running slice of black rhetoric alive today. Its origins go back to Gullah talk of three centuries ago, as a term of reverence and admiration for any slave that dared to flout Ole Maussa's rules. "That nigga is baaaad."

bammer: phony, poor quality. Example: RBL's classic "Don't Give Me No Bammer Weed." Aka "bootsie."

bangers: violent gang members.

banging: gang fight; also used in street basketball to describe highly aggressive play.

bank: (1) money. (2) a bad situation or idea. "Forget that job, man, it's bank."

Bad Is Good

So much of the youth culture slang of the last twenty years rests on "bad is good." It's the sine qua non of youthful rebellion—if they say it's bad, let's try it. Here are some words in use today that signify excellent, beautiful, and good, though they literally say "bad."

apocalyptic	filthy	nasty
bad	foolish	retarded
badass	furious	rude
cold-blooded	gnarly	the shit
crazy	harsh	sick
deadly	hype	stupid
dirty	ill	vicious
fat	killer	wicked
fierce	kooky	

the beast: the police. Aka "the poe-leece," "Jake," "Little Boy Blue."

beeyatches: sexy women.

bitch: woman, female, girlfriend. This demeaning term is so prevalent among black male youth and their wigger counterparts, some women just take it for granted.

bitch slap: a backward and forward slap on the face. "When he comes home, I'm gonna bitch slap him for making me wait."

bitch up: back down.

blow up: promote or become famous.

bluebird: something that's nagging you, a nuisance.

buggin': getting too excited or crazy. Aka "buggin' out."

burner: an illegally obtained cell phone.

bust: chide or make fun of someone.

bust a move: make a sexual move on someone.

buster: wannabe gang member. Also, a poseur, someone not worthy of respect.

butter: women. Aka "biddies," "Betties."

the butters: excellent, smooth. Aka "butter."

Captain Save-a-ho: a dude who will do anything for a woman thinking he'll get some "bootie" in return but who invariably ends up alone anyway.

chassis: a woman.

check it out: "listen up, my good man, I have something to say."

chickenhead: a not very attractive or desirable girl. There are several kinds of chickenheads, also known as "KFC brand chickenheads." "Original recipe" is a girl from the projects or an ugly girl in ugly clothes. "Extra spicy" is an ugly girl in pretty clothes. "Rotisserie Gold" is a pretty girl with a gold digger mind-set.

chill: take it easy, cool out. As an adjective, "chillin'" (massively hip).

chillin': as a verb, hanging out.

chip: a stolen cell phone, used to make free or illegal calls. Aka "faulty" or "burner."

chump: asshole, loser. Not a term of endearment. "Get outta my face, chump, before I kick your ass."

The Dozens

THE DOZENS IS THE ORIGINAL NAME FOR THE black game of busting, a vicious sport of personal attacks that often revolve around a unifying theme of "your mama" (or, in today's vernacular, "yo mama"). A gentler variant is known as signifying (an attack on the person, but not their mother). Here are examples of both busting and signifying:

"Yo mama so ugly, when she walks in the bank they turn off the cameras."
"Well, yo mama so ugly she has to sneak up on the mirror."
"If ugliness were bricks, yo mama would be a housing project."
"You so ugly when you were born, your parents named you 'Shit Happens.'"
"Yo mama so fat she's on both sides of the family."
"Yo mama so fat she's got her own area code."
"Yo mama so fat, when she goes to a restaurant she doesn't get a menu, she gets an estimate."

And so on.

Caveat: the Dozens has many possible roots. Two explanations are: (1) the slave owners' practice of selling the sickest or most disabled twelve slaves after the trip from Africa; (2) a direct association with the number 12, which is a bad roll in craps.

Wiggers

"Wiggity wiggity wack, you think you're black."
—LISA LIBERATORE, BANGOR, MAINE

M Y USE OF "WIGGER" CAME ABOUT FROM MY OBSERVATION of how middle-class white kids interacted with black rap culture. There was such a complete and total "copping" of black language and attitude, I realized these lily white kids had evolved into a whole new breed of human being (the wigger), with a general attitude of defiance, dismissal, and superiority, hand gestures that totally mimicked those of black rap stars, and, strangely, a common bond of basketball. But lately, on the other side of the fence, I've started to see increasing numbers of black teens skateboarding, snowboarding, and generally adopting the mores and attitudes of "dude culture." When you merge the elements of rap and dude, as more and more teens seem to do, you essentially have 90% of today's youth vernacular.

Therefore, I've now decided that a wigger is no longer just a "white nigga" but rather a hybrid of the two prevailing youth cultures: the anticapitalist, no-stress rebellion of the California dude merged with the gangsta rap posing of black ghetto youth to become the defining role model of late-20th-century youth culture. Over two hundred years of linguistic evolution have gone into his development. As the millennium approaches, the wigger can now stand tall, thin, and defiant, ready to laconically dismiss his place in history.

clock: to watch something or someone very closely, or to get soundly punched or beaten up.

cracker: a white person.

crazy: cool, excellent. Aka "cold-blooded."

crib: a house or apartment.

D-boy: a drug dealer.

da bomb: most excellent. "MJ is da bomb."

dead presidents: paper money. Aka "papes." "Honeybee" = $100; "dime" = $10; "nickel" = $5; "bone" = $1.

def: excellent, talented. Aka "thick."

dope: stylish, the truth.

dune piece: a pretty gal.

fat bank: rich, riches.

federal: successful. To have "gone federal" is to have "made it."

fetti: money. Short for "federal." Aka "scrilla."

flammy: flamboyant.

flex: show off.

flossin': driving a car fast. Example: "He's flossin' through the 'hood."

flossy: a very cool person or thing.

flow: money.

flygirl: an attractive girl.

free it up: come on and tell me.

fresh: stylish. Aka "dap," "dip," "dope," "phat," and "flave."

G: male friend, homeboy. "S'up, G?" Origins go back to the 1940s jive term of "hep gee" (someone in the know). Aka "Slim," "Cuz," or "B-Boy."

gear: clothing.

glock: a gun. Aka "gak" or "piece."

ho: (1) a loose woman (aka "skeezer"); (2) girlfriend (aka "biddie"). Caveat: having a black "biddie" is the absolute sure sign of homeboy status to a bona fide lily white wigger; (3) any woman. From "whore." A "milky ho" is a white woman.

Holmes: a good friend. Same as "homey."

homey: a friend from your neighborhood. Comes from the '40s jive term "homey," a friend from your hometown. Aka "home," "home biscuit," "home slice," or "homegirl."

hottie: a good-looking woman.

hubba: crack cocaine.

hypest: the newest.

ice cream man: a crack dealer.

janky: phony. See also "bammer" or "bootsie."

'jects: cheap things. From "projects."

jimmy: condom. Aka "jimmy hat."

kickin': takin' it easy. Aka "kickin' it," "marinating."

Kill-a-ho: a subgenre of rappers from Hunters Point, in SFC.

Lex Luther: Lexus, the newly coveted car in the 'hood.

mack: dress up. Once dressed, you are "macked out" or "pressed out."

mail: money. Aka "fetti."

Nathan: nothing.

new jack: a novice rapper.

nickel shot: a five-story housing project in "the Fillmoe" (the Fillmore district of San Francisco).

A Rapper's Guide to the U.S.

A-Town: Atlanta, the home of Arrested Development.

Boogie Down: the Bronx.

Bricktown: Newark.

Bucktown: Brooklyn. Aka "Crooklyn," "Chocolate City," or "Gunsmoke." Neighborhoods of Brooklyn include "Dead-sty" (Bedford-Stuyvesant, aka "Do or Die") and "'Bush" (Flatbush).

C-Town: Cleveland.

Chill-Town: Jersey City.

Crestside: a neighborhood in Vallejo, California.

'Dale: Sunnydale, a public housing project in South San Francisco.

Double Rock: the 254-unit Alice Griffith Housing Development across the street from 3Com, formerly Candlestick, Park. Double Rock was the site of the largest concentration of murders in San Francisco in 1994 (six were near Griffith and Fitzgerald). All the Double Rock murders are unsolved, even though many had witnesses.

Eastside O: East Oakland.

Fillmoe: the Fillmore District of San Francisco. Aka "the Western Addition." Or simply "Moe." Home of rappers Rappin' 4-Tay, JT the Bigga Figga and the GLP, and Dre Dog.

$\rightarrow$

nigga: short for "nigger," a heretofore pejorative term for black person reappropriated by black people as a term of endearment among themselves. Warning to European tourists: we know you want to be down with the homeys, but this is not a cool word to use under any circumstance.

Oreo: a black person whose soul is white. An "Uncle Tom." The opposite of an "X-Man."

peeps: my people, my tribe. "I gotta get with my peeps."

Penelopes: police. Aka "Popos." See E-40 and the Click.

pervin': drunk.

phat: fantastic, truly great, cool. Aka "dope," "flavor," "fresh," "hype," "da bomb," "all that."

ph'in: the act of playa hatin'.

playa hater: someone who hates "players" (i.e., "gangstas"), at least when they stop posing as gangstas and start being criminals. What deluded gangstas mistake as jealousy.

posse: friends, group of friends. Aka "crew."

props: proper respect. Aka "big ups."

punk: an asshole, loser. "Yo, punk, I'm gonna mess you up." Can be used as either authentic disparagement or a playful tease. A direct borrowing by black gangsta rappers from the real gangsters of the '30s and '40s.

rap vs. hip-hop: rap is a specific kind of music whose modern roots probably go back to Jamaica. Hip-hop refers to a whole way of being, with rapping and rhyming just one element of a lifestyle that includes tagging, break dancing, and djing.

represent: stand up for.

shut the fuck up!: like it says. This one is straight out of the 'hood, from parents to kids to other kids. Ironically, in the inner-city world where love and hate are so casually intertwined, this expression is usually taken lightly, often as a

---

H-Town: Houston.

Hillside: a neighborhood in Vallejo, the home of E-40 and the Click.

HP: Hunters Point, a neighborhood of SFC. Home of Herm Lewis, 11/5, and U.D.I.

Illtown: East Orange, N.J.

Jungle: Harlem.

Killa Cali: California.

Killin' Fields: East Oakland. So called because of the many random murders that occur there. See Black Dynasty's "Deep East Oakland."

New Jack City: New York City.

New Jerusalem: New Jersey.

Now Rule: New Rochelle, N.Y.

O.C.: "Outta Control" public housing projects formerly in "the Fillmoe" district of "SFC."

Oaktown: Oakland.

Poe: Baltimore.

SFC: San Francisco City or Sucka Free City, depending on what kind of a sucka you are.

Shaw: the Crenshaw district of L.A.

Swamps: the Sunnydale Projects in South San Francisco.

V-Town: Vallejo. The home of E-40 and the Click and Potna Deuce.

How to Talk American

playful taunt. As in "I'm gonna pop you upside the head, nigga, if you don't shut the fuck up!" Followed by laughter and playful wrestling.

stacking: making money.

stay black: a customary farewell. Akin to "keep the faith."

straight up: the real deal, no baloney. Aka "legit."

threads: clothes.

tight: excellent.

vega: a "vega" is to the West Coast what a "blunt" is to the rest of the nation: a cigar with the tobacco poked out and replaced with marijuana. From Garcia y Vega.

wassup: what's up? Aka "S'up" or "Zup." Alternately, "Wassup widdat?" (when used as more of a direct question). As in, "Wassup widdat curfew shit?"

whack: not a good thing. Aka "pork."

wigger: white black male wannabes. Stands for "white nigga." Think Marky Mark, Vanilla Ice, and most white kids on your block. Aka "yo-boy."

word up!: I agree; this is true. Aka "word to the mother!"

yo!: all-purpose term, though most often used as "listen up," "pay attention," "I've got something to say." What black slang users may not realize is that the ubiquitous "yo!" may go back to Italian immigrants in South Philly. In the Neapolitan dialect, *guaglione* (pron. "guahl-yo-may") meant a young man. The immigrants of the 1930s shortened it to "guahl-yo" (which they pronounced "whal-yo"), which was eventually abbreviated to "yo." A common greeting among South Philly's Italian Americans was "Hey, whal-yo" and eventually just "Yo!" Made popular by Sylvester Stallone in the movie *Rocky*.

Boston

Botown, St. Botolph's Town, Beantown—however you want to call it, Boston is the cradle of the American Revolution and the source of one of the most distinctive, if dying, regional accents in America. I note a few of its hallmarks here ("pahking" and "arear," for instance), but I also provide a lexicon of highly unique terms one finds only in the town that both Tommy Heinsohn and Billy Ruane call home.

Back Bay: you got the money, you can stay.

Bean Town: Boston. From Boston Baked Beans, a traditional dish here. Used only by outsiders. No true local would be caught dead saying it. Like "Frisco" for San Francisco.

Bird: Larry Bird, former star of the Boston Celtics. Like his archrival, Magic Johnson of the L.A. Lakers, what Bird lacked in speed and jumping ability he made up for in grit, determination, and an uncanny grasp of the game. In a town as racially polarized as Boston, it also helped that he was white. Aka "Larry Legend."

boot: a yellow steel wheel attachment locking your trusty vehicle in place due to your avoidance of Boston's vigilantly enforced parking codes. Aka "Denver boot."

Bosox: the Boston Red Sox. One of the great old professional baseball teams, with tremendously loyal fans, a colorful ballpark in the heart of the city, and a penchant for blowing every possible chance they have to win a World Series (see "the Curse of the Bambino").

Brahmins: the upper-class descendants of Boston's original aristocracy: 19th-century captains, ship owners, railroad magnates, and robber barons.

breakdown lane: ostensibly the highway shoulder but a complete misnomer. You do not want to break down in a Boston breakdown lane, especially during rush hour, when the breakdown lane becomes a high-speed lane.

bulkie: a sandwich bun.

the Bury: Roxbury, the home of "Vanilla Joyce."

the C's: the Boston Celtics, white America's favorite pro basketball team. Aka "the Celts" (pron. "Seltz").

cabinet: a milkshake.

candlepin bowling: a strange Boston phenomenon, where bowlers try to knock over slender little pins with tiny little balls. I'm tellin' ya, this town is "wee-id."

Cantabrigian style, elements of: buy a Volvo or Toyota and a big frame house, aspire to a MacArthur Fellowship or Washington appointment, maintain some semblance of radical chic through participation in a variety of PC causes, dabble in Eastern religions, have a few carefully chosen pieces of African art, and you've got it.

Cantabrigians: residents of the People's Republic of Cambridge.

the Car Guys (pron. "the Kah Guys"): quintessential Bostonians "Click and Clack" (i.e., Tom and Ray Magliozzi), the acerbic and hilariously opinionated hosts of NPR's "Car Talk." In a piece of astounding irony, several *Southern* stations pulled "the Kah Guys" off the air because listeners couldn't understand their thick Boston accents.

Central Artery Project: either the greatest boondoggle to beset the city since the days of Michael Curley or the long-awaited and costly answer to Boston's downtown traffic woes.

Charles River blowfish: sewage.

chef on premises: Bostonians are convinced that having the owner "on the premises" is a sign of culinary greatness. Having the owner also be the chef is a sign of even further greatness.

the Combat Zone: the Midtown Cultural District, Boston's shrinking porn and vice neighborhood.

Cooz: Bob Cousy, a former star guard and subsequent TV announcer for the Celtics.

the Curse of the Bambino: any dyed-in-the-wool Bostonian knows full well that the Red Sox have not won a World Series since Babe Ruth was traded to the New York Yankees, back in 1920. However, they have come close—in 1946, 1967, 1975, and 1986—but invariably something goes horribly wrong (such as ex-Cub Bill Buckner's bungling of a routine ground ball in the sixth game of the 1986 World Series).

directional: a car's blinkers.

Dot: Dorchester, where superstar rapper Marky Mark grew up.

the Duke: Michael Dukakis, the short, combative Massachusetts governor who ran for president in 1988 not so much on a platform as on the premise of "good government." Needless to say, he was trounced by George Bush.

elastic: a rubber band.

Evacuation Day: a statewide holiday on March 17 celebrating the day the Redcoats finally evacuated Boston.

frappe: milkshake to the rest of us.

give her some business: do her up nice in Boston beautician speak.

go to the packy: go to buy liquor. Aka "packy run."

the Green Monster: the towering green left field wall in Fenway Park, the oldest major league ballpark in America (along with Tiger Stadium).

the Head of the Charles: the world's largest crew regatta, held every fall on the Charles River on the last weekend in October.

hermit: a molasses cookie.

the Holy Trinity: roast beef, lamb, and "poc" (options for Sunday "dinnah").

Hoodsie: a small cup of ice cream eaten with a small wooden spoon. From the legendary local dairy, H. P. Hood.

the Hub: *Variety*'s term for Boston, the economic and cultural vortex of New England. Some local wags insist it actually came from Oliver Wendell Holmes, who referred to the State House as "the hub of the solar system." A plaque in front of Filene's commemorates the point. However, only newspaper people really use the term anymore. As in the apocryphal headline: "2 Hub men die in blast; New York also destroyed."

the Irish Hurricane: Boston's very own heavyweight prizefighter, Peter McNeeley, who in 1996 lasted a total of 89 seconds in the ring with Mike Tyson, though his poetry no doubt will survive well into the next century: "I'm Peter McNeeley, from Medfield, Mass. / On Saturday night, I'm going to kick Mike Tyson's ass." Whatever happened to "float like a butterfly, sting like a bee"?

jimmies: chocolate flecks placed on top of ice cream cones. Used throughout New England. Known as "sprinkles" in other parts of the country.

JP: Jamaica Plain, "the most integrated neighborhood in America." Aka "the poor man's Cambridge."

Kilroy was here: perhaps the most well-traveled expression

How to Talk American

ever to come out of Boston. According to one popular explanation, James J. Kilroy, an inspector in a Quincy shipyard, wrote the expression on ships and crates to indicate they had passed his inspection. Subsequently, "Kilroy was here" traveled all over the world, scribbled by GIs wherever they landed.

liberal: a person who believes government can and should do something. Boston is one of the last few cities where "liberal" is not a dirty word.

live 'n' kickin': the only kind of "lobstah" you'll find at area delis.

Mass.: short for Massachusetts.

Mass.-Ave.: Bostonians always abbreviate any avenue with a long name. As in "Comm.-Ave." for Commonwealth Avenue.

Massachusetts: a Native American word meaning big spending—excuse me, big hill people.

Massive Genital: the Massachusetts General Hospital. Aka "Mecca."

Tommy "Mumbles" Menino: the current "mayah" of Boston.

the MFA: the Museum of Fine Arts.

Micks with Dicks: a pejorative name for the *Boston Herald*, this town's version of the *New York Post*. The nickname comes from the alleged coterie of white, male, and gleefully politically incorrect Irish guys who make up the upper echelons of the tabloid's management, presumably including, but not limited to, arch-conservative publisher Pat Purcell and "homosexual agenda"-ranting columnist Joe Fitzgerald.

the Montreal Express: a fierce northern wind that determines much of Boston's winter weather.

NINA: No Irish Need Apply. A common sign around town in the late 19th century. In this blue-blood capital, racism of all stripes has still not quite gone the way of all flesh.

the North End: the oldest part of Boston, originally settled by the Puritans, and since 1920 the primary neighborhood for the city's sizable Italian-American restaurant community.

OFD: Originally from Dorchester. "The South Showah is swarmin' with OFDs."

the otha side: what an East Boston resident (or "Eastie") calls the rest of Boston because it's on "the otha side" of the Sumner Tunnel.

P-Town: Provincetown. The gay mecca of Massachusetts.

packy: packaged liquor store.

the Patsies: Boston's historically lame professional football franchise, the New England Patriots, aka "the Pats." In recent years, with Drew Bledsoe at quarterback, the team made an impressive turnaround.

perambulate the bounds: a Massachusetts surveyance custom. Every five years, town leaders walk their perimeters to make sure nobody has moved the boundary stones.

the Pru: the Prudential Center, a giant *Lost in Space* robot in Back Bay.

quahog (pron. "co-hog"): chemically saturated, oil-slicked, lawn-fertilized, UV-treated, hard-shelled red tide clam, preferred by Bostonians for its taste.

the Rat: the Rathskeller, Boston's old school punk and alternative club.

Rozzie: Roslindale, one of Boston's premier neighborhoods, containing houses with "plenny a chahm."

scrod: a small cod. There is no fish officially known as a "scrod."

Shawmut: the Indian name for Boston.

smoot: a unit of measurement. In 1958 a drunk pledge at MIT's Lambda Chi Alpha fraternity was required by his brothers to measure the length of the Harvard Bridge using his own body. Thus the 5'7" Oliver R. Smoot became the first human ever used as a unit of measurement. The smoot plaque on the Cambridge side of the bridge commemorates Smoot's singular achievement and the yearly Lambda Chi tradition. The Harvard Bridge is 364.4 smoots long.

soft: courageous, bold. "You were pretty soft to challenge the guvnah."

Southie: South Boston, a traditional Irish-American enclave and a breeding ground for politicians, cops, and homophobes.

spa: a mom-and-pop convenience store. Also used in New York City.

spuckie (pron. "spooky"): an Italian "sub" (from "spucadella").

strangers: the name given by the Puritans to *Mayflower* passengers motivated by money more than God. A belief system that turned out to be not so strange in the New World.

sub: a submarine sandwich. In Western Mass., "subs" are called "grinders." In Philadelphia, "hoagies." In New York, "heroes." In Rhode Island, "wedgies." In Miami, "Cuban sandwiches." In Wisconsin, "Garibaldis." In Los Angeles, "torpedoes." And in New Orleans, "po boys."

the T: Boston's rapid transit system. Aka "the rattler."

TA: Trans Am.

Taxachusetts: a label used by outsiders and a growing number of insiders for the state's liberal "tax and spend" tradition.

time: a party, usually to celebrate some major life event. "We're throwin' a time for the Kid down at Jimmy's. Count you in?"

tonic: soda pop or, specifically, a Coke. In some supermarkets, there are signs directing you to the "tonic" and "diet tonic" sections.

townies: most often, residents of Charlestown, but also those from "Reveah" and "da Point" (Whiskey Point in Brookline), so it's also a state of mind, or maybe hair. You can tell townies by the way they add "'n shit" to the end of many sentences. "Oh my gawd, like yestihday, right, he was totally down polishing his TA 'n shit."

the Triangular Trade Route: Harvard Business School to Wall Street to the witness protection program.

a Triple Eagle: someone who attended Boston College High School, Boston College, *and* B.C. Law School.

umbrella graveyard: a huge wind tunnel on Clarendon Street in front of the notorious John Hancock Tower (remember, the one where the windows kept falling out). The company has taken to placing barrels in front of the building, where angry pedestrians can chuck their broken umbrellas.

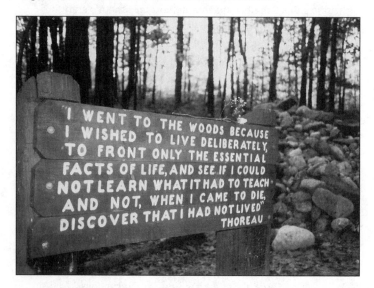

Walden Pond: a lake near a trailer park and the Lincoln town dump, where locals who live lives of quiet sexual frustration go to feel backwoodsy and "Thoreauvian." A preteen summed it up best when he came upon the archaeological monument to the remains of Thoreau's chimney: "It looks like a pile of dumb rocks."

WGBH: the pride and joy of PBS. Produces *Masterpiece Theatre, Frontline, Nova, Mystery,* and *This Old House.*

Wormtown: Worcester (pron. "wistah"), the second city of Massachusetts, an hour west of Boston.

Yaz: Carl Yastrzemski, Hall of Fame right fielder for the Red Sox.

Traditional Bwostinese

THE RULE IS SIMPLE: JUST DROP AN *R* BEFORE *CERTAIN* consonants and certain vowels and add it to the end of others, but *only* if the next word begins with a vowel sound. Confused? Read on.

ah: the letter between *q* and *s*. As in "Hahvuhd," "the Cahdnal," and "chowdah." Just think of that tongue depressor down your throat at the doctor's office and try this: "Pahk the cah near Hahvuhd Yahd."

Ann Tenor: the device that transmits radio waves to your car.

arear: an area. (The *r* at the end of certain words is a phenomenon also found in the outer boroughs of New York.) "What arear of the city you live in?"

awed: the opposite of "even."

ba-ba: the man who trims your hair.

bah rum: where you get liquored up.

boa: a dullard.

Bonnie: the purple dinosaur kids either love or hate.

Broons: the Boston Bruins, my favorite hockey team growing up. Former stars include Bobby Orr and Phil Esposito (aka "Espo"). Aka "the B's."

bud: bird. "That Larry Bud rarely makes an era."

Bwostin: Boston. Remember the *w*; only Brooklyn residents pronounce it "Bawstin." For example: "We ate hwot dwogs and pwop cwon at the Mahshfield Fayah." A sure sign of a native "Bwostinian" is that they know "Copley Square" is pronounced "Cop-ley (not "Cope-ly") Squayuh," Tremont is "Treh-mont" (not "Tree-mont"), and that the Boston Common and the Public Garden are both singular (never "Boston Commons" or "Public Gardens").

bzah: strange. "Willie Loco Alexander is bzah."

cahnt: pronounced like German philosopher Immanuel Kant, but it means "can't."

characta: an interesting personality.

clabbids: the wooden boards that cover houses.

con: a sweet, starchy yellow vegetable served during the first Thanksgiving near Plymouth Rock and popular ever since.

Coolidge Connah: Coolidge Corner.

cotton: typically, a container for milk.

dinnah: the meal served on Sunday between noon and 2:00 p.m. (depends when "the Pats" are playing). Traditionally consists of a roast of "the Holy Trinity."

draw: "the paht of a dressah where yah keep yah socks and sweatahs" (Sheila Pierce Stevens).

Dwochestah: Dorchester.

era: a mistake.

fah: not near.

How to Talk Harvard

"You can always tell a Harvard man, but you can't tell him much."

THOUGH A RECENT *U.S. NEWS & WORLD REPORT* SURVEY has people debating the point, Harvard University is still regarded as the pinnacle of American academic achievement. Think about it—Cheryl Wagner and Kate Tews went here. I even spent a summer here by some strange fluke. Here are terms used in the commons, in the Houses, and around the Yard by those rare Americans who can actually distinguish structural geology from structural linguistics from structural unemployment (which, if you have a Harvard degree, you probably need worry little about).

A.B.: a B.A. An "S.B." is a B.S. Harvard does everything just a little bit differently.

the Action Man: a legendary figure among Harvard students, who would call up rooms at random and mumble in a lascivious manner, "Looking for some action?" One student, a product of the New Canaan Country School and Andover, once confronted the Action Man with this very proper retort: "Do you have any fat boys I can hurt?" The Action Man stopped calling after that.

Bahnie: what Cambridge and Somerville "townies" call "Hahvuhd" students or any geek from Cambridge. From "Barnyard," the townie nickname for Harvard Yard.

comping: joining an organization. "I'm comping the *Crimson*."

concentration: one's major.

crump: when things don't come through. "The research crumped on that paper I was writing."

15-point scale: used instead of the customary 4-point grade scale. As the joke goes, "Yes, we're just that much smarter."

final club: Harvard's version of a fraternity, the most exclusive being "the Porc" (short for "Porcellian").

first years: freshmen.

Harvard man: an extremely confident and clean-cut *white* fellow. One of those enduring, if not necessarily endearing, Harvard stereotypes.

→

House: "dorm" is used only for freshman housing. It's Dunster House, Lowell House, Eliot House, etc.

legacy: you're a son, daughter, or close relative of a Harvard graduate. You may not be qualified to attend, but you most likely will.

the Statue of Three Lies: the bronze statue of John Harvard in Harvard Yard. The inscription at the bottom reads: "John Harvard, founder, 1638." All three of these points are false. First, it is not a statue of John Harvard, who lived in the 1600s. It was cast in 1884 by Daniel Chester French, using a student as a model. There were no known drawings of Mr. Harvard. Second, Harvard was not the founder. The Great and General Court of the Massachusetts Bay Colony established the school. Third, the "colledge" (*sic*) was founded on October 28, 1636, not 1638. In 1638 Harvard left more than half his estate to the new school, including his entire library. Because of this generosity, it decided to name the college after him a year later.

teaching fellows: teaching assistants. Aka "TFs."

Wig: Wigglesworth, a freshman dorm. Where your humble author once resided.

foddy: the numbah aftah thirdy-nine.

-fud and -kud: place name suffixes, as in Chelmsford (pron. "*chums*-fud"), Medford ("*mehd*-fud"), and Concord ("*kahn*-kud").

the Gahden: Boston Garden, home of the Celtics and Bruins before the construction of the FleetCenter.

gahkablahka: gawker-blocker. Coined by traffic reporter Kevin O'Keefe, referring to a traffic jam caused by folks who slow down to gawk at an accident or other roadside spectacle. O'Keefe also came up with "cram 'n' jam" and "stall 'n' crawl."

guvnah: the governor, chief executive of the state.

hahbuh: the harbor. Some argue that if the "er" sound in Bostonese ends as the final syllable it should be phonetically spelled "uh," not "ah." I mix it up throughout this section. You "Bwostinians" can fight it out.

hahf-ahst: half-assed.

Hahvuhd: Harvard University, Al Gore and Jerry Harrison's alma mater. And where Jim Crotty went to debate camp.

I-an-eah: the Massachusetts Eye and Ear Infirmary.

khakies: car keys.

Kwinzee: Quincy. A big-hair suburban outpost.

light dawns ova Mahblehead: when one finally grasps the obvious. "I was asking Ricky and Dave why they were always together. 'Are you brothas or somethin'?' And they said, 'In a sense.' And then I was, 'Light dawns ova Mahblehead! They're gay!'"

"Mawtha a' Gawd!": the signature exclamation of Kevin White, a former mayor.

onna-conna: on account of. Like New Yorkers, Bwostinians occasionally leave out a few consonants, such as *t* and *d*.

owah: our. As in "owah neighbahs."

Pete sir: "pizza" in other parts of the country.

poc: pork.

Red Owahback: Red Auerbach, coach of the Boston Celtics during their dominance of professional basketball in the 1960s. A bald, cigar-chomping local legend.

reefah: refrigerator.

s-word pronunciation: "PSDS" (pierced ears), "CS" (Sears), "GS" (jeers), "VS" (veers: "this cah VS to the right"), "PS" (pears), "TS" (tears: "the TS of a clown when no one's around").

Saddadee: the seventh day of the week.

sssta: sister.

Tea Potty: the seminal event that launched the American Revolution.

wah: war.

wottah: water.

wottah bubblah: a water fountain.

How to Talk American

Car Culture

AMERICA IS THE GREAT DRIVING NATION. We invented the first mass-produced automobile and made driving an integral part of our national culture. Here're some "boss" terms our car drivers *and* car salesmen use.

advertisers: the low-priced cars featured in promotions in order to lure buyers to the dealership, where, it is hoped, they will then be "stuffed" into higher-ticket vehicles by the sales force.

art car: a wildly decorated automobile or bus, often using discarded tschotkes of pop culture.

bang a left: make a left turn.

bang a right: make a right turn.

beater: according to Beater Bill of Portland's Beater Car Club and Beaterville Café, a beater is a beat-up old car, any car with over 100,000 miles on it, or a "second owner car" that's been in the family awhile. Example: a '67 Rambler.

Beamer: a BMW. Aka "Bimmer," "Bumwah."

blow the brains out: install a sunroof, in car dealer parlance.

blue book: a guide that lists the value of a used car. "The blue book says this '68 Chevy is worth $550 at best." Or, "What's the blue book on that '77 Buick Century?"

boat: a big, comfy American car.

Bott's dots: raised reflective pavement markers that alert drivers to slow down. Invented by Dr. Elbert Bott. Aka "idiot buttons."

brain bucket: a racing helmet.

brodie: a screeching stop that leaves noticeable skid marks. Interestingly, the origins of the word go back to July 23, 1886, when, on a bet from some friends, a New York newsboy named Steve Brodie allegedly jumped off the Brooklyn Bridge. Unfortunately, he had no witnesses to corroborate his amazing feat, which was believed to be a fake. Though arrested for attempted suicide, Brodie was later released and paid $100 a week to exhibit himself at the Brooklyn Museum as "the world's most courageous man." By the 1930s, "brodie" had come to be known as a "mistake."

bushing: raising a car's price after a customer has bought it.

buy-n-die: a Hyundai.

Caddie: a Cadillac.

California car: any vehicle that hasn't been exposed to harsh weather and is thus a better resale.

cancer: rust or corrosion.

cream puff: a used car in excellent condition.

diamond lane: a traffic lane reserved for buses or vehicles with two or more passengers.

dimple: dent.

doing doughnuts: spin a car 360° in a snow- or ice-covered parking lot.

doughnuts: tires.

the family car: "the four-door" wagon or sedan one uses for a Sunday drive.

fender bender: a minor traffic accident.

flip a bitch: make a U-turn. Alternately, "flip a U-ee."

high rider: a vehicle structurally adjusted to ride very high off the ground; e.g., a "monster truck."

Honda-Bago: a Honda motorcycle with all kinds of accessories.

hoopty: a big and cheap older American car. The '78 Caddie and '67 Impala are classic hoopties. Aka "slab-sided cruiser."

jenny: a generator.

jug: a carburetor.

lay-down: an easy sell in dealer parlance.

lick paint and suck chrome: when a potential buyer falls totally in love with a car.

lip: a potential car buyer.

Louie: a left turn.

How to Talk American

low rider: a souped-up automobile whose chassis is adjusted to ride very low to the ground. They have a long history in this country, though they have most recently been made famous by Hispanic Americans.

paperweight: an unpopular make a dealer has trouble "moving" (selling).

pickin' the cherry: running a red light.

rice burner: a Japanese motorcycle. Aka "rice rocket" or "crotch rocket."

riding the turtles: riding the raised lane dividers to stay awake.

the rig: a pickup. What "the husband" drives.

roach: a prospective car buyer with credit problems.

roach motel: a dealership that specializes in selling to roaches.

roadkill: any and all animals smashed to smithereens by traffic.

a Roscoe: a right turn.

rust bucket: a thoroughly rusted car.

shotgun: the front passenger seat. "I got shotgun!" is a frequent teenage refrain.

slow-and-go: traffic announcer term for traffic that is "stop and start."

squeezing the lemon: speeding up to make it through a yellow light.

tailgater: a driver who follows too close to your back bumper. Also, a party held in the parking lot of a sporting event.

thumb: hitchhike. "I thumbed my way up to Philly."

tranny: the transmission.

U-ee: a U-turn. "Drive up here and make a U-ee, and it will be down a few blocks on your right."

valve job: making love in a car. Aka "testing the shocks."

wheels: a car. "Fred's got wheels. Let's go with him." Aka "ride."

RV Vernacular

I'VE LIVED ON THE ROAD FOR OVER 11 YEARS, FIRST in a '72 Ford van and then in a 1986 Fleetwood Bounder motor home. The Ford held up pretty well for a couple years; the Bounder was nothing but trouble from the get-go. Lesson 1: do not buy any make of vehicle in the first year of the model. Lesson 2: do not buy a motor home from a dealer called Leach Camper Sales.

Having broken down 40 times (including 80 flat tires, 3 new transmissions, 1 new engine, 12 new starters, 2 radiators, 22 new batteries, 4 carburetors, 9 fuel pumps, 12 fan belts, and 13 sets of windshield wipers), I know all there is to know about the RV lifestyle. So much that you might never catch "this motorhomeboy" near an RV park for quite some time. When I travel now, I prefer the luxury of Plaza Motel 6.

black water: the "you know what"!

caravan: road clones who eat identical microwaved breakfasts, share identical lawn ornaments, relax on identical AstroTurf, then unplug and wheel off into the sunset with all their buddies in identical RVs. It's the 1990s version of the wagon train. When you stop, they stop. When you pull into Wal-Mart, everyone follows. From tourist trap to tourist trap, RV park to RV park, it's the life!

dump: "What a dump!" said Joan Crawford (or was it Bette Davis?). If they could only get a load of this. It's the downside of an otherwise sanitized camping experience. The truth is, you're actually a septic tank on wheels. The dump is the payback for never leaving your RV to use a toilet. At some point you gotta let her fly. And trust me, it's not a pretty sight or smell.

dump station: the collective toilet of the RV set. Usually an innocuous hole in the tarmac that goes into an even larger septic tank. You have to follow protocol to avoid those messy spills.

full hookup: if RV parks were hospitals, then full hookup would be intensive care with full life support. This clearly separates the campers from consumer queens. With full hookup, you plug in the big plug to turn on the microwave, TV, Cuisinart, air conditioner, hair dryer, toaster, waffle

$\rightarrow$

iron, and electric blankets. You hook up the water so you can run the dishwasher, take a bath, wash your panties, and water your plants. And you hook up your sewage so you can take five baths, two showers, and flush the toilet every hour without filling up the holding tank. Effectively fosters the illusion of home.

full-timer: people so enamored of the RV lifestyle, they do it all year long.

Germans: the most common foreign contingent at RV parks. Kraut couples just love to tool around in those "over the cab" rental numbers, usually with little Berendt and Stephan in tow. They do the whole plug-in procedure with military precision. And when finished, they invariably walk to the front desk and ask, "Do you know ze vay to ze Fisherman's Varf?"

Good Sam: the AAA of the RV set. To join, you swear to abide by a host of rules that sound frightfully close to Boy Scout slogans. You get a special sticker of a smiling Sam, a plastic ID for those fabulous discounts, invites to all the Good Sam Jamborees, and the reassurance that wherever you go, Sam is looking after you. I have to admit that as often as I broke down, the $89 Good Sam Emergency Roadside Service was a pretty good deal.

gray water: dishwater, bathwater, and all the gunk that you try to force down a sink—leftover food, toothpaste spittle, hair, phlegm, old coffee, and soured milk. This all adds up to one big ugly mess, and to think that some RVers think it's cool to let the gray water flow into a backcountry ditch.

jamboree: a gathering of middle-class white RV owners

who fire up the microwave, play croquet (boule if they're Canucks), sit in lawn chairs, and talk about their new security systems. Aka "rally."

KOA: Kampgrounds of America. The McDonald's of RV parks.

partial hookup: electric, but no sewer or water. You shower with all the Germans. And you use the dump station every three days.

pull-behind: the generic term for any vehicle you tow behind your car or truck, such as a giant "fifth-wheel trailer" or a "pop-top trailer."

pullthrough: like a circular driveway, you just park it, and when you leave? "Keep moving forward, Frank. FORWARD FRANK, FORWARD!"

the RV foxtrot: when you first drive your motor home after the nylon tires have sat for a few days, it will start rocking for a few miles while the tires warm up. This is the RV foxtrot.

Know Your RVs

RECREATIONAL VEHICLES CAN BE VERY SPORTING. The idea is simple. Take everything you have at home, miniaturize it, put in four walls, an engine, and tires, and you have an RV. It's a condo on wheels, with several varieties to suit your income and aesthetics.

Let me step you through the hierarchy.

---

slideout: when George and the little lady have guests, this is where the visitors sleep. The walls slide out to turn a run-of-the-mill single wide into a "double wide" motor home. Just don't forget to slide her back in before heading on down the road or your extra space will be splintered along the highway.

snowbirds: wonderfully sweet and midbrow Minnesotans, Michiganders, and Manitobans—or any Northerner, for that matter—who heads south for the winter.

Winnebago: a popular name for an RV, though it is actually just one RV manufacturer and neither the coolest (the Airstream gets the nod there) nor the most popular (Fleetwood is tops there).

Airstream: a silver, top-of-the-line RV popular with not only your average RVer but with hip artists seeking that retro road culture thing.

art truck: a cargo van (often a bread truck) that has been converted into a colorful living space on wheels. I see mostly Dutch and Germans in these captivating "wohnwagens."

fifth-wheeler: the giant trailer home you're towing behind your vehicle.

hippie bus: essentially, any stripped-down and outfitted school bus. Kesey's "Further" is the classic example. Though lots of Deadheads, Rainbow people, and aging hippies still prefer this mode of transport, anybody can drive one. However, if you seem in any way countercultural, your vehicle, even if it is a class A motor home, is invariably referred to as a "bus." This has always been the case with the Monkmobile. As in, "We saw that bus of yours parked near the Safeway on Market."

minicabs with a camper: all the luxuries of a dollhouse compacted into a cheesy plywood interior (no toilet; they came later).

minicabs with a shell: you've seen them, the Datsun pickups with just enough room in back to crawl in and sleep.

over-the-cab van or pickup: you're standing in your own house on wheels (unless you're over 6'2"; then you're bumping your head a lot). There's a decent bed protruding over the driver's roof, which is fairly roomy but claustrophobic for the one sleeping in the corner, and a good attempt at a kitchen, with a cute little dinette that makes into a bed, and even a wet bathroom (basically a toilet in a stall with a shower overhead).

pop-top trailer: a dinky little pull-behind that blossoms into a tacky tent structure when parked.

pop-top van: as the name implies, a top pops up when you stop, allowing for an overhead bed and standing room. Commonly found on VW and Toyota vans.

Rock Star buses: humungous old converted Greyhound buses. A world unto themselves, they are stereotypically associated with musicians and their crew, though they were popularized by President Clinton on his campaign bus tours, and they have been used by everyone from Greenpeace to the Green Tortoise.

→

Finally, there's the . . .

Class A motor home: even the name implies you're at the top. Mounted on a Class A steel frame chassis (let's hope they're still using steel and not aluminum or plastic when you buy one), you've got a 2-ton house on wheels. It separates the weekend campers from the serious RV set, because it takes a bit of know-how, not to mention a pretty good-size loan, to drive off the lot with one of these beauties. The common denominator in all Class A's is a full kitchen (stove, microwave, stand-up fridge, and double sink), a bath, a separate bedroom and closets, plus a "living area" with TV, stereo, and optional VCR. From there it's just a matter of where lies your threshold of comfort (you can add a cell phone, video surveillance, an elaborate alarm system, and more). There are several makes of Class A's, including Fleetwood's Pace Arrow, sporty Southwind, and goofy Bounder, the nostalgic futurism of the silver Airstream, the no-frills Honey, the captivating Holiday Rambler, and the old standby, the Winnebago. I made the mistake of choosing the Bounder.

Chicago

"Chicago is the ultimate American city—rich, deep, insane."
—STUART ROSENBERG

"I got two rules. The first one is—Don't make no waves. The second is—Don't back no losers."
—BERNARD NEISTEIN

CHICAGO CARRIES A LOT OF WEIGHT WITH ME. My first big city. The city of my alma mater, Northwestern. The city of my true academic love, the University of Chicago. The city of Hemingway, Sandburg, and Skafish, a hermaphroditic New Waver who first showed me the twisted mise-en-scène at this city's core. The city where Elke fell in love with me after meeting my mother. As only she could put it, here's "Sheee-kah-go."

Big John: the John Hancock Center. At the time of its construction, the tallest skyscraper in the world. One of the highlights of my childhood was going to the top of "Big John" (aka "Top of the Cock").

bleacher bums: rowdy fans who commandeer the bleachers at Wrigley Field.

the Boss: an old nickname for Mayor Richard J. Daley, who ruled the city in the '50s and '60s and is most fondly remembered for commandeering the police crackdown on demonstrators at the 1968 Democratic National Convention.

Bridgeport: any Chicagoan will know what this traditional Irish neighborhood stands for. RACISM, baby. The home of the Daley clan and other political insiders. Same as it ever was?

Chi (pron. "shy"): Chicago. Aka "Chi-town."

Chicago: the classic American city in all its brawn, bluster, and bigheartedness. From the Potawatomi Indian word *Checaugou*, which translates as "wild onions" or "swamp grass."

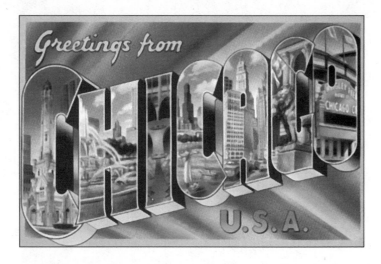

Greetings from CHICAGO U.S.A.

Chicago majority: 110% of the vote. A holdover from the days of rampant political corruption.

the Chicago method: the Great Books curriculum pioneered at the University of Chicago.

Chicago pizza: a deep-dish pizza, with the fillings stuffed inside the dough rather than placed on top. Pioneered at Chicago's Pizzeria Uno.

Circle: the University of Illinois at Chicago, because the campus is just south of the Loop.

City of the Big Shoulders: the city as industrial powerhouse, so called by Chicago's poet laureate, Carl Sandburg. Today it has been modified to Chicago, "City of the Women with Big Shoulder Pad Dresses."

City of the Big Smell: sardonic nickname for "Chi" when it was the meatpacking capital of the planet. Aka "Porkopolis" (a title it shared with Cincinnati).

come wit: come with. The pure Chicago expression par excellence. "We're going to Berghoffs. Wanna come wit?"

the Cubbies: the Chicago Cubs baseball franchise. Chicago is a rough town. In fact, a well-known S&M town. You might say that if the late Richard Daley supplied the sadism, being a devoted Cubs fan most assuredly supplies the masochism. The boys of Wrigley have come close many times but have never brought home a World Series championship. Still, they are Chicago's team, even with the South Side White Sox faring far better. The Sox won the Series in 1917; the Cubbies haven't won since 1908 (the longest drought in Major League Baseball).

da Bears: the Chicago Bears football team.

da Bulls: the Chicago Bulls basketball dynasty, the finest set of superstars Jerry Krause could buy.

da Hocks: the Chicago Blackhawks hockey team.

da Jeffer: the CTA 6 Jeffery Express, from the Loop to the South Side.

downstate: any part of Illinois south of Chicago. Akin to Nebraska's "out-state."

duh mare: the mayor. As opposed to New York's "de mayah."

eye bee: an Italian beef sandwich.

Fast Eddie: the Chicago political insider Eddie Vrodolyak. Once a powerful alderman from the 10th Ward, now a local radio commentator.

Fightin' Jane: former mayor Jane Byrne, a chain-smokin' tough blonde from the 'burbs who was the first to go up against the vaunted "Machine" and win.

501: an inebriated driver. The code number for drunk driving in the *Illinois Revised Statutes.*

Folk and People: the two major North Chicago rival gang alliances, big in the 1980s and to some extent still today. "Folk" consisted of the Royals (whites, Puerto Ricans, and blacks) and the Disciples (all-black). "People" consisted of the Gaylords (white ethnics) and the Latin Kings (Mexicans). The memorable Folk slogan was "Folk poppin', people droppin'." "Family" referred to unaffiliated individuals neither alliance wanted to mess with.

Friday shipment: the scheduled relocation of convicts from the Cook County Jail to the state prison system.

the friendly confines: Wrigley Field, where the Cubbies play.

gapers block: a traffic jam caused by a Dennis Rodman billboard.

ghost payrolling: the latest twist on the age-old Chicago custom called "patronage." But this isn't just rewarding your supporters with plum city jobs, this is rewarding your supporters, your family, and your extended family with jobs where they don't even have to show up!

the Giant Orange Juice Squeezer: the nine-sided Baha'i House of Worship in Wilmette, a favorite Northwestern student hangout.

Go-ee-thee: Goethe Street, as said in Chicago.

the Gold Coast: the stretch of Lake Shore Drive winding north along Lake Michigan that includes many of the city's most illustrious residences and real estate. Aka "the Magnificent Mile."

goo-goos: reformers. Ostensibly, those who don't follow the rules of patronage. In actual fact, a reformer is simply a new face on the same old Machine (Byrne, Washington, Daley; the system stays intact).

the Great Fire: the Great Chicago Fire of October 8–10, 1871, which remains the pivotal turning point in the city's rough-and-tumble history. Any true Chicagoan will know that it started in Patrick and Catherine O'Leary's barn, though it is still debated whether the conflagration started when a cow kicked over a lantern while Mrs. O'Leary was milking it.

His Airness: Michael "Air" Jordan, star of the Chicago Bulls. Aka "Michael."

Howard Street: a literal and symbolic Maginot Line between the forces of sobriety and the forces of fraternal inebriation. On the sober north side you have Evanston (home of the Women's Christian Temperance Union and Northwestern University)—until ten years ago a "dry" town, with no bars except in the Orrington Hotel (now expanded to restaurants), though always plenty of booze at campus "keggers." On the south side you have Chicago, where booze flowed happily and continually right through Prohibition. Northwestern students regularly make the trek over to Howard Street to hit the bars there. Thus the expression, "We're heading to Howard Street."

Illinois State Circus: the state government in Springfield.

Juneway Jungle: a crime-ridden neighborhood in Rogers Park.

the L: the elevated transit line of Chicago. What local author Nelson Algren called Chicago's "rusty iron heart." There is absolutely nothing more painful to the ears than the screeching of an L train as it makes a 90-degree turn.

the Lab School: the high school on the campus of the University of Chicago. You do have to wonder about what kind of student comes out of a school with the name "Lab."

the lake effect: the extremes of heavy snowfall and rain produced by cold arctic air passing over the warm waters of Lake Michigan (or any of the Great Lakes, for that matter). The reason Chicago or any Great Lakes town can suddenly experience over a foot of snow in just a few short hours. Heard frequently on weather reports.

Leo the Lip: Leo Durocher, for over 41 years a legendary player and then manager of the Cubs. Known for letting umpires know quite clearly where he stood on a call.

the Loop: downtown Chicago. So called because the subway loops around the downtown area before it connects with "the Magnificent Mile."

LSD: Lake Shore Drive.

"A Lithuanian won't vote for a Pole, and a Pole won't vote for a Lithuanian. A German won't vote for either of them—but all three will vote for 'a Turkey,' an Irishman." —A CHICAGO POLITICAL INSIDER

---

the Machine: Chicago's version of New York's Tammany Hall. You have not experienced orchestrated control of the voting populace until you've experienced Chicago ward politics. Less corrupt than in years gone by, the Machine still operates but is better disguised under the current mayor, Richard M. Daley, son of the city's most notorious mayor, Richard J. Daley. The whole mind-set and terminology at the heart of the old Machine can be summed up in this sentence from a Mike Royko column on "Chiconics": "There was a beef from some goo-goos about a deal we had running, and I was gonna be vised from my spot in Streets and San. But then my chinaman used his clout, and the fix was in." Translation: "There was a complaint by some reformers about a swindle in which we were engaged, and I was about to be fired from my job in the Department of Streets and Sanitation when my political sponsor used his influence to have the complaint dismissed." Or, as the Boss himself explained, it's "organization, not machine. Get that. Organization, not machine."

Maxwell Street: one of the last funky people's markets in the country, now run by the city. Home of Jim's Polish, open 24 hours every day of the year, whose prominent feature is a pile of fried onions that look as if they've been around as long as Maxwell Street itself.

the Merc: the Chicago Mercantile Exchange.

Michael: Michael Jordan, star player for the world champion Chicago Bulls. Other black celebrities from Chicago include Oprah Winfrey, Jesse Jackson, numerological genius Louis Farrakhan, and friend of Sani Abacha, Senator Carol Moseley-Braun.

Monsters of the Midway: 1940s name for the Chicago Bears football team, still occasionally used. Aka "da Bears."

North Siders vs. South Siders: The monied, educated North Side of town versus the poor and working-class South Side.

off-Loop: the designation for smaller, independent theaters north of downtown. Like New York's "off-off-Broadway."

over by: to. "We're goin' over by Willie's place."

Pip: Scottie Pippen of da Bulls, the leading actor in Michael's "supporting cast."

Polish Broadway: Milwaukee Ave. between Diversey and Belmont. Chicago has the largest number of Poles outside Warsaw.

Ritchie: the local pundits' name for Mayor Richard M. Daley when he was rising through the Democratic ranks.

Royko: Mike Royko, the late beloved columnist for the *Chicago Tribune* and the quintessential Chicago cynic. Frequent refrain: "Did you read Royko today?"

s at the beginning or end of a word: this uniquely South Side trait is found in sentences like "Did you go to the Jewells?" (the supermarket chain called Jewell). Or "Did you go to the Oscos?"

708ers: Chicago's equivalent of New York's "bridge and tunnel people," mid-brow, middle-class folks who populate the city's clubs, bars, and restaurants on weekends. Based on the new area code that covers the Chicago 'burbs.

the show: a film. You never go to "the movies" in Chicago.

Sout Side: the South Side. South Siders tend to drop the *h* on certain words.

Studs: Louis Terkel, a beloved Chicago writer, radio commentator, and man of the people. Author of *Working* and other oral histories.

this is going to be the year: the hopeful, if largely futile, mantra one hears every year come spring training from Cub fans.

the U. of C.: the University of Chicago, the city's true intellectual powerhouse, where Jim Crotty was the film critic for the *Grey City Journal* and where Fermi produced the first nuclear chain reaction. The first experiments were conducted right under the football field.

where do you stay?: where do you live?

the Windy City: Chicago, even though it is not even among the ten windiest in the country. Aka "the Second City," even though it's been replaced by Los Angeles as the country's second most populous. Caveat: "Windy City" was created by a *New York Sun* reporter in response to all the Chicagoans' bragging about their city after the 1896 World's Fair.

wine candy: Jolly Ranchers hard candy. Another South Side word that never makes it up to the North Side.

yer: the. "That would be yer Music Box over here." And "That would be yer Biograph over there."

youse guys: you guys. A ubiquitous expression also heard throughout the northeastern U.S., though there's nothing like hearing it from a true blue Chicagoan: "Hey, youse guys, I tell ya how to tawk Cheek-ah-ga."

Crime

THE U.S. IS RANKED FIRST AMONG THE ADVANCED industrial nations in the number of people in jail or prison—well over a million at last count. Chances are very high that you are acquainted with one or more of these current inmates or with someone else who has spent sizable time behind bars. Knowing the vernacular of this incarcerated subculture as well as the system that surrounds them will tell you more than any news report or get-tough-on-crime propaganda about the true nature of the American criminal justice system.

Cops

Almond Joy theory: used when the suspect's behavior can't be explained. From the Almond Joy advertising line "Sometimes you feel like a nut, sometimes you don't."

ate his gun: when a cop commits suicide with his own gun.

boost: to steal or break into a car.

bow and arrow squad: unarmed police.

choir practice: partying with fellow cops.

choo-choo: a police van.

chop shop: where thieves strip a car for salable parts.

code 7: a lunch or doughnut break.

D and D: Drunk and Disorderly.

ERA: Earned Ram Average. The number of blows a SWAT team takes to bust down a door.

get small: run away, disappear. "When the perp saw the Christmas lights, he got small real fast."

gimme: a handgun.

Gray Bar Hotel: jail. "I just checked the perp into the Gray Bar Hotel. He won't be leaving for a while."

heater case: a high-profile case that's getting lots of publicity; e.g., Nicole Brown Simpson vs. Orenthal James Simpson.

IBM: an Italian businessman. A member of the Mafia.

Juvie: Juvenile Hall or any juvenile detention facility.

Kojak light: the temporary flashing red light police put on the roof of an unmarked car. From the TV series *Kojak*, which used one.

the Mamas and the Papas: a family deeply enmeshed in a life of crime.

Missile X: the small orange card police in some areas fill out when they respond to a call that brought about no arrests.

Mutt and Jeff act: good cop, bad cop.

on the muscle: a nervous or agitated suspect.

patsy: a fall guy for a crime. Example: Seattle police officer Mathias Bachmeier setting up James Wren as the arsonist who destroyed his home.

perp: the alleged perpetrator of a criminal offense.

pinch: an arrest.

popcorn machine: the flashing lights on top of a police car. Aka "cherries" or "gumballs."

prone-out: assume the prone position when asked to do so by a police officer. Regular instruction given by parents to kids in south-central L.A., though rarely in Simi Valley.

rap sheet: the record of a perp's crimes, convictions, and arrests.

short: a car.

smoker: a stolen car.

spot: where drugs are sold.

10-13: police radio code for an officer in distress. Aka "code 0."

weight: a large amount of either cocaine or heroin.

Lawyers

drop: phone in bits of criminal gossip from inside the slammer.

flipper: an accused criminal so eager to cooperate with the D.A. that he offers testimony against his pals in exchange for a lighter sentence.

has Mr. Green shown up?: does the perp have money on him?

jocker: the victim of a love triangle, with the assailant being a jealous husband fighting for his unfaithful wife.

jury tax: the insinuated threat of a longer sentence if a defendant rejects a plea bargain and decides to have a jury trial.

L.O.G. (Low on Green) motion: a continuance whose hidden agenda is to give a client time to raise money for his attorney.

package: consolidate multiple charges into a single court appearance.

paper: the ultimate reducer every perp hopes for—probation instead of prison.

reducer: a strategy by which an accused is enticed to waive his right to a trial and plead guilty to a lesser charge.

scooped off the floor: the no-waiting service by which a perp who loses at his trial has his bond revoked and is immediately remanded into custody.

the vic: the victim of a crime.

Private Investigators

IN AMERICA THE PRIVATE DETECTIVE IS DEIFIED. SAM Spade was one. Columbo was one. Jim Rockford was one. Over the decades we've become used to the colorful vocabulary of these characters. Words like "gumshoe" or "private eye" for the investigator. More modern terms follow.

burned: to be seen tagging someone.

competitive intelligence: going to the opposing side to find out what they know. An informal form of "discovery."

exacts: mundane facts about a subject, such as birthdate, address, phone numbers, etc. Aka "background."

popping: uncovering hidden or classified information, such as a person's bank records. "I popped her bank account."

Russian deal: what should be a source of free information, such as the library or a bureaucratic organization, but you get shaken down for a small amount of cash.

the subject: the person you're investigating.

tagging: tracking someone. Investigating them. Aka "surveilling," "tailing."

Jail Talk

ad seg (pron. "ad sec"): a special cell for the "administration segregation" of problem inmates. At the far end of the "mainline" on each floor, this sizable tank houses "trannies" (transvestites), transsexuals, and crazies as well as murderers and other violent types.

backup: an inmate or group of inmates who will fight for a friend. It might take six candy bars, a dozen bags of corn chips, and a few late night favors, but once you've bought some backup, you can start to relax.

What Our Law-Abiding Civilians Call Cops

squidlies, squirlies, rollers, the heat, fuzz, pigs, bacon, the man, popeye, long johns, and *Dickless Tracy* (for female cops)

blister: a totally "out" and practicing homosexual. A "house mouse" is a "blister" who never ventures out of his cell. A "bandit" is a "blister" who checks out men's buttocks in the shower.

boy: an inmate who puts out sexually. Not necessarily gay. There are plenty of perks to being someone's "boy," such as automatic backup and lots of free food. Aka "punk," "queer," "queen."

bullet: one year in jail. "Can you believe it? I did two bullets for stealing a damn stereo."

cellie: an inmate who shares a cell with another inmate. Since this is a forced situation, not unlike an unwanted seatmate on a flight to Sydney, this detail really counts as the months, if not years, peel off the calendar. The only two things that really matter (since looks, smell, and sound you'll adjust to) are what they're gonna take from you and what you can get in return. It's a classic take-take scenario in which everyone loses. Aka "bunkie."

county: jail. Not unlike the bum on *Mayberry RFD*, there's plenty out there who feel jail's a picnic. What with free food and a bed that doesn't resemble a ratty cardboard box, it's a definite improvement to some. However, jail is considered far worse than prison. There's a big difference in all areas—from visitation rights to library access to exposure to the outdoors. Aka "the country," or "three hots and a cot."

daddy: a male inmate who takes a dominant role in a relationship. Not exactly all it's cracked up to be, a "daddy" has to do plenty of overtime watching out for other predators and defending the roost. Big muscles are a must, but that takes work too.

down: time served. It's definitely not up, unless you're on the penthouse floor of a "glamour slammer" in some of the newer urban correctional facilities. Down is definitely down, locked away from the world. It's a badge of honor to say "two years down" with a grimace or smirk.

dry run: a trip to court that proves futile. The miracle of our legal system is that not only is the inmate clueless about his case, but so are the judge, D.A., and public defender. Hence the frequency of dry runs—inmates pulled out of a cell, cuffed and shackled, then paraded into court for a no-results appearance reset for a future date.

fish: new arrivals. Every eye reads a fish for the giveaway signs of vulnerability and then acts accordingly, taking what they can before the fish gets his bearings.

gladiator farm: a maximum security prison. Aka "gladiator school."

gump: a homosexual male guard. Used by female convicts to describe someone who poses no threat. Also used by cops to refer to a male prostitute who dresses as a woman.

guns: fists or biceps.

the hole: a basic, solitary cell where an inmate is sent for rule violations. Is it punishment or relief from the crowded cells? Sure, you can't hang in the yard or play cards, but you aren't breathing other men's body odors, either.

jiggler: a long thin wire used to trip up pay phones so you can make calls for free. Jigglers are almost as hot a commodity as lighters. Can't smoke contraband without the light, nor can you keep up business without the phone, and who the hell is going to pay Ma Bell. Didn't pay her on "the outs," why start when you're "down"?

joint: prison. Aka "pen," "big house." Universally agreed by all inmates, "county" jail is bad news. The "pen" is where the easy life is (greater access to education, work, weight rooms, and other programs that can take the edge off incarcerated life).

keeping store: stockpiling commissary, money, and contraband to trade or sell at a high markup on the black market. It's the ultimate scam—a captive market with limited supplies. You start by saving lunch meat and move up from there.

keistering: smuggling contraband by hiding it in the anal cavity. Slightly inconvenient, but the most efficient way to waltz through a strip search holding a month's worth of heroin. Also great for holding money, cigarettes, matches, pipes, and illicit photos—all wrapped in plastic and carefully removed.

lockup: to be locked in a cell as an extra measure of punishment without privileges or freedom to exercise. The seeming revenge for bad behavior, the lockup actually gives the green light to lie in bed all day, eat candy bars, drink pruno, and read trashy novels without the nuisance of leaving the cell.

mainline: a main corridor of cells. Where the action is. Like being on the Strip versus an obscure alley. The best deals, fights, sex, views, are always on the "mainline," but the noise level can be deafening.

man: police. Aka "beat walkers," "pig," "popo's," "black-and-white." Whatever the name, they are the *enemy*, plain and simple. The adage "the only good pig is a dead pig" prevails, no matter how much community policing there is or how progressive and open they make the jails.

man down!: a fight or accident that results in an inmate's falling to the floor. A "man down!" is better than TV. Everyone will drop what they're doing to see the bloody details. Medics will be the last to arrive. Guards live for this moment and come swarming like locusts, with pepper spray drawn and choke holds flying.

nabbed: arrested. Aka "busted." Though an inconvenience, to be "busted" isn't the end to a life of crime. It's more likely the beginning. More deals, connections, like-minded partnerships, are forged in jail than outside, thereby helping to bolster one's status in the underworld.

8 Great Lines of Guilty Americans

1. "The bitch set me up" (Marion Barry on his arrest for possession of crack cocaine).

2. "100% Not Guilty" (O. J. Simpson at his trial for the murders of Nicole Brown Simpson and Ronald Goldman).

3. "Because that's where the money is" ("Public Enemy Number One," John Dillinger, when asked why he robbed banks).

4. "Let's do it" (convicted killer Gary Gilmore just before he was to face a Utah firing squad).

5. "I am Tania" (armed robber Patty Hearst, aka "Tania," on a videotape sent to the press by her captors, the Symbionese Liberation Army).

6. "We thought they were going to kill us" (the murdering Menendez brothers, on why they shot and killed their parents).

7. "Only the little people pay taxes" (tax evader, hotel empress, and undisputed "Queen of Mean," Leona Helmsley).

8. "I am not a crook" (nearly impeached Watergate ringleader and duplicitous commander in chief, Richard Milhous Nixon).

O.G.: an original or old gangster. Used to refer to older inmates. Amazingly, even in our youth-obsessed culture, an old criminal is given some amount of respect. Not that he can teach the young homeys new tricks or bend their ear with escapades they haven't already done themselves. It's just that in a fatherless culture, where prison is *the* rite of passage, an "O.G." might be the closest thing many young men ever have to a mentor or role model who might give them more than the time of day.

pruno: an alcoholic drink made from fermenting fruit. Absolutely the ultimate in brain rot, only the desperate go here, but hey, this is jail, and there are some desperadoes on board, so expect extra batches of the stuff. Recipes vary, though it's basically the same coast to coast. Save your fruit or fruit juice, pour it in a plastic bag, add lots of sugar, and leave it to ferment for a week or longer. Tastes like flavored rubbing alcohol. Can send the cellies into a heady tailspin and have them hugging the steel goddess for a long, long ride.

pulling plastic: when an inmate packs all his belongings in a plastic garbage bag and carries it around when relocating. One more grain of humiliation to remind the prisoner that he is nothing more than a state-supported piece of refuse, a mere step away from homelessness.

putting water on it: flushing the toilet after each new "deposit." In the tight quarters of one's cell, this is a must.

roll up, rolled up: moved within the jail, released from jail, or rolling up your blankets and belongings. The barking order "Roll up!" can arrive at the most inconvenient times, sending shock waves of terror through an inmate's nervous system. Like, "*Now* where are they sending me?" On those rare occasions when "Roll up!" means a case was dropped, someone posted bail, or, best of all, the computer made a mistake, the adrenaline rush of imminent freedom is the best high a "con" can buy.

shakedown: a full search, used when something is missing or if contraband is suspected. Probably as entertaining as a "man down!," this is when the guards get serious about the right to search and seize anything in sight. Things can get tense as they come awfully close to finding contraband. But the cons invariably win, because hiding evidence is a natural-born instinct that gets even better in jail.

shank: as a noun, an implement for stabbing. Examples: a toothbrush, paper clip, or #2 pencil. Storing a "shank" in one's anal cavity is known as "slamming." As a verb, to stab. All it takes is a point, a little push, and some raging hormones to drive the message home. It still remains the quickest way to end an argument.

sitting on steel: using the seatless stainless steel toilet. Low to the floor with a flush strong enough to suck out intestines, it's the ultimate degradation used to deprive a man of his rightful throne.

snitch: one who gives information to the police or guards regarding illegal activities. Aka "narc." The lowest of the lows, which is an irony considering the back-stabbing, self-centered, dog-eat-dog world that the average convict hails from. But this is just one thing that you never do behind bars. If you do decide to snitch, you better have one hell of an escape plan, because no one cooperates with "the man" and gets away with it. Caveat: in women's jails, a snitch is known by the more colorful "cheese eater." Allegedly, a "cheese eater" will find cheese crumbs in her bed following a snitch. This usually precedes a "blanket party" (when the "cheese eater" is covered with a blanket and pummeled, strangled, or knifed by her fellow inmates). Isn't jail fun?

the tank: a holding cell where a suspect goes when first arrested. This is the pits. This is foul. This is where jail is all it's cracked up to be and worse. You're stuck in a cramped cell with no idea what the hell is happening as the bureaucracy slowly turns. Crazed drug fiends, lice-infested homeless, bleeding homeys, and the stench of fear set the tone for the bottom rung of jail life. With up to five days on a floor, no shower, and puking junkie pals, it's a major relief to finally make it into a cell.

testing dirty: a drug test that shows up positive. Couldn't ask for a worse nightmare than a random drug test during a probation visit. Nine times out of ten, "testing dirty" is the violation that keeps the revolving door to jail spinning.

tray monster: an inmate who steals food from other inmates' trays.

trays: cafeteria food served on hideous plastic trays. Imagine eating out of a really, really dirty dog tray with a mound of miscellaneous meat products, overcooked vegetables, and soggy slices of bread as the main course. Throw in mystery hair and unidentifiable flavoring as appetizers. And you thought Denny's was bad.

write-up: a written notice of a rules violation. One of the greatest ironies of jail. As if criminals give a squat about petty rules such as no hoarding of sugar (could be used to make alcohol), no sex between inmates (yet condoms are passed out), no food in your bunk area (where else are you going to eat snacks?). The big *threat*, something to really make "cons" shake in their boots, is the "write-up." It's like getting a parking ticket. The inmates just tear it up and laugh.

yard: an outdoor area for exercising and trading contraband. Sure, the fresh air is good, and a little exercise always improves the attitude, but the yard is really nothing more than a marketplace where deals are made, schemes plotted, escapes attempted, and old debts settled once and for all.

Cyberspeech

How many programmers does it take to change a light bulb? None. That's a hardware problem.

HAVE YOU EVER LISTENED TO A COMPUTER HACKER? It's not speech; it's not even language per se. It's code. Cyberheads have grave difficulty communicating as normal people do. I know this from direct experience—try getting a hard-core gearhead to talk candidly about emotions or relationships, and you can literally see sparks fly as their brain short-circuits. It simply doesn't compute. But get these folks talking about Lego minifigures, Java applets, or bugs in the System 23.725 software, and you will have immediate rapport.

Some would claim that the style of speech attributed to men and women in the computer industries, what is commonly called cyberspeech, originated in that great dweeb laboratory known as Silicon Valley. But with the arrival of the Internet and the widespread proliferation of desktop, not to mention dashboard, publishing, cyberspeech has spread like wildfire throughout the world.

Altavista: where you go after you can't find what you're looking for on Yahoo.

banana problem: a process that doesn't know how to stop. From the joke about spelling "banana": "I know how to spell it, I just don't know when to stop."

bandwidth: the holding capacity of an information pipeline, whether fiber-optic, copper wire, or cable. The bigger the bandwidth, the closer to God. The size of one's bandwidth is the surest sign of one's status in the digital world. 9600 = pauper; ISDN = prince; T-1 = knight; T-3 = *Stud or Babe of the Information Superhighway.*

barf: malfunction.

baud: the speed of a modem. Named after telecomm pioneer Émile Baudot. Aka "bits per second" or "bps."

beta: the testing stage of a digital product. "I'm sorry, Jim, we can't make any more changes in the CD-ROM. We're already in beta."

bi star: any two things that are apparently inseparable, for whatever reason. "Agents and cell phones: totally bi star!" From "binary star configuration."

Bill: Bill Gates, the founder of Microsoft and future owner of your brain. "Bill's so smart. Bill is wise. Bill is kind. Bill is benevolent. Bill, be my friend . . . *please!*" (from *Microserfs,* by Douglas Coupland).

bio-break: a techie euphemism for using the commode.

bit flip: a 180-degree personality shift. "Carolyn did a major bit flip and became a born-again Christian." Aka "morph." "She morphed into a monster babe."

bitraking: a new form of Net-based investigative journalism. Becoming popular as journalists from major magazines and dailies "troll" the Net for hot stories. A spin on muckraking.

bit-spit: any form of digital correspondence (text, bit-mapped images, fax transmissions) or the act of sending same. "Did you bit-spit that file to Ian yet?"

body shop: in computer software, a small business that supplies talented workers to high-tech companies on a short-term basis. These temps are often foreign born, bred, and educated and easily taken advantage of.

bozo filter: a program that allows you to filter out unwanted Usenet posts.

buggy: a program that is full of flaws or "bugs."

bugs: glitches in the software, causing it to malfunction.

the BUNCH: acronym for Burroughs, Univac, NCR, Control Data, and Honeywell, who, along with IBM, were the leading companies in the mainframe computer revolution of the 1960s.

byte-bonding: when computer users get together at social events and discuss things that nonusers don't understand. When the "byte-bonded" start playing on a computer during a noncomputer-related event, they are "geeking out."

CD-ROM: Compact Disc–Read Only Memory. A CD-ROM can hold up to 600 megabytes of memory, allowing for the quick and easy storage and playing of video, audio, animation, and text on a monitor. Now superseded by the Internet to become "the 8-track of the multimedia age."

cheese: computer software.

cheesebox: a computer.

Online Shorthand

cul8r: see you later.

f2f: face-to-face. Meeting someone in person. Used in discussion groups or by hackers. Aka "face time."

FAQ: Frequently Asked Questions. There's usually a FAQL (Frequently Asked Questions List) at the beginning of Usenet groups.

FOAF: Friend of a Friend.

FTR: For the Record.

HHOK: Ha, Ha—Only Kidding.

IMHO: In My Humble Opinion. A frequent comment.

IMNSHO: In My Not-So-Humble Opinion.

MorF?: acronym for "Male or Female?" Used in the People Connection "rooms" of America Online as conversants try to determine the sex of other occupants. "Sandy—MorF?" Replies often include age and geographical location: "F/24/Akron."

PITA: Pain in the Arse.

ROTFL: Rolling on the Floor Laughing.

RTFM: Read the Fucking Manual.

SIG: Special Interest Group.

TLA: Three-Letter Acronym. Cyber people love acronyms.

TOSsed out: dismissed from a chat room on AOL for breaching its Terms of Service (TOS) agreement. The persons doing the TOSsing are sometimes called "cybercops." The person who's been TOSsed is "under mouse arrest."

TYPING IN ALL CAPS: SHOUTING. To be avoided.

User Eye-D: a personal, face-to-face (f2f) meeting with someone you've only known on the Net. "The User Eye-D with Brook was not what I hoped for. He's a man."

YMMV: Your Mileage May Vary.

---

chips and salsa: chips = computer hardware; salsa = software. "First we gotta figure out if the problem's in your chips or your salsa."

client–server action: sexual relations.

coaster: an unsolicited software disk, such as AOL software.

CodePie: a pizza ordered to celebrate a debugged and completed program.

crash: your computer system has suddenly ceased to function.

Far worse than a "bomb," it can suddenly make you armed and dangerous.

crypto: encryption. The codes and passwords that maintain the privacy of digital communication—in a perfect world.

cuspy: excellent; a program that runs neatly, cleanly, and efficiently without any "bugs."

cyber-: this proliferating prefix joins the ranks of other overused and now almost meaningless words like "natural," "free," and "alternative" as a popular linguistic icon. William Gibson is credited with bringing the word into popular usage in his seminal work, *Neuromancer* (1948), though it was actually used first by Norbert Wiener, a mathematician who coined the term "cybernetics" (the science of automated systems) by toying with the Greek *kybernan* (to steer) earlier in the '40s.

cyberpork: government money that finds its way to well-connected Internet contractors.

cybertot: a youngster raised in the digital age.

cypherpunk: (1) an Internet activist, concerned primarily with access and privacy; (2) an Internet outlaw, who tries to break government security codes.

dawn patrol: programmers who are still at their terminals when you return to work the next morning.

dead end users (DEUs): consumers who call technical support with painfully dumb questions, such as "How do I turn on my printer?"

decompress: wind down. "I'm still decompressing after that wild weekend at Burning Man."

deep hack: the deep state of concentration hackers get into after long hours of hacking. Akin to being "in the zone."

digerati: the technical elite. From "literati."

domain dropping: giving someone your cooler-sounding e-mail address in an attempt to impress them, even though you rarely use it.

Easter egg: a surprise goodie buried in software or a computer game. "There were several cool Easter eggs in that Residents CD."

firefighters: Net users who try to put out "flame wars" early in their gestation.

flame bait: through taunting or outrageous comments, a person just asking to be flamed.

flame mail: nasty e-mail.

floodgaters: individuals who send inquiring e-mail and, after

receiving only a slightly encouraging response, begin flooding you with multiple messages of little or no interest.

404: someone who is totally clueless or ignorant on a subject. Example: "Janet is totally 404 when it comes to multimedia. I'm going to have to get a new assistant." From the "404 File Not Found" message on the Web when a site is closed or is temporarily inaccessible.

full-on honkey handshake: a standard protocol that allows peripherals to connect "without a lot of street jive" (no complicated configuring).

gearhead: a computer programmer. Aka "propeller head."

geek: a term of endearment for a computer nerd, aka "chiphead." In recent years, computer hackers and aficionados have started to wear the "geek" or "nerd" label with immense pride.

geekfest: when a bunch of nerds with minimal social skills get together and play networked computer games for days on end. Aka "blahrfest."

Ghod: preferred hacker spelling of God. Like science fiction fans (which many hackers are), hackers like to add an *h* to words whenever possible.

GIGO: Garbage In, Garbage Out. An age-old computer truism. It pretty much sums up the drivel spewing forth, like waste from a sewage overflow pipe, from the bastions of commercial Web sites these days.

glass-roots campaign: a cyber grassroots campaign that uses Usenet groups, computer networks, and e-mail to get the message out. Example: the online campaign against the clipper chip.

gritch: complain.

grok: to completely grasp the cosmic meaning of it all. From Robert Heinlein's *Stranger in a Strange Land*.

gweeps: humanoids who use computers only to do their jobs. The opposite of "hackers."

hacker: one who finds creative fulfillment tinkering with and getting to know computers. Also, a highly skilled programmer who enjoys creating mischief on the Net and elsewhere in the technological world. Aka "cracker."

hash: unwanted, unnecessary data.

Holy Wars: chat room debates that never end, with points of view that never change. Favorite Holy Wars are fought over abortion, pornography, and gun control.

ice: security software. Origin: William Gibson's *Neuromancer*.

identity hacking: posting anonymously, pseudonymously, or by giving a completely false name, address, or phone number with the intent to deceive.

"I'm not excited, but I'm experienced": joke making the rounds in Silicon Valley about search engine Excite's ad campaign slogan, "Are You Experienced?"

Infobahn: the information superhighway.

information superhighway: a pipe dream that goes by various other satirical names, such as the Pixel Parkway, Al's Joint, Poor People Go Fish, and Big Ol' Interactive Thingama-jig.

killer app: a very useful, even transformative, application of computer technology.

kludge: a functional but unwieldy solution to a computer problem. The opposite of "elegant." Similar to "jury-rigged."

knowbots: software agents who search the Internet for requested information.

link: send an e-mail. "I'll link you on that."

LRF support: Little Rubber Feet. Used to prank computer salespeople. "Does this system come with LRF support?"

Macintoy: a pejorative term for a Macintosh, implying that it is not suitable for serious, hard-core computing.

meatware: the human body.

mouse potato: a computer addict. The online generation's answer to the couch potato.

multi-mediocrity: dull, inferior CD-ROMs or other multimedia platforms.

mung or munge: irreparably harmful.

netiquette: acceptable behavior on the Net, especially in the use of e-mail and Usenet groups, learned through trial and flaming.

notwork: a network in its nonworking state.

ohnosecond: that minuscule fraction of time in which you realize that you've just made a BIG mistake, such as deleting your e-mail address book irreversibly.

pona: person of no account. Someone who is not online.

porn speed modem: a 33,000-baud modem. Fast enough to handle large porn files.

port-per-pillow: the goal of a university that wants to install network connections in the bedroom of every student on campus.

RAM: the short-term memory of the computer. In the '90s, masculinity is measured by the size of one's RAM.

random: "nonlinear" behavior, such as extreme anger or any unpredictable emotion. Can really upset the apple cart in a hacker's highly linear world.

Rasterbator: a compulsive manipulator of digital images. For instance, a frequent user of Photoshop.

romming: programming for CD-ROMs.

Sagan: a very large quantity. From the late astronomer Carl Sagan, who was known for his "billions and billions" line on the TV show *Cosmos*.

salami attack: computer crime performed in small increments to avoid detection.

screenager: today's teens, who've grown up in the computer age. "Damn screenagers drive me nuts!"

shovelware: (1) low-quality software that is released to the public before all the bugs are worked out; (2) a CD-ROM title comprising old material shoveled in to fill up the 600 megabytes of available disk space. Aka "kitchen-sink title."

Silicon Valley: the area around San Jose, California, where the bulk of the American computer and computer chip industry is clustered. White bread and *borrrring*.

Siliwood: "Silicon Hollywood," the coming convergence of movies, interactive television, and computers. When the locus of power is Silicon Valley, use "Siliwood." When the locus is L.A., "Hollywired" is preferable.

single-systemitis: being so loyal to one computer system that one categorically refuses to learn or even acknowledge any other. People so afflicted are known as "hedgehogs."

slag: bring a network, especially a local area network (or LAN), to its knees by overloading it with data traffic. "We slagged the net last night by playing Spectre while the MIS department was trying to reindex the accounting file."

slave: a computer that is controlled by another computer, known as the "master."

Smileys: clever, if sometimes annoying, visual ways to add punch to online discourse; e.g.,]:-{o is a barbershop quartet singer.

snailmail: U.S. Postal Service mail.

spam: as a verb, to fill someone's brain space with useless information. Also, to post inappropriate information to a huge number of inappropriate newsgroups. As a noun, the junk mail of the online world. From the Monty Python sketch featuring Vikings in a restaurant singing "Spam, Spam, Spam, wonderful Spam, marvelous Spam" over and over *ad nauseam.* Aka "roboposting."

spelling flame: criticizing someone's spelling on the Internet. The lowest level of attack, used when someone has nothing of substance to offer. Aka "dictionary flame."

stop words: words so common, it is useless to include them in a word search. Example: "and."

surfing: searching through the Internet or online services for interesting stuff.

technogentsia: people who appear to know more than the rest of us about all things digital. Aka "the digerati."

telco: the telephone company. Cyber people *love* to toss this word around. "It's really up in the air right now whether the telcos or the cable guys are going to run with this."

thrashing: clicking helter-skelter around an interactive computer screen in search of hidden buttons that might trigger actions.

time bomb: instruction built into a program that tells it to destroy all data at some designated point in the future. Used by disaffected hacker employees.

Toasternet: cheap Internet routers made with old PCs. May have been inspired by the Video Toaster desktop editing device for the Amiga or by that ubiquitous home appliance, the toaster. "Grunge computing" has been proposed as a general term for the repurposing of old PCs and other trashed digital technology.

trap door: an opening in computer programs that allows you to bypass the system's security protection.

troll: search the Internet for specific information. As opposed to "surfing," which has a more random quality.

true blue: an IBM-only office.

vaporware: a product that is announced well before it actually appears on the market.

wave a dead chicken: to perform a useless and irrelevant repair on a severely damaged computer to prove to the customer that you at least tried to fix it.

webjam: according to media artist Ebon Fisher, a webjam is a "rhythmic event integrating humans, technology, and nature." Superficially similar to "raves," "happenings," or "be-ins," a webjam is actually more ecological at its core. In other words, you have to be there to get it.

Webmeister: the person in charge of a Web site.

WELL-being: a participant in the Sausalito-based online service called the Well.

wired: plugged into the cyberscene. Also, *Wired* magazine, a hip, stylish, cyber rag.

World Wide Wait: an increasing popular nickname for the World Wide Web because of the enormous delays in accessing sites.

Zero Bug release: roughly, the bugs in the current software have merely been "postponed." A Microsoft misnomer.

zorch: move speedily through a task.

Great Cyberquotes

"I have traveled the length and breadth of this country and talked with the best people, and I can assure you that data processing is a fad that won't last out the year."
—*editor in charge of business books, Prentice-Hall, 1957*

"But what . . . is it good for?"
—*engineer at the Advanced Computing System Division of IBM, commenting on the microchip in 1968*

"There is no reason anyone would want a computer in their home."
—*Ken Olson, president, chairman, and founder of Digital Equipment Corporation, in 1977*

"640K ought to be enough for anybody."
—*Bill Gates, 1981*

Deadheads

"The Grateful Dead without Jerry is like four guys without a job."   —JOHN EXWORTHY,
      WHO BUILT THE ALTAR FOR JERRY GARCIA'S FUNERAL

"We will survive. We will get by."   —"TOUCH OF GREY,"
                        THE GRATEFUL DEAD (1987)

WHETHER YOU LOVE OR DESPISE THE GRATEFUL
Dead (and there are equally valid reasons for both), you
cannot ignore them. Here is the vernacular of the most successful
progeny of the Summer of Love and the all-time official San Francisco House Band, whose spirit and vernacular will live on long
past the last bootlegged memory of Bob Weir singing "Sugar Mag-
nolia."

With a flip of the tape to David Shenk and Steve Silberman, authors of *Skeleton Key: A Dictionary for Deadheads.*

AUDs: audience tapes of Grateful Dead shows, ostensibly not for
    profit. A visionary hallmark of the Dead experience. There's
    even a "tapers' section" at Dead concerts (aka "the pit"). Clear
    recordings are "the kills." Taping is known as "spinning."
the Bogus Bobby: Randall Delpiano, a Bob Weir look-alike, who
    conned gullible Deadheads out of dope, dough, and food even
    after serving two years for impersonating Weir.
bota bags: flask-shaped leather pouches for carrying various
    kinds of "dosed" refreshments into a show. Since they are not
    bottles, bota bags are never confiscated at the door. A lasting
    relic of '60s hippie culture.
the Boys: a nickname for the band, which has been all male, ex-
    cept for Donna Godchaux's stint from 1972 to 1979. "The Boys
    were on fire tonight." Aka "the Boyz."
Captain Trips: the late Jerry Garcia. Aka "the Old Man."
the Community: one of the many whacked-out spiritual com-
    munities that feed off the Dead experience. A cross between

the Hare Krishnas and the Love Family, touting a strange Judeo-Christian stew. Its members are not so much fans of the Dead as "fans of the *fans* of the Grateful Dead." In other words, missionaries, offering free medical help and propaganda to any Deadhead in need. Aka "Yahshuas."

the Dead: the Grateful Dead, the greatest hippie road band of all time. Their live concerts were the stuff of legends. And so were their drug habits.

Dead sled: a VW bus.

Deadbase: the complete guide to the Dead live oeuvre, with set lists from every show the band has played. Aka "the bible."

Deadhead: strictly speaking, a follower of the Grateful Dead, though I think Blair Jackson adds the proper perspective: "I wish I had a dollar for every person I've met who said, 'I like the Grateful Dead, but I'm not a Deadhead,' as if the word 'Deadhead' was a synonym for 'leper.' That's because these

people have bought into the straight media's portrayal of Deadheads as stoned, tie-dye-wearing, VW-van-driving, stringy-haired, patchouli-scented, weirdly named, mono-syllabic crazies who sell veggie burritos and crystals. Of course, there actually are a fair number of Deadheads who fit that description, but anyone who bothers to look even the slightest bit beneath the Day-Glo veneer finds so much more." Believe me, I know. Bill Weld, Rick Crotty, and Tipper Gore are all Deadheads.

false Jerries: Jerry Garcia look-alikes, frequently spotted at shows.

Jerry: Jerry Garcia, demigod of the Deadheads. His every move, thought, word, gesture, has been eulogized, pondered over, and regurgitated by serious fans of the band and in all Dead-head discussion groups. This guy was a talented musician, but does he deserve this much adulation?

Jerry's side: the right side of a concert hall floor, in front of Garcia's customary concert position. The opposite of the "Phil

Know Your Deadhead

Outside the Auditorium

Gawd Squad: truly high people who are, unfortunately, always dysfunctional. A Gawd Squad usually consists of an older dude who's probably a vegan, who probably did some time with the Hare Krishnas, who no doubt pretends to be celibate, and who thinks he's God, with younger "chickie-poos," who believe he's God too, fawning all over him. This dude is inevitably sleeping with the young chickie-poos, though they wonder what's wrong with *them*.

According to Heather Wakefield, "The Gawd Squadders often have a food thing going on in the parking lot or can be seen in long lines giving each other massages, oohing and aahing because they are so deprived of SEX."

hall gawkers: the "philosophers" of the Dead experience, often found leaning against a wall, watching the scene go by.

hall people: a general category of Heads who hung out on the periphery of "shows." Most hall people never went in to actually watch the band. As Heather Wakefield put it, "Every once in a while I had to go down to see if the band was still there."

Inside the Auditorium

aisle gawkers: similar to "hall gawkers," except they tend to hang out in places that are usually right where you need to walk. They tend to have little or no focus, so they also tend to have complete and total meltdowns right in the aisles.

behind-the-stage people: pretty simple, really. They bliss out behind the stage.

chair people: Heads who navigate around a specific seat. Chair people get territorial by section (Jerry's side, Phil's side, etc.). Everything is organized by where members of the band are stationed. "I'll meet you on Phil's left."

floor people: everyone who hangs out on the floor. The opposite of "chair people."

heavyweights: a subset of "parking lot people" who are heavy into heroin and in a direct polarity with the "wharf rats." Origin of the expression: "I used to be a heavyweight, but now I'm a wharf rat."

tapers: usually men with lots of equipment and a singular

Zone," which is the left side of the floor, where fans of Phil Lesh congregated. When Phil hit a particularly loud bass note, it was known as a "Phil Bomb."

miracle: a ticket to the show. From the Dead song "I Need a Miracle."

Netheads: Grateful Dead fanatics who populate Internet sites and "Dead boards" on services like the Well.

no, but I've been to shows: what you'll probably hear from a Deadhead if you ask if he or she is, in fact, a Deadhead.

on the bus: you've acid-tripped. Wavy Gravy invented the term. Then Kesey made it popular with his bus, "Further." A metaphor for people with a clue. "Who are with us, not against us."

railrats: seriously devoted Deadheads who want to get as close to the band as possible, hanging out right in front of the stage. They are distinguished from other Heads who prefer "space dancing" or "swimming" (roaming around the concert hall, taking in the show from a variety of perspectives—what I call "attention Dead disorder"). To get "on the rail," a railrat must do some serious "line duty" (waiting in line for hours before the concert).

sacraments: drugs.

Shakedown Street: Dead album #15, which also refers to the main drag of vendors in the parking lot of a Dead show.

spinners: people who spin to the right while dancing to the Dead. Those who spin to the left are "twirlers." Twirlers are known for "twirl-byes" and "twirl-by-twirlings." Some argue that the "spinners" screwed up the world, so the "twirlers" have to unscrew it. Roots go back to the whirling dervishes of Sufism.

stubbing down: trading tickets in order to secure a better seat.

total family kine: extraordinarily good. "How was the show?" "Total family kine, sister."

Touchheads: the sizable contingent of young Deadheads drawn to the scene by the popularity of the 1987 hit "Touch of Grey," the best-selling Dead single of all time.

tour rats: Deadheads who religiously follow the Dead around on tour. They are often in concert parking lots, peddling merchandise to keep their trip afloat. At the end of a tour, a tour rat is faced with the ominous prospect of "reentry" into normal society.

West Coast Deadheads: supposedly mellower and freer than East Coast Deadheads and thus closer to the original spirit of the band.

wharf rats: an organization of clean and sober Deadheads (an oxymoron?). Their motto: "One Show at a Time."

the wheel: the wheel of karma. From the lyric "the wheel is turning, you can't slow down."

Detroit

You really have to like darkness and despair to move to Detroit, Michigan, "America's First Third World City." This is a city most natives are glad to be *from* and damn glad to be *away from* now. Yet, despite its rotten rep, Detroit has that cool, dark, industrial vibe that I've always found perversely beautiful. I remember Detroit with overcast skies and either cold or humid. I remember a giant Uniroyal tire plus a humungous ferris wheel peeking out of the mist. Coming from Omaha, I was always impressed by Detroit as an invitingly butch place to live. Eventually learning that MC5, Patti Smith, and Iggy Pop also came from Motown only added to its cachet.

Some Tips to Get You Oriented in Our Nation's Auto Capital

1. If you live in Detroit proper, you say "*Deee*-troit." If you're a suburbanite, you say "Detroit" (very sharp and to the point). If you're making fun of the whole idea, you say "Day-troi."

2. In a town that manufactures most of America's autos, it's no surprise to find a vibrant teenage car culture. "Cruising" is still an honored pastime. East Siders cruise on Gratiot ("Grash-it"). West Siders cruise on Telegraph (what is affectionately called "goin' Graphin'"). The major cruise street in the city is Woodward (what some locals call "Woodard"), a huge north-south thoroughfare that divides the east from the west side. If you're looking to cruise there, you'd say, "I'll be 'cruisin' Woodard' tonight."

3. You can tell what side of town Detroiters are from by the way they pronounce street names. Example: Schoenerr is a German word whose correct pronunciation is "Shaner." Depending on where you live, however, it can also be pronounced "shoner" or "shawner." The correct pronunciation of Lasher is "Lawsher." But only half the street signs in the city spell it "Lasher." The other half spell it "Lahser," thus the alternate pronunciation, "Lawser." Of course, that doesn't stop other locals from pronouncing it "Laser."

4. In Detroit there's the automobile workers and there's every-body else.

5. Michigan is shaped like a hand. One of the most delightful things you will encounter when approaching a Michigander for directions is how they use a hand as a map. A Michigander might say, "I'm going to Alpena for the weekend." You'd say, "Where's that?" The Michigander would then hold out a hand and point to where Alpena is on the palm. Remember: when using the Michigan hand map, you must always have the thumb sticking out. And if you want to signify the Upper Peninsula, simply position your other palm horizontally on top of the first palm.

6. Because of the primacy of the automobile industry and the fact that the Ford family started here, there is still a sense of working for an individual rather than a vast corporation. People who work at Ford will say, "I work at Ford's." As if Henry Ford were still running the place. As if they had a relationship with the man. Others will say, "I work at Chrysler's."

7. Detroit may be the only major city in America where, if you go south, you're in Canada. Windsor, to be precise.

A^2: Ann Arbor, home of the University of Michigan.

the Bad Boys: the old nickname for the Detroit Pistons, when Rick Mahorn and Bill Lambier were chairmen of the boards. Now they might just as well be the "nice boys," with well-adjusted all-American good guys like Joe Dumars and Grant Hill on the team.

the Big 3: Ford, GM, and Chrysler. Many Americans think all the divisions of the Big 3 (Buick, Pontiac, Dodge, Chevrolet, etc.) are separate companies. A local never makes that mistake. Alternately, Little Caesar's, Domino's, and Hungry Howie's.

Black Bottom: where Coleman Young grew up.

COLA: Cost-of-Living Allowance. Bitter locals complain that nobody else in Detroit gets it but the auto workers. But there's no use arguing the point, because the auto worker unions get whatever the hell they want.

Coneys: chili dogs. Aka "Coney Islands."

the Corner: Tiger Stadium, on the corner of Michigan and Trumball. Used by diehard fans.

da Dead Wings: the Detroit Red Wings hockey team when they lose.

Devil's Night: as if things weren't bad enough in Motor City, on the night before Halloween, locals used to make it a habit to engage in several hundred acts of arson.

downriver: the area south of metropolitan Detroit, home of nouvelle muskrat cuisine.

downstate: everywhere in Michigan except the Upper Peninsula. The area south of Bay City is known as "down below."

the Fab Five: the legendary five University of Michigan basketball players, featuring Detroiters Chris Webber and Juwan Howard, who led the Wolverines to two straight NCAA finals in their freshman and sophomore seasons.

flip-flops: turnaround lanes. In most of Detroit you don't have left turns. You have "flip-flops," which are positioned past a traffic light as an indentation in the meridian. It's very important to grasp this concept so that when a local says, "Go past Nine Mile, do a flip-flop, and take a right," you know what to do. Aka "Michigan turnarounds."

Hizzoner: former mayor Coleman Young.

in the thumb: the area near Saginaw and Bay City, seen when using the Michigan hand map.

the Joe: the Joe Louis Arena. "The Stones concert will be held at the Joe."

Madonna: the archetypal Detroit girl, though she was born in Bay City and went to college in Ann Arbor. Every Detroit girl has something of Madonna in her—that gum-chewing, streetwise, punk kid who is gonna get the hell out of this hole and make something of her life.

the Motor City Madman: Ted Nugent.

the Pussycats: what the Detroit Lions are called when they aren't faring well on the football field. Aka "the Pontiac Pussycats."

the Ren Cen: the Renaissance Center. The city's shopping, hotel, and business complex, with a "classy" rotating restaurant on top.

650 Lifer: Michigan's notorious mandatory sentencing law, which sets a life sentence for the possession of more than 650 grams of cocaine.

the Somerset Collection: according to one local, "the hugest, swankiest mall imaginable" (Needless Markups, et al.), taking up two whole sides of the street. The name speaks volumes about Detroit's desperate yearning for "class."

the U.P.: the Upper Peninsula of Michigan. The northern part of the state, reached by crossing the Mackinaw Bridge. Surrounded by three of the great lakes (Superior, Huron, and Michigan), the U.P. has its own language and heritage, which have formed the basis of several secessionist movements. See "Yoopers."

up north: anything outside the Detroit area. Even if you're going due west to Grand Rapids, you say you're going "up north."

Uppie: what Michiganders from the Lower Peninsula call Upper Peninsula residents (aka "Yoopers").

Vernor's: a ginger ale drink made in Detroit. Outsiders have no clue about the emotional lock it holds on a local's psyche. For instance, when a Detroiter is sick, he might say, "I need some Vernor's to settle my stomach." If you move here from out of state, it's the nastiest thing you've ever tasted. The second way to tell a local is whether he will die for a scoop of Sanders Hot Fudge. Outsiders think it's nothing special. Detroiters swear by it.

Windsor ballet: the strip clubs across the river in Windsor, Canada.

Yoopers: residents of the U.P. They take pride in their isolation and have created their own culture, which celebrates the contours of their life—blizzards in winter, mosquitoes in summer, and lots and lots of beer guzzling. They have also invented a unique idiom, dubiously called "Yoopanese," which is an amalgam of the "bad English" used by Finnish farmhands and French-Canadian trappers mixed in with Cornish and Italian miner talk. The most notable features are anything but foreign—expressions like "let's go store" ("let's go to the store") and "da" for "the." Perhaps the most notable contribution is "Trolls," which stands for southern Michiganders because they live "below" (or south of) the Mackinac (pron. "Mackinaw") Bridge.

Diners

Diners are a truly American institution, serving comfort food to weary travelers in small, box-car settings. You'll find diners all over the country, but especially in the Northeast. While the old, highly descriptive diner vernacular is dying fast, I encourage you to keep this fantastic tradition alive by using the words listed here as you navigate through the fascinating diner landscape.

Points to Remember

1. A great deal of what I call "diner vernacular" started with "the soda jerk," the fare well and hale met fellow who manned the soda fountain in the early part of this century, constantly dreaming up new ways to name his concoctions and woo the ladies with his speedy wit.

2. Diners were America's first standardized fast-food joints. Not as fast as today's Burger King or Taco Bell, but they launched the concept into the American mind-set.

Beverages

Adam's Ale: a glass of water. Aka "moisture" or "one on the city" ("hold the hail" if no ice).

baby: milk.

balloon juice: champagne or seltzer.

billiard: buttermilk, because it always has little white lumps. Aka "Arizona."

drag one through Georgia: Coca-Cola (Atlanta is the home of Coke).

draw one blonde: coffee with cream.

go-go juice: coffee. Aka "tar" or "midnight."

hug one: squeeze a glass of orange juice.

lacey up with spla: hot chocolate with whipped cream.

M.D.: Dr Pepper.

make it moo: coffee with milk.

scandal soup: tea. From the Boston Tea Party.

snow shoe: a cup of hot chocolate.

sun kiss: orange juice.

Breakfast

Adam and Eve on a raft: two link sausages on a pancake.

army strawberries: prunes.

bailed hay: shredded wheat.

bangers: sausage. Aka "grunt."

bear claw: a sweet bread shaped something like its name implies.

bird seed: a bowl of cereal.

blowout patches: pancakes.

cackleberries: eggs.

collision mats: waffles.

complete chicken dinner: two hard-boiled eggs.

eggs in the dark: eggs fried on both sides.

elephant dandruff: corn flakes.

hope: oatmeal.

looseners: prunes.

mother and child reunion: fried chicken and fried eggs.

sinkers: doughnuts.

slaughter in the pan: beefsteak for breakfast.

spoil 'em: scrambled eggs.

stain 'em: put blueberries in the pancakes.

tire patches: pancakes.

wrinkled dough and ole black joe: waffles with coffee.

Condiments

breath: onions.

Bronx orchids in May: coleslaw.

dog biscuits: crackers.

frog sticks: french fries.

grass: lettuce.

lighthouse: catsup. Aka "hemorrhage."

may: mayonnaise.

Mike and Ike: salt and pepper shakers.

Mississippi mud: mustard.

red lead: catsup.

rush it: Russian dressing.

sea dust: salt.

skid grease: butter.

yum yum: sugar.

Desserts

brown derby: a chocolate doughnut topped with a scoop of chocolate ice cream covered in chocolate syrup or hot fudge.

Canary Island: vanilla soda with chocolate ice cream.

Chicago: a pineapple sundae.

Dagwood special: a banana split.

Dionne Quintuplets surprise: five small scoops of vanilla ice cream topped with whipped cream and a cherry on each, crushed pineapple on one side and crushed strawberries on the other. Named after the popular 1930s quintuplets, who even had toys named after them.

dusty miller: a chocolate sundae sprinkled with powdered malt.

gedunk: ice cream (from the sound it makes plopping into a soda).

George Washington: cherry pie. Aka "Virgin."

a guinea football: a jelly doughnut.

ice on rice: rice pudding with ice cream.

ice the blue: blueberry pie à la mode.

magoo: custard pie.

monkey: coconut pie.

roach cake: raisin cake.

shivering hay: strawberry Jell-O.

shivering liz: Jell-O.

sleigh ride special: vanilla pudding.

white horn: a vanilla ice cream cone.

Dinner

angels on horseback: oysters rolled in bacon and served on toast.

bloodhounds in the hay: hot dogs and sauerkraut.

bossy in a bowl: beef stew.

C.J. Boston: cream cheese and jelly. In part from Boston cream pie.

chewed fine with breath: a hamburger with onions.

Cincinnati oysters: pigs' feet. "Cincy" was once known as "Porkopolis."

duck a half: oyster stew containing six oysters (a half dozen).

Hebrew enemies: pork chops.

hot swimmers: catfish.

Italian hurricane: spaghetti.

prairie oysters: bull testicles.

radio sandwich: tunafish sandwich.

rock island: Irish stew.

sewer trout: pink salmon.

slab of moo, let 'em chew it: rump steak rare.

a splash of red noise: tomato soup.

sweep the kitchen: a plate of hash.

whistleberries: baked beans.

yesterday, today, and tomorrow: corned beef hash.

People

bubble dancer: a dishwasher.

cloud: the headwaiter.

hummingbird: a talkative fountain man.

lady bug: a fountain man popular with the ladies.

pie pusher: an inexperienced counter man.

soup jockey: a waitress.

Miscellaneous

fix the pumps: a well-endowed female just walked in.

love box: a booth.

ninety-five: a customer is leaving without paying.

pitch till you win: eat all you can.

thirteen: the boss just arrived.

with wheels: get it to go. Aka "put wheels on it."

Disney

"THE HAPPIEST PLACE ON EARTH"? YEAH, RIGHT. Several decades ago Disneyland had a mythic power over my psyche. It was a swell place, filled with innovative rides, psychedelic imagery, and a heady degree of hype that had me believing it was all actually fun. Back then, I liked Disneyland.

Then came the corporate sales pitch of EPCOT Center. And suddenly the magic was gone from the Magic Kingdom.

Here is the inside vernacular on the vast entertainment conglomerate that turned the hallucinogenic visions of Master Walt into the disingenuous, white bread family fun of Brave New Disney World.

backstage: all of the cast member–only areas, such as the cafeteria.

the Big One: nickname for the earthquake ride at Universal Studios. The ride actually subjects one to an 8.3 Richter quake.

cast members: employees.

Celebration, Florida: a 20,000-citizen town owned by the Disney corporation, with a town hall designed by protomodernist Philip Johnson, who's obviously too senile to contemplate the implications of this Huxley vision come to life. Bill Bennett is the honorary mayor (just kidding).

costumes: uniforms.

Disney dollars: greenbacks bearing Mickey's image in $1, $5, and $10 denominations accepted at Disney World.

Disneyland Paris: the new name for EuroDisney.

EPCOT: corporate advertising under the guise of "fun, Fun, FUN!" Visit "the American Adventure!" (sponsored by Coke and American Express). Witness the amazing "IllumiNations!" (sponsored by GE Lighting). Travel inside the 180-foot-high "geosphere" known as "Spaceship Earth!" (sponsored by AT&T).

EuroDisney: the troubled foray of the Mouse into hostile international waters. Otherwise known as the revenge of the French on low-brow American culture.

guests: visitors.

the Hub: the area in front of Cinderella's Castle in Disney World.

imagineering: dreaming of fun things for all of the guests to do that mesh well with the corporate sponsorship.

the Magic Kingdom: not only a specific park at Disneyland and Disney World but a name for Disney as a whole.

mouschwitz: an inside term for Disney used by some of its employees.

the Mouse: Wall Street's nickname for Disney.

Mouseville: what the few alternative-minded people in Orlando call the family values capital of the South and hometown of Disney World.

onstage: the areas one can see as a guest.

passport: an all-day ticket.

the Space Mountain Dash: the mad sprint riders make to get back in line after a ride on Space Mountain.

spokes: the bridges coming out from the castle going to different lands.

stacking: queuing passengers outside a ride to relieve congestion inside. Gives the illusion of a long wait when there isn't.

20K: The 20,000 Leagues Under the Sea ride.

we request: do not do that.

widowmaker: gruesome nickname for the vaunted Matterhorn roller coaster, where several folks have met their maker on one of those "magical, happy days" in Disneyland.

Drugs

AMERICANS ARE THE MOST OVERMEDICATED PEOPLE on the planet. The medical establishment, and likewise the general public, thinks most mental, physical, and spiritual problems can be solved pharmaceutically. Thus, the widespread use of both licit and illicit drugs to "cure" all that ails us.

Given this state of affairs, it should come as no surprise that Americans have a variety of fascinating terms to go with their drugs of choice.

acid: lysergic acid diethylamide-25, a derivative of ergot, a fungus that grows on rye. Alternately, "LSD." Aka "liquid" (when dissolved in liquid), "blots" (when absorbed into blotter paper), and "sheets" (perforated hundred-hit squares of blotter paper).

acid test: way before Mr. Kesey gave us the term, it referred to miners testing the gold content of objects by scratching them and applying nitric acid.

Alice: LSD or shrooms. From the line "Go ask Alice" (Jefferson Airplane).

angel dust: the powdered form of PCP, an animal tranquilizer that is either sniffed or smoked. Aka "dummy juice," "rocket fuel," "water," "angel hair."

Augustus Owsley: a high-grade variety of LSD, named in honor of the man who first produced it.

B: Benzedrine. Aka "Benny."

back in the box: back in business after a drug arrest. A dealer term.

barbie dolls: barbiturates. Aka "barbies," "goofballs," "downers," "Geronimos."

barrels: saccharine tablets that absorb more than 75 micrograms of liquified acid.

Bart Simpsons: LSD. Aka "conductor," "contact lens," "Lucy in the Sky with Diamonds," "strawberry fields."

basehead: one who "freebases" cocaine.

Belushi cocktail: the combination of cocaine and heroin that killed John Belushi and River Phoenix. Aka "speedball" (speed and heroin).

blow: snortable cocaine. Aka "nose candy," "snow," "powder," "paradise," "paradise white," "Ye Olde Peruvian Marching Powder," "girlfriend," "pimp." Prisoners use two additional names, "blanco" and "cheese."

booty juice: MDMA dissolved in liquid.

boxed: in jail for drug use or selling. The majority of those in American jails or prisons are in for drug-related offenses.

brewery: where drugs are manufactured.

button: a hit of peyote, which is shaped like a button in its natural state.

candy flip: an acid and ecstasy combo popular at rave parties. Aka "X&L."

cat: methcathinone. An amphetamine analog that is popular in Michigan and Wisconsin. Often made from solvents found at any hardware store (perfect for the Upper Peninsula). AKA "goob" or "morning star."

check out: overdose and die. "He decided to check out."

clocker: a street-level drug dealer. Aka "retailer."

cocktail acid: the less potent variety of acid sold today (20–80 micrograms), compared to the far more potent type (150–500 micrograms) sold in the 1960s, when acid first became popular.

coke: cocaine. Ironically, Coca-Cola (i.e., Coke) was known as "dope" back in the 1930s.

coke blunt: a rolled combination of pot and cocaine. Aka "coca puff."

come home: conclude an acid trip.

cookie: a cigarette laced with crack.

coolie: a cigarette laced with cocaine.

the copping zone: a shadowy world in which drugs are freely dealt. Involves a whole network of support personnel, including neighbors (to stash drugs and money and feed the sellers), cabbies (to bring in buyers), kids (to run the drugs), and cops (paid to lay low).

crank: methamphetamine. Old term for "speed." Aka "go fast," "wizard," "water," "cartwheel," "truck driver," "road dope."

crashing: coming down from a drug high. Aka "sinking," "kicking."

DMT: dimethyltryptamine, an LSD-like hallucinogen that doesn't last as long.

dose: a hit of LSD. Aka "paper," "square," "cloud," "tab."

Dr. Feelgood: a physician who indiscriminately prescribes drugs.

CAPTAIN JACK EXPLAINS HIS BONG TO BILLY

drugola: the bribes drug dealers pay to the police for protection.

Dust Bunny: someone high on PCP or a frequent user of PCP.

E: Ecstasy. Aka "X." The true chemical is MDMA, an amphetamine that is purported to open up "the heart center." See *Wayne's World* ("I love you, maaaaaan"). The ghastly physical effects that E exerts on the nervous system have led to a decline in the drug's use in recent years, though not in Europe, where techno ravers think it's the latest "rage."

fiend: a heavy drug user. Aka "dope fiend."

freebase: smoke chemically altered cocaine hydrochloride. Caveat: there is a subtle difference between freebasing (which Richard Pryor burned himself doing) and crack smoking. As Professor Terry Williams explains, "Freebase" is made by boiling powdered cocaine in water, which yields a residue that is put in cold water, where it "forms an off-white odd-shaped hard mass. Pieces of this mass, which is called base or freebase, are then chipped off" and smoked. Base makes a crackling sound when smoked, which accounts for the term "crack." However, while freebasers tend to prepare their own base from powdered cocaine, crack users tend to buy their base "precooked and mixed with other cheaper chemicals, including baking soda." The popularity of crack is due precisely to its ease of use, lower quality, and concomitant lower price.

glass: very pure crystal methamphetamine ("crystal meth"). Aka "sparkle," "shards," "oda," and "ice" (the purest form of all).

go out: overdose. Aka "O.D.," "go down."

ground control: one's guide during an acid trip.

high beams on: high on cocaine. Aka "coked up."

Hinkley: PCP (phencyclidine). Aka "O.P.P.," "purple rain," "Peter Pan," "soma," "elephant."

hippie crack: an inhalant. Aka "poor man's pot."

huffer: someone who inhales chemical vapors to get high. Aka "gas huffer." As a verb, "huff," "Elmer," or "Clinton."

ice: smokable super-pure methamphetamine, with prolonged highs (some lasting as long as 24 hours) and highly addictive.

ice cream habit: the occasional use of drugs. Aka "Pepsi habit."

internals: people who smuggle drugs inside their body, often by swallowing condoms filled with the drug. Aka "bodypackers," "mules."

jelly beans: painkillers.

Jonesin': an intense craving for drugs; needing a "fix" really really bad.

the K hole: a flattening of the emotions from an overuse of ketamine. Hard to get out of. The drug is so euphoric, it can also cause a loss of interest in breathing. Users have to be reminded of this.

the kind: marijuana. From the Hawaiian, and some say original, pronunciation, "da kine, Brah." Aka "the kind green bud."

love boat: marijuana dipped in formaldehyde.

mad spun: high on LSD. "That dude's mad spun."

the man: a drug dealer. Aka "connect," "source," "doctor."

meth monster: a person who has a violent reaction to methamphetamine.

Miss Emma: morphine.

moon rock: a potent blend of heroin and crack cocaine. Aka "parachute."

mortal combat: high-potency heroin.

mule: a person who smuggles drugs on or in his or her body. The practice came to light when surgeons discovered dozens of drug-filled condoms in the intestinal tracts of two survivors of a Columbian airline that crashed in New York City. Aka "internals."

nail: a hypodermic needle.

nickels and dimes: $5 and $10 bags of your drug of choice.

on the nod: under the influence of narcotics.

on the pipe: addicted to smoking pure cocaine; i.e., "freebasing."

one and one: a package with two small balloons, one holding heroin, the other cocaine.

pancakes and syrup: a combination of glutethimide and codeine cough syrup.

Crack

Back in 1989–90, I spent many nights in the East Village of New York hanging out with "crackies" of all stripes around makeshift bonfires of the insanities. I never tried "rock," and I'm always boggled by anyone who would, but I was always fascinated by the complex world that surrounded its use.

Though smack has taken over as the drug de jour, crack still soldiers on as the poor man's cocaine. Here's a look inside the crack world, with a tip of the pipe to Professor Terry Williams (*Crack House*).

beamer: crack user. Aka "Prudential." See "Scotty."

bottlers: women who divvy crack into vials.

chocolate ecstasy: crack made brown by adding chocolate milk powder during processing. Aka "chocolate rocket."

crack: extremely addictive smokable cocaine. Aka "rock," "ice cube," "kryptonite," "breakfast of champions," "Rocky III."

crackie: the outside world's name for a crackhead.

the cracking hour: that time during the early morning, usually around 7:00 a.m., when the crackhead is staggering around, out of drugs and out of his or her mind.

the devil: crack. Aka "devil's dandruff."

geek: a crack addict.

Germans: crack dealers who are overly rigid or controlling in their conduct. Aka "the Enemy." In New York circles, usually applied to Dominicans.

ghostbusting: the futile examining of all white particles to see if they are crack cocaine. See "searcher."

the glass diet: using crack cocaine.

the great white hope: crack. Given its decimation of the black community, it has a rather poignant double meaning.

hubba: crack in a vial.

keeblers: crack user's term for white folk.

lookouts: people who alert other gang members via walkie-talkie when the police are coming. Usually found on street corners or any high place, such as a rooftop.

manager: dispenses crack to the pitchers, oversees financial accounting as well as the hiring, paying, and arming of "lookouts."

→

messengers: kids who run errands for the dealers, such as taking crack to pitchers, guns to managers, and cash to stashers.

on a mission: searching for crack. Aka "tweak mission."

perp: fake crack, made of candle wax and baking soda.

pitchers: the sales force, often crackheads themselves. They work out of designated locations considered their "turf."

pseudocaine: phenylpropanolamine, an adulterant for cutting crack.

rock star: a woman who trades sex for crack or money to buy crack.

Scotty: crack cocaine. From the character on *Star Trek*. Other words also come from *Star Trek*, including terms for getting high ("Beam me up" and "I'm going to see Scotty"), and going from one crack house to another in search of "rock" (an "interplanetary mission"). Certainly this would never meet with Scotty's or Mr. Spock's approval.

searcher: a crackhead who searches for lost crack particles. Like a diehard smoker in search of a butt.

skeezers: women who prostitute themselves for crack.

slab: overly adulterated crack.

spaceship: the glass pipe used to smoke crack.

spotter: one who warns sellers about the police.

stashers: people who offer their apartment to stash cash, drugs, and guns. Their rent is covered in return.

strawberry: a completely gonzo crack-addicted woman who often sells her body for "rock." Aka "raspberry."

tax: price paid to enter a crack house.

taxing: charging more per vial depending on the race of the customer.

tension: crack cocaine. Aka "white girl."

thirsty: an intense craving for crack.

trey: a small dose of crack ($3 worth).

twitchers: crackheads so far gone they start to develop quirky little tics or twitches. Some, completely unable to stay still, jerk and fidget uncontrollably, or in some cases pull on arms, ears, or legs (aka "pullers").

yahoo: crack. Does David Filo know about this?

Yale: crack. What's that make Harvard—smack?

zoomers: individuals who sell fake crack and then flee.

Names for the Herb

MARIJUANA IS A COMMON DITCH WEED THAT PRODUCES some rather uncommon results. It seems to be enjoyed by many good folks around the planet, hence a name for it in several different languages. It was also farmed and enjoyed by Thomas Jefferson, principal author of the Declaration of Independence, and some claim by George Washington, "the father of our country." Here is the American argot for the sacred plant known in Costa Rica as "la bonita," in Brazil as "Dona Juanita," in South Africa as "dagga," in India as "guaza," in Denmark as "hampa," in Columbia as "hoja," in Israel as "shesha," in Mozambique as "suruma," and in Nigeria as "wee wee."

airplane	grass	Mary Jonas
alfalfa	hash	Mary Warner
baby	herb	moon cabbage
baby bang	hooch	owl
bud	jazz	pot
budda	KGB	rasta weed
Buddha	kind	reefer
chronic	kind green	tweeds
da kine	kind green bud	weed
dank	Mary Anne	wood
ganja	Mary Jane	

Using the Herb

Alice B. Toklas: a brownie laced with pot. Aka "hash brownie."

baked: high on pot. Aka "stoned" or "lit" ("I'm nice and lit off just one hit, man").

baking like Betty Crocker: getting stoned *frequently.*

Benny Mason: super-strong pot. Aka "Mr. Mason."

blunt: a huge joint rolled in cigar paper without tobacco. Aka "spliff" or "fatty." From the Philly Blunt brand of cigar.

Bogart: the ultimate stoner admonition not to hog the joint. Quite humorous to hear from slackers, many of whom haven't a clue who Humphrey Bogart was or seen any of his films. "Hey man, don't Bogart it, I haven't even got a hit."

bong: a specially fitted water pipe used to gain the maximum hit from a "bowl" of marijuana.

cornhusker: a joint rolled in corn husks. For special occasions.

doper: someone associated with smoking marijuana who shows all the "dazed and confused" characteristics of a stereotypical pot smoker. Aka "pothead" or "stoner."

goo-ball: any sweet treat laced with marijuana.

hold: possess pot.

joint: a marijuana cigarette. Aka "doobie," "hooch," "reefer," "stick," "rope," "splint," "spliff" (pron. "spleef"), or "Bob."

KGB: killer green bud, i.e., marijuana.

killer weed: extremely good marijuana. Aka "killer pot."

lid: an ounce of marijuana.

lost farm day: so stoned one cannot function. Someone might say, "Are you plowing the fields of the lost farm?"

Maui wauie: marijuana from Hawaii.

munchies: hunger pangs engendered by smoking pot. "Hey man, I got the munchies."

panatella: a large marijuana cigarette.

purple hair: a special strain of extremely potent Afghani pot. So named because of the purple hairs on the buds.

roach: the butt end of a "joint."

roach clip: a metal tweezers-like clip that allows a user to hold and smoke a "roach."

schwag: very bad marijuana. Made popular by Manny the hippie, star of *Late Night with David Letterman*. Aka "ditch weed."

sens: sensamilla, a potent strain of pot.

skunk weed: strong-smelling marijuana.

spark a fatty: light up a joint. Aka "spark a hoon."

stoner chick: a woman who hangs out with "stoners" whether or not she smokes.

swisher: a cigar emptied and filled with marijuana. Not as large as a "blunt."

twist one up: roll a joint.

up against the stem: addicted to marijuana.

walk the dog: smoke pot. Aka "get stoned."

zombie: a chronic user of marijuana.

Names for the Nag

HEROIN IS A HIGHLY ADDICTIVE AND REFINED FORM of morphine. Ironically, it was first developed as a cure for morphine addiction. As a friend so aptly put it, "Another one of those good ideas gone bad."

Since so many of our fine youth, in pathetic imitation of recent superstar heroin casualties (heroin came from the Greek word *hero*), prefer H over other addictive substances, and with everyone cashing in on the obsession, from Quentin Tarantino (*Pulp Fiction*) to Calvin Klein (a perfume called Opium, with pale, anorexic models looking like they need a fix), I decided to clue you and them in on the language and mind-set that goes with "the drug of the '90s."

Running with the Nag

biscuits: methadone. Drug used to kick a heroin addiction.

black tar: the less pure Mexican "brown" heroin. Aka "chiva," "mud," or "tar." Popular on the West Coast.

bunk: bad heroin. Aka "stepped on," "cut up," "gank."

chasing the dragon: addicted to heroin. Used also when one inhales the smoke from an opium cloud.

chip: occasional heroin user. Aka "chipping."

code blue: when someone temporarily (or permanently) stops breathing due to a heroin overdose.

cotton fever: when a piece of cotton used in cooking heroin gets drawn into the needle and shot into a vein, causing extreme sickness.

donkey dick: a very strong and lasting erection, attributed to heroin use.

euphoric recall: dreaming about your next hit of heroin.

fix: a shot of heroin.

give wings: inject or instruct someone on how to inject heroin properly.

gotta cap, hook up, hook me up, get well, get my sick off: various ways to express the need for a fix. Aka "I'm dying to have a balloon."

hype: a heroin addict. Aka "hophead," "junkie." There are two types of "hype": a "gutter hype," who lives on the street, and a "house hype," who lives in a stable dwelling.

$\rightarrow$

jab: inject heroin. Aka "hit," "fix," "drive iron," "bang," "slam," "mainline," "shoot up."

P-dope: 20%–30% pure heroin.

paper boy: a heroin peddler.

popping: shooting heroin into the skin when you can't find a vein. Aka "muscling it."

rig: the syringe used in shooting drugs. Aka "point," "outfit," "tommy gun."

slammed back: high on heroin. Aka "wasted," "gowed."

take in the sky: shoot up heroin and space out.

tie me off: help me shoot up.

tracks: needle marks on a junkie.

turned out: getting someone completely addicted so you can use them for money or companionship. "He got her turned out so he could get her dad's dough."

the works: all the paraphernalia used in shooting drugs like heroin or speed (such as the cooker, the syringe, the tie-off). Aka "the kit," "the set," "artillery."

Heroin Through the Ages

A-bomb	Henry
antifreeze	hero of the underworld
Aunt Hazel	him
big boy	jack
big daddy	jazz
big H	junk
big Harry	lady in white
black stuff	Lady White
blue sky	liquid sky
China White	moon rock
Chinese Red	number eight
courage pill	racehorse Charley
dog food	red chicken
ferry dust	smack
foolish powder	snowball
galloping horse	tecaba
George Smack	tragic magic
H-caps	triangle stuff
Harry	white God
Hazel	

→

Heroin Terms Today

Aries	mud	scag
boy	negra	stuff
death	ogoy	tar
dope	Old Steve	white boy
H	outfit	the witch
hop	Peg	
horse	perfect high	

peaking: at the top of your trip. "Fully inflamed," in the words of Kym Trippsmith.

peanut butter: PCP mixed with peanut butter. Also, a type of brownish methamphetamine

permafried: high all the time.

pig killer: PCP. From the violent reactions caused by the drug.

pizza toppings: psilocybin mushrooms.

poppers: isobutyl nitrite or amyl nitrite, which is "popped" open and inhaled. Popular as a "sexual training tool" in '70s gay culture.

potato chip: crack cut with benzocaine.

primos: marijuana joints mixed with crumbled pieces of crack.

puddle: a substantial dose of liquid LSD.

quack: Quaaludes. Aka "ludes."

rat boy: a human guinea pig, who tests the purity and potency of a drug before giving everyone the green light to use it.

riding the E train: feeling the effects of Ecstasy.

riding the train: using cocaine.

Robo-ing: drinking Robitussin with codeine.

roid rage: aggressive behavior caused by the excessive use of steroids.

roofies: Rohypnol, an extremely powerful sedative slipped by cads into a woman's drink, rendering her pliant. Aka "the forget pill" because victims of "roofies rape" cannot remember any details of the crime.

Sam: federal narcotics agent.

sandwich: two layers of cocaine with a layer of heroin.

schedule one: drugs that have no currently accepted medical use. Includes most hallucinogens.

schwilly: a person who drinks alcohol.

shaman: peyote.

sheet rock: crack mixed with LSD.

sherm: a cigarette that has been dipped in embalming fluid.

shermed: loaded on PCP. Aka "dusted."

shooting gallery: place where injectable drugs are used, primarily heroin.

shrooms: psilocybin mushrooms. Aka "magic mushrooms."

skeeze: to use cocaine.

slinging: selling drugs. Aka "swinging," "grinding," or "running."

space dust: crack dipped in PCP.

special K: ketamine hydrochloride. Discovered in 1965, it's typically used in the U.S. as a veterinary anesthetic, though it's also used recreationally to experience altered states of consciousness (seeing angels, tunnels of light, immortality, yadda, yadda, yadda). Aka "super acid," "super c," "purple."

stash: one's personal supply of drugs.

step on: "cut" or dilute a drug.

tab: a single dose of acid. AKA "hit." Current varieties go by several brand names, including "Mr. Natural," "Mickey Mouse," "Black Pyramid," and, yes, "Bill Clinton."

Tammies: Tamazepam, a popular sleeping pill that doesn't give you a sleeping pill hangover.

taste: heroin. Also, a small sample of drugs.

tolley: toluene, a potent paint solvent popular with the *Citizen Ruth* set.

tripper: a person high on LSD or a person who routinely "drops" acid.

tweaked: completely amped on speed. Aka "sketched," "spun," "geeked."

tweaker: speed freak.

utopiates: hallucinogens.

weight: a package of drugs.

wounded soldier: a half-drunk beer.

wuwoo: marijuana and cocaine in any combination.

yuppie flu: the ongoing effects of a cocaine-snorting habit.

Zen: LSD. I don't *think* so. Then again, Doc Ellis pitched a no-hitter on acid, so anything's possible.

zero: opium.

zoinked: intoxicated on drugs to the point of uselessness.

Ecobabble

"An activist is the guy who cleans the river, not the guy who concludes it's dirty."
— Ross Perot

As a rule, I divide up the environmental mind-set into two competing categories: (1) environmentalists, who go to painstaking extremes to clean up their neighbors' backyards but whose own homes are often a complete mess (motto: I *am* my brother's riverkeeper), and (2) polluters, who generally don't give a damn how much they foul up the commonweal but whose own homes are as neat and clean as a pin (motto: I did it my way).

Keeping in mind that Lex the Cosmic Psychic predicts in the future "a consortium of environmental extremist organizations will evolve into an extremely powerful religious cult after merging with former Scientology leaders," here's a quick way to keep tabs on your favorite conservationist or all-out bad guy polluter. With a pole stroke to Donald "Sasquatch" Francis for all his Piscean help.

BANANA: Build Absolutely Nothing Anywhere Near Anything. The rallying cry of communities categorically opposed to environmentally unfriendly uses of their land (landfills, waste disposals, nukes, etc.).

basic brown: a person who is largely uninterested in environmental issues and most definitely will not be basing purchasing decisions on them.

beach nourishment: a disingenuous term used by industry publicists for placing toxic dredged sediments on the shorelines of rivers.

bunny cop: a derogatory term for a park ranger. It comes from the NYPD officer who laughingly referred to Katie Weil, then a park ranger, as a "bunny cop" while issuing her a speeding ticket.

Cascadia Free State: a renowned nonviolent occupation of an ancient forest near Oak Ridge, Oregon, scheduled to be logged under "the salvage rider." A community of punks, hippies, and homeless kept up the fortress-like encampment from September 1995 to August 1996, using blockades, bridges, and moats. A role model for future encampments and road blockages up and down the Cascades.

catch and release: catching fish with barbless hooks and then releasing them back into the waterway. A type of angling practiced by "hook" people. Many animal rights activists consider "C&R" a form of fish torture, since the angler simply drags it up on the shore to take its picture while the fish gags. Many fish die after release from the trauma of the experience.

crunchy: adjective for those who adhere to the au naturel look from the late '60s, such as body hair or serious dreadlocks. Often refers to those who have spent a great deal of time following the Grateful Dead and/or hiking. From the longstanding hippie habit of feasting on granola (thus "crunchy").

deep ecology: the belief that one can literally find God in a grain of sand.

dolphin safe: tuna fishing in which no dolphins were killed.

ecodork: Vice-President Al Gore, considered a leader of the modern environmental movement. Aka "Captain Ozone," a more pejorative nickname for Big Al repeatedly used by John McCain of Arizona, the "angry white guys" representative.

environmental justice (aka "EJ"): a grassroots reaction to the disproportionate dumping of pollution in low-income communities and communities of color. According to Don Francis,

"EJ" is "such a broad and inclusive movement, it needs to become the new model of environmentalism as a whole, or the environmental movement will die." Dumping pollutants in poor or minority areas is known as "environmental racism."

environmental wacko: one who considers unpolluted water and air more important than corporate profit. A term used to describe environmentalists, ecologists, conservationists, and preservationists by extra-plump radio talk show host Rush Limbaugh.

environmentally friendly: a product that will cost you 15% more.

Ewok Village: a type of West Coast ecoterrorism that involves sabotaging logging operations by using nature-friendly supplies to prevent the entry of modern machinery. A key component is a system of rope bridges between trees, which allow tree-sitters to navigate an old-growth logging site without touching ground. From the *Star Wars* characters the Ewoks.

FODs: Forces of Darkness (not to be confused with Friends of Don). Essentially, the timber, mining, grazing, and aluminum industries. According to environmentalists, FODs make most of their money from extracting or decimating public lands and national forests at far below market value, then leaving the cleanup costs to the taxpayer. Associated terms for these practices include "welfare ranching," "welfare mining," and "welfare logging."

Freddie: a U.S. Forest Service employee.

God Squad (aka "Gang of Four"): a small group of scientists assembled to decide if saving a species on the brink of extinction will lower corporate profits. If the decision is yes, then the proposed development can be built despite the eradication of the species.

greenlock: traffic gridlock at national parks and forests, particularly in the summer.

greenwash: misleading advertising and promotion that makes a corporation seem environmentally sensitive when it isn't. Example: ads that congratulate a company for protecting a wetland when it was required by law to protect it anyway. Oregonians for Food and Shelter is a "greenwash" name of an environmental lobby for agricultural and wood product industries.

hook and bullet crowd: anglers and hunters who also care about the environmental impact on fish and game animals. These are the original white American conservationists who, decades ago, worked to protect their favorite hunting and fishing spots. Teddy Roosevelt is the father of this group and one of this country's earliest and most successful conservationists.

Los Angelization: unplanned, car-centered, decentralized urban development, with concomitant air pollution, land abuse, and social alienation. Examples: Las Vegas, Orlando, San Diego.

new forest: a timber industry term for a crop of row trees that will be cut down within several decades.

oil war: a conflict to preserve and protect vital oil supplies. Classic example: the Gulf War.

old-growth forest: a large mixed-age stand of trees (containing many over 100 years old) surrounded by diverse flora and fauna. Less than 10% of America's old-growth forests remain.

overmature forest: a term used by timber industry flacks to cajole the public into supporting the cutting of old-growth forests.

pollution rights: when companies pay localities a fine for the right to pollute. The idea that profit is more important than public health.

regulated organic nutrients: sewage.

the sacred trinity of the modern environmental movement: David Brower, Rachel Carson, and John Muir.

the sacred trinity of the modern Wise Use movement: Charles Hurwitz, Dan Quayle, and James Watt.

salvage logging: logging healthy trees in national forests because they will probably die on their own. . . in the next 500–600 years.

the salvage rider: a federal statute that circumvented most logging restrictions and effectively eliminated citizen participation, allowing what environmentalists called "logging without laws."

selective cutting: a logging industry PR term used to describe clear-cutting where a few trees per acre are left standing.

SLAPP: Strategic Lawsuits Against Public Participation. An attempt by a powerful special interest or individual to dissuade activists from opposing their plan for development. Recently environmentalists have successfully resorted to "SLAPP-backs" to thwart the impact of any SLAPP.

they get the gold, we get the shaft: environmentalists' catch phrase for the consequences of the 1872 Mining Act, which has allowed multinational corporations to mine billions of dollars' worth of precious metals from federal land for as little as $5 an acre. Many of these mines have polluted nearby rivers when runoff carried toxic metal and chemicals into the waterways.

treated: a misnomer used by Exxon after the *Exxon Valdez* spill in discussing the pools of oil covering rocks and bushes. Aka "environmentally stabilized."

tree-hugger: derogatory term for people who feel passionately about protecting America's forests and forest-dependent wildlife, especially old-growth forests of the Pacific Northwest. Also a Republican word for any environmental activist. Aka "bunny-hugger."

tree-sitter: someone who constructs a simple stoop high in an old-growth tree targeted for cutting. "Ground support" provides food, water, clothing, and escape help if the tree is cut.

tuna laundering: misrepresenting tuna as "dolphin safe" when it is not.

unwise abuse: the Wise Use movement, which cautions voters about the long-term impacts of environmental measures on jobs and property rights.

Film and TV

WE ARE A NATION OF HAMS. WE ARE ALSO A NATION of spectators. The film and TV industry serves both.

Abby Singer: the next-to-last shot of the day. From the first assistant director who routinely announced "Last shot," then would add, "No, wait. Just one more."

above the line: costs incurred before filming even begins (usually from payouts to directors, actors, and producers). "Below the line" is everything else.

AD: Assistant Director. The director's right-hand person, essentially relieving him of mundane duties so he can focus on pure creativity and chasing chicks. For instance, the AD will "call" the crew and actors to work and keep track of who must be on the set, when, and for how long. ADs are also in charge of crowd scenes, and will most likely shout, "Hey everybody, quiet on the set!"

Alan Smithee: the pseudonym directors hide behind when they want to dissociate themselves from a film. Predicted to increase in use as directors grow increasingly irate at the alteration of their original visions to suit the demands of the digital era. Some of Mr. Smithee's films include (with real directors): *Fade In* (Jud Taylor), 1968; *Ghost Fever* (Lee Madden), 1987; *I Love N.Y.* (Gianni Bozzacchi), 1988; and *Catchfire* (Dennis Hopper), 1991.

animal wrangler: the person in charge of managing animals on and off the set.

ankled: when an important player leaves one studio for another. Once he or she has arrived at the new studio, he or she is said to "put up a shingle."

apple box: the plywood building blocks of a film set. When it is used for a short actor to stand on, it is known as "the manmaker."

associate producer: defined by comedian Fred Allen as "the only guy in Hollywood who will associate with a producer" (from the credits to the 1940s movie *In the Bag*).

How to Talk American

attached: when an actor or major player signs on to a film project. "We're almost set to go—we've got Joe Eszterhas attached as screenwriter."

author: (verb) to write, also "to ink."

baby legs: a short-legged tripod. Aka "shorty."

baby wrangler: a child acting coach.

bananas on bananas: a TV or film "gag" that is so overdone it loses its punch. "Just have Mike and Jim fall off the boat. Having Ellen do it too is just bananas on bananas."

BCU: Big Close-Up. A shot that fills the screen.

best boy: support person for the gaffer or key grip. In the hierarchy of film, the director of photography oversees the camera and lighting departments. Under lighting there is a gaffer and key grip, each of whom has a best boy.

biopic: a film or TV show about a famous historical person.

B.O.: Box Office; i.e., actual or potential ticket sales. As in, "*Home Alone* had strong box office." Or, "The new Stallone flick will be good box office."

bomb: a box office failure.

bow: open, premiere.

boy-meets-girl: a standard cinematic love story. *Romeo and Juliet* is the classic "boy-meets-girl" story.

buck: $100,000 in Hollywood parlance. "For ten bucks, Uma will do your picture."

the business: the television industry. As opposed to "the industry."

C-47: a wooden spring-loaded clothespin. Used in large quantities on a film set (e.g., affixing gels to the "barn doors" of lights). The name derives from the ordering number for clothespins in the catalogue of a major film expendable supplier.

cable-access: community-based television programming that often has low production values but high entertainment value. Its existence is mandated by a federal law requiring cable companies to provide at least one channel of free, noncommercial programming to any and all citizens in the viewing area that get on the waiting list for three years and request it.

cattle: Hitchcock's term for actors. Still used today. A "cattle call" is an open-call audition (in modelspeak, a "go-see"), to which many "cattle" have been invited.

chopsocky: *Variety*-speak for a martial arts film.

corrective surgery: quietly getting a difficult or weird contestant off the set of a TV game show.

craft: actors' wonderfully annoying term for their life calling. "Since *Dante's Peak* I've been really working on my craft." The day I heard myself say this, I knew the saccharine city had won.

craft service: the snack food table on a film set. Not the catering company, as is sometimes assumed.

crash and burn: kill the story.

D-girls: development girls. They read stupid plot ideas and pitch them to the players. Aka "trackers," "D-heads."

deal memo: the statement of intention between "the talent" and the producer that precedes a final deal. Also used in the publishing world.

DGA: the Directors Guild of America.

doughboys: caterers.

ducats: tickets.

earwig: the radio listening device a sound technician puts in an actor's ear to prompt him or her with lines or music. Used a lot in *Mr. Holland's Opus* to synchronize the miming of piano playing with the actual soundtrack.

elbow grabber: the model who escorts contestants off the set of TV game shows.

event movies: gigantic blockbuster productions that more resemble thrill rides than "films." *Jurassic Park, Independence Day,* and *Twister* are classic "event movies."

eyeballs: television viewers. "Any idea of how many eyeballs we got on that Ann-Margret Christmas special?"

Fishtar: nickname for Kevin Costner's riotously overbudget flop, *Waterworld,* for its similarity to another infamous failure, *Ishtar.* Aka "Kevin's Gate."

the fluffer: the person on the set of a porno movie who keeps the actors erect between takes.

Foley artist: the person in charge of "Foley," the process by which sound effects are added to a movie soundtrack.

frankentits: ridiculously large surgically enhanced breasts. Found in adult movies and magazines.

fresh air exhibitors: drive-in movie theaters. Aka "out-doorers," "open air operators," "underskyers," "rampitoriums," "mudholes," "cow pastures," and "passion pits."

gaffer: a lighting director on a film or TV set.

grip: the muscle of the lighting department, where high tech and low life collide. Handles everything short of construction (shadows and screens in front of lights, rigging, etc.).

gross player: a big enough star to command a percentage of the gross receipts on a film (or "points on the gross") rather than a percentage of the net profit. The latter is the largest ripoff in the entertainment business, to which any creative talent can attest, since there is nothing stopping a studio or production company from declaring a net loss on a project even if it grossed big-time bucks. "Don't even talk to me about net. Carolyn Reese is a gross player, and that's all there is to it."

hang the black and poke the eyes out on the babies: a command from an AD, cinematographer, or gaffer to hang up a black cloth and remove the Fresnel lenses.

helmer: the director. As a verb, to "helm" (direct). "It looks like Van Sant might helm *The Mayor of Castro Street* after all." Aka "CB" (after Cecil B. De Mille).

hickey: a favorable review in the press.

high concept: a film with a clearly defined and easily explained plot. Examples: *King Kong, The Poseidon Adventure, Airplane.*

high schmooze: a Hollywood event with a high proportion of "players" in attendance.

HINT: Happy Idiot News Talk. The vacuous and silly banter that occurs between anchors on local TV news broadcasts. When used to fill up the end of the broadcast, it's known as "drooling."

Hollywood: as an adjective or noun, highly commercial, superficial, or tacky. "I suggest you shoot in New York. Otherwise, it will become all Hollywood and lose any depth."

a Hollywood minute: one year.

Hollywoodland: Decades ago, the name of the housing development in the Hollywood Hills, which erected the prominent Hollywoodland sign to advertise itself. After years of neglect, the sign was restored, sans the last syllable, to become "the Hollywood Sign."

horse blanket: any device a cameraman uses to make the actor look more appealing. "She's a do, better throw a horse blanket on it."

hot set: a set completely "dressed" and ready for shooting. "Stay out of the bathroom. It's hot."

if it bleeds, it leads: mantra of TV news producers, who are keenly aware of the public's appetite for death and mayhem.

in the can: a completed but not yet released film.

How to Talk American

the industry: the film business. As opposed to "the business." Aka "Hollywood."

jet: to go. "Look, I gotta jet. Can we hook up tomorrow?"

juice: a little extra something added to a TV report to give it pizzazz.

kamikaze: the prop master.

key grip: head person in the grip department.

the Kodak: any motion picture camera. "Move the Kodak over here."

leg: longevity at the box office.

legit: to be in "legitimate theater" rather than film (which is considered even by those in "the industry" to be not as classy or demanding).

the majors: the top film distributors.

Makita: a popular cordless drill found in most grip departments. As a verb: "Hey, come over and Makita some screws for me." Any cordless drill is called a Makita. As an adjective: "Hand me some of those Makita screws" (a hardware store wouldn't know what you were talking about).

Maliboobs: *Baywatch,* the most popular TV show in the world, featuring babe-a-licious bikini-clad lifeguards sporting prominent fake boobs. It's really hard deciding who to hate more—television's clueless bonehead hunkulus, David Hasselhoff (the founder and star of "Babewatch"), or film's overrated, overexposed, pop culture junkie, "Cretin" Tarantino, so I just make it easy and unconditionally hate them both.

marquee: a highly recognizable star who will attract considerable public interest. "No question about it—Jim Carrey is a marquee talent." Also used in sports ("We feel Shaq is a marquee player") and politics.

meat puppet: an actor.

Mickey Rooney: a short movement. From "short creep." "Just as John opens the car door, we'll do a Mickey Rooney."

monster: a huge success. "*E.T.* was a monster hit."

M.O.S.: a script abbreviation to indicate a scene without sound or sound effects. Comes from "mit out sound," an expression used by a German director, Erich von Stroheim, in Hollywood in the 1930s. Aka "wild picture."

murder-your-wife brick: fake brick from the 1965 Jack Lemmon film *How to Murder Your Wife.*

net: one of the four major television networks (ABC, NBC, CBS, and Fox). Aka "web."

nine iron: a shovel. If you need a shovel from the grip truck, you say, "Get me a nine iron."

nostril shot: unflattering footage of a subject.

numbers: performance at the box office; i.e., how many tickets sold. Alternately, a TV show's Nielsen rating (how many households watched a given program).

Oscar nod: an Academy Award nomination.

painter: a makeup person.

Pasadena: to pass on a script.

player: a major industry heavyweight, usually a producer or executive producer. Aka a "wheel."

props that eat: extras. Courtesy of Rob Dalton (the TV exec who *didn't* discover Oprah).

PUC (pron. "puke"): a Previously Unknown Child who is suddenly tossed into the life of a soap opera character.

punch up: to add verve and excitement to a script. "That second act needs to be punched up a bit in the laugh department."

the Rachel: a popular hairstyle pioneered by Jennifer Aniston on the TV sitcom *Friends.*

reel: one's latest and best video pieces spliced together on one tape. "I'll send you a reel."

rip-o-matic: a video of storyboards used to entice production companies into investing in your project. Alternately, editing existing movie footage to show one's editing style. Also called a "rip."

Rudin: throw a complete and total tantrum. From the notorious rageholic producer Scott Rudin.

Rupert's World: Fox Broadcasting, after its CEO and infamous "Sun King," Rupert Murdoch.

SAG: the Screen Actors Guild.

Salvador: a "dolly," the wheeled vehicle that carries a camera around a set. From Surrealist painter Salvador Dalí.

screwperstar: an adult film celebrity.

sked: a schedule.

skin flick: a pornographic movie.

slasher: a film with gratuitous amounts of graphic violence. Examples: *Night of the Living Dead, Texas Chainsaw Massacre.*

snuff: a film where people actually die. Completely illegal.

sound bite: a short, pithy quote suitable for the nightly news.

spaghetti western: a western shot in Italy with an Italian cast, a few major American actors, and English dubbed in. Sergio Leone was the quintessential spaghetti western director.

sparky: the electrician on a movie set. Alternately, a "juicer" or a "juice boy."

spec: to do work for future pay.

spec script: a writer's version of a "spec"; i.e., putting together a few key scenes for presentation. A writer is not paid to do a spec but uses it to sell his idea. As in, "Are you being paid for this or is it a spec?" "Spec scripts" are never written for the show one is applying for but for another popular show with which people would be familiar. "Spec scripts" all used to be *Cheers*. Then they were all *Seinfeld*. Now they're all *X-Files*. Aka "treatment."

stag film: one emphasizing explicit sex. What at one time was also called an "art film."

the star system: the grooming and marketing of individual actors and directors as the focal point of entertainment products. A brutal, elitist, winner-take-all system that is fundamentally inefficient, narrow-minded, and cruel— unless, of course, you're a star.

starrer: a film in which a known actor appears. Aka "star vehicle."

sticks: a tripod.

stretch: go beyond one's normal thespian schtick, often into uncharted waters. The ability to "stretch" successfully is what separates true "actors" from mere "personalities."

strip show: a program airing five days a week in the same time slot.

the suits: the executives in an entertainment company. Aka "the higher-ups." As opposed to "the talent." All "talent" must inevitably answer to "the suits" on one key point: "the numbers."

sweetening: improving the sound of a film in the final mix.

swing gang: the workers who put up the furniture and set dressing before a shoot and "strike" a set afterward. The "swing gang" works the exact opposite shift from a shooting crew. Aka "set dressers."

tabloid TV: television news programs that mirror the lurid and sensational content of tabloid newspapers. Example: Fox's *Hard Copy*.

talking head: shot from the head up. Also, a television reporter.

the trades: the daily *Variety* and *Hollywood Reporter*, the entertainment industry's bibles.

undercrank: operate a camera at a lower film speed than normal.

vamp: an early name for a Hollywood sex symbol.

Vanilla Oprah: Ricki Lake, the hilarious and beloved former John Waters star (*Hairspray*) turned earnest daytime talk show host.

vanity show: a project put into development to placate a major star.

video moment: a heartwarming shot or sound bite.

wallah: background voices, movements, and other sounds added to a soundtrack to provide authenticity. Aka "wallah, wallah rhubarb." Comes from the way a large group actually sounds to an audience. A "wallah group" creates the background dialogue in a studio, often tailoring their banter to the specific theme of the scene (e.g., a law firm scene might have lots of legalese).

wet stuff: sex and/or violence.

wrap: finish or wrap up a project. "That's a wrap." Also used beyond the film business in the sphere of relationships (L.A.'s other obsession): "Tim's been a real pill lately. I think I'm going to wrap that up."

yo, Hollywood!: a term of endearment from one player to another.

Florida

If there is one state the rest of the country could do without, it would certainly be Florida—the ticky-tacky taste, the fundamentalist hoo-hah, the complete disregard for the environment, and, if you're a sports fan, the annoying success of the college football programs. In fact, in my conversations with Americans, Florida keeps coming up as the one state they want "bombed." Still, people move here—for the sunshine, the beach, the bedrock of family values, and, if you're heading for Key West or Miami, the decadence.

Alligator Alley: Route 84 between Fort Lauderdale and Naples.

the Back Country: the islands of Florida Bay, northwest of the Keys.

butt floss: a pretty skimpy bikini that fits neatly between "the butt cheeks." Women wear them on the beach, though they're banned (along with 2 Live Crew and topless doughnut shops) in Fort Lauderdale.

cesspool of the South: Jacksonville. Aka "Jax."

Die 4: Interstate 4, which cuts through the center of the Sunshine State.

Everglades: Pa-hay-okee, or "grassy waters," according to the native Miccosukee Indians. This 50-mile-wide, 100-mile-long, and only 6-inch-deep river of sawgrass barely hangs on as America's largest remaining subtropical wilderness. Aka "the Glades."

God's waiting room: a nickname for Florida because of all the elderly who have moved there. Politicians don't want to even *think* about cutting Social Security in this state.

Grapefruit League: preseason pro baseball. Found throughout Florida.

hammocks: semi-elevated, tree-covered islands in the "river of grass" known as the Everglades.

walking trees: the mangrove trees throughout the Everglades and the Keys.

Key West

"I've been as far south as you can go. I've been to Key West. And Key West is a holiday island. Wide, flat, white, sunny and no one ever works. There are eternal guest houses and piano bars. And it's a shrine to Mister Hemingway. Every bar has a life-sized photograph and the words 'Hemingway lived here, Hemingway drank here, Hemingway fought here.'" —QUENTIN CRISP, THE MONK'S GUIDE TO NEW YORK CD-ROM

THE INDIGENOUS LANGUAGE OF THE KEYS IS CONCH, a nickname for the locals. But some say there's so much cockney in Conch that one might rightly call the language "Conchney." Alas, many of these words and expressions are no longer heard regularly on the street, for radio, TV, and unbridled tourism have pretty much leveled out any idiosyncrasies. The original flavor can still be heard, however, in a conversation between two Conches raised in Key West before electronic media came to town.

Blood Beach: the former name of Smathers Beach. So called because livestock were brought from Stock Island, slaughtered on the beach, and the fresh meat delivered to Key West homes.

boatel: it's not just a boat or a hotel. It's a boatel. And it's unique to Key West.

bolios (pron. "boy-ohs"): a Key West version of southern hush puppies made with mashed, shelled black-eyed peas instead of ground cornmeal.

booger: cocaine.

boogered up: high on cocaine.

Bubba: a friendly greeting reserved for old Key West friends, as in "Hey, Bubba." Similar to "Hey, Bud."

Bubba system: when old Conches control city government.

Bubbagate: any Conch-related controversy, usually involving the ever-present Conch patronage system.

bug: crayfish. Aka "Florida spiny lobster." "You'll see lots of bug traps down around MM #63."

Cayo Hueso: the original name of Key West, "little island of bones." Legend has it that when the Spanish settlers arrived, they discovered bones left over from Indian battles. Today one of the popular Conch trolleys is called the Cayo Hueso Express.

Conch (pron. "konk"): (1) A chewy pink shellfish that comes in those huge spiral shells you blow as horns and put next to your ear to "hear" the ocean. This Bahamian specialty is customarily served as an appetizer either plain, in chowder, or battered and fried as "fritters." (2) Anyone born in Key West. The story goes that the nickname dates from a time when the natives proclaimed that they'd "rather eat the meat of the Conch than pay the high tax to King George."

Conch cruiser: an old rusty bike with a basket, no fenders, and high handlebars, or a beat-up car, sometimes stolen from up north, used for getting around on the island.

Conch houses: built in the 1850s by the original settlers, who came from Great Britain via the Bahamas.

the Conch republic: a fictitious nation born on April 20, 1981, in reaction to troublesome roadblocks set up at Florida City. Now another annual Key West tourist celebration, called Conch Republic Days.

cuda: barracuda, ubiquitous in the Keys. Cuda does not make good eatin', as it inflicts the eater with "cigutera," violent fish poisoning.

Dixie farm: pejorative term for an unkempt property.

downtown 76: the mid-'70s restoration fever still going strong in old Key West.

Fat Albert: a 1,400-foot, radar-equipped blimp tethered to the ground that hovers over the area around Cudjoe Key to detect drugs and drug smuggling. Occasionally it blows away and has to be shot down—only to be replaced by "Son of Fat."

grits box: a stove.

grunt: a fish you can easily catch but don't want to unless you're awfully hungry. Named from the sound it makes.

Grunt Bone Alley: where locals tossed their grunt bones during the Great Depression (when Key Westers ate only "grits and grunts").

how ya doin', cuz?: a familiar Conch salutation.

the hurricane: the storm of September 2, 1935, that blew across the Matecumbe Keys with 18-foot tidal waves and 200 mph winds, leaving 800 dead in its wake. Ironically, "Matecumbe" is probably a corruption of the Spanish *mata hombre*, "kill man."

Key lime: the scrubby key lime tree, with its thorny branches, grows to about 15 feet. Key limes (aka "true limes") are greenish yellow, resemble small lemons, and are more tart than other limes.

Key lime pie: the area's signature dessert, featuring the small limes native to SoFlo, a yellow meringue topping, and a graham cracker crust. Little-known fact: a pie with true Key limes will set immediately without any gelatin because of the limes' high acid content.

Keys: from the Spanish *cayos*, meaning "small islands."

kitchen safe: pantry.

Little White House: President Truman's vacation cottage at the Key West Naval Station.

Mananaville: Key West. As Jack Moyer of the historic Conch Tour Train notes, "Nobody's on time in Key West. There's nothing that can't be put off till tomorrow."

Margaritaville: Key West, as immortalized in the Jimmy Buffet song of that name.

Mile Marker: sign on the side of the road telling you how far you've gone on a given highway. One of the primary means of navigating in the Keys. Often written as "MM."

natural sponge: a dishcloth.

orse: a horse.

Red Cross houses: industrial-strength, super-thick concrete houses built in towns like Tavernier after the horrific hurricanes of the 1930s. Aka "hurricane houses."

a saw: a native of Nassau, in the Bahamas.

sea pissers: sea cucumbers, because of the way they squirt.

sportfishing: one of the sickest pastimes in the Keys—catching fish solely for their looks or, worse, for the show they put on when they're caught (example: tarpons and sailfish). There's no intention to eat them, only to mount them.

sugarloaf: name for pineapple in the Bahamas. Key West used to be a distribution point when Henry Flagler's railroad came through town, supplying canned pineapple to most of eastern North America.

the tourist tree: a gumbo-limbo tree at Watson's Hammock off MM #31, whose limbs look as if they have a bad case of peeling sunburn.

treenails: wooden pegs used to build the early houses in Key West. Ship's carpenters used treenails because regular nails would bend in high winds and had to be imported from England.

turtle kraals: the northern foot of Margaret Street on the Key West waterfront, where the now-endangered green sea turtle was butchered for its veal-like meat. *Kraals* is an Afrikaans word for "enclosure" or "corral."

wisit: visit.

Miami

MIAMI IS A POLYGLOT—PART COLONIAL CARIBBEAN, part Eastern European, part working-class English, part good ol' Dixie. There are perhaps a dozen language groups in Miami. If I really wanted to be specific, I'd create lexicons for Little Havana, Little Haiti, South Beach, Coconut Grove, and a host of other ethnic enclaves. But I'm going to go easy on ya. You're going to have a hard enough time dodging the coke traders and South Beach fashion mafia.

barbacoa: the original name for barbecue. So named by those inveterate campers, the Seminole Indians, the first tourists in Florida. They used their barbacoa to cook meat, fish, and fowl on wood gratings over a hot fire.

bodega: a store specializing in Hispanic groceries.

cafe cubano: a very strong black brew, served in thimble-size cups with lots of sugar.

Calle Ocho: SW 8th in Little Havana, the street that literally and figuratively divides Miami—with Coral Gables to the south and Hispanic, Haitian, and African-American neighborhoods to the north.

the Canes: the University of Miami Hurricanes, once a mighty football powerhouse now playing second fiddle to the likes of "the Gators" (University of Florida) and "the Noles" (the Florida State Seminoles).

crackers: people born and raised in the Sunshine State. According to Joyce LaFray Young, the test of a true blue cracker is whether they have eaten swamp cabbage, the "terminal bud of the Sabal palm."

Cuba: a mythical storybook kingdom of feudal capitalism where everybody is Latin, everybody speaks Spanish, everybody hates the Communists, and everybody is happy.

Cuba B.C.: Cuba Before Castro. A daily fantasy time warp for a good portion of the 250,000 right-wing Cuban Reaganauts of Miami-Hialeah.

dolphin fish: don't be misled when you see this in local fish markets. Floridians are as a rule unconscious about endangered species, but not *that* unconscious. A SoFlo specialty, this plump, white-meat fish has nothing to do with the marine mammal.

flamingo: the totem bird of South Florida, once seen on everything from garden ornaments to bookends. Now a lawn ornament in "camp lite" suburbia.

jai-alai: a sort of Spanish indoor lacrosse, with gambling and game fixing.

Kennedy: the boogie man of Little Havana. After JFK abandoned the Bay of Pigs invasion, all Cuban Americans suddenly turned Republican.

La Brigada: a misguided attempt by gonzo right-wing Cuban exiles to retake their country, eulogized by equally misguided American authors like Joan Didion.

Latinized: roughly translated, "honkies, blacks, and Puerto Ricans no longer in charge."

lychee: a popular fruit in SoFlo; its pulp has the texture of a grape and a luscious, sweet, aromatic flavor.

Mariel boatlift: Castro's revenge. The pompous Cuban dictator, in the grand European tradition, cleans house in 1980 and

dumps unwanted exiles on the bad-blood capital of the universe, America.

Miami: gateway to the Americas, capital of the Caribbean, Babel-by-the-Bay, Sun, Fun, and Cocaine Capital of the South.

palmetto bugs: cockroaches.

pan cubano: famous, long, denatured, white crusty Cuban bread.

pastel: gives Miami a soft, creamy, inviting look in the tourist brochures but can send you screaming for Brooklyn brick if you get too much of it.

Pullmanette: '40s lingo for a hotel room with a fridge, stove, sink, and roaches.

Radio José Martí: Ronnie's brilliant idea of anti-Castro propaganda.

SoFlo: South Florida. Aka "Baja New York."

Tropical Deco: Architectural style unique to SoFlo. Essentially Art Deco adapted to Miami's climate. Features flamingos, palm trees, alligators etched in glass, and nautical elements (shiplike porch railings, porthole windows). According to one Deco tour guide, "No one building in the Art Deco District is completely Art Deco. They are a fusion of Streamline, Zigzag, and Art Deco."

worms: Castro's name for the Cubans who left his island paradise for Florida.

Yanquis: Yankees.

Ziggurat: Art Deco "yuppie porn" term for the stair-stepping, lightning flash effect on Deco rooflines. Just drop it casually into late afternoon chats about porthole windows and pink houses.

Orlando

UNABLE TO DISCOVER ANY EXTRAORDINARY EXPRESSIONS from a breakfast meeting at the Dr. Phillips Rotary Club, nor any astounding argot from a surprise appearance with the band Men with Mortgages, nor any interesting idioms from a visit to the Sand Lake Dermatology Clinic or Dennis Scott's place downtown, or the YMCA, or the Turkey Lake RV Park, I decided to send my able Dartmouth interns, Thomas Jawetz and Benjamin Sternberg, on a week's reconnaissance mission to determine if Orlando, Florida, is indeed the first slang-free metropolis on the planet. Here's what they found, as written by future Washington insider Ben Sternberg.

Searching for "Orlando" in WebBrowser and Yahoo yielded many results, some of which could have helped me with a paper I wrote about Virginia Woolf. Unfortunately, all pages regarding the city dealt with the Orlando Magic, which I gather is the largest form of entertainment in the city after Disney World. Online searches of the New York Public Library system indicated that no one had microfilm of the *Orlando Sentinel;* what's more, being New Yorkers, they didn't give a rat's ass. E-mail and phone calls to people from the Orlando area turned up nothing.

We then perused the numerous travel guides written about Florida and Disney World. *An Adult's Guide to Disney World* and

Disney World for Lovers yielded surprisingly poor results. (We thought we might find some term for hanky-panky Disney style.) Other travel books were incredibly boring. The format was as follows: "This is a 'land.' This is a fun ride. The whole family will love it. Stay at this hotel. Enjoy your stay. Buh-bye." I half-expected to see that the book was written by Jim Bob Beauregard, Delta pilot.

So, after invoking premature male-pattern balding from tearing our hair out at the roots, we finally acted like the teenagers we are and used the phone. The Disney World Information Center was helpful, but workers at the Orlando Chamber of Commerce spoke English poorly. We tried EPCOT, MGM, et al. Nothing. I called two hotels, the Contemporary and the Grand Floridian. Crystal worked at the former and Kim, the latter. Crystal wasn't too helpful. She said she "wasn't too good with that kind of stuff" and promptly hung up on me. Kim asked me to hold on while she thought, and I vaguely detected the whirring of the one Disney mind at work. Just like *A Wrinkle in Time*. After a minute of holding I said, "Hello?" She said, "Hi. I'm still thinking." After another two minutes she said, "Nope. Nothing. Thanks for calling and have a good night." That's how all sentences ended, "Have a good morning" or "Have a good night." I don't think they really cared about me—after all, I wasn't staying there—but they always ended the conversation with a congenial brainwashed farewell.

Interestingly, after Ben and Tom struck out, I did uncover one gem of Orlando speech.

O'Rena: Orlando Arena, home of the Orlando Magic basketball team.

Footbag

IT'S NOT HACKY-SACK. YOU'RE "SNIFFIN' FOR scoobies" if you think it is. It's footbag, one of the fastest growing "sports" in America. One Portlander practically lives the sport. His girlfriend says that until recently he slept with his bag under his pillow. He's 26-year-old "Little Mike" Parker, the inspiration for the River Phoenix character in *My Own Private Idaho*, an actor in it himself, and the tenth best amateur footbagger in Oregon. Here are the key terms used by Mike and his fellow baggers.

bagger: a footbagger. If you want to play, you ask, "Do you want to go 'kick'?"

Beaver Open: the annual celebration of Old School footbag. Probably the only time and place you'll find the pioneers of the sport, including Jeff "the Animal" Johnson.

brain fart: when the bag hits the ground because you couldn't remember or decide on a move.

butter: a great move. "That's butter. That was Parkay. You're ready for the Aunt Jemima Classics."

circle: a group of people playing footbag. Aka "posse."

drybagging: normally, a footbag sticks to your foot nicely when it is a little wet. If it's dry, the bag slips off easily, making it hard to execute any moves. That's "drybagging."

foot sex: someone who is having an incredibly good day or routine.

4:19 and holding: a bagger who wants to smoke pot but doesn't have any.

4:20: a police term for people smoking pot, used by baggers themselves. Caveat: while at least half of all baggers smoke pot, there's a serious debate whether it actually improves performance. Mike Parker says it hinders his.

fuck the circle: widen the circle because it's getting too close.

going on a voyage: smoking pot and then playing footbag.

gravity check: when the bag hits the ground after you totally miss a move or after someone tosses you the bag and you aren't paying attention.

grind: an attempt to flip the bag up from the ground using your toes. This is never done by serious footbaggers because it destroys the bag.

hackalogical: trying to get into somebody's head to teach them a complex move.

hackalogical liar: somebody who says they can hit certain moves but can't.

hackasm: a move way beyond your normal ability.

hack slacker: standing in a circle and being totally lazy, exerting no effort at all.

Hacky Sack®: a brand of footbag.

hacky sacker: someone not into the sport of footbag, just a "kicker."

minimal space shredder: a supremely excellent bagger. He can stand in one place and tie himself in a knot and then untie himself before you can say "eggbeater." Generally, a bagger who comes up with moves you've never seen before.

prodigal boy: an excellent footbagger. Examples: "Saul the Shit," "Brian the Big Man Bagger," and "Shredrington" (Little Mike Parker).

psycho hack team: people who play all the time, as if it's their life.

rocks in the pocket: you need to chill out.

rogue hacker: a circle kicker, not a professional bagger. One who doesn't know the game. Aka "hacky sacker."

sick: a kicker who is clearly getting better. Alternatively, "Somebody get this guy to the hospital."

sniffin' for scoobies: a really lame person.

that's psycho: really intense.

torqued: very excited about a move.

Other Points to Remember

→ Footbag was ostensibly invented by Mike Marshall and John Stahlberger back in the early '70s in Oregon City, though some American Indians claim it's been played in this country since the 1800s.

→ Unlike other popular pastimes, footbag is not elitist or exclusive. Everyone is encouraged to enter the circle and give it a try.

→ Many baggers personalize their bags by giving them names. Mike Parker calls his "Clarise," and adds, "She's good to me." If you're not playing well on a given day, it means "your bag is not being good to you."

Sample Moves

add: anything you add to a basic move. Great baggers can do up to six "adds" at a time.

butterfly: a leg-over to the instep clipper.

clipper: a "set" that starts from behind the instep of the foot.

clipper double leg-over: hitting the bag off the instep followed by two leg-overs.

an eclipse: a midair stall with a leg-over.

an eternity: a leg-over clipper to the other side leg-over clipper. Almost like a figure 8 in motion.

the mirage: toe catch leg-over.

neck stall: the bag stalls on your neck.

the osis: an instep move executed from the back of the body.

the pendulum: where you grab a foot and pull the bag all the way around the front side of the body.

the pinch: catching the bag right behind the knee.

the rake: a sweep executed from the back of your hip and then raked in front of you at high speed. It's known as a "set move"—you can execute practically any move from it.

torque: a whole body-twisting move.

a whirl: an instep clipper hopping leg-over.

whirling swirl: an instep hopping leg-over.

Gambling

I REALIZE THAT BY INCLUDING THIS SUBJECT I AM essentially aiding and abetting a serious addiction of millions of Americans. But this is the land of the free, darn it, where money *is* God, money *can* buy you love, and the middle-class shills just love to spend their paychecks chasing the illusory dream of phat bank. Here's the language to get you inside the mind of a gambler.

action: the sum total of all wagers placed on a given hand, roll, or game. "There's lots of action on that Kentucky-Arizona game."

bankroll: the total amount of money a player has allotted for gambling, as opposed to the specific amount placed on the table at any one time.

basic strategy: one of many computer-generated strategies for blackjack based on the best odds for a player's hand against the dealer's up card and the known cards played to date.

Big Dick: in craps, a dice roll of 10. Aka "Big Dick" or "Big Dick from Boston, the Ladies' Friend."

black chip: a $100 casino chip. Aka "blacks." "I was playin' with a stack of blacks."

boat people: Las Vegas casino workers' term for the throngs of Asian gamblers who arrive by bus from all points on the map.

bones: the dice. Also used in dominoes.

book: place a bet or make a reservation. Or (noun) a room where sports and race wagers are made, as in "the sports book."

boxcars: a roll of 12 in craps.

boxman: a craps dealer who supervises the game and handles bets and payoffs.

buy-in: the sum of money a player exchanges for chips.

cage: the main casino cashier.

carpet joint: a luxury casino catering to high rollers. Opposite of a "rotten rug."

checks: casino chips.

comp: reduced (or free) room rate, meals, drinks, golf, airfare, and other extras (used to include sex before the recent corporate casino makeover). Once reserved for high rollers, now open to any old plebe who gambles enough. Related verb: "RFB" (to offer free Room, Food, and Beverage).

compulsive gambler: a person who will gamble on anything and everything, anywhere and at any time, who has no control over the urge to gamble, and who will not stop until all the money, credit, assets, and hope are gone.

crank games: games of chance won or lost based on a single event. Roulette, faro, acey-deucy, wheel of fortune, are all crank games.

dead man's hand: aces and eights. First used more than 120 years ago: James Butler "Wild Bill" Hickok was holding aces and eights when a hired assassin, Jack McCall, burst through the door of Saloon 10 in Deadwood, Dakota Territory, and shot him in the head.

degenerate gambler: a gambler who will play until his or her bankroll is gone but is able to stop (unlike a compulsive gambler).

drop: the total cash traded for chips at the gambling table (i.e., the total that goes in the drop box).

drop box: a box, fed through a slot in the table, which holds the money players have exchanged for chips.

envelope: illegal payoffs made to influence the outcome of a game.

eye in the sky: cameras and/or employees hidden above the casino ceiling to watch for cheaters. Think Sir Mix-A-Lot in "The Watcher." Welcome to the new world.

fin: a $5 tip.

folding money: greenbacks.

Blackjack

burn: when a dealer takes one or more cards off of the top of the cut deck and places them in the discard pile.

busting: going over 21 and thus losing the round.

double exposure 21: a variation of blackjack in which both of the cards originally dealt the dealer are dealt face up.

doubling down: when you take one, and only one, extra card and "stand," with your previous bet being doubled. You can only double down immediately after the two initial cards are placed on the table and before "hitting."

first base: the player to the dealer's immediate left, who receives the first card. Many experts prefer this position because bonehead plays by others cannot affect them. Also, a key player in any cheating scam involving the dealer. "Third base" (the chair directly to the dealer's right) is the last player to get cards.

flat bet: betting the same amount every time.

front loading: when the dealer inadvertently exposes the hole card to a player.

hard hand: a hand that includes an ace that is counted as 1, not 11.

hit: to be dealt another card. "Hit me."

hole card: the dealer's unexposed card.

insurance: a 2-1 bet made when the dealer's second card shows an ace. You are betting that the dealer has a natural 21, or a blackjack. Though the dealers say it is a wise move, experts say that insurance is a sucker's bet.

natural: two-card 21.

→

funbooks: books of gambling coupons that ostensibly save you money.

gaming: a gentler and more benign industry term for gambling.

George: a generous tipper. Aka "Super George" or "King George." A generous female tipper is known as a "Georgette" or "Female George." Placing a bet for the dealer is a kind of tip also called a "George."

getting rated: a method by which casinos assess the status of a player, based on his "buy-in" and "action." If these are high enough, the player may receive comps, generally amounting to half his average bets per hour.

 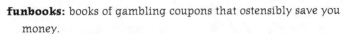

paint: a face card.

pips: the number of spots on a number card.

push: tie with the dealer. No money is lost by either party.

round: a complete hand, start to finish.

soft hand: any hand containing an ace valued at 11.

splitting: when the two initial cards dealt have the same
point value, one may "split" them into two separate hands.

standing: stopping and taking no more cards.

stiff: a hand totaling between 12 and 16.

surrender: fold after seeing the first two cards. Permitted in
some but not all casinos; you get half your money back.

tells: a dealer's mannerisms after checking the hole card.

to the farm: when the dealer's hand goes over 21.

---

green: a $25 casino chip. Aka "quarter." Uniform color coding is
used in all casinos in any given town. In Vegas, white = $1, red
= $5, green = $25, black = $100.

grind joint: a casino that caters to low rollers. Aka "sawdust
joint."

grinds: less affluent folks who grudgingly bet their money a
nickel or quarter at a time. Aka "low rollers."

handle: the sum total of all monies moving in a casino on a
given night.

hard count: counting the change from slot machines. As opposed to "soft count" (counting the folding cash).

heads up: in blackjack, one player vs. the dealer. In poker, one
player vs. another in a game or in an active hand. Aka "head
on head."

high rollers: wealthy visitors who come to gamble in earnest.
Technically, this is any gambler able and willing to spend
$5,000 or more on a weekend; there are an estimated 35,000
bona fide high rollers in the world (almost all of them men).

hold: the house profit from all wagers.

house advantage: the mathematical winning edge that the
casino gives itself by manipulating the rules of the games to
ensure profitability. Also called "percentage," "P.C.," "vigorish,"
or "vig."

juice: power, influence, knowing da right people. Also, the casino tax on a bet (aka "vig").

junket: a group of high rollers, usually flown in on a plane
chartered by the casino and accorded full "RFB."

ladderman: baccarat supervisor. Sometimes stands on a small ladder to view the whole pit.

Little Joe: in craps, a dice roll of hard 4 (i.e., 2–2). Aka "little Dick Fisher." Contrasted with "Big Dick."

loose slots: slot machines that are programmed to pay off more frequently (aka "higher payback percentages"). Some casinos actually hire independent CPA firms to verify this. A "loose slot" is a safer gamble than a "tighter" slot machine, but the payoff is generally less. In addition, the so-called loose slots often amount to one unidentified machine or bank of machines somewhere in the casino, so, on average, you still come out on the bottom.

low roller: a typical tourist making $1 and $2 bets. Aka "grinds," "suckers," "tinhorns."

marker: a gambler's IOU. Also, one who keeps track of a gambler's tab.

nickel: a $5 chip.

on the rim: on credit.

on the wood: when a marker is taken to the cage to revise a player's tab.

overdue to hit: a common phrase about a slot machine that has not paid off in a while. Because the numbers generated are completely random, however, there is really no such thing. Each game is independent of the previous games, just as the probability of getting heads when you flip a fair coin that has landed tails nine times in a row is still 50%.

overflow joint: a hotel or resort where visitors end up when the more popular hotels are "booked out."

the pencil: having the juice to write comps.

percentage (or P.C.): the house advantage, measured in percentage points.

pit: the area for casino employees behind the table games.

pit boss: an employee who oversees a cluster of dealers and tables and watches out for cheating.

pit critter: any pit employee.

play: gamble. True "players" never use the g word.

plungers: gamblers who increase their bets when they lose in an attempt to compensate for previous failures. This act inevitably plunges them into a deeper hole. Aka "screamer."

points: the percentage of ownership in a casino.

progressive slot machines: grand jackpot or payoff that grows until somebody "hits it" or wins the jackpot and resets

WOOING LADY LUCK IN NEVADA

the machine. The opposite of a nonprogressive slot machine (where the payoff stays the same no matter how many use it).

property: a casino. Gambling overlords never say "casino."

rack rate: the standard room rate. You can rent a room in a casino for a lower price if you intend to gamble. If you want a complimentary or discounted rate, you will be asked what game(s) you intend to play, the amount of your average bet, how many hours a day you usually gamble, where (at which casinos) you have played before, and how much gambling money you have on this trip. Once you procure such a deal, your actions will be monitored closely to ensure that you live up to your end of the bargain. If you gamble too little money, too infrequently, or too much at other casinos, you will find your rate altered by the time you check out.

railbirds: people who watch poker games from behind the rail around the room that separates the gaming area from the rest of the room.

random number generator (to computer folks) or **black box** (to the layman): the computerized number system that determines which stops come up on a slot machine.

RFB: Room, Food, and Beverage. A full "comp."

rotten rug: a low-life casino. The Klondike in Vegas is the quintessential "rotten rug."

sawdust joint: a casino catering to the proles. Aka "rotten rug."

shills: Back when there was such a concept as an "empty casino," "shills" were those folks paid to gamble in order to make a place look busy.

Cheating

arms smuggling: concealing cards up your sleeve.

bath: a huge loss by a casino. "The casinos took a bath on the Tyson-Holyfield fight."

black and white: a casino dealer, because of his or her customary black and white attire.

black book: a list of people who have incurred the wrath of the Nevada Gaming Commission for corrupting that paragon of Mormon virtue, Nevada's gaming industry, and who are banned for life from the state's casinos. Aka "the List of Excluded Persons."

bug: a device for concealing cards attached to the underside of a card table. "Mac was holding a jack of hearts in his bug clip when he got busted." A "hand mucker" is a cheater who holds out cards sans device.

cap: add chips to a pot surreptitiously after winning the hand. Stealing a few chips back after losing the hand is known as "dragging."

card counting: an advanced technique that tracks the cards played and determines if the remaining pack is favorable to the player. The often tried and not so true method of beating the casinos at blackjack.

chip dip: an adhesive applied to a dealer's palm which allows him to swipe chips while shoving a winner's pot across the table. The opposite of "capping."

cosmetics: subtle markings on the backs of cards to indicate their value. The marking substance itself is often known as "juice." When an entire pack of cards is marked it's known as a "juice deck."

crossroader: a cheater who travels from casino to casino, city to city.

gaff: jury-rig a roulette wheel so that the ball falls on a desired number (a favorite method of inside scammers).

heat: when a casino's attention is attracted by a cheat or by a blackjack card counter. However, card counting is not officially illegal, though people will end up on the black book for it anyway.

knuckle mash: an indentation in a card, deliberately made with a player's knuckle.

mechanics: highly skilled blackjack dealers hired by

disreputable casinos to tilt the odds in the house's favor. For example, by stacking the deck.

needle ring: a finger ring with a projection used to mark cards with a raised dot, as in Braille.

screening out: a scheme wherein a gambler or other cohort blocks the view of the wheel while the dealer uses sleight-of-hand to switch the number (as in roulette). An effective trick used by gambling cheats.

shiner: a secret mirror used to observe cards being dealt to other players. Often placed in cigarette packs, pipes, or other objects one is allowed to place on a table.

silent partners: in poker, two players that are in cahoots. Typically, one will bet heavily to build up the pot for a partner who signals a likely winning hand. They split "the take" at the end of the night.

stacking the deck: a cheating system in blackjack where the dealer shuffles the deck in such a way that a good sequence of cards is dealt to the cheat.

subway tickets: cards dealt from the bottom of the deck.

turns: the portion of the cheating team who distracts "the heat" from the cheaters.

shoe: card-holding device for table games such as blackjack or poker.

the skim: the illegal parsing of casino profits by employees. The primary way the Mob made a living when it ran Vegas.

soft count: counting the folding money.

spotter: an employee who watches games and looks out for cheats.

the spread: how many points the favorite team gives up to the opposition in sports gambling. Aka "the line."

stickman: the craps dealer who handles the dice, using an L-shaped stick.

stiff: a winning player who doesn't "toke" or place side bets for the dealer. Or, in blackjack, a hand with a poor chance of winning no matter how it's played, usually adding up to between 12 and 16.

stops: positions where a slot machine reel can come to rest. Generally, a reel has 20, 25, or 32 stops.

toke: a gratuity, tip.

turkey: a gambler who's unpleasant to the dealer.

under/over: betting against the line on how many total points will be scored in a given sporting event. You bet either "under" or "over" the estimate. In some casinos it's even broken down to how many points will be scored in a given half by a given player.

vig: short for "vigorish." An extra 10% added to a bet placed with a bookie. This means you'd bet $1,100 to win $1,000. Aka "juice."

vigorish: the house advantage. Comes from the 5% commission on all wagers charged by the original bank–craps operators, who brought in money with "vigor." Gamblers added a syllable of jargon.

warp: a slightly bent card.

who do ya like?: a sports gambler's mantric conversation starter. Also used by bookies when you walk up to "the book."

working: bets that are in action and can win or lose on the next roll. Aka "live."

Gays

"If homosexuality is a disease, can I call in queer?"
—Michael Albert

 Impress all your straight but not narrow friends. Learn to speak gay. And become queer for a day.

the A-list: the "in" crowd. As opposed to the "B-list."

ACT-UP: the AIDS Coalition to Unleash Power. Founded by Larry Kramer to bring a more militant and in-your-face attitude to the fight against the Reagan-Bush inertia on AIDS.

Amy-John: a lesbian who plays the dominant role in a relationship.

attitude queen: someone with a really snobbish air.

basket: a well-filled crotch area. "That's a nice basket." Alternately, "The Easter bunny's been good to you, hasn't he?"

bear: big, weighty, hairy gay man. Pursued by "bear-chasers" and envied by "cubs."

beard: a straight friend posing as a gay person's spouse so that the gay person can pass as straight.

Bette: Bette Midler, the ultimate "fag hag."

Drag diva Paige Turner

bisexual: go both ways. Aka "confused."

booger drag: a man in drag who keeps a key part unshaven (such as a mustache or hairy legs).

bottom: the passive or receiving partner.

boy: a gay man. Almost never used about actual boys.

breeders: heterosexuals. Particularly the homophobic, Kinsey Zero variety that congregate in "singles bars." Aka "the Zima People." See "San Francisco."

but cha are, Blanche, you are!: absolutely the cruelest line ever delivered in American movies (spoken by Bette Davis to the crippled Joan Crawford in *Whatever Happened to Baby Jane?*), used by gay men whenever a campy dramatic moment strikes. Full quote: "But cha are, Blanche! You are in that wheelchair."

butch: a macho-looking or -acting fag or dyke, often signified by a short "butch" haircut. Now applies to tough straight women as well.

chicken: young gay man. There's "corn-fed" (take it anally) and "milk-fed" (do it orally).

chubby chasers: men who like fat men.

clone: a type of gay male known for wearing the same basic "uniform" day in and day out. "Castro clone" refers to the homogeneous look of the men who cruise Castro Street in San Francisco.

cow catcher: in the looks-centric world of '80s gay men, this device was used outside pretty boy bar doors to exclude "the wrong kind of gay men." If you didn't fit between the two poles without turning, you couldn't get in. Gave birth to the militant bear movement.

cruising: discreetly or not so discreetly checking out a "boy."

Danish pastry: a transsexual.

den mother: the paternal leader of a group of male homosexuals, often an older man.

dish: the latest gossip. Or a "hot guy" in drag queen parlance.

does he like boys?: another way to ask "is he gay?" Variants: "Are you a sister, Dorothy?" "Is he family?"

domestic partner: one's lover. Not solely a gay term, but used when it comes to legislation protecting the rights of "long-term companions."

don't take me there: "I wouldn't bring that up if I were you." If the person persists, the response would be, "You want to go there? I'll go around the block with you on that one, girl."

Usually used by black drag queens or their white speed freak imitators. A mild variation, "Don't go there," was made popular by Whoopi Goldberg at the 1996 Academy Awards presentation and is now used everywhere.

double-gaited: bisexual.

drag: dressing to look like the opposite sex as parody, without the total "realness" of a transvestite. A man who does this is a "drag queen." A woman is a "drag king."

East German swimmer: pejorative breeder term for a lesbian. Aka "donut bumper," "muff muncher," "rug eater."

fab: excellent, fabulous, wonderful.

faerie: a peace, love, and mother-earth hippie "fag." Prefers glitter dust to gold digging. Aka "radical faerie."

fag: a pejorative breeder term for a gay person now reappropriated by gay people to describe each other. Don't use unless you are a bona fide member of the club.

fag hags: straight girls who like to hang out with gay men and whose love interests are also, frustratingly, sometimes gay.

fellagirly: a lesbian with both "butch" and "fem" inclinations.

fem: a more effeminate lesbian. Aka "femmy."

galimony: alimony paid by one lesbian to another.

gaydar: the well-honed ability to know when there are homosexuals in the house.

girlfriend: a gay male term of endearment. Like so much of recent gay speech, it started out with straight black women, was brought into gay culture by black male transvestites, and is now popular everywhere.

good to his mom: a gay male. Aka "friend of Dorothy's."

Gump: a passive homosexual.

guppie: a gay upwardly mobile professional.

gym queen: a gay man desperately seeking Adonis.

het: a heterosexual.

heterosexuality: "morbid sexual passion for one of the opposite sex" (*Webster's Dictionary*, 1923).

hydrogen bond: a gay encounter in a college locker room.

in the closet: when a person chooses to keep sexual proclivities a secret or is not yet fully cognizant that he or she is in fact gay. "Oh, honey, he's so far in the closet, he doesn't know there's a door."

in the life: what black queers say they are. Now used also by black drug dealers.

in transition: a transgendered person on the way to becoming a full-fledged transsexual.

Jesse: the tobacco industry's poster boy, Jesse Helms, the pathologically homophobic North Carolina senator who actively seeks to curtail not only sexual diversity but most sexual expression. Any gay man knows who "Jesse" is. Ironically, in England a "Jesse" is a gay person.

jocker: an aggressive homosexual.

Joey: a "kept" lover. Primarily young.

joy boy: a male prostitute.

Kinsey Six: a thoroughly gay male. "I'm a Kinsey Six, hon. I can't even *think* straight."

lipstick lesbian: a more feminine acting and dressing lesbian. Opposite of a "bull" or "butch" dyke.

Liza: the ultimate drag queen persona, Liza Minelli.

log cabin Republican: an organization of gay Republicans. A contradiction in terms.

Miss Thang: a gay man. Aka "Mary." "Oh, Mary, he's straight."

NAMBLA: the National Association of Man-Boy Love. The outer fringes of the modern gay liberation movement, though the one tiny segment picked on and blown clear out of proportion by right-wing anti-gay crusaders.

Nellie: a pejorative term used by gay people to describe overly prissy and bitchy gay men. Aka a "Sally."

outing: deliberately disclosing a public figure's homosexuality. Allegedly coined by *Time* magazine but made famous by the work of ACT-UP and the writings of Michelangelo Signorile. A more voluntary form of outing is encouraged by the annual National Coming Out Day.

pass: come across as the opposite sex. "He passes as a woman."

P.E. teacher: a lesbian who doesn't know she is one . . . yet.

people like us: gay people.

pink angels: gay anticrime patrols now found in urban gay areas all over the country.

pre-op/post-op: whether or not the transsexual has had the operation to surgically alter the genitals.

queen: a generic term for a gay person used by gay persons, but usually more specific to an effeminate, "prissy," often overdramatic type of queer. Aka "drama queen."

queer: used by the straight culture to insult gay people, now reclaimed by more righteous gay folk to distinguish themselves from more establishment "gays" and "homosexuals." "Queers" like to view themselves as the vanguard of the gay rights movement, having given birth to once powerful organizations like Queer Nation.

queer as a football bat: very gay.

S&M bar: a Stand and Model bar, where people stand around looking gorgeous for one another.

severe queers: those who possess a shaven head, ten or more piercings, radical tattoos, and an ability to look extremely mean when necessary.

she: any gay man. "What does *she* want now?"

shot to the curb: drag queen parlance for an ugly or badly dressed girl. A variation, "to the curb," is used by talk show maven Ricki Lake.

the Sisters: the Sisters of Perpetual Indulgence. Gay men in nun drag who creatively campaign for various gay causes.

size queen: a gay man who bases his preference in partners on the size of their penis. "I'm sick of all these size queens."

sneakers and makeup: an S&M bar.

sweater queens: gay men in nicely pressed sweaters and slacks who look as if they are ready to head off to work at Macy's.

T.S.: a transsexual.

tea room: a venue for public sex. Most commonly a bathroom.

Trannie

there go her pearls: she (i.e., he) just got rebuffed.

top: the dominant partner.

trannie: a transsexual.

transgender: the annoyingly PC way to say transvestite or, for that matter, cross-dresser and transsexual.

trolling: on the prowl. Looking for meat.

trolls: older gay men.

TV: a transvestite.

unclipped: an uncircumcised penis.

veal cake: somewhere between chicken and beef when it comes to taste in men.

versatile: gay men who can go top or bottom.

work it: a word of rousing encouragement from one gay man to another trying to pick up some action or at least attention. "Work it, girl."

"I've discovered the best protection against HIV is what I'm doing—have extremely high standards and be a big fat slovenly pig."   —URBAN HUTCHINS

Graffiti

DESPITE THE CONCERTED EFFORT OF CITY OFFICIALS across the country to wipe it out, graffiti is here to stay. Here's a look at the vernacular of "tag bangers," those swift and prolific subway car and wall defacers who've influenced not only the style and sensibility of rap culture but the entire zeitgeist of the teen and twentysomething generation.

acronym: name. Sometimes a graf name is an acronym, as in KRS-ONE (Knowledge Rules Supreme Over Nearly Everyone) and MCA (Making Cops Angry). Lots of times there'll be meanings behind the letters even if it's a word on its own.

bite: steal other people's style without giving proper credit. It ain't the done thing.

black books: books in which graffers write their outlines and plan pieces. It's not uncommon for them to meet and write in each other's books. When a crew of graffers conspire to do a wall, they will meet to make sure their styles correspond. Aka "piece book."

bomb: write your tag everywhere. You can also spray-paint (same result). REVS + COST are "sticker bomb" kings in Manhattan (i.e., they plaster stickers of "REVS + COST" all over town). Their fame is not related to style.

bombers: taggers or graffiti artists.

the buff: the ways NYC transit officials strip subway cars of graf.

burner: a good piece, with all the elements. To burn is to completely cover the work of another graffer or tagger. This is a major insult and can lead to violent retribution. It's proper to highlight the pieces of dead writers, but not cover them.

caps: nozzles that fit on spray cans to diffuse or concentrate spray. "Fat caps" cover large areas with paint. Caps range from "German Fat Caps" (expensive) to household cleaner caps (free). You can't "write" without them.

characters: not necessary, but they often enhance the piece. Some writers have "bomb" characters and "whack" letters and vice versa. Characters are sometimes derived from comics, sometimes "bitten" from other writers, or, in the best cases, created. They should correspond with the piece and often take the place of letters.

COMIX: comics, used as inspiration for graffers' characters. For example, a halo is traditional, harking back to the Saint, as in, "Beware the sign of the Saint." A crown is also popular. An arrow below the tag isn't from the comics but means "attack from below."

crew: graf team. Letters added below or near a tag to indicate the tagger's crew. ESK = East Side Krew; UW = a big crew in the Bronx; FC = Fantasy Crew, also from the Bronx. Crews are very tight and often competitive. They may "get up" (cover with their graffiti) a neighborhood, or "go over" (cover) other crews until they command an area. For graffers like John Love, it's GNK (Got No Krew).

flat: old, smooth-sided subway car that is much more conducive to the tagger's art; the newer "ridgy" or corrugated cars are harder to work with.

get up: cover with graffiti. Aka "burn," "hit," "kill," "terrorize," or "get over," especially applied to successfully tagging a train.

go over: paint over someone else's tag.

graf: graffiti. Aka "piecing," "style," or "junk."

graffer: a graffiti artist as opposed to a "tagger." Aka "writer."

head: an accomplished writer.

ice down: completely cover a wall or subway car with a piece.

king: an excellent piece.

lay up: tagging subway cars when they are in the yard. The safest way to go. As opposed to "motion tagging" (graffing on a moving car).

markers: fat ones like Magnum 44s (black) and paint pens (silver and white) are the choice.

mentors: older and more accomplished graffers who help aspiring writers with their style in exchange for paint. The mentor sometimes provides his charge with "outlines" (inked-out plans for pieces). Writers will also give outlines to one another. It's rumored that legendary graffer SCOPE's most popular style was given to him.

method: in truly great graffiti, there should be a movement in the structure of the letters that takes your eye along in a fluid

How to Talk American

way. Many writers use arrows to exaggerate this movement. The letters should be creative but discernible, at least to other writers. Positive-negative space is crucial and important to consider when deciphering. (SCOPE, for example, creates letters out of the space between letters as well as the letters themselves.) Colors should be blended carefully to create depth. Bright colors and whites are used for highlights and shine. A cloud often serves as a background for a piece. The character should correspond to the piece stylistically and thematically. No drips. No fuzzy lines. No holes.

ONE: a common suffix for writers (e.g., SUM-ONE, KRS-ONE).

piece: the actual graf.

the politix: the facts.

presidents: masters of style, with history. Presidents run crews. They are also usually "kings" (they have "gotten up" so prolifically in an area that it becomes their own).

racked: stolen, as in "racked paint."

scratcher: a person who "tags" train windows with either keys or a strip of sandpaper attached to a block of wood.

tag: write your pseudonym in a way that indicates your style and marks your turf. Taggers who simply tag are not graffiti artists.

throw ups: abbreviations of a piece filled in with simple depth. Throw ups are usually black + white, or red + white, or green + white, etc. And they are often quite large.

whack: an ugly or badly done piece.

wild style: very complex, multicolored and interlocking. Preferred because people who don't "write" can't usually figure it out.

window down: a piece on trains painted from the window down.

write: create graffiti.

writer: tagger, graffer.

Gutter Punks

GUTTER PUNKS ARE TEENS AND TWENTYSOMETHINGS who deliberately live a trashy, homeless life. Known for their missing teeth and funny smells, they are so disgusting, they actually turn off dopers and slackers. The following is a small snapshot of their language as well as a broader look at the punk ethos in general.

be like Ted: a joke phrase that is a beautifully ironic corruption of the "be like Mike" Jordan commercials. Refers to Theodore Kaczynski (the suspected Unabomber).

black and green: gutter punk who is both an anarchist and an environmental activist. From the heading of the 'zine distributed at "the West Coast Anarchists Gathering" in North Bend, Oregon.

Boneheads: Nazi skinheads. White racist Aryan youth who are about as far away from being the master race as one can get. Quite pathetic.

boot party: a generic "skins" term (including SHARPs) for when a bunch of skins gang up on someone, with one skin holding down the victim's head while anywhere from one to a dozen or more kick the daylights out of the person with their steel-toed boots.

car-shop: bust into cars.

crusties: plural of "crusty punk." A step beyond gutter punk (if you can imagine such a thing). Refers to kids who ride the rails, don't bathe, get obnoxiously and violently drunk, and don't use their brains very often.

denk: good stuff.

Dumpster: as a noun, it's a trash receptacle. The revered source of many of the essentials in a punk or gutter punk's life. As a verb, short for "Dumpster dive," which means to search others' refuse for food, clothes, furniture, appliances.

emo: a genre of emotive (some say "sappy") punk love songs. You can actually hear the lyrics.

goth: gothic/ethereal/noise music; or, those who play it, listen to it, or make up their face in goth style (dark shadows, black lipstick, lots of white powder).

grommets: gutter punk wannabes. Lifted from dude lingo.

groundscore: as a verb, to score something off the ground; e.g., on the floor of a hall after a concert (for the scrupulous) or during one (for the unscrupulous). As a noun, whatever is thereby obtained.

hoppin': using cargo trains or boxcars for free transportation. Synonymous with "ridin' the rails." Or "hoboin'."

hotshot: a priority train, which makes fewer stops and arrives at its destination earlier than other trains. Favorites of "hoppers," of course, though they tend to be more heavily patrolled.

kick down: provide for another (willingly or reluctantly). As a noun (usually plural), that which is donated. As in, "Yeah, Food Not Bombs got a shitload of kickdowns from that health food store last night."

on tour: if said by hippies or "peace punks," they're usually being nostalgic about the good old days, when they crossed the country with other Deadheads. If said by members of a punk band, they're making the concert circuit of halls, teahouses, punk houses, and warehouses.

on tour with SP: hopping across the country on Southern Pacific trains.

panning: panhandling.

peace punk: a punk who is into pacifism, antinuclear work, and nonviolence, or a hippie who hangs out with punks.

piercings: plentiful and everywhere you could imagine. Punks have now taken to stretching them as far as possible, often in the style of *National Geographic* tribal photographs.

saucy: horny-drunk or flirtatious (drunk or not drunk).

schnickered: silly, laughing at self drunk. Or others laughing at you drunk.

schwag: foul, not cool.

score: as a verb, to obtain, possibly illegally (usually at least via nonmonetary means). As a noun, whatever is thereby obtained.

SHARPs: Skinheads Against Racial Prejudice. According to Ellen Klowden, who works in Eugene, Oregon, with at-risk youth, "It sounds great, and they do succeed in running Boneheads the fuck out of Dodge, but they (around our scene) are also known for getting drunk and violent against punks and hippies (and

allegedly sometimes men who are perceived as gay or effeminate). . . . Keep on your guard around them, but organize with
them against the fascists."

skinheads: white racist youth. Often lumped with punks by outsiders, and though they sometimes occupy similar niches, they
are often antagonistic to punks and hippies. According to
Klowden, this is often a question of "class and style." She explains that in Eugene, "the skins look kinda like old English
mods (as in *Quadrophenia,* by the Who) with their clean-cut
looks and button-down shirts, trousers, jackets, caps, and sus-
penders. They put on Ska shows (a type of music similar to
reggae), although some are more into 'Oi' (supposedly political, class-conscious skin music, which is really often racist,
sexist, and violent). The skins are working class but employed,
whereas punks are antimonetarist and therefore perceived as
lazy sponges by skins. Life-threatening territorial-respect
squabbles thus ensue."

smiley: a thick padlocked chain worn around the neck or arms.
Made famous by Sid Vicious way back when and by all punks
since.

spaynging (pron. "*spayn*-jin"): spare-changing, panhandling.

spent: exhausted, wiped out, from sleep deprivation or overexer-
tion, often but not necessarily due to excessive intoxication.

spun: way too high. If someone uses it about themselves and
seems happy about it, it tends to refer to hallucinations from
psychedelics and/or ganja. If someone uses it derogatorily, especially about others, or with "out" afterward, it tends to refer
to heroin.

squat: a place where people can "crash out" (stay). Or to take
something over for the purpose of sleeping or residing there.
Refers to anything from a lean-to to abandoned, dilapidated
houses to fully equipped warehouses. The equivalent of urban
homesteading. "Squatters" are those who occupy "squats."

tablescore: take leftover food from restaurant tables. As a noun,
whatever is thereby obtained.

tat: tattoo. The latest vogue is facial tattoos, similar to those of
the Maori of New Zealand.

zip: methamphetamine. Can be snorted or injected. The ideal
gutter punk drug, since it gives them energy. Unfortunately,
the hard-core addicts usually end up selling their bodies to
scrounge money for more "zip."

Hoops

Old men, sports stars, and rock-'n'-rollers all claim to play golf, but the ruling game in the streets, parks, and driveways of America remains "b-ball." Even soccer, newly popular, will not make a dent any time soon. Basketball is one of the most beloved participatory sports because it elicits the greatest emotion, talk, and player involvement. In recent years, as the game has loosened up and a wide assortment of folks have come to play, there's evolved a fascinating speech to accompany it. If you want to play serious "hoops," it pays to know your "hops" from your "stops" and a "run" from a "game."

airball: a shot that completely misses the basket, hitting "nothing but air."

and one!: said by shooter after being fouled while making a basket. In regular basketball, the shooter would earn a trip to the free-throw line. But since there are no free throws in pickup basketball, this statement is the best anyone can expect—an affirmation of an amazing play.

ball: the game of basketball. "Let's play some ball." Or, "Been playin' any ball lately?" Aka "B" or "B-ball." Also, the actual basketball.

bangin': intensely physical style of play. Usually refers to rebounding. From the street term "bangers" (violent gang members).

basket: a score. From the origins of the game, when balls were literally tossed into peach baskets.

Billy Hoyle: the character played by Woody Harrelson in *White Men Can't Jump.* Used to describe pesky, somewhat geeky white players who don't appear to have a game but actually do. Case in point, yours truly.

brick: a shot that misses badly. As opposed to an airball, a brick actually hits some part of the basket.

bucket: a basket, a score.

burn: playing time, as in "I gotta get some burn, maaan."

bust: great shot. "Good bust, man."

call, next!: reserve the next game. As in "I got next." Or "I called next" (aka "Next!"). Also said when one is fouled. As in "Call," or "I got a call." Caveat: it is considered bad form to "call" offensive fouls in pickup basketball, especially charging. The best you can hope for is the ball "up top." In addition, unlike in regular ball, there are no three-second violations, illegal defense calls, or time possession rules in pickup ball.

cash: good shot.

cheap: debatable. "That was a cheap call. I barely touched him!"

check: letting the opposing player or team touch the ball before inbounding in half-court games. One checks it to make sure the defensive team is "set" or ready. As the defensive player returns the "checked" ball, he will often shout, "Ball in!"

cherry picker: a player who discreetly hangs back around his basket waiting for a long pass and an easy bucket.

choke: you screwed up big time. Example: you are driving uncontested to the basket for the winning bucket and you choke, i.e., you miss the easy layup. Aka "clutch." Example: "Dude, I choked on that layup."

clear: taking the ball "back" to a designated point after each change of possession in half-court games. Usually either the foul line or the 3-point line, though can include an imaginary line 10 to 20 feet from the bucket on both sides. "Hey, Mark, you've got to clear that."

clutch: coming through when most needed. "That was a clutch play, maaan."

count: score. The question "What's the count?" occasionally yields some profound disagreements.

D: defense. "C'mon, let's 'get back' on D."

D up!: an exhortation from a teammate to get tough on "D."

dish: pass. "Nice dish." Aka "look."

don't trip: don't beat yourself up for making a bad decision. Just keep playing. It gets metaphysical out there.

downtown: shooting from far beyond the basket, usually beyond the 3-point line. Used more often by announcers in college or pro ball. "He's hitting from downtown."

facial: making a basket despite a serious in-your-face defense.

fill it up: when a team or player is hitting a series of shots from the outside. "They're filling it up tonight."

game: one's unique style of play. In some circles how one's game looks is as important as how one plays. There are several expressions that go along with the notion of game. (1) "Hey man, that's not your game." Said by one teammate reprimanding another who is trying to go beyond his ability or who's not playing his role (i.e., a big rebounder trying to take 3-point shots he can't hit). (2) "Hey man, don't let him mess up your game." In other words, don't let the opponent get "inside your head" and get you to do things you don't routinely do well. One of the key concepts of basketball is to stay within your game, i.e., your limits (which a true hoopster, as well as a realized human being, knows intimately). The longer one plays "ball," the more one sees it as not only a metaphor for life but a direct mirror of an approach to life as well. My game? "Throw up" shots from all over the court, loud and aggressive "D," infectious enthusiasm, and total inconsistency.

game point: if a given team makes one more, it wins. In street ball, games are usually played by 1s to 12 or 16. When one team has 11 or 15 and leads by at least a point, it's game point.

garbage: ugly-looking shots that go in the basket.

get in my head: disturb someone's "game" by taunting. "Maaan, I'm not going to let you get in my head."

get that shit out of my house!: used when a player makes a thunderous block in his defensive zone. In San Francisco, substitute "condo" for "house." In L.A., "gated community." In New York, "crib."

go off: play at an extremely high level, far superior to anyone else on the court. "Dak just went off, man. He was jammin', dishin', stealin', poppin', hittin' everything in sight."

got one: I've been fouled. Aka "got it." "Top" is also said to indicate I've been fouled and want the ball "up top."

gunner: a player who shoots a lot, often from far outside. My nickname during my Christ the King grade school days. Just ask Dave "Evie Da V" Evans.

hack: routinely foul; i.e., "hacking." Example: "Jesus, Bob, take it easy, you're hackin' me all over."

hacker: a player who routinely fouls, often flagrantly. Aka "Bob Hackadoo" or "the Hackness Monster."

handles: the ability to dribble. "That guy's got handles."

help me out: guard my man if he gets past me on defense. Aka "help" or "li'l help."

hit: score. "He's hitting everything."

hole: the basket. "Take it to the hole."

hoops: the game of basketball.

hops: excellent jumping ability.

house: the painted key around the basket. As in, "Get that shit out of my house."

hutch: an individual game played by two or more people; the first person to score 21 or 32 wins. You get 2 points for a regular basket, 3 points for a 3-pointer. If you make a basket, you get to shoot up to three free throws. Make all three, you keep possession. No out-of-bounds. No fouls (unless it's flagrant). It's what you play when there aren't enough people to form a full-tilt game. Aka "hooch" or "21."

in-your-face: a seriously up-close and confrontational style of defense.

it's the shoes: a lampoon of shoe commercials that foster the impression you will be a better player if you wear a certain brand. Said when a player is doing really poorly or really well. Player: "I can't hit a thing, man." Spectator: "It's the shoes." Alternately, "It's the girlfriend," "It's the hair."

j: a jumper or jump shot. "I got my 'j' working today."

kick it out: pass the ball to a player on the outside. Used when a player in "the post" (aka "inside"), i.e., near the basket, is double-teamed and a player "outside" or "on the perimeter" is open for a shot.

kicks: shoes. "Hey, Tim, nice kicks."

lightin' it up: tremendously good field goal shooting ("They were just lightin' it up"). Often applied to one shooter in particular who is hitting all kinds of shots from "the outside."

make it, take it: you make a basket, you keep the ball. Used in half-court games of 2–10 players.

man: short for man-to-man defense. "Let's play man. No, let's play zone, maaan."

money: shot that goes in or is about to go in. As in "money in the bank," a sure thing. Often said by those on the sidelines before an excellent shooter lets go of the shot. "That's money." After the shot goes in, "See what I mean?" Aka "cash."

my bad: my fault or mistake. Said after a bad play, like not calling out a pick or letting a player get by for an easy bucket. Just one of the many examples of "incorrect" English that permeate the sport. If overused, can devolve into a grating attempt by white players to achieve some bogus form of street cred.

nothin' but net: a perfect shot that doesn't even touch the rim on its way through the basket.

paint: used mostly in indoor ball, it represents the painted area around the basket or the free-throw lane in regular basketball (aka "the lane"). If you include the area above the free-throw line up to the top of the semicircle, that is called "the key." There are no 3-second violations for being in the "paint" in pickup basketball. And no foul limit or free throws.

pill: the basketball.

pinned: when a player's shot gets blocked and the ball doesn't leave his hand. Aka "stuffed."

rainin': when one is routinely hitting long-range "j's." Aka "drillin'" or "drainin'." Example: "Pete was rainin' threes."

the rock: a new, popular term for a basketball. "Gimme the rock."

run: play a game. "Can I run with you guys?"

schooled: get seriously beat on a play or in a game. "You got schooled, Alex." Aka "burned."

shirts and skins: a way to distinguish teams (male teams, that is)—one wears shirts, the other doesn't. In France, one wears cologne, the other doesn't.

shoot for it: in the absence of a referee, disputes over fouls and possession are often resolved by a member of one team shooting from the top of the key. If the shooter makes it, his or her team gets the ball. Disputes can also be resolved by screaming, shoving, or a simple gunfight.

shooter: the guy on the team who can hit the outside "j." "You better guard him, he's a shooter."

shootin' blanks: badly missed shots taken from the outside. Aka "air," "airballs," or "bricks."

skunked: when the losing team doesn't score a single point. "We got skunked!"

slap: slapping the backboard after a dunk or layup.

stop: when you keep the opposing team from scoring during a critical point in the game. "C'mon, let's make a stop here." Or, "Guys, we need a stop."

swing it: pass around the perimeter of the defense. I usually hear coaches shouting this, not players. "Swinging it" fast and sharp is absolutely essential in beating a zone defense.

take him to the butter: take him to the basket.

take it to the hoop: drive to the basket.

a three: a 3-pointer. Aka "a trey."

throw it down: dunk with authority.

throw up: take difficult shots or simply to shoot.

top: said by a player when fouled. "Top!" means "I'll take it at the top of the key."

trash: irreverent, contentious speech designed to unnerve the opposing team (e.g., "You ain't got no moves"). Aka "shit." Can also refer to an ugly style of play or a cheap basket. In some circles, talking trash is often as essential to a good game as dribbling or defense.

ugly: a player who doesn't have the best form or style. "Crotty's got an ugly game, but he can score." Can also refer to the quality of a run. "That game was ugly."

walking: took more than two steps before dribbling the ball. "C'mon, man, you walked with the ball." Aka "traveling," "carrying the ball," or simply "carrying." Or, in Jim "the Mad Monk" vernacular, "Goin' walkin' after midnight."

water: a smooth shot.

what's the count?: what's the score?

who's got next?: who has the next game? Alternately, "we got next" when it's your turn to play. Or simply "next." Disputes often arise on busy street courts over who "called it." An interlude might go something like this. "I got next." "No, man, we was here first." "No way! I called first before you even got here." "That's bullshit, man." "Well, go ahead and ask my man there." "Alright then, we got the game after you." "That's cool."

whose man is that?: roughly, "Who's supposed to guard that guy?" Said by a teammate when an opposing player makes an easy, uncontested basket.

win by two: the winning team must win by two baskets. No longer a universal rule in street ball.

zip: zero. "We're ahead, 10–zip."

zone: a style of defense in which players guard a particular zone of the court rather than a particular player. Also refers to those magical moments when a player is hitting every shot and making every play. The equivalent of basketball nirvana; one feels totally happy and at peace with the world ("Man, that dude was in a zone"). Enjoy it, because as soon as you think about it, it usually disappears.

Las Vegas

"Rose was Vegas born and raised, and if the town had tried to teach him anything in his forty-two years it was, go for the money—drunk or sober, in fear or for fun, go for the money and the personal would take care of itself."   —FROM THE DEATH OF FRANK SINATRA
BY MICHAEL VENTURA

THIS IS THE TOWN WHERE ITS MOST FAMOUS native son was once asked: "What do you want out of life?" And Liberace answered: "The whole enchilada."

That is precisely what Vegas has provided since "wide-open" gambling was made legal here back in 1931. There's a lot more than gambling in the new Vegas—a procession of Centurions at Caesars Palace, exploding volcanoes outside the Mirage, a sea battle outside Treasure Island. No matter what the entertainment, however, all passageways invariably lead back through the slots. Here's a lexicon to help you understand the sensory overload.

Amarillo Slim: a legendary Vegas gambler, Thomas Preston, known for winning many outrageous bets. He defeated Minnesota Fats in pool using a broom for a cue and bested Evil Knievel in golf using a hammer for a club.

Area 51: a vast expanse of desert where new and exotic weapons are tested (e.g., the Stealth bomber). Rumored to be the place where aliens are housed.

the Big Shot: the 921-foot-high reverse bungee jump atop the Stratosphere Tower. Caveat: I once rode the positively evil Big Shot up the 228-foot spire of the Stratosphere Tower. This was not fun. This was torture. This was INSANE! At G forces up to 4 and fewer than 0, this was not so much a ride as a test of astronaut-level endurance.

the biggest little city in the world: Reno, Vegas' poor cousin to the north.

Boulder Dam: the original name for Hoover Dam, located outside Boulder City, the only Nevada town where gambling is illegal (because it was built by the federal government). Harold Ickes, the secretary of the interior in 1935, insisted on calling the dam Boulder, noting that "this great engineering achievement should not carry the name of any living man, but, on the contrary, should be baptized with a designation as bold and characteristic and imagina-

tion-stirring as the dam itself." Alas, no one could come up with such a bold and imagination-stirring designation, so Boulder Dam became "Hoover's Dam" and later simply "Hoover Dam." Caveat: contrary to widespread misconception, it was Hoover Dam that fueled interest in Las Vegas, not vice versa. The year the dam was completed, 750,000 people came to see it, and all of them had to pass through "Sin City." The famous Vegas saying from the 1930s says it all: "My life wasn't worth a damn until Uncle Sam gave us the Hoover Dam."

Boulder Strip: the string of casinos along Boulder Highway, including Sam's Town, Boulder Station, Showboat, Joker's Wild, and Nevada Palace.

Carson: what northern Nevadans call Carson City.

COMDEX: the Computer Distribution Exhibition, one of the largest trade shows in the world, held twice a year (once in Las Vegas), with over 200,000 in attendance. Visitors know it all too well because every hotel room in town is booked way in advance. "CUMDEX" is the side exhibition of adult entertainment that was forced to spin from COMDEX.

D.I.: Desert Inn Road.

enhancements: serious repairs or a makeover to improve a failing casino or attraction.

eye in the sky: one-way mirror surveillance. Pioneered in Vegas, now commonplace throughout surveillance nation.

five points: the intersection of Charleston, Boulder, Fremont, Easter, and 25th streets.

Flamingo Wash: a flood channel cutting through the middle of

Las Vegas that fills with muddy water every time it rains. People have drowned in it before, and there is always a trickle of water flowing in which one can observe buried wreckage.

Fremont Street Experiment: the Fremont Street Experience, a flashy attempt to lure business back downtown and make tourists feel more comfortable, featuring an overhead canopy used for light shows and lots of ticky-tack, bric-a-brac, and T-shirt shops. It ruined the funky authenticity of Fremont Street, the closest thing Vegas had to Main Street USA, turning it into an indoor-outdoor pedestrian mall.

gamboling: promenading along the Las Vegas Strip.

Glitter Gulch: the main strip of casinos downtown. Lots of neon, lots of white trash, lots of cheap, sleazy motels. Until the recent mallification, the last authentic strip of Old Vegas.

the Lake: Lake Tahoe, which means "big water" to the local Native Americans. Caveat: Lake Tahoe lies partly in California and partly in Nevada. At the Cav-Neva swimming pool, you can do the breast stroke in California and the flutter kick in Nevada.

Las Vegas total: the typical Vegas experience of room, food, gambling, show, and commercial sex.

Lost Wages: Las Vegas.

Marryin' Sam: a wedding chapel minister.

mucker: a miner.

Nevada: "snowy" in Spanish.

Nevada Highway: what Boulder Highway is called in Boulder City.

proving ground: where the bombs are tested.

the Radiant City: a brand-new term for Vegas. Gaining in popularity.

the Rat Pack: the entertainers Frank Sinatra, Sammy Davis, Jr., Dean Martin, and Joey Bishop, among others, who raised the naughty, loungy alkie schtick to new heights and put Vegas on the map.

Richard "the Fixer" Perry: notorious local sports "fixer" who was once caught in a hot tub with several UNLV basketball players.

scared money never wins: the mantra of Vegas gambling.

Sin City: an old-school term for Vegas.

Slummerlin: Summerlin, a cookie-cutter yuppie and old people tract house burb. Green Valley II.

the Strip: the 3.5-mile stretch of Las Vegas Boulevard South that holds most of the top hotels and showroom entertainment. Named after L.A.'s Sunset Strip.

Tark: Jerry Tarkanian, former coach of the UNLV Runnin' Rebels basketball team. Known for taking very good care of his inner-city players. So good he was ousted as coach, despite one of the best winning percentages in college basketball history. Afterward, the bald, towel-chewing Armenian took a job as a sports commentator and threatened to run for mayor. In 1995 he became head coach of the Fresno State Bulldogs. Aka "Tark the Shark."

touron: tourist. The go-on-predictable-vacation, leave-brain-at-home variety, with the glazed automaton look.

the Tower of Bobel: the Stratosphere Tower, Bob "Vegas World" Stupak's ultimate attempt to upstage the local Vegas deity Steve Wynn (Treasure Island, Mirage, Bellagio). Ironically, Stupak has completely bailed from the financially troubled enterprise. Grand Casinos, out of Minneapolis, is now the effective owner.

Trop: Tropicana Boulevard.

How to Talk Paiute

BEFORE RAFAEL RIVERA AND HIS PARTY CLAIMED Vegas for the white man, there were tribes of Indians roaming "the meadows." Here are some of their words that survive to this day.

ahdam du'r etz: the voice of nectar.

cach-kumai it mama'its: a virgin.

ma'ah vee'en: a fearless leader.

mantoxo'avi: a rattlesnake.

marukats: the white man.

moxoam: spirit.

numpicant: crazy.

o'si: a cactus.

pah'al say'mel: a pot-bellied wizard.

sangwav: sin.

t'ack'ee marukats: Paiute prophecy of the coming of the white entrepreneur Bob Stupak.

UNLV: the University of Nevada at Las Vegas.

Vegas: Las Vegas, L.A.'s bastard child. With more glitz, less glamour.

Vegas Vic: a 60-foot-tall talking neon cowboy at the Pioneer Motel who used to wave an arm and say, "Howdy, partner, welcome to Las Vegas," every few minutes (he no longer waves due to the overhead canopy of the Fremont Street Experiment). He inspired River Ric and Wendover Will. It is said that he watches the area 24 hours a day, guarding its tackiness. It's also said that Sassy Sally is his main squeeze.

Wilbur Clark's Desert Inn: We're Not Italian.

yuppie gulag: Green Valley, another horrendous Vegas residential development. Hasn't this town learned *anything* from L.A.?

Los Angeles

"Los Angeles, the town built on the horrifying reality
that reality is so horrifying we need an industry to
recreate it."
—Jerry Stahl

THERE'S A CERTAIN SATISFACTION IN DRIVING
into a smog-induced L.A. orange sunset—it's tranquil in
a perverse way. But one must never forget that this is a very sick
city, filled with very tacky, selfish, and greedy people, chasing
and manufacturing every possible samsaric illusion. In other
words, I love it.

Some Important Tips

1. Long waits in L.A. offices are legendary, especially in the
offices of anyone associated with the film industry. A rule
of thumb: the shorter the man, the longer the wait. Plan
accordingly.

2. "Nobody walks in L.A." Not only a song by Missing Persons
but an obvious truism.

3. Almost every single stretch of this city you've seen in a
movie or on TV. You are literally living inside a set.

4. Everyone in this town is "writing a screenplay." And they
will say so without a shred of irony. Get used to it.

amateur night: L.A.'s version of "bridge and tunnel people."
"I'm sorry, honey, the show is sold out. Must be amateur
night."

the American Riviera: the self-proclaimed title of Orange
County.

AMW: Actress, Model, Whatever. Aka "Wammie." Alternately,
"MAW."

Angelenos: residents of L.A.

Angelyne: a silicon-breasted, shameless self-promoter who uses
billboards to extol her availability. Not for sex or any other
palpable talent. But for being, well, "Angelyne." Used as in

"Call Angelyne." Also used to refer to anyone determined to be famous in spite of their lack of talent. "She's so Angelyne."

behind the mountain: "I'll be going behind the mountain," i.e., the San Gabriel Mountains.

the best-policed six square miles on earth: Beverly Hills.

Bev Cen: the Beverly Center shopping experience.

Beverly Hills adjacent: real estate term for any rental unit remotely near Beverly Hills, even if it's a South Beverly Hills gang area.

the Big Orange: Los Angeles. Aka "La-La Land" (though no true Angeleno ever uses the latter).

the Blue Whale: the Pacific Design Center, in West Hollywood.

Bompton: the "Crip" word for Compton, a major ghetto south of L.A., which is seen as a "Blood" stronghold. As a rule, Crips have an aversion to using the sacred C letter.

the Boo: Malibu, where many "celebrities" live.

boulevard boys: male hookers on Santa Monica Boulevard. "Gas queens" are the men who pick them up.

Buk (pron. "Booook"): L.A.-based writer Charles Bukowski, the late alcoholic demigod of twentysomething poets and writers.

a California roll: rolling through a stop sign without coming to a full stop.

call sheet: a list of calls to be returned. Your position on the list says everything about your status in a town ruled by status consciousness.

Camp O.J.: the veritable encampment of trailers and journalists behind the Criminal Courts Building in downtown L.A. during the 1995–96 "trial of the century" of O. J. Simpson for the murder of Ronald Goldman and Nicole Brown Simpson. The trial generated some other notable O.J. vernacular, including "O.J. shoes" (Bruno Magli shoes allegedly worn by Simpson at the scene of the crime).

can't we all just get along?: the memorable line uttered by Rodney "the Human Piñata" King during the height of the L.A. riots. Now used tongue-in-cheek anytime there's a squabble.

Carsonigen: Carson, a major oil refinery center.

the Château: the Château Marmont, Hollywood's hotel of the stars . . . and star casualties (John Belushi and Jim Morrison both died here).

Chuck: Charlton Heston (*Ben Hur, Omega Man*), an old-school GOP poster boy. New school: Bruce Willis.

the City of Angels: Los Angeles. With residents like Stacey Koon, the Menendez brothers, and O. J. Simpson, this place is such a far cry from angelic it's not even funny. But the name continues to be tossed around in the hope that one day it might stick.

city shamans: popular practitioners of alternative medicine, such as Janet Zand, or New Age human potential gurus like Louise Hay.

closing the deal: sexual intercourse. In a town of major "deals," it's an appropriate metaphor. Aka "getting busy."

coast 'n' toast: a drive-by shooting. The preferred way to settle scores in "Angel City."

cocaine-contra: the alleged introduction of crack cocaine into the L.A. black community by CIA operatives trying to raise money for covert operations in Nicaragua. Of course, none of it is true. Not a shred.

the Colony: Malibu Colony, an ultra-exclusive beach community that counts several stars as residents.

Crips and Bloods: two rival L.A. gangs who have maintained a truce since 1992. The Bloods wear red; the Crips, blue.

Cruise control: excessive control of one's media image. Coined in honor of Scientologist Tom Cruise, who in his producing debut on *Mission: Impossible* wrested control of the PR from Paramount Pictures to his own publicist, Pat "the Pit Bull" Kingsley.

cut to the chase: get to the point. From the silent era in movies, when almost every film was a pretext for an elaborate chase scene.

devil winds: the Santa Ana winds—hot, dry, fast-moving gusts that allegedly wreak havoc with the psyche. Aka "Santa Anas."

dialed in: in the loop. An appropriate metaphor for "the City of Angels," given its residents' love affair with the telephone.

do: L.A.'s verb of choice. Lunch, meetings, and drugs are "done," not eaten, attended, or taken.

eight-trey: L.A. rapper-speak for 83rd Street.

El Toro Y: a traffic term for where the freeways form a Y in El Toro.

faaaaaabulous: a Westside adjective of approval.

fierce: all-purpose adjective of approval.

fruit and nut run: what pilots call a flight to L.A.

G: a Gulfstream jet. "Hey Al, have them send a G, will ya?"

gat: gang term for "gun." Aka "glock."

gated community: a real estate term symbolizing L.A.'s paranoiac obsession with security.

a Gates man: a fascist cop. After the notorious former police chief Darryl Gates.

ghetto bird: a police helicopter. Ubiquitous in "the City of Quartz."

glassphalt: bright speckles of stardust placed for the benefit of tourists on Hollywood Boulevard.

going Richter: blowing one's top, getting very angry. Refers to the Richter scale, which is used to measure the strength of earthquakes, of which there are plenty in Southern California.

the Golden Triangle: a ridiculously wealthy Beverly Hills district defined by Santa Monica Boulevard on the northwest, Wilshire Boulevard on the south, and Canyon Drive on the northeast.

got: gradually bumping "do" as the verb of choice. "I've got a lunch tomorrow."

got you on my car speed dial: sure sign of über status. You've arrived.

harsh a mellow: mess up a calm or groovy mood. One is

frequently called on it by earnest, New Age, irony-free Angelenos.

Heidi chicks: high-class call girls. After Heidi Fleiss, former madam to the stars.

Hispo-trash: Hispanics with mysterious sources of disposable income trying to emulate Eurotrash, of which there are thousands in L.A.

the industry: the film industry. If you are not somehow directly associated with "the industry," you are literally a nobody in this town.

juice: power, influence, connections. If you got "juice," you "da man."

the Juice: the former football great and probable murderer, O. J. Simpson.

jurassic: old-fashioned, no longer cool.

L.A. burn: a pain in the throat felt by new arrivals when they first encounter the intense L.A. smog.

the L.A. farewell: a smile followed by:
→ I'll call you: "get lost, you'll never hear from me again."
→ let's do lunch: "I like you, but you're a loser."
→ let's do sushi: signifies the beginning of a serious commitment.

La-La Land: another one of those taboo city nicknames. Its use is a dead giveaway you're some out-of-it laid-off bricklayer from Poughkeepsie. Just don't use it.

like, and, all, go: "Like, I'm way into this L.A. thing, and she's all 'Yeah, but.' And I go, 'It's like way cool. Like, c'mon.' And she's like all into this regret trip. So I go, 'Babe, let's get in my ride and check out the sunset.' And she's all mopey. So I get all lovey. And she's 'okay,' and I'm all 'yowzer!'"

the Little One: the 1994 L.A. earthquake. For "the Big One," see San Francisco.

mad skills: very talented. Not a requirement for success in this town and always a big surprise when encountered.

map the heavens: tag hard-to-reach freeway signs. L.A. graffer term.

marine layer: moisture leading to haze, which outta-towners mistake for smog.

MAW: Model, Actress, Whatever. The same as "AMW." Take your pick.

a Michael Jackson: a badly botched plastic surgery.

Miracle Mile: the continuous wall of tall buildings in the Wilshire District of West L.A.

mud flows: mudslides.

multi-culti: multicultural.

my boyfriend's in rehab: according to former smackhead Jerry Stahl (*Permanent Midnight*), the ultimate career-enhancing cachet for the upwardly mobile "d-girl."

my people/your people: a speedier, '90s version of the classic L.A. player line: "I'll have my people call your people." Aka "my peeps/your peeps." Now used mostly tongue firmly in cheek. If not, it's a sure sign of a complete moron.

No Hoe: North Hollywood.

Normandie-adjacent: a real estate term for young urban trendoids who really want that multiculti thing.

the Orange Crush: where several major freeways (the 5, 22, and 57) intersect in Orange County. Heard on traffic reports.

the Orange Curtain: a cultural, political, and physical barrier separating L.A. proper from Orange County. "Behind the curtain" lies Republican-land, with scads of white folk, a brand-new airport named after John Wayne, traffic snarls for days, defense contractors, family values paranoia, and golf.

orange men: street vendors, usually Hispanic, found at intersections all over L.A. selling bags of fruit and nuts.

over the hill: the drive from the San Fernando Valley "over the hill" to Hollywood, the home of heavy metal rock 'n' roll.

pan-hassling: in-your-face panhandling.

the People's Republic of Santa Monica: the last holdout of '60s L.A. consciousness, which has been almost thoroughly quashed by corporate development, real estate speculation, and the Santa Monica Promenade. The only '60s remnants are the large number of homeless people scattered near the beach, pockets of rent control, and some juice bars.

place: mansion. "We've got a place in Malibu and another place in Palm Springs."

power (lunch, dinner, drinking, sweating, running, etc.): nauseating L.A. yuppie term for doing anything with a high degree of intensity or dedication.

the Promenade: the Santa Monica 3rd Street Promenade. Has replaced Westwood Village and Beverly Center as the yuppie food, folks, fun, and annoying street performer destination of choice.

ride: your car. Aka "wheels."

rig: fake breasts. "Man, check out the rig on that chick over there." Aka "put on weight" (as in, "Looks like Cindy put on some weight recently"). L.A. is truly the "Silicone Valley."

Rodeo Drive: the ridiculously overpriced shopping street that cuts right through "the triangle." See "the Golden Triangle."

Samo: Santa Monica. More specifically, Santa Monica College.

Shakey Quakey: a van that educates youngsters about earthquakes. Yogi Bear lectures while the vehicle vibrates.

Sigalert: traffic is completely stopped. Invented by a traffic reporter named Sigmund.

Silicone Beach: the Playa del Rey–Venice area, home of a large number of silicone-breasted beach babes.

Slimey Valley: the Simi Valley.

smog: smoke + fog. And, folks, there's no way around it. It's bad.

the Strip: the Sunset Strip in Hollywood, the home of rocker boys and chicks for the last three decades. A standard sight: heavy metal singers in pointy cowboy boots, multiple bolo ties, and skull and dagger tattoos, with their Pamela Anderson–clone babe support, who seems to have walked right out of Playmates, Hollywood's premier source of slutgear.

Surfer U.: Pepperdine University in Malibu.

the Swish Alps: Silverlake, the second largest gay enclave in the city.

the 3 Bs: Brentwood, Bel Air, and Beverly Hills. Rich, white, star-studded enclaves.

tradin' paint: a car accident.

transition: when one freeway merges into another.

trust me: do not trust this person. In the world capital of disingenuousness, it's a dead giveaway.

TV parking: finding a spot exactly where you want to be. A phenomenon that only happens on TV shows. Aka "Kojak," as in "nice Kojak!"

Uncle Tom: Tom Bradley, former mayor of L.A. For over twenty years, he was credited with wimping out on several issues important to the black and Latino communities and in general sucking up to the prevailing white power structure. But he had a nice smile.

University of Spoiled Children: USC, the University of Southern California. Along with UCLA, it counts many film directors as former attendees. Caveat: film director is widely regarded as the profession of choice for spoiled rich kids.

the UV index: the ultraviolet ray index. Los Angelenos' answer to the weather report.

the Valley: the San Fernando Valley.

Weho: West Hollywood, L.A.'s answer to the Castro. "Where the gay boys pose."

Will Rogers: major gay beach where Santa Monica Canyon meets the ocean.

the Wizard of Westwood: the legendary UCLA Bruins basketball coach John Wooden, who won ten NCAA Division I championships—by far the most successful career of any college coach. His players included Lew Alcindor (aka Kareem Abdul Jabbar), Jerry West, Bill Walton, and the all-time Crotty family sharpshooter of choice, Lynn Shackelford.

yarmulke burn: the bald spot on the back of the head.

Given an initial boost by Frank Zappa's "Valley Girl," featuring banter by his daughter Moon Unit at the Sherman Oaks Galleria, plus a recent kick by the film *Clueless*, Valley Girl seems poised to last a long while, or at least as long as teenage girls with attitude are hanging out at, like, the mall.

as if!: yeah, right. In other words, I do not believe you.

bitchin': most excellent.

fer sure: certainly.

gag me with a spoon: unpleasant or disturbing. Aka "barf out," "gross," "grody."

I don't <u>think</u> so: give me a break, not a chance.

I'm sure: sardonic; means completely the opposite. "My mom asked me to change my baby sister's diapers. Like, I'm sure." Aka "I am *so* sure."

like: a word preceding every, like, well, almost, noun and verb. Sample sentence: "I was all like . . . and then he was all like. . . and then I was like. . . ." This is *the* fundamental Valley Girl expression, where one is supposed to understand what the other is saying by the look they give you after "like." Scholars interpret this peculiarly Southern California phenomenon as the triumph of the media culture over imaginative speech, where popular images are so well understood, no one even has to make a comparison anymore. It is simply understood by the context of "like."

mellow: calm, like, you know, sedated.

no way!: you're kidding me. Exclamation used like, whenever. Like, "Deirdre is going steady with that gross debater guy." Your response: "No way!" In recent years, a popular retort has evolved: "Yes way!" Or simply "way."

oh my God: very excited, happy.

oh right: disbelieving. Akin to "give me a break."

okay, fine: something that's not fine at all, but I have to put up with it.

totally: completely. Aka "to the max."

way: very; yes.

whatev: short version of "whatever."

whatever: emphasis on second syllable. Frequently made with a *W* hand gesture (thumbs together, index fingers up, other three down) with a meaning so profound and inexplicable it almost sums up an entire generation. Like, whatever.

Love

"I love being consumed by a lover so overpowered with lust, he's operating on pure instinct." —GILLIAN BONNER

"Never trust a woman, even if she has borne you seven children."
                                        —JAPANESE PROVERB

THOUGH I HAD BROKEN UP WITH HER ABOUT a dozen times before, Elke put the kibosh on our whole affair after she concluded we weren't "soulmaids." She was right. How could we be? In comparison to any German, I am a complete slob.

It was just one of many cross-cultural romantic misunderstandings. For starters, Elke didn't understand that "I LOVE YOU, I LOVE YOU, I LOVE YOU!" said repeatedly after going out for three hours was mid-American Irish Catholic for "Give me some time, I might get to like you." By contrast, "Ich liebe Dich" (German for "I love you") is said quite sparingly, for it means "Not only do I love you, but I want to die for you, make babies with you, merge with you, blood to blood, soul to soul, for eternity upon eternity and then some."

Fortunately, neither Elke nor I used some of the more embarrassing examples of love talk that characterize my native tongue. Here they are, along with some esoteric concepts you might find useful next time around.

against the law: an extraordinarily good-looking woman. Usually applied to a woman who probably knows it.
babe: a good-looking person, though usually applied to women. Also, "total babe," for those of us with a penchant for hyperbole. Understanding the babe concept is absolutely essential to understanding how American men look at women. Like it or not, men will spend huge hunks of time debating whether a woman is, in fact, "babe material."
babe-a-licious: very good-looking, a knockout. Made famous

by Dana Carvey and Mike Meyer in *Wayne's World*. Alternately, "babe factor," "babe material."

breakdown: a date that didn't live up to expectations. "We had a breakdown on the 101."

Clydesdales: a great-looking guy accompanied by a great-looking gal.

the Code: a straight male's answer to the Rules. The Code says a man must be a beast to snare a woman.

cutie: a swell-looking guy. Used by women. As in, "He's a cutie." Similar to a straight guy's use of "babe."

fatzilla: an extremely overweight individual. Aka "munchasaurus." As in, "What about Tom?" "You expect me to go out with *that* fatzilla? I mean, that guy is a total munchasaurus."

fishing fleet: a posse of women on the prowl for men.

fox: a very good-looking woman. Aka "stone fox." Akin to "babe."

fresh talent: a new love. "He's not interested in getting back together. He's after fresh talent."

Helen Keller: a blind date.

henpecked: a man dominated by his wife.

high maintenance: a person or relationship that is quite taxing on one or both partners. Or a love interest whose emotional ups and downs sap all of your time and energy. "The sex was phenomenal, but Susan was just too high maintenance."

I want to date other people: I wanna see if I can find someone better.

Kama Sutra: a Hindu sex manual many people talk about but few actually read, let alone use.

Ken: a meticulously well groomed male. Also, a teenage term for a gay man.

kitchen pass: permission from your wife to go out with your buddies. Here's the scenario. Buddy calls asking you out. Your response: "Hang on, let me see if I can get a kitchen pass."

let's be friends: in other words, "You're good enough to hang around for me to use, but you're not good enough to be my lover" (Dominic Boswell).

love handles: rolls of flesh protruding from the side of one's belly. Great for squeezing.

Monet: someone who looks gorgeous from a distance but not up close.

Mr. Right: the guy who knows "the Code" and lets you play by "the Rules."

Mr. Right Before: the guy who loves you more intensely than you've ever been loved, which, if you are a thoroughly modern career woman, is just too damn much.

PMS: Putting Up with Men's Shit.

the Rules: a female's answer to "the Code." Says a woman must play hard to get in order to snare her dream man.

scary: extremely good looking. "You know that tall blond English chick? She's scary." Alternately, "damage." As in, "That chick could do some serious damage."

scene: a relationship. "He doesn't want a quickie, he's looking for a scene."

she gave me the Heisman: she broke up with me. Because the Heisman Trophy (given to the best college football player every year) shows a running back fending off tacklers. Aka "brown helmet."

she thinks he hung the moon and stars: she's deeply, perhaps blindly, in love. My kind of gal.

smooch: kiss.

split the sheets: break up. Also, "split up."

tie the knot: get married.

tonsil hockey: kiss passionately.

tzaftig: Yiddish for a "curvy" gal. Aka "Rubenesque."

whipped: someone who is totally flat-out bonkers in love, often pathetically so to those who are mateless.

Maine

"Love ya dahlin' cuz ya wicked smaht . . . knew it when I saw ya at the ole Kay Maht." —THE WICKED GOOD BAND

IF YOUR IDEA OF MAINE IS AN OLD-MONEY porchbreaker, you've got a rude awakening coming, cappy. Yes, there's that summer WASP contingent up around Bah Hahbah, but it's a tiny fraction of a state that has far more in common with the stories of Carolyn Chute than the measured sentiments of Lady Astor.

away: (1) not from Maine in general or that particular Maine town; (2) that vast netherworld free of pickups, black dogs, and lobster traps. You are "from away" unless you and your parents were both born and raised in Maine. Similar to "Northerner" in the South.

ayuh: a common colloquialism, like New York City's all-purpose "Yo!" Can mean "you betcha," "that's right," "hello," "don't know," or signals a transition to a new thought or pause in the conversation.

the back door trots: diarrhea.

the Back Side: Southwest Harbor, the poor side of Mount Desert Island.

Bah Hahbah: Bar Harbor, tacky T-shirt, get-rich-quick mirage of New England, with 155 hotels and B&Bs all lined up and ready to gouge.

balled up: constricted, confused. "I got all balled up and couldn't make it."

Bean boots: footwear designed by Leon Leonwood

Gorman, aka "L. L. Bean." Launched what is now a popular and overpriced Maine line of shoes and sportswear. Boasts the most frequently visited store in what has become the outlet mecca of Freeport.

blowin' out endways: a gale, as known only on the Maine coast.

bug: a lobster. "Had me a bunch of bugs last August."

buoy: an important line of demarcation for lobstermen. Like a cattleman's brand, it has different colors and lines for each owner.

canned tuna casserole: the totem food of white trash Maine one finds everywhere except on "MDI." Only those "from away" eat fresh fish on a regular basis.

Cape Porpoise: an early name for Kennebunkport, George Bush's real hometown.

cappy: friend or acquaintance.

changing water: taking up the lobster pots to put new bait in.

chowdah: chowder.

clammer: one who digs for clams.

close as the bark to a tree: stingy.

COA: the College of the Atlantic, in Bah Hahbah. Evergreen State College East. Long stringy hair capital of Maine.

corker (pron. "cocker"): the very best. Aka "finestkind."

cottage: a WASP summer home, containing at least twenty rooms, eight bathrooms, and a carriage house for the servants.

cow puncher: veterinarian. So called because of the practice of punching cows in the stomach to release trapped gas.

cow's tongue: rough on one side, smooth on the other; being two-faced. "He's got a real cow's tongue."

crackleberries: eggs.

crocus sacks: burlap bags.

cruncher: hunterspeak for a very large deer.

cunnin': cute. "She's awful cunnin'."

dinner bucket: lunch pail.

Disgusta: the capital of Maine.

dow!: ah, c'mon! Can also mean no.

down cellar: the basement. Where one keeps the washer and dryer.

Down East, Down-Easter: you actually go east when you head south from Maine. Coined by sailors because the coastal winds made traveling from Boston to Maine the easy or "downhill" run. "Down-Easter" can also refer to a full-rigged wooden ship.

downstreet: downtown.

Dr. Green's: a liquor store.

driver: a hard worker.

duffah: character. "He's a real old duffah."

Maine Jokes

Q: What's a Maine virgin?
A: A 10-year-old who can outrun her pappy.

Q: Why wasn't Jesus born in Maine?
A: God couldn't find three wise men and a virgin.

Q: How is a nor'easter (a wicked Maine storm) like divorce court?
A: Either one could take away your trailer.

---

dust bunny: balls of dust that collect behind doors or under beds. Aka "dust kittens."

either fish or cut bait: shit or get off the pot.

empties: returnable bottles.

feedy: fisherman's term for when a fish's gut is so full of food it's only good for lobster bait.

fetch: (1) to be pretty. "She's a fetchin' young lady." (2) to get. "Jerry, fetch me that beer."

finestkind: the very best.

fishbones and mare's tails: rain is coming. Refers to the shape of the clouds.

flakes: wooden frames used by Euro fishermen to carefully cure their fish before returning across the Atlantic.

Floridy: Florida, the great getaway for half of Maine. The inspiration for most of Ellsworth. And, according to one reliable source, "the only state that compares to Maine in the quality of its cheap merchandise."

fresh enough to flop: very fresh fish.

gawmy: clumsy, awkward, big and dumb.

groundfishermen: those who fish for halibut and flounder, as distinct from lobstermen.

grunters and groaners: a "groaner" is a foghorn with one prolonged tone; a "grunter" has two tones.

gulls an' buoys: lasses and lads.

gurry: fish cleanings or guts.

gurry buckets: containers for empty clam shells and lobster debris. Used by diners in some Maine restaurants.

gut bucket: a very untidy place.

guzzle hole: a store that also peddles gasoline.

hardscrabble: an extremely rocky area, hard to farm. Also refers to a hearty, rough-hewn personality.

haul: how you move or lift things in Maine.

he skims his milk at both ends: a stingy man.

he's got his own zip code: spaced out.

Ice Cream and Cake School (ICCS): those who pronounce "Mount Desert" with the accent on the last syllable. Now the official MDI pronunciation. See "Sahara School."

Jackson mice: Syrian hamsters used in cancer research at MDI's Jackson Laboratory, the largest genetics lab in the world and the largest single employer on "the island."

Quintessential Maine Expressions

LIKE MOST RURAL TERMS IN THIS BOOK, MANY OF these Maine expressions are found in other ports of call. Nevertheless, I heard them first in Maine, and for that reason they've always been associated in my mind with Maine.

"Well, dahlin, you wanna keep your wheels up on the berm, and when you get to that tree, you wanna be shovelin' the coal to ah."

Keep the wheels of your truck out of the ruts and step on the gas when you get to the tree.

"That fella over there look like he been rode hard and put away wet."

Someone who's hung over or all tired and nasty-looking.

"You talk about a boy who don't know nothin'. That boy don't suspect nothin'."

He's mighty stupid.

"You see my daddy's new pickup? Don't she go." Pause. "Can't I drive her. Corker." Pause. "You just slap her in drive and clamp down on her. Don't she go."

That new pickup is a mighty fine vehicle.

"Cute as a bug's roller skate."

Very cute.

"Jumpin' around like a flea on a hot rock."

Agitated, spastic.

"It's raining pitchforks and barn shovels."

It's raining hard.

"I remember when you were knee high to a grasshopper."

When you were very young.

"I have to piss so bad my back teeth are floatin'."

I've got to urinate *baaad*.

"Your ass is sucking wind."

You're full of hot air. You're not saying anything worth listening to.

"He's a good boy, but he shits a little close to the house."

He's not too bright, but I like him anyway.

→

> **"He's two [fill in food choice] shy of a picnic."**
> He's not quite with it.
> **"Tougher than a boiled owl."**
> Very tough.
> **"Nervous as a long-tailed cat in a room full of rockin'
> chairs."**
> Very, very nervous.
> **"Get yer feet off the dashboard. How'd you like a snap
> on the beak."**
> Or as a northern Maine virgin might say to her male suitor:
> "Get off me, Dad, you're crushin' my smokes."

jag of wood: a full load.

jizzicked: too far gone to be fixed. "That tire is jizzicked."

Kee-Reist: Jesus Christ.

khaki: the regimental fashion of mainline MDI WASPs.

light in the loafers: a gay person. "That Charlie's a little light
in the loafers, don't you think?"

Little Jerusalem: the area on Long Pond on Mount Desert Island settled by wealthy European Jews who came to America
during World War II and were denied access to the clubs and
property in Northeast Harbor.

lobster car: a floating raft in which lobsters are stored at sea.

'magine: Maine form of "I about imagine," meaning "I think so."

Massachusetts driver: any bad driver on the road.

Massholes: people from Massachusetts.

MDI: Mount Desert Island.

the mink mass: the 10:30 Sunday service at St.
Mary's-by-the-Sea Episcopal Church in Northeast Harbor,
where, depending on how well you are dressed, cocktail party
invitations are issued like holy communion.

"mon bud": as in "Come on, buddy" shortened to "Come on, bud"
shortened to "mon bud." Used when a threat to fight is in order.

moxie: courage. Though the word has spread into general usage,
I mention it here because its namesake, a gentian-rich soft
drink called Moxie, was bottled in Maine. Allegedly, the taste
of the "tonic" was so sharp, one required courage to drink it.

Nasty Gansett: Narragansett beer, a totem drink of Maine locals.

New Hampshire screwdriver: a hammer. Used when one
doesn't want to take the time with an actual screwdriver.

Northeast Harbor: a wildlife sanctuary for endangered WASPs on MDI.

number than a hake: you're stupid. A hake—a variety of codfish—is considered fairly dim-witted.

on your beam ends: you're in bad shape, like a shipwreck that rests on the ends of her beams.

PFAs: People from Away.

pistol: a lobster that has lost one or two claws.

poke: the stomach.

porchbreaker: a summer WASP cocktail party.

pot: a lobster trap.

prayer handle: a knee.

punt: a blunt-nosed boat, almost rectangular, used to row around harbors and coves.

Red Sox: even in remote Maine, the Boston Red Sox are next to godliness. Which says a lot about the self-abnegating Puritan soul of this region. The team hasn't won a World Series since it sold Babe Ruth to the Yankees.

red tide: poisonous rust-colored algae occasionally ingested by clams and mussels, which can cause permanent paralysis in humans. Not killed by cooking.

Rockefeller roads: the 57 miles of carriage roads in Acadia National Park built by MDI philanthropist John D. Rockefeller.

How to Pick a Fight, Maine Style

MAINE, BEING A RELATIVELY HARDSCRABBLE STATE, has several expressions for "put up your dukes," such as "come aboard, swampah" or "you feel froggy, you leap." Maine also has several ways of saying you're not too bright: "dumber than a box of hair," "number than a pounded thumb," "uglier than a hat full of assholes," "wick cut a little close to the candle," "running on a lean mixture." Of course, after you've effectively countered the offer to fight and insulted the other person's intelligence, it's time for a little Maine braggadocio, as in: "I'll hit you so hard it'll kill your whole family," "I'll rip your head off and shit down yer neck," "I'll knock you flatter than a cow turd," "You think you're hot shit on a silver platter, but you're nothing more than a cold fart on a paper plate."

Quite clearly, this state does not concern itself with restraint and propriety.

Conversation with Maineiacs

U: Urban Hutchins, all-time great Maineiac, C: Chris Dorr, aka "Geech," Urban's loyal liege; M: Jim Monk.

C: Howzbout 'nutha story, cappy? The drinkin' crowd, we are the drinkin' crowd.
M: Yes!
U: OK, it's a small family restaurant, and a friend of mine from Florida—from away—is managing it, and this baaad-ass clan from the backside of the island comes into the restaurant, they's havin' a helluva good time—whoopin' it up, poundin' back the suds— and my friend comes up to 'em and asks if they wouldn't keep it down jest a tad, y'know, till "the drinkin' crowd" comes in. Well, ol' Gertie, the matriarch, stands up and pounds her fist on the table and bellows, "Drinkin' crowd? *We are* the drinkin' crowd!" Well, then he calls the police who inform him that, yes they can, in fact, get this lovely large family—one of 'em's passed right out on the floor, snorin' away, ya know the little tourists are, oh, slightly appalled—the police tell him, "We'll get 'em out of there for you, but you realize you'll probably have $1,100 worth of damages to the place in the process." Still, my friend elects to have them come on over, and Gertie finds out that the police are on their way and she stands up and points her crooked bony finger—as Chuck and Bubba are carrying out ol' Cousin Earl—she points her finger at my friend and with this evil squinty grin croaks, "I knew yoah name before you crossssed the Trenton bridge."
C: This being the bridge that connects the island to the mainland, of course.
M: What part of Bar Harbor is this happening in?
U: Straight from the Back Side, cappy, right from where you wanna count the toes on 'em.

M: Oh my God. That's great.

C: Here's a brief one. My friend Sam just told me this-un the other day. His mutha had just gotten hired on over to this Down East school and was talking with the vice principal about the students and had inquired about student behavior and discipline and was assured that the students were generally well behaved although "there were a few 'decency' calls you have to make, like the girl I sent home the other day, the skirt she wore was so short you could see the fringes on her benefits."

rusticators: the early well-heeled summer folk who took to visiting MDI for a break from the heat and humidity in their normal ports of call (e.g., Newport, R.I.). They were particularly drawn to the rustic qualities of the island.

Sahara School: those who pronounce "Mount Desert" like "Operation Desert Storm." See "Ice Cream and Cake School."

scouse: clam chowdah made without clams.

scrid: a tiny portion.

shagimaw: a fictitious animal that is a cross between a mouse and a bear, allegedly found in remote parts of northern Maine.

she goes with her head up and her tail over the dashboard: a proud woman.

steamers: steamed clams, the second most valuable Maine saltwater crop (after the lobster).

stove up: anything that has been damaged severely. "We was hanging out down on the pier, started harassing some of those fishermen, and they opened up a can of whup-ass on us, and we were some stove up."

summer: the six weeks between mid-July and Labor Day.

summer people: the MDI blue-blood WASP contingent, one fourth of the economy in places like Northeast Harbor. Aka "gnats." Can also refer to the droves of summer tourists. (Aka "summer complaints." As in, "Don't ask me for directions, hon, I'm just a summer complaint.")

ten-fowah: 10-4 in Maine CB lingo.

tippin': collecting pine boughs to make wreaths.

touchin' up: stealing. "They caught him touchin' up Hal's motorbike."

Tremont: the redneck side of MDI. Where an outlaw motorcycle gang might live. Very working class, yet knows its place. According to local lore, many kids grow up in Tremont and never visit Northeast Harbor because Dad said, "It's not for us."

twitch road: a winding road that snakes through the woods and is used to haul timber.

two burnt holes in a blanket: your eyes, with bags underneath.

warp: the rope used to connect the lobster trap to the surface buoy.

whup-ass: beat someone up; see "stove up."

wicked: as in "wicked good," "wicked fun," "wicked sharp," "something wicked." Totem expression of Maine. Similar to "awesome" or "totally." You get "wicked gas" after one of those Saturday bean suppers.

windflagging: when the white pine, the state tree, shows the direction of prevailing winds by sprouting branches on the downwind side of the tree.

wood-eaters: an old name for moose.

yahd: the non-cement area around a house.

yaht: yacht.

Yankee: from the Abnaki Indian word *yenghi*, meaning "white people of New England."

you better bring your lunch: used when you're facing someone who vows to kick your ass.

The Midwest

TRAVELERS TO THESE UNITED STATES usually focus on the exciting but ephemeral beauties of the East and West coasts with maybe a trip to Graceland thrown in for good measure. Ignored is the vast hinterland in the middle known affectionately as the Great Plains—land of corn, soybeans, and BIG BEEF. It is quite literally the breadbasket of the world. Seen from an airplane it's awesome—miles upon miles of manicured flatness, with all manner of "fields" arranged in beautiful, quiltlike mosaics. For me, a native of Omaha, it's the most astonishing sight I can imagine—unless, of course, we're talking of those broad Nebraska sunsets, which put all other sunsets from Key West to San Diego to shame.

The natives of this proud agrarian land, like the natives of all the other unique regions of America, have their own style of speech. But not a lot of attention is paid to it because (1) snobby bicoastal types consider the Midwest not worthy of their attention and (2) with the exception of those from Minnesota and Wisconsin, Midwesterners do not have an easily recognizable accent. Allegedly, this is why most major league announcers, from Johnny Carson to Tom Brokaw, hail from these parts—their accent-free anchor talk will offend no one and welcome everyone.

Midwesterners view this innocuous quality with a degree of pride. It seems to suit the region. For the goal of most Midwesterners is *not* to stand out. Warren Buffet, the second richest man in America, lives in Omaha. But you wouldn't know it. He lives in a relatively modest house, plays bridge with the locals, and generally eschews big-time publicity.

Midwesterners aren't showy. But they are eminently down-to-earth, testing the rapid-fire intellect of the East and the unconventional spirit of the West against the eternal verities of sun, snow, and mud. Which is why I say, if America is truly the new Buddhaland, then the Midwest is the Middle Way.

Some Pointers

1. A sure sign you're dealing with true, rural Midwesterners over the age of 50 is that they don't have an e-mail address or, God knows, a Web site.

2. There are three midwestern vegetables: corn, potatoes, and green beans, all either from a can or a box.

3. At most midwestern bars, especially outside the major cities, don't expect microbrews. The only import is Heineken, and the only sounds come from Top 40 radio.

4. Until recently, on a big-city FM radio station you might hear some Kansas or, if you were real lucky, some Bachman-Turner Overdrive. On AM radio you could expect oldies but goodies like "Born Free" and "Winchester Cathedral."

5. Many people in the Midwest are FAT. And in some rural areas they are EXTREMELY FAT. While this may seem abhorrent to a New York social x-ray or an L.A. aerobics queen, Midwesterners do not look on this with a great deal of alarm. If you are a man and you are fat, you can always play for the Nebraska Cornhuskers. If you are a woman and you are fat, you can always marry one.

Keep in mind that in the Midwest, fatness is not a weight problem, it's a geographic problem. If you weigh 250 pounds and you live in a big city, you may be considered overweight. But if you move to the country, you'll fit right in. Colon, Nebraska, might be a good destination. Or, if that's too congested, try Funk (named in honor of P. C. Funk, a Civil War veteran).

6. In all the major midwestern cities, there's invariably a tiny community of tasteful hipsters who pride themselves on listening to NPR, knowing about Beuys and Grotowski, and eating at the two groovy restaurants in town. Years of butting up against an entrenched square culture has made these folks very, very *weird*.

7. Topics to discuss with men: weather, the route you took to get here, sports, the route you're taking to get home. Topics to discuss with women: what Rush said yesterday, "the kids," and what Rush said this morning. Caveat: though she may be smarter,

upon arriving at the relatives', a midwestern wife always lets her husband get in the ceremonial heartfelt introduction: "So, how you do like that new Chevy?"

8. Conversational faux pas. Never begin a sentence, "I think that new Ebonics program over at Central High is . . ." However you stand on the issue, Midwesterners will not let you go without at least a 20-minute harangue on the topic. Though some suspect racism is at the root of the midwestern aversion to Ebonics, I suspect something more benign—an aversion to any speech that isn't middle-of-the-road and accent-free. And don't even *think* of broaching the subject of abortion.

9. Giving directions is a big deal in the Midwest. Along with the weather, it's a required conversation-starter. In fact, if you can segue a discussion of the weather into a description of how you got to Ponca City, you'll be a big hit in these parts.

10. Never ever put a midwestern man in the wholly uncomfortable position of having to discuss, let alone express, "feelings."

11. Never ever expect a midwestern man to discuss the real condition of his health. "Oh, I've got a little tumor over there I guess, can't walk much from the chemo, but I'll probably outlast all of ya." And you know what, he probably will.

12. What to expect for dinner: meat, more meat, and, of course, Jell-O. Midwesterners do wonders with Jell-O. And we're not just talking dessert here. One of the essential courses at any rural feed is green Jell-O stacked with all kinds of vegetables. Yum, yum.

Some Quintessential Expressions to Get You Started

THESE ARE NOT ALL STRICTLY MIDWESTERN EXPRESSIONS, but I heard them here first.

→ "The best fertilizer for the soil is the owner's own footprints."

→ "If you plant your crop in dust, the bins will bust. If you plant it in mud, your crop's a dud."

→ "He ain't heavy, Father, he's my brother." Saying beneath the famous statue at Omaha's Boys Town depicting an older boy hoisting up a younger one.

→ "She's so homely she'd scare a mule away from his oats."

→ "She's so cross-eyed, when she cries, tears run down her back."

→ "He's as tight as a bull's ass in fly time."

→ "Two types of people raise cattle: a millionaire and a guy who has nothing."

→ "Bulls make money, bears make money, hogs go broke."

ag: agriculture. "Yeah, Jimmy's headin' to that ag program at Iowa State."

ax handle wide: a woman with "a broad beam." That is, she's fat across the fanny.

beans: soybeans. There really aren't any other kind of beans that matter much here. Most soybeans don't even go to humans and certainly not to tofu. They go to hogs.

big on: a fan of, devoted to. "Jimmy is big on soccer. I've never really been into it much myself."

the biggest boobs in the barnyard: turkeys. Domestic turkeys are so stupid, if you let them outside in a hard rain they'll drown from gaping in shock at the droplets. As one local put it, "They are so inbred they have no instincts left whatsoever."

How to Talk Like a Midwesterner at a Formal Dinner Party

Spos'ta git down to freezin' tonight.

I got my storm windows on last week.

Well, a snowstorm in May is a wagonload of hay.

Right as rain.

black as the inside of a cow: very dark.

bring home the bacon: make a good amount of money.

bumper crop: a very good crop.

button: a pig's nipple. "There's eight buttons on that sow."

caught kind of cornered: don't know the answer.

chew the fat: kibbitz.

corn: three main types are grown in the Midwest—seed corn (what they'll be planting next year), feed corn (for the hogs and cattle), and sweet corn (fed to humans). Most corn grown here is feed corn. And most sweet corn preferably comes from cans.

How to Talk Like a Midwesterner at a Funeral

Nice day for a funeral.

Well, it's a little cloudy, but it's s posta' clear by tonight.

corporate farming: when a farm is owned by a large corporation, which hires, fires, and supervises farmers as if they were paid laborers. The farmer does not rent the land, nor does he have to supply his own equipment. Decisions are made by the "corporate farm manager," though the farmer can still choose the seed cap he wears.

cry your eyes out: a hard cry.

Dakota: South Dakota. For most Midwesterners, not to mention most of the country, North Dakota doesn't even exist.

deal: a situation or thing. As in, "That new inflatable stadium's quite a deal, isn't it?" Or, "That tornado they had over there in Dunlap, that was some deal, wasn't it?" Some ascribe this important noun to Minnesota, but it's actually used throughout the Midwest. Aka "heckuva deal."

drop the neck yoke: it's time to quit.

feed: a large meal.

4-H: Head, Heart, Hands, and Health, an educational organization for rural kids. Given the spate of troubles back on the farm, the 4-Hs might now represent Hell-raising, Hickies, Heavy Metal, and Hemp.

get a move on: get moving. "You better get a move on, son, the Corn Palace closes in an hour, and we have 30 miles of driving ahead of us."

gettin' into: a major business move. "Yeah, we're gettin' into hogs now."

got: the Midwest is a very self-effacing culture, so "I" is rarely used. "Got a shipment in the other day."

grandpa cats: huge gnarly channel catfish that grow to more than 6 feet and will bite your arm if you get too close. If they do bite you, they hang on for dear life, and you have to pound a nail through their head to kill them.

grass widow: an unmarried gal with children.

gutless wonder: a person without backbone.

head: quantity of cattle. As in, "How many you got now?" "I'm runnin' about 2,000 head."

the Heartland: the Midwest in general, often Nebraska in particular. That part of the country where bicoastal hype and hoopla just don't fly. Aka "the Midlands."

he's a good feeler: hale-met and hearty fellow. Someone who enjoys a good time.

he's got a leg up on Joe: he's ahead of him.

---

5 Classic Midwestern Ways to Say "I Love You"

That's some rain we've been havin'.
What about them Huskers?
You think the Bluejays have a chance?
You're from Tyndall, eh?
Do you like corn?

---

how'd you get here?: this is by no means as innocuous as it sounds. The first 30 minutes of any conversation in the Midwest must be spent discussing "the route you took." There will invariably be other opinions on why that particular route is not necessarily the best, in which case you are required to validate the wisdom of taking this alternative route while defending the route you in fact took. Always indicating, of course, that the next time you might try another route not even discussed.

in: can only be explained in context: "Yup, got 50 acres in clover out there in the back 40."

in the bin: never count your income from crops until they are "in the bin." Or "in the elevator."

it's a nice night for an old sow to have pigs: it's a bright, moonlit night.

it's raining pitchforks and hammer handles: it's raining very hard.

jim dandy: a well-dressed man.

John Deere: a corporate farming deity, one of the largest manufacturers of farm equipment in the country. You'll see a lot of farmers wearing yellow and green John Deere caps. Many go into major debt procuring the latest John Deere equipment. If, for some reason, you can't afford John Deere equipment, or some corporate farming entity is paying for it, it's still good form to wear a John Deere hat. Otherwise it's acceptable to be seen in a seed company hat (DeKalb, Funks, and Pioneer will do just fine).

a knuckle sandwich: a punch in the face. "How'd you'd like a knuckle sandwich?"

kwitchurbellyachin': stop complaining.

let's cut the bellyband: let's get going. The "bellyband" is the strap that goes around a horse's stomach to hold the harness on. "That's enough. Let's cut the bellyband. Supper's waiting."

meet and greet: a political reception.

the Midwest: Kansas, Nebraska, Iowa, northern Missouri, southern Minnesota, and South Dakota.

the missus: a rural expression for someone's wife.

nuttier than a fruitcake: one whose words don't make a heckuva lot of sense. "That fella they got runnin' that elevator now, heck, he's nuttier than a fruitcake."

on account of: because. Midwesterners, a little like Southerners, don't seem to use "because." It doesn't seem to have the right rhythm or maybe it's just too direct. "He had to delay the harvest on account of the rain we've been havin'."

organic farming: a communist plot.

outfit: a company or place of business. "That John Deere outfit over in Laurens has got some pretty good deals on combines right now."

Pier: the capital of South Dakota, Pierre. It is not pronounced "Pee-aire."

pigs: there are four main types of pigs in the Midwest—"sow" (a female); "boar" (a non-neutered male); "hog" (a fixed male); and "swine" (a juvenile pig, or pigs in general).

pool hall yield: an exaggerated crop yield. Used by farmers who go down to the local bar and, after a few Millers, start bragging about their yields.

pop: called "soda" on the East Coast.

puttin' out to flower: planting sunflowers or alfalfa in a field formerly used for beans and corn. This is a way of giving the field a rest, helping it replenish itself. Part of a farming system known as "crop rotation."

reachin' out there: that's a bit of a stretch for me.

riverboat gambling: sounds romantic but definitely isn't. This is the Old West–sounding pretext that gaming interests have used to win over legislatures in several midwestern states. The casinos are supposed to travel up and down the river every few months, but the law is easily circumvented or ignored.

rocky mountain oysters: the fried testicles of a young male pig. Considered a delicacy by some, though not by anyone in my family.

round the bend: a geographical pointer or someone who's turned a bit nutty. "He's gone round the bend."

route (pron. "root"): the roads you took.

Rush: porcine radio commentator Rush Limbaugh, the Father Coughlin of '90s America, propaganda arm of the "Republican guard," and the all-knowing pontificator almost all Midwesterners swoon over. "Did you hear what Rush said this morning?" Or, "You know what Rush said—he said he'd like to hear those tapes of Newt to see if they weren't planted by the Democrats." Proof that all those gorgeous midwestern gals just loooove those porky midwestern guys.

sack: what is known as a "bag" in other parts of the country.

Sears Want More Buck: the late Sears, Roebuck catalogue, in years gone by the primary way for farm families to procure all manner of supplies. Caveat: the bra illustrations provided horny farm boys with their first glimpse of the nearly naked female form.

see: the transition word of choice in the Midwest, though made popular by Ross Perot. "Now, Jimmy, Iowa State has all their starters back, see, so we're expecting great guns out of them." Or, "See, Debbie can't walk worth a darn, so we moved her to the home there in Sioux City, see." The ideal midwestern sentence would incorporate "see" and "deal" in a discussion of directions and weather: "See, here's the deal, it was snowin' pretty good, so we took 29 there out of Mo Valley, heading to Mount Damien, then we headed north through that keep-on-truckin' town and on up through Moorhead, Charter Oak, and on into North Denison there, see, but next time I think we'll just go the ole way on 30

🦆

through Logan and Dow City and miss that whole construction deal down around Soldier."

Silicon Plains: Fargo, North Dakota, now that Great Plains Software has moved to town. As the saying goes, before Great Plains arrived, the most exciting thing in Fargo was the $5 bingo night at the Holiday Inn.

Siouxland: the total area that comprises Sioux City, South Dakota, and Sioux City, Iowa, all of which once belonged to the large and mighty Sioux Nation.

spread: the total collection of land. "Oh, he's got a good spread there, about 700 acres."

Stuckey's: the 7-Eleven of the great midwestern roadway. You'll know you're in the heart of the Heartland when you see one. Famous for their peanut brittle (yuk!).

up ta [fill in name]: to. For example, when referring to an entire family, you simply say, "We're going up ta Scott's" (though you are, in fact, referring to Scott's entire family). And it's always "up ta," never "down ta." Aka "over ta."

vertical farming: when a corporation controls all aspects of the farming operation—from growing the feed to raising the cattle to butchering the meat.

volunteers: corn stalks from the year before that grow in this year's field of beans. Or vice versa.

walkin' the beans: when you walk through the field of soybeans with a small hoe or bean knife, cutting out weeds and "volunteers." Growing up, whenever we visited Uncle Paul and his family up in Havelock, Iowa, this particular brand of character building was inflicted on city slickers like myself. It essentially confirmed my suspicion that I was a spoiled and lazy brat.

Wallace's Farmer: the *Time* magazine of the farm belt.

weather: farmers listen more to the weather report than the news. A lot of thought and conversation is directed toward it. Be prepared.

Iowa

"We're friendly ducks." —THE MOTTO OF MALLARD, IOWA

the Athens of the Midwest: Iowa City. Because it is so ethnically diverse and because of its fairly strong state university (most notable for its Writers' Workshop).

the Big Boar: says one Iowan, "You have not seen balls in your life until you've seen the balls on a 900-pound pig." Along with the butter cow, the main attraction at the Iowa State Fair.

Bill the Cat: a character in the famous cartoon strip set in Iowa, "Bloom County." Though a feline in the strip, there is a real Bill the Cat, a seriously fried and nonfunctional Vietnam vet who lives on the streets of Iowa City.

the boobs: a tall sculpture on the capitol grounds in downtown Des Moines featuring four bare-breasted broad-beamed Iowa gals, one of whom is holding her breasts as a gesture of fertility.

the Capital City: Des Moines. Pronounced "deh-*moyne*," never "dez *moy*-nez" (unless satirically).

Cat: the Caterpillar tractor company. For years Cat hats, clothing, and yellow boots were popular in Iowa, but now they've become trendy with gay boys in New York, Portland, and San Francisco.

CB: Council Bluffs, a ghetto of Omaha.

corn-fed spread: the gradual widening of the lower extremities on any woman born and raised in the state. At age 14, during March Madness, most Iowa girls look like cute, thin, spunky cheerleaders. By 19, after they've had the first child, the weight has gone up at least 25 pounds. By 25 and two more kids it's doubled, and it goes up exponentially from there. By the time an Iowa gal has achieved "broad beam" status, she has entered that hallowed realm of the "corn-fed spread." Much prized by Iowa men, even though doorways and beds have to be expanded accordingly.

dinner: lunch. In Iowa the noon meal is called "dinner," and what regular people call "dinner" is called "supper," which invariably includes leftovers from lunch—I mean, dinner.

funnel cake: super-sweet pancake batter that's poured through a funnel into a vat of extremely hot oil. Similar to fritters, but they weigh close to a pound. You have not fully experienced the Iowa State Fair until you've lunched on a corn dog and funnel cake. Never mind the cholesterol.

girls' basketball: forget the Hawkeyes, this is the real Iowa spectator sport. Iowans raise the strongest, healthiest, most capable gals in America, in large part because of the attention they give to their extracurricular activities.

the Gofer: Fred Grandy, a former Iowa congressperson, Harvard alum, and star of *Love Boat*.

have you seen the butter cow?: an essential rite of passage—
seeing the cow made entirely of butter at the Iowa State Fair.

it's good for the corn: the Iowa state mantra. Used earnestly
by old-timers, as in, "Heck of a storm we're having." Reply:
"It's good for the corn." And satirically by high schoolers, as
in, "Those March Madness idiots are blocking the road!"
Reply: "It's good for the corn."

March Madness: when the small-town teams and fans around
the state descend on Des Moines for a month-long sports bonanza—the first week is the state wrestling tournament, the
second is girls' basketball, the third is boys' basketball, and
the final week is the Drake Relays, one of the oldest and most
prestigious track-and-field events in the country. You see
more seed coats, seed hats, and farmers cooperative hats during March Madness than you see all year in the capital.

Packy: Iowa's former governor Harold E. Hughes. So called because of his renowned ability to "pack in" large quantities of
liquor before his political days, when he sobered up to become
one of the finest public speakers in Iowa history.

the Ped Mall: the Pedestrian Mall in Iowa City.

we don't grow potatoes and Cleveland's in another state:
in other words, this is Iowa, dang it.

what's the corn up ta?: how high is it?

the Workshop: the Iowa Writers' Workshop. If you can say, "I
got read at the Workshop," you're a big star in this town.

Kansas

Kansas became a state at the same time as
Nebraska. But there the sameness ends. Kansas is about
wheat. Nebraska is about corn. Kansas had Hickock and Smith (of
In Cold Blood). Nebraska had Starkweather and Kopechne (of *Bad-
lands*). Kansas has national champion college debate teams. Nebraska has national champion high school debate teams. Kansas
has great college basketball. Nebraska has great college football.
Kansas has Burroughs. Nebraska has Cather.

Missouri

Missouri is a transition state. A hybrid of
North and South. Tom Sawyer meets East St. Louis. The
Ozarks meet crack cocaine. *Hee-Haw* meets Marty Schottenheimer.

It's called the Show-Me State, owing to a stubborn awnriness, best personified by former president and favorite son Harry S. Truman (aka "Give 'em hell, Harry"). I think it's a crankiness born of being in the middle, not sure if you are part of the Union or the Confederacy.

been on the boat?: have you been riverboat gambling?

fishbowl: a large mug of beer at Rigazzi's restaurant in St. Louis.

Fo Po: Forest Park, in St. Louis.

the Gateway City: St. Louis, owing to the St. Louis Arch, the city's notable landmark.

Hoosier: in Missouri, a redneck.

Italian Hill: South St. Louis.

Jeff City: Jefferson City, the state capital.

Kan City: a major city in Missouri, home of the Chiefs, Royals, and Larry Drahota. Aka "KC."

L.A.: Lower Arnold, a suburb of St. Louis, where Hoosiers hang out.

Missoura: Missouri. The pronunciation the southern part of the state allegedly prefers. Caveat: because of its agrarian backbone, I put Missouri in the Midwest, though the distinctly southern accents you'll hear at the state university in Columbia might make you think you're in the heart of Dixie.

Missouree: Missouri. The pronunciation allegedly preferred by most "Missourans."

Mizzou: the University of Missouri. Known for its journalism school, not its football team.

Nashville of the Ozarks: Branson. All the country-and-western has-beens eventually find their way here.

New Madrid: the site of the largest earthquake in world history and the name of the earthquake itself. Everybody in "Missoura" knows about it.

the Plaza: the Country Club Plaza in KC, the nation's oldest and some say most beautiful shopping center.

pond-filler: a heavy rain. Aka "ditch-washer."

the Rena: where the St. Louis Blues hockey team plays.

Sauget ballet: a topless dance area in Sauget (pron. "saw-jay"), Illinois, just east of St. Louis.

show me: one of the more popular theories claims that this Missouri nickname dates from the Civil War. A Confederate general from Missouri was confronted by a Union general,

who demanded the Confederate army's surrender, boasting
that he had several thousand soldiers to back him up. To
which the proud Confederate commander replied, "I'm from
Missouri. You'll have to show me."

Slew: St. Louis University.

slider: a hamburger.

St. Louie: St. Louis. Never used by residents but often by visitors.
Like saying "Frisco" in San Francisco.

Nebraska

"Omaha [is] west of civilization, which stopped in Des
Moines, and east of the scenery, which began with the
Rocky Mountains. It was distinguished only for its
'conformity'; extreme only in its weather. Its contribution to culture was the Swanson dinner."

—Saturday Evening Post, September 10, 1949
(paraphrased by Roger Lowenstein in Buffett)

Aksarben: Nebraska spelled backward. Also, the largest horse
racetrack in the region until it closed (a casualty of the riverboat gambling boom across the river in "CB"). This predilection for backward spelling is popular in the Midwest. The
major racetrack in South Dakota is Atokad.

Archie: the extraordinarily large *Archidiscodon* mammoth at the
University of Nebraska State Museum in Lincoln.

Bee-at-trice: Beatrice. A midsize Nebraska town.

the Big O: Omaha, my revered place of birth. Marlon Brando,
Henry Fonda, and Gerald Ford were also born here. When referring to other parts of the
city, one uses "O": "South O,"
"North O," or "West O."

the Blackshirts: Nebraska's
vaunted starting defense.
The players wear black
shirts during practice.

Bob Devaney: the late revered
Nebraska football deity, former coach, and athletic director, who led "the Huskers"
to their first national championship back in 1971. I once

Go Big Red

Q: What does the <u>N</u> on the side of the Nebraska football helmet stand for? A: Knowledge.

O F ALL THE SPORTS PROGRAMS IN THIS PROUD AND sports-obsessed country, Nebraska football comes closest to the Greek ideal of rugged physical prowess. This state is characterized by big farms and even bigger ranches, populated by big men and big women doing serious big-time labor. The biggest and mightiest sons of these hardworking rural parents go on to play football at "the Program," the most vaunted and consistently successful college football program in the country.

It is a matter of great pride on the Great Plains not only to support the team but to get one's son on it. Like the pride in sending an Athenian warrior off to conquer Troy. Or the more perverse pride in sending off a Muslim suicide bomber, who might never come back again.

Which is why every summer and fall so many small-town Nebraska boys try out for Coach Osborne's squad. Many don't have a scholarship. Many weren't recruited at all. They are "walk-ons." And because of sheer desire and determination, many end up making the grade.

Make no mistake—this is about war. At times, holy war. Nebraska vs. Oklahoma in years gone by. Nebraska vs. Colorado today. Like any true Nebraskan, every Saturday of my childhood I tuned in to Lyle "Man, Woman and Child!" Bremser announcing the Cornhusker games on Omaha's AM radio powerhouse, KFAB. I listened religiously for a solid decade until debate tournaments usurped my interest in football, only to see it return like a crop of kudzu a decade later. I am now hopelessly addicted to the fortunes of Big Red.

I am not alone. During every home game in the fall, Lincoln's Memorial Stadium becomes the third largest city in the state, with over 80,000 in attendance. More than 20,000 fans follow the team to away games as well. These people are devoted—sitting in their requisite Big Red attire, cheering the team on through rout after rout of hopeless and hapless Big 12 opponents, then journeying home to McCook or Kearney or

North Platte to rework the rout in their weekday conversations and in the fantasy football world in their heads. Being a fan of Big Red is the sine qua non of being a true Nebraskan. So when the team loses, as it invariably does to top-ranked opponents ('94 and '95 were the fluke years), it puts the entire state in one Big Red funk.

Win or lose, however, the beautiful thing about Husker football is that it so perfectly mirrors the zeitgeist of Nebraska. Take a look at these similarities:

1. The Cornhuskers use a steady, methodical running game that over four quarters eventually wears down the opposition. Passing through the vast expanses of western Nebraska has the same effect on drivers. It's the origin of the expression "I've never stayed in Nebraska, but I've driven through it."

2. While the Cornhuskers always have a few tricks up their sleeves, most of what they do is not that flashy or unpredictable. They just do it very consistently and very well. The same can be said about the love life of Nebraskans as well.

3. Nebraska is a proud agrarian state. Year after year, the Cornhusker offensive front line looks as if they were fattened up on one of those "outstate" feedlots, with extra helpings of Czech *kolache* and trips to the local Runza Hut. These men, with names like Zack Wiegert and Brenden Stay (pron. "sty"), are as big and strong as a cow and as impervious to attack as the meanest bull. They literally move entire defensive lines several yards off the ball with just one push, mimicking the action of a large combine.

4. The Cornhuskers are the pioneers of what has become known as "smash mouth football." Just run the football right up the middle of the field over those huge behemoths at tackle and guard. This is also the Nebraska approach to life— middle of the road, middle of the country, nothing too extreme.

5. In the words of one Omaha native, Kurt Anderson, "The idea that terrifies Midwesterners the most is that they are too big for their britches." The same applies to Cornhusker football. There are no flamboyant stars on any Nebraska squad. Only team players, all hard working and all interchangeable. Lost the starting "I-back"? There's five more waiting in the wings, with just as much speed, desire, and even longer criminal records.

shook hands with him when my mom was president of the Omaha Symphony Guild. For Nebraskans, shaking hands with Bob Devaney is the equivalent of Bill Clinton shaking hands with John F. Kennedy—an event that marks you for the rest of your life. In my case it ensures I will always be remembered for my option-oriented approach to work and my grind-it-out selling game.

the Cemetery of Lights: Council Bluffs, Iowa. Pejorative term used by Nebraska teenagers in years gone by because they would never venture over the bridge to "CB" were it not for the lower drinking age. My preferred destination was the Depot Lounge, where under the influence of several Sloe Gin fizzes, I would dance the night away under the Depot's spinning crystal ball to the cutting-edge sounds of Foghat and REO Speedwagon.

Coach Osborne: Tom Osborne, the minister's son turned football coach. He has received flack in recent years for allowing players with questionable pasts and criminal records to play on his team. But the stoic philosopher-coach weathers on. There is something quintessentially Nebraskan about his humble and noble approach to the game. When an enemy has been soundly defeated, Osborne consistently refuses to run up the score. The act of downing the ball on the last play of the 1996 Florida-Nebraska national championship game was a testament to this quality in the man.

Duchesne Dolly: student at the Omaha Catholic girls' high school, Duchesne, run by the Sisters of the Sacred Heart and paid for by the Fathers of the Bleeding Bank Account.

Hollywood High: pejorative old name for Omaha's Westside High School because the student body was considered rich, spoiled, and prone to driving around in red convertibles.

how's your taters?: how are ya? Popular in the area of western Nebraska just before the Sand Hills, where potatoes are allegedly grown.

the Huskers: the University of Nebraska Cornhuskers football team. Aka "Big Red." Nebraska's state religion.

the Jet: Johnny "the Jet" Rodgers, a legendary Husker football star, Heisman Trophy winner, and armed robber.

Lincoln: the state capital, home of the Cornhuskers, and that place on the map where all the dialects of America become null and void.

the Luv Guv: Bob Kerrey, a former Nebraska governor who

received this name when he was cohabiting with film star Debra Winger. Kerrey, now a U.S. senator, is also known as "Vietnam Bob" for his tendency to play up his Vietnam service in courting votes.

Mrs. B.: Mrs. Rose Blumkin, the 103-year-old founder of Nebraska Furniture Mart, the largest retail furniture facility in the Midwest, who's known for driving a golf cart around the store to serve customers. A local legend, who escaped her native Russia at the age of 23, Mrs. B. is jokingly referred to as "the only business partner of Warren Buffett's to ever run out on him." (Buffett's Berkshire Hathaway owns the Nebraska Furniture Mart; Mrs. B. now runs Mrs. B.'s Carpet.)

the option: the cornerstone of the Nebraska Cornhusker offense. The quarterback runs down the line of scrimmage and has the option to either "pitch" the ball to a trailing back, step back and throw the ball downfield, or run it himself. For an option freak like myself, this style of offense was always quite appealing.

outstate: every part of the state west of Omaha. Which is most of the state.

the Red Guard: University of Nebraska football fans. Because of their total, almost militant, devotion to the football program despite gross violations (e.g., allowing running back Lawrence Phillips to return to action only five weeks after pummeling his girlfriend). To show the fascinating priorities of the university, the library is not open during home football games.

the Red Phone: the phone that sits at SAC, used only when the president calls for an all-out nuclear war.

SAC: Strategic Air Command in Bellevue, which would be the first place attacked in a nuclear war and the last place you want to be caught speeding to pick up your Bellevue high school sweetheart.

the scoring explosion: the potent offensive combination of Turner Gill, Irving Fryar, and Mike Rozier from the 1983 Cornhuskers.

the Tower on the Plains: the beautiful state capitol in Lincoln, home of the nation's only unicameral legislature.

the Wizard of Omaha: Warren Buffett, the second richest man in America, an investor noted for his common-sense musings on investments and modest living. Aka "the Oracle of Omaha." My parents invested $10,000 with Mr. Buffett back in the 1960s. Then they pulled out their investment to pay for their children's education. If they had not done so, their initial investment would be worth $80 million today. Mitigating factor: my dad gets to occasionally play bridge with Mr. Buffett.

South Dakota

MOST OF THE PEOPLE IN SOUTH DAKOTA TRACE THEIR roots back to the early part of this century, when farmers in Iowa, Nebraska, and Minnesota were coaxed to explore the cheap new opportunities waiting in "the Dakota Territory." What the new arrivals forgot to check was that the average annual rainfall here was about half of what they got back home. For this reason, South Dakota was hit the hardest during the Depression Dust Bowl, sending many of its new settlers scuttling home for good. Those who remained are a hearty, frugal, and surprisingly happy bunch, making do without many of the luxuries enjoyed in the surrounding farm states—including, often, indoor plumbing and toilets.

South Dakota (or "Dakota," as it's called by its residents) has about half the population of states like Iowa or Nebraska, and it's not going up. However, it boasts America's largest drugstore (Wall Drug in Wall), a sculpted rock bust of Teddy Roosevelt, Jefferson, Lincoln, and Washington (Mount Rushmore), the TV announcer Tom Brokaw, and the most liberal presidential candidate in U.S. history, George McGovern. In the vast sameness of the Great Plains, South Dakota is most definitely the black sheep.

The Military

SORELY MISSING FROM MY LATE TEENS AND early twenties was the discipline, camaraderie, and hard-headed vernacular that previous generations of Americans gained from the military. Because most young Americans, like myself, never have to pass through such a character-building initiation, these days the military has become just another business competing for premium ad space in *Rolling Stone,* whereas in the past it represented a sacrosanct attitude and an argot implicitly understood by most American males. So listen up, folks, here's what you're missing.

Bubbaville: a camp of southern soldiers stationed in Saudi Arabia during the Gulf War.

the Butcher of Baghdad: Saddam Hussein. Aka "Sammy."

butter bar (Army): straight out of the service academies, the first rank you can make as an officer is second lieutenant (aka "second louie"). While you are supposedly a great leader, you are actually just as raw as a private. You are called a "butter bar" because you wear a gold bar on your uniform (a first lieutenant, "first louie," wears a silver bar). "Oh no, looks like we got a butter bar today."

cherry (Army): a newcomer to the military. Aka "new-boo" (new from boot camp). This is your name for six months whether you like it or not. If you protest, all you'll hear is, "Shut up, cherry."

crabs: Air Force personnel.

the dark side: people who work covert operations. Aka "black op" or "black side." Often used in situations where the U.S. is officially not supposed to be. For example, Nicaragua. Typically, a dark-sider's name is dropped from the rolls so nobody can point a finger.

Dixie: code word for Israel or Jerusalem. Used during the Gulf War to avoid offending our freedom-loving Arab supporters.

dogface: a soldier in the Army.

don't ask, don't tell: a policy developed toward gays in the military that now unofficially covers everyone. Which is why some cynics concede that the military let it pass. For example, when an NCO screws up, the unwritten code now is "don't tell." The actual roots of the phrase go back to the old Army slogan "Better to ask forgiveness *for* than permission *to.*"

drop your cocks and grab your socks: get out of bed immediately.

fat boy program: according to the Army's old "tape test," if a soldier is deemed overweight, he is put on a special diet, with extra required exercise and PT (physical training).

fatty (Marines): anything of large proportion in experience or size.

frag: revenge taken on an officer by enlisted soldiers. Quite common during the Vietnam War. From "fragmented grenade," which has a wide "kill area," making detection nearly impossible. As in, "Better watch it, LT, before you get fragged." Used today in a more casual sense: "She started fragging me for calling her stupid."

GI Jo: a female soldier.

got one on the hook (Army): got a car literally on your tow.

grunts (Army): the low soldiers on the totem pole (usually infantry or anybody who has to "hump," i.e., walk).

gun bunny: anybody in Army artillery.

gunny (Marines): a gunnery sergeant.

headache: a journalist.

HMFIC: Head "Military Figure" in Charge.

hooah (pron. "hooo-ah") (Army): yes sir. A motivational term, said when you're excited. "We going to win this battle, men?" "Yes sir, hooah!" Can also be said when someone asks you a stupid question.

intelligence center: the latrine.

jarhead: a derogatory term for Marine, also used self-referentially. The Marines are the vaunted elite branch of the military characterized by insanely devout beliefs about honor, discipline, morality, duty, and elitism (only the Airborne Rangers are as gung-ho). Known for their intense pride (they claim to "guard the gates of heaven"). Unknown to most Americans, the Marines are officially under the jurisdiction of the Navy because they are amphibious and do land assaults from the sea. The Marines are also responsible for security on naval ships.

K mart: Kuwait. Used in the Gulf War.

leatherneck: a Marine. Because old Marine uniforms had leather collars.

leg Ranger (Army): old term for foot Ranger, before every Ranger was required to be an "airborne Ranger."

legs (Army): non-airborne personnel (aka "naps"). The soldiers that walk, as opposed to fly and parachute. The airborne are the elite.

little brass (Army): a lieutenant or captain.

noncommissioned officer (NCO): sergeant through sergeant major. Commissioned officers receive their rank from the president. A "noncommissioned officer" rises through the ranks. It used to be that an NCO could rise to become a commissioned officer (known as a "battlefield commission," for outstanding performance in the field). Now the only way to become a commissioned officer is through ROTC, a service academy, or OCS (Officer Candidate School).

180 out: a false answer or information.

oxygen thieves: soldiers considered so worthless that they may as well be stealing the oxygen they breathe because they haven't earned it.

pogue (Army): a worthless soldier. Aka "REMF" ("Rear Echelon MotherFucker").

poguey bait (Army): stuff bought at the PX to carry into the field because the rations are so disgusting, e.g., Top Ramen, smokes, chew, Velveeta cheese (it mixes well with Ramen), any kind of candy, coffee, Kool-Aid. So called because anyone considered lame is called a "pogue" (like herring bait).

pop smoke: to leave. From military exercises: when it's time to "x-fil" (exfiltrate or leave), a soldier pops a designated smoke grenade, which says that the coast is clear and it's cool to come get us. Veterans will say "let's pop smoke" (it's time to leave) in a variety of civilian situations.

profile (Army): injured and can't perform. A "profile slip" confirms as much. "Private Profile" is derogatory, for a soldier who's always complaining.

PX: postal exchange. The store on an Army base.

PX soldier: wearing unearned badges of skill or rank. Also applied to other branches, in which case said person is known as a "BX [from "Base Exchange"] soldier." Admiral Jeremy "Mike" Boorda, the chief of Naval Operations who committed suicide on May 16, 1996, is the classic and most tragic "BX soldier."

rotorhead: a military helicopter pilot.

Saddamize: forcefully control and/or destroy a person, a people, or a situation.

Scudavision: CNN during the Gulf War because of its extensive coverage of Iraqi Scud missile attacks.

semper gumby: always flexible. A play on the Marine motto, *Semper fidelis* ("Always faithful").

SERE: Survival, Evasion, Resistance, and Escape. Everyone gets SERE Level A training in boot camp. But only Special Forces, aviators, and high-ranking officers (or anybody with a high risk of being captured) go through SERE Level C, a very intense, mind-bending high-risk program that teaches a soldier how to really survive when captured.

smoke: trouble. As in, "You got 5 minutes to get this area clean or I'll bring smoke on you."

snake-eaters: the Special Forces (aka "Green Berets"). The military's go-anywhere, do-anything guys, who are expected to survive on whatever food they find.

squid: Navy personnel.

SRO: the Senior Ranking Officer.

tree-eater: a member of the Special Forces.

war baby: the youngest guy in a POW camp.

you can't smoke me (Army): you can't make me quit doing the exercise. You can't burn me out.

Minnesota

IF YOU'VE SEEN *FARGO*, YOU KNOW THE accent. If you've heard Garrison Keillor, you've grasped the attitude. Until you've lived here, however, you simply do not know the depths of SCANDIE HELL! Welcome to Minnesota. Have a little lunch?

The 9 Handy Rules of Minnesota Living

1. Do not, under any circumstance, forget to recycle. It doesn't matter how high your income. In fact, the higher your income, the more you are *expected* to recycle. Recycling applies not only to consumer waste but to food. If the Olsens serve you turkey tonight, you will be eating turkey sandwiches for lunch tomorrow and turkey soup for dinner. If there's any turkey left, you'll find it in the next morning's omelette. Caveat: in general, never throw anything away—either recycle or keep it (you never know when your great-grandchildren might need it).

2. Do not display your wealth. This is the land of the Midnight Liberal, the home of the Happy Warrior, Hubert H. Humphrey. And Walter Mondale. And Paul Wellstone. Just think, Dukakis carried Minnesota! Keep these points in mind:

   A. No matter your income bracket, do most of your shopping at garage sales and consignment shops (a great source for baby clothes and curlers). This stems from a fundamental Minnesota shopping corollary: Never Buy Anything New.

   B. If you must venture farther, shop at either the Mall of America or one of the discount malls. Rarely, if ever, set foot in a Neiman Marcus or Saks. Dayton's is okay if it's having a "13-hour sale."

   C. Do not be caught in a Mercedes. The preferred Minnesota vehicle is a beat-up Volvo. Think about it—a Volvo is extremely safe, practical, and unpretentious, and it's made by Swedes!

   D. Minnesotans, no matter how wealthy (and generally you can't possibly tell up here, anyway), will never look down at a Friday night out at Long John Silver's. Better yet, the $2.95 Friday fish specials at Byerly's. Forget Goodfellows.

E. Fashion tips. *For women,* I recommend a big Coach purse (to hold all the Minnesota essentials—a flashlight, a car phone in case you break down in 40 below, jumper cables, flares, a fleece blanket). *For men,* sweat pants, Sorel boots, and a prominent sports team sweatshirt will do just fine.

3. Neither rain nor sleet nor snow can stop a true Minnesotan from riding a bike. It's 24 below windchill? "I'll take the bike, hon."

4. Minnesota is built on the altar of permanent agreeability. Do not confront. Do not raise your voice. Do not act shocked or too dismayed. As Frances McDormand in *Fargo* ably demonstrates, all of life's tragedies and ghastly calamities can be met with the same understated Minnesota informality: "Okay, so we got a trooper pull someone over, we got a shooting, and these folks drive by, and we got a high-speed pursuit, ends here, and this execution-type deal."

5. If you want to keep peace with your neighbors, do not salt your driveway come winter. The salt may melt the ice better, but it eventually finds its way into the water stream and pollutes the lakes and rivers. Minnesotans do have a point; the lakes in a city like Minneapolis are quite swimmable.

6. Use what linguists call "the terminal rise" in the voice. Old Minnesota gals are so good at it, they actually squeak. This is reported to turn Minnesota men completely wild with passion.

7. This is not Los Angeles. Minnesotans hate celebrities and anything that reeks of celebrity privilege. For instance, a Minnesotan will walk twenty blocks in 20-below windchill instead of paying a guy two bucks to valet-park the car. And forget about drawing rave reviews for building that mansion on Lake Minnetonka. Nobody's impressed.

8. Summer pastimes: (1) going to garage sales; (2) holding garage sales; (3) going to "the cabin"; (4) going to someone else's cabin. Remember: everybody in Minnesota has a cabin.

9. If you want to get along, never admit you enjoyed *Fargo.* Though I do recommend a visit to the town of Margie, in the heart of Koochiching County.

blacktop: a paved road. A freeway is a "four-lane blacktop." Still said, even though most roads are now paved.

Boundary Waters: a wilderness area on the Minnesota-Ontario border, frequented by serious canoeists and outdoorsmen.

the cabin: one's cabin.

da Ranche: the Iron Range, an area in northern Minnesota centered around the iron ore deposits of the Mesabi Range. Until
1965 it was the land of milk and money. Wages were better
than almost anywhere else in the country. With the arrival of
cheap Chilean steel, however, the Range went into decline.
Though it's a shadow of its former self, the hardworking,
fiercely proud natives of the area still call themselves
"Rangers." Caveat: in the great Minnesota tradition of
world-known performers (the Artist Formerly Known as
Prince, Hüsker Dü, Debbie Koenen), both Bob Dylan (born in
Duluth, grew up in Hibbing) and Judy Garland (from Grand
Rapids) hail from "Da Ranche."

Every Day I Need Attention: Edina, a wealthy suburb of
Minneapolis. In general, people in Minneapolis despise the
suburbs.

Finndian: the Finnish people around the town of Detroit Lakes
have intermingled so long with the Chippewa of the nearby
White Earth Indian Reservation that they've acquired a bit of
their accent and vocabulary.

the Five-State Area: Minnesota, Wisconsin, Iowa, and the
Dakotas. Used by weather people.

flurries: a blizzard.

Fritz: Walter Mondale, former Minnesota senator and vice-president under Jimmy Carter.

going up north: going to "the lake." The tradition between
Memorial Day and Labor Day up here is, come Friday afternoon when Dad gets home, you pack up Mom and the kids
and head north. Nobody considers it anything special. And

nobody demands to know precisely where you're headin'. It's kept purposely vague, for this is your getaway after all, your secret little paradise. "So where's your cabin then?" "Oh, it's up north." Up north is anywhere from 60 miles north of the Twin Cities to the Canadian border (about 300 miles).

the Gophers: the nickname for the University of Minnesota sports teams. "Hey, how 'bout them Gophers?"

the Happy Warrior: the former Minnesota senator and presidential candidate Hubert H. Humphrey.

the Homerdome: the Hubert H. Humphrey Metrodome, where the Twins play.

hotdish: a casserole. This isn't some stereotypical joke. Minnesotans definitely use the term.

the lake: one's lake.

the Land of 10,000 Lakes: there are actually 14,000 lakes in Minnesota. "Scon Sin" has 8,000 more. As a child, I went to Camp Foley on Whitefish Lake, north of Bemidji. Besides being "the land o' lakes," Minnesota is also "the land o' camps."

lunch: the main meal of the day (what the rest of the country calls "dinner"). "A little lunch" is any snack between breakfast and "lunch."

lutefisk: a smelly Scandinavian delicacy of dried cod rehydrated with lye. The brunt of restrained Minnesota jokes but rarely eaten.

the Mall Brawl: former Timberwolves basketball star Isaiah Rider's notorious thumping of a female sports bar manager at the Mall of America in Bloomington (aka "the Mega Mall"). Say what you want about "the Timber Pups," but dumping the talented miscreant (theft, intimidation of witnesses, obstructing justice, plagiarism, marijuana possession, illegal cell phones, and alleged rape) ranks as one of their greatest on- or off-court moves.

Mini-Apple: Minneapolis. Residents like to kid themselves it is a small New York City.

mini-sober: because of the many treatment centers in the Twin Cities area—Hazelden, St. Mary's, etc.

Mining: the 3-M Corporation. As in, "I work at the Mining."

Minneapaulitans: residents of either Minneapolis or St. Paul.

the Minneapolis Sound: Minneapolis was the first "Seattle," a midsize liberal American city that produced a bevy of creative musicians in the 1980s, including Prince, the Replacements, and Soul Asylum.

A Primer on Talking Minnesota

1. Begin a sentence with "so" and end it with "then." "So are you going to college this year then?" Or, "So is Bob still doing carpentry work then?" Minnesotans know it sounds hokey, but they can't help themselves.

2. Minnesotans, being largely of Scandinavian descent, are not known for being extra loquacious or emotional. Sometimes 15–30 minutes of a conversation can go by in complete silence. When a Minnesotan finally decides to speak, it's often completely out of the blue with a statement like "oh, I suppose" or "yessir," which signifies nothing, foreshadows nothing, and really means nothing at all.

3. Though the rest of the country thinks Minnesotans respond in the affirmative with "yeah, sure," the more common reply is "I hope to shout." You'll seem far less like a rube if you start using the latter. However, "yep," "you bet," and "you betcha" are so common, you'll only draw attention to yourself if you don't use them.

4. When a Minnesotan comes in from a fishing trip, you don't say, "Have any luck?" You try to be as low-key as possible: "So-they-bitin'?" (said as if it's one word). "Yup" comes the reply. Your rejoinder: "Any-size-to-'em?"

5. As a rule, Minnesotans err on the side of understatement. For instance, if a Minnesotan was extremely happy, he or she would say, "I can't complain." Meaning, of course, that they could complain and probably will be complaining when life returns to its normally difficult and uneven course.

6. If you had to sum up the Minnesota mind-set in one word it would be "conservation": of energy, resources, emotions, leftovers, speech, and restaurant tips. You wouldn't say, "I can't believe this happened to me. What a total living nightmare!" You'd say that "things are not so good."

Minnie Snowda: what those California transplants call "Minnie Soda" come winter, spring, and fall. As the local joke goes, there are two seasons in Minnesota—winter and road construction.

the mother of vice-presidents: Minnesota. Both Humphrey and Mondale are natives. Interestingly, so is 90-year-old

Harold Stassen, the father of all presidential candidates. The
former governor (1939–43), a self-styled "progressive Republican" and one of the eight original signers of the UN Charter,
ran for president every four years from 1948 to 1992, a total of
ten times. In 1996, at the age of 89, Stassen offered to be Bob
Dole's running mate, telling local WCCO-TV that "the fact he is
continuing to work productively should show that Dole [at 72]
is young enough to be a successful president." Go Harold, go.

North Dakota: Minnesota's poor cousin.

Rudy: Rudy Perpich, the most popular governor in Minnesota's
history. Even when the Republican Rudy Boschwitz was a
senator, when you said "Rudy" everybody knew you meant
Perpich.

Sconnies: residents of "Scon Sin," the neighboring state of Wisconsin.

Senator Welfare: Senator Wellstone.

stop-and-go lights: traffic stoplights.

that's different: a Minnesotan's self-contained way of expressing disdain, discomfort, or disagreement. Alternately,
"whatever."

the Twin Cities: Minneapolis and St. Paul. I do not recommend
grouping the two. Minneapolis is very Lutheran, very Scandie,
very "manifest destiny," very cosmopolitan (the "easternmost
western city in the Midwest"). In contrast, St. Paul is very
working class, very neighborhood-oriented, and *very* Catholic.

the Upper Midwest: though they share several traits with
Midwesterners (their political and environmental conscious-

So What About Wisconsin?

THERE WILL BE SOME SERIOUS DEBATE ON THIS point, but you can safely say that northern Wisconsin and most of Minnesota share the same linguistic traits. As a lifelong resident of both states, Jay Peterson, puts it, "The divisions provided by the St. Croix and Mississippi rivers don't mean as much" as you'd think. However, there are some noticeable differences south and east of Madison as you head to Chicago, most notably in the hilarious Germanic deviations from English grammar found in Milwaukee ("Put me in a sack for five cents of kiss candy" or "Come from out the yard in, I tink a tunder shower is pulling up"), and the rampant use of "hey" to end a sentence:

"Where you from?"

"Madison, hey."

"Are goin' the cities?"

"Goin' to Platteville, hey."

ness definitely not among them), Minnesotans in general, and northern Minnesotans in particular, don't consider themselves part of the Midwest but part of the "Upper Midwest," which seems to include Minnesota, Wisconsin, North Dakota, and possibly even Manitoba and Ontario, Canada.

uptown: the Hennepin area of Minneapolis.

what's going around: a cold or flu. "Hey, I won't be able to play hockey this Saturday. Guess I caught what's going around."

wood ticks: conservative Democrats in northern Minnesota. A spin on boll weevil. Lately called the "blue dogs."

the Zoo: the University of Minnesota, one of the largest state universities in the country.

The Mountain States

I'VE DIVIDED THIS AREA INTO THREE STATES: Colorado, Idaho, and Montana. Some might include Wyoming (part of the Bland Belt) or Utah (part of the Mormon Belt), but I decided these states best characterize the three main elements of the region: ranchers, racists, and nouveau riche.

Colorado: Big Ski Country

THE HOME OF HUNTER S. THOMPSON, JOHN ELWAY, and my beloved Aunt Mary and Uncle Milt. Also one of the least fertile territories for innovative speech in America. Still, like a persistent lead miner, I persevered and uncovered what might be termed the mother lode of Rocky Mountain banter.

Aspen foot: about 2 inches of snowfall. Aspen radio stations lie about the snowfall to get people to ski.

bag a fourteener: to climb one of Colorado's 14,000-foot peaks.

the Big Mac: McNichols Arena, where the Stanley Cup champion Colorado Avalanche play hockey. This town has amazingly good luck with expansion teams.

the Blake Street Bombers: the Colorado Rockies baseball team. One of the highest octane batting teams in the majors. For good reason: in Mile-High City, the balls travel very far.

the brown cloud: the yellow-brown layer of air pollution observable above Denver during cold weather.

champagne: beautiful sparkling snow.

diet snowstorm: a light snowfall. Aka "Snowstorm Lite."

dump: a heavy snowfall.

the f word: flurries. Nice snow but poor visibility.

flatlanders: out-of-towners.

the Front Range: the eastern part of the Rockies, which holds Colorado's increasingly interlinked urban areas, ranging from Greeley to the north to Pueblo to the south. Over 80% of the people in Colorado live along the Front Range.

Gonzo: Hunter S. Thompson, the coke-snortin', pot-smokin', booze-drinkin', gun-poppin' legend of Woody Creek. And author of *Fear and Loathing in Las Vegas*.

Henry John Deutschendorf, Jr.: John Denver, Colorado's major contribution to pop music.

hootenkacking: buttonholing people into doing something they clearly do not want to do.

ivory snow: perfect snow.

Jeffco: Jefferson County, west of Denver, the second largest and second richest county in the state.

LoDo: Lower Downtown Denver.

the Mile-High City: Denver.

the mousetrap: the intersection of I-25 and I-70 in Denver. So named because it paralyzes traffic.

NORAD: the North American Air Defense command center in Colorado Springs, home of the Air Force Academy and the largest per capita concentration of right-wing fundamentalists in America.

the Orange Crush: dated yet still accurate name for the Denver Broncos defense.

Silicon Mountain: Colorado Springs.

snow-eaters: the warm, dry chinook winds that come out of the mountains at up to 143 mph and are responsible for some of the most radical climate shifts in the country. One day there can be a foot of snow on the ground and two days later grass and chirping birds.

South Platte River: "the St. Peter's Basilica of trout fishing," according to *Time* magazine.

Idaho: Big Spud Country

Though the Klan, the Aryan Nation, and Mark Furman (formerly of the LAPD) all make their home here, Idaho is known for primarily one thing: spuds. Most of the lingo centers around it.

America's Alps: the Sawtooth Mountains.

Bo: Bo Gritz (pron. "Grites"), a former Green Beret who is a major leader of the modern militia movement. He warned of govern-

Know Your Spuds

1. Spuds come in two different varieties in Idaho: "fresh packed" (10-pound sacks of spuds) and "processed" (mashed potatoes and french fries).

2. Idaho's specialty is the Idaho Russet Potato, which is oval and grows well in the volcanic soil here.

3. "Spuds" is actually a bona fide acronym for "Some Potatoes Under Desirable Standards." After the disastrous Irish Potato Famine, the term garnered a second meaning ("the Society for the Prevention of Unwholesome Diets").

4. Besides eatin', spuds have several practical purposes, according to diehard Idahoans: (1) to get a broken light bulb out of a socket, simply cut a spud in half and jam it into the broken bulb, which allows for safe twisting and removal of the bulb; (2) to remove a wart, rub the spud on the wart and then bury the spud (this remedy may not go over real big with one's dermatologist father and brother); (3) to dye or darken hair, take a comb from a basin of water that has been soaking in spud peelings and brush through hair; (4) to remove wrinkles, take 2 teaspoons of grated raw spud, place in gauze, and make a warm-water compress out of the spudified gauze and place over the eye; and (5) to rid oneself of migraine headaches, sleep with a spud under one's pillow.

ment conspiracies to restrict freedoms and instructed his followers to move to the hills of Idaho and arm themselves for the coming struggle. His political arm, the Center for Action, is based in Kamiah. Briefly, David Duke's running mate in 1988.

Boysee: Boise. How the locals pronounce it; not "Boyzee," as the rest of us do.

Charlie Sampson country: Charlie Sampson was an Idaho City piano teacher who made it his personal mission to signpost unmarked country roads leading to his music store.

the City of Trees: Boise. So dubbed in 1833 by French trappers, who were ecstatic at the sight of trees after seeing nothing but lava and sagebrush for weeks on end.

covenant communities: the armed far right–wing Christian communities proliferating throughout the mountain states who live "off the umbilical" (i.e., independent of the government). Prototype: Bo Gritz's Christian Patriot Movement.

Euzkaldunak: the Basque people of Boise, who have a language all their own, including words like *ongi-etorii* (welcome), *osa garria!* (salut!), and *biltoki* (gathering place). The Basques, Europe's oldest ethnic group, are found mostly in Spain (c. 600,000) with a smaller number in France (c. 100,000). They speak Euskara, the last remnant of the Neolithic languages of Stone Age Europe that were over time displaced by today's Indo-European languages. Because of the demand for wool during World War II, the U.S. made a special exemption, allowing Basques to immigrate as sheepherders. As a result, today large numbers of Basques live in the sheep country of northern Nevada, southern Idaho, and southeastern Oregon.

Haileywood: the nickname of the town of Hailey, near Sun Valley. Because of all the rich celebrities who use it as their winter playground.

jockey box: the glove compartment. Also used in Montana. As in "Get the map out of the jockey box."

Niagara of the West: Shoshone Falls.

outfit: vehicle. Aka "rig."

Picabo (pron. "peek-a-boo"): champion women's downhill skier Picabo Street, who was named for a small area near Sun Valley.

the Potato Capital of the World: Bingham County, Idaho, which produces 30% of our nation's spuds. Caveat: Shelley Spud Days, held every September, feature a tug-of-war over a pit of mashed potatoes.

pride: a posse of tourists. Especially around Lake Coeur d'Alene come summer. Aka "unkindness."

the River of No Return: the Salmon River's nickname ever since the 1954 Marilyn Monroe and Robert Mitchum film of the same name.

river rats: water sport enthusiasts. Aka "floaters."

Ruby Ridge: the site and name for the 11-day standoff in 1992 between federal marshals and survivalist Randy Weaver that has become a cause célèbre among the Timothy McVeigh set.

sacks: bags.

Sho-Bans, Sho-Pais: the Shoshones (whose official homeland is now the Fort Hall Indian Reservation near Pocatello) share their reservation with the Bannocks to form "the Sho-Bans."

The Shoshones and Paiutes (on the Duck Valley Indian Reservation on the Idaho-Nevada border south of Boise) make up the "Sho-Pais."

slack: the period between Labor Day and Thanksgiving at the Sun Valley Ski Resort, when tourists are at a minimum.

spud cellar: where you store your spuds.

spuds: no one calls them potatoes in Idaho.

Tad: Idaho's answer to Meatloaf.

that deal over there: whatever it is you're pointing at.

you bet: the quintessential Idaho expression.

Whitewater Capital of the World: Salmon, Idaho.

Montana: Big Sky Country

JANE AND TED. THE FREEMEN. ELIZABETH CLAIRE Prophet. Ted Kaczynski. Steve Albini. Is there a pattern here? Welcome to Montana, the home of bona fide American originals as well as the last place in the continental U.S. where, if you are sick of "civilization" and have a few "mill" to spare, you can buy a little piece of "the real West."

Albini: Hellgate High grad Steve Albini, the second punk rocker (after Randy Pepprock) in the history of Montana. His first high school band name? Just Ducky. Aka "Albini the Weenie," "Bino," or "Bean."

America's Outback: the upper Great Plains and Rocky Mountain area in general, and eastern Montana in particular, so named in a 1989 *Newsweek* article. The nickname is now used with great pride by residents. Aka "Buffalo Commons."

Big Sky Country: eastern Mountain, as opposed to the more mountainous western part of the state (and source of the name "Montana"). Aka "Big Dry Country" and "the Big Open."

the Bob: the Bob Marshall Wilderness Area, along Highway 83 in the Seeley-Swan Valley. With the Great Bear and Scapegoat wilderness areas, it forms the largest wilderness area in the lower 48.

chattery: a place where one can eat, sit a spell, and hear gossip and tall tales.

chupta pod?: what are you up to, pardner?

CUT: the Church Universal and Triumphant, Elizabeth Claire Prophet's bunch up near Corwin Springs. As in, "He used to be in CUT, but now he's sharpening saws." Not to be confused with BUT (the Band Universal and Triumphant, out of Bozeman). CUT is the source of one of the great New Age mantras: "I am a being of violet fire, I'm the purity of God's desire." Start chanting that real fast, and you too will start feeling universal and triumphant. Though the state lives by the motto "Mind your business, I'll mind mine," Montanans can't help but wonder why a Christian organization like CUT has stockpiled arms, tanks, and diesel fuel and has built gun towers and huge underground shelters around its property.

dry farmers: farmers who work non-irrigated farms. Found mostly in eastern Montana.

flatlanders: people from eastern Montana.

goat roper: your stereotypical Montana ranch dude. Typically he wears tight Lee jeans, a cowboy hat and boots, and a nice tight western shirt as he gets into his new Ford pickup, drinkin' a beer with his buddies. He is the very symbol of Montana machismo that drew all the rich yuppies here in the last two decades.

the Golden Triangle: the barley- and wheat-growing area between Great Falls, Havre, and Cut Bank that is considered the breadbasket of Montana.

Griffles: Great Falls.

the Hi Country: northern Montana, a vast open area filled with ranchers, farmers, six different Indian tribes, and two dozen German-speaking Hutterite communities. Also, Highway 2, which cuts through the region. Aka "the Hi-Line," an area that goes from Browning in the west to Glasgow in the east.

the Hmong: Laotian mountain people, several hundred of whom settled in Missoula after the Vietnam War.

hooky bobbing: grabbing the bumper of a passing car on slippery winter streets, using your feet as skates or skis. Aka "skitching" in other parts of the country.

the Hoots: Hutterite farmers who live in colonies in eastern Montana.

the Last Best Place: Montana.

Lincoln: where the Unabomber set up shop. Right in the heart of the Scapegoat Wilderness.

the Man of Surgical Steel: Evel Knievel, native son of the copper mining town of Butte. The world's most famous daredevil artist spent a lot of time trying to scale major landmarks, such as the Caesars Palace fountain and Snake Creek Canyon. In the course of 15 years he sustained over 433 broken bones; he has 10 steel plates and several metal pins inside him.

Montana double date: two guys and two dogs riding in the cab of a pickup.

mountain canaries: mules and donkeys.

muckademuck: a high-ranking official. From Dashiell Hammett's *Red Harvest*, which is set in Butte (though he calls it Poisonville).

the Ox: a famous bar–café–gambling room in Missoula. Short for "the Oxford." The Ox serves brains the way other places serve hash browns. The joke was that whenever anyone ordered brains, the waitress would yell to the cook, "Needs 'em!"

pishkun: a place where Indians used to drive buffalo off cliffs and then eat those that fell. At Madison Buffalo Jump State Park, one can see many skeletons.

Rat Boy: Robert Dorton, the crazed Freeman who fired at federal officials when they tried to seize his extra-large cats.

the Richest Hill on Earth: Butte. Because of the huge open-pit copper and mineral ore mines right in the heart of town, one of which is so full of water it has been designated a Superfund site. Aka "Little Chicago," because in the late 1800s it was not only the most populous city in the West but was also inhabited by strong, tough, European immigrants, who worked the mines.

study the bark: what you do when you're camping and you need to pee. "I'll be right back. I'm just going over there to study the bark."

to go cup: in Montana the bars close at exactly 2:00 a.m., not a minute before. The bartenders know better than to take away someone's drink when it's time to leave, so they place a plastic cup over the drink, tip it over, and hand the plastic "to go cup" to the exiting patron. Happy trails!

umm vrr or **um brr:** for shame, for shame. Used mostly by kids in Missoula when you are spotted doing something you could catch hell for (such as stealing or smoking a cigarette). In other words, I've caught you and I could use it against you, but instead I'll use it as a bargaining chip in the future.

up the Yaak: along the (very remote) Yaak River valley in the extreme northwest corner of the state.

you got cut: said when you step in a cowpie.

The Music Biz

"We don't like their sound, and guitar music is on the way out."　　　　　—DECCA RECORDING COMPANY, ON REJECTING THE BEATLES IN 1962

"I wasn't aware that the world thought I was so weird and bizarre."　　　　　—MICHAEL JACKSON AT THE 1993 GRAMMY AWARDS

AS YOU READ THIS, ALTERNATIVE ROCK IS ON full life support, ready to be buried once and for all. Grunge, whatever the hell that was, died a full decade ago. I stopped listening in earnest after a Martha and the Muffins concert at the Brighton Pavilion back in 1980. Still, pop soldiers on. And so does the industry that keeps it afloat.

alterna-nation: a snide industry term for the big bucks marketing of alternative rock over the last decade and the predictable look and attitude that accompanies its merchandising. The term arose "post-Nirvana," when you could find the mainstreaming of "alternative" in every crevice of the country. When kids started wearing Docs in Dubuque, the "alterna-nation" was whole and complete.

alternative rock: the music of the young, mostly white, slacker. Here's how one heavy metal rocker reacts: "Man, it's just depressing mopey crap with depressing mopey fans who drool over these losers. Let's go back to real rock 'n' roll, when rock was FUN! Groups like Motley Crue, Poison, Dokken, Bang Tango, Baton Rouge, Warrant, Ratt, Cinderella, White Lion, McQueen Street, Twisted Sister, Slaughter, Trixter, Skid Row, Jackyl, Kiss, Anthrax, Lita Ford, Britny Fox, Love/Hate, White Snake, Mr. Big, Faster Pussycat, Shotgun Messiah." Hey, you forgot Foreigner.

ax: guitar.

beautiful audience: lots of good-looking guys and gals who are prime pickin's for a promoter's pickup line. "There's a beautiful audience out there tonight."

the big six: the biggest music distributors, which control most of the labels and most of the product "moved": BMG (Agenda to Windham Hill), CEMA (Barking Pumpkin to SBK), UNI (Chess to Varese Sarabande), Polygram (Bulletproof to Victory), Sony (Blackheart to Word), and WEA (Atco to Titanium).

blastissimo: rock 'n' roll slang for extremely high volume.

bumrush: when a group of kids bolt past security to get good seats where they're not supposed to be.

bus face: the worn, beat-up face of a musician or roadie after sleeping on the tour bus all night. "I gotta get rid of this bus face; I go on in an hour."

cock rock: heavy metal rock 'n' roll. David Coverdale of White Snake is the quintessential cock rocker. An alternative is Vince Neil of Motley Crue.

contest pigs: people who try to win prizes in radio contests by tying up the phones with multiple lines or speed dial.

Courtney: Courtney Love, widow of the late Kurt Cobain and lead singer of Hole. Can be seen as either a trashy, second-rate punk version of Madonna or the willfully messed-up offspring of Valerie Solanas (take your pick). Spreads holy terror and a kind of perverse masochistic attraction in anyone who enters her orbit. Evidence: she will aggressively rail at this description. Claim to fame: has turned serious unbridled dysfunction into celebrity cachet (see *The People vs. Larry Flynt*).

crowd surfing: being passed around in a mosh pit. Aka "head walking."

doughboy: a catering company.

drop: when a record is released. "Monday at midnight U2's *Pop-mart* will drop." "Live's new record dropped on Tuesday and moved 235,000 in the first day." Also, "drop an artist" (the contract is canceled).

drop the bomb: smoke pot with a rock star. As in, "Let's go drop the bomb with Tricky."

86ed: kicked out of a concert.

flight attendants: humungous guys manning the barricades at rock shows. They keep the "crowd surfers" from crashing.

floral arrangement: pot for the band. "Did the floral arrangement arrive yet?" "Did you enjoy the floral arrangement?"

gak: cocaine.

gig: a show. A term that has crossed over to the mainstream, most notably to refer to an occupation. "What's your gig?" "I'm a financial analyst downtown."

GIT: Guitar Institute of Technology in Los Angeles. A cutting edge "riff school" that Mark Kates requires all his bands to attend. A "GIT band" is a band that is overplaying.

the green room: the area in a concert hall, often near the stage, where performers can relax, tune their instruments, and meet visitors. At an outdoor concert, it's usually a trailer or tent. It's also where the band can do a final "production meeting." Or, better yet, "drop the bomb with the floral arrangement in a production meeting before going onstage." Ironically, the gas chamber at San Quentin is also called "the green room."

groove culture: what used to be called disco. Now subdivided into "house," "deep house," "techno," "progressive house," "jungle," "drum and base," "trip-hop, "Brit-hop"—it's all 4-4, and it's all disco, er, I mean "groove culture." Aka "electronica."

hair farmer: a heavy metal band with big hair, who are still living in the days when big hair was remotely acceptable. Particularly the "W bands" (Warrant, White Snake, Great White, White Lion, and Winger).

hardcore: very loud, fast, aggressive punk rock birthed in the early 1980s as a militant reclamation of the original spirit and energy of punk. Aka "HC." Classic hardcore bands include Minor Threat, Scream, Deep Wound, and the Fartz.

hit the post: in radio parlance, to talk over the lead-in of a song, then stop just as the vocalist starts to sing.

homocore: gay punk music. Popularized by the Canadian Bruce

Le Bruce and the San Francisco indie label Outpunk. Classic examples: Team Dresch and Pansy Division.

I'm doin' it for the kids: used cynically by music insiders, who are too tired to rock 'n' roll but too well-fed to get off the lucrative money train.

indie: a major label waiting to happen.

indier than thou: an independent label or band that admonishes other labels and bands for their crass commercialism while appearing to stand for the pure and untrammeled virtues of artistic freedom and integrity. In a positive sense, the Kill Rock Stars label out of Olympia would be considered "indier than thou" because, in the words of Nils Bernstein, "they refuse to align themselves with corporate culture in any of its sneaky guises." On the other hand, seriously misguided folks might call Touch and Go Records founder and Black Flag front man Steve Albini "indier than thou" because he allegedly preaches an indie line but produces major label bands like Bush, king of the Nirvana clones. But, oh my brothers, how terribly wrong they would be. For these troublemakers may not know that Mr. Albini was lead guitarist for the Poster Children (the most unheralded indie band *of all time!,* which briefly featured your humble narrator as lead screamer).

it's AG: it's all good. "So how's your life?" "It's AG."

the King: Elvis Presley.

Kurdt KO-Bain: the late, great Kurt Cobain, lead singer and guitarist for the Seattle grunge sensation Nirvana. And unofficial Good Sam Motor Club member.

Lollapalooza: an alternative rock event founded by Perry Farrell of the band Jane's Addiction, held in cities around the country every summer. Interestingly, the word first appeared in the 1930s Swing Era, meaning "anything out of the ordinary" (Tom Dalzell, *Flappers to Rappers*). Aka "Lalapaloozer" or "Loser-palooza."

markets: formerly known as cities. Now broken down into "primary markets" (cities that sell a lot of records, such as New York, San Francisco, L.A., and now Seattle), "secondary markets" (St. Louis), and "tertiary markets" (Eau Claire). The term is also used in other industries.

MC: the performer in a rap group who does the actual rapping.

mersh: way too commercial. Refers to a band that is a complete "sellout," whose music is too "mershy." "Those Pearl Jam guys used to be cool, but they've gone totally mersh, man."

mosh pit: the space in front of the stage used for slam dancing at punk and alternative rock shows. Though these days there's one at practically any show. Especially at the Hollywood Palladium, where Mark Kates once saw kids moshing to the Cocteau Twins! It would have to be Throbbing Gristle to get more unmoshable than that. Caveat: the mosh pit family tree dates back to early punk pogoing, which became slam dancing, which gave birth to the full-scale mosh pit during the heyday of hardcore and, like all things "alternative," went stratospheric with the rise of Nirvana.

the mullet: a haircut that is short in front, long in back, and, lately, razor short on the sides. The "do" that arrived in the mid-'70s, when declining longhair hippie culture butted up against glam rock and nascent punk. Think David Bowie *Aladdin Sane*. Or, better, think Larry Fortensky. Though its roots date from the pre-Egyptian era or at least back to the Cowardly Lion, today's "mullet" is most commonly associated with heavy metal bands and stylish World Cup soccer heroes. "The mullet" is known in Coos Bay, Oregon, as "the schlong," in New York as "the Bridge and Tunnel," and everywhere else as simply "the shag." See issue 2 of *Grand Royal* for a full exploration of the "history, mystery and meaning of. . . the mullet."

paper the house: give away tickets to make the show look respectable.

pay for play: just another way to reem gullible mulletheads. The concept is as American as bad apple pie: the band sells tickets to its own show. If it doesn't sell enough, it pays the club the difference. What drove the heavy metal era on L.A.'s Sunset Strip back in the '70s and '80s.

pirate: as a verb, to take over. "We'll pirate the airwaves once we get a transmitter." As a noun, a rebel/clandestine/unauthorized radio broadcast, station, or frequency.

pre-production: an advance given to a band, ostensibly for actual rehearsals, though it's generally understood it will be used as party money.

product: actual CDs, records, or tapes. "Hey, ask your friend over at Warner if he can get some product for me."

production meeting: when the promoters and/or tour manager sneak off to get stoned. "Time for a production meeting." Aka "pre-production."

punk houses: ratty houses where bands can perform and stay. A whole circuit of bands go from city to city, playing in punk houses. Examples include the Powerhouse in Portland and the Goat House in Seattle.

riot grrrls: I am woman, watch me snarl. A social movement of teen punkers that tries to communicate a radical feminist agenda through music. Bikini Kill is the prototypical "riot grrrl" band. Interestingly, "riot grrrls" are divided on the subject of Courtney Love of Hole. On the one hand, she is viewed as a "riot grrrl" role model. On the other, she is castigated for using sex to advance her own career. Similar to the feminist debate over Madonna.

rock star: derogatory for an egomaniacal rock performer.

the room: any venue. A "good room" means it's crowded. When the "gig" is packed, a heavyweight like Alec Peters might say, "The room is flush."

Seagram's: Universal Concerts, MCA Concerts, Universal Amphitheatre, etc., all of which are owned by Seagram's.

seat surfing: moving from one unoccupied seat to another at a concert, trying to get the best vantage point.

shoegazers: musicians who do not engage in pleasantries with the audience between songs but remain totally focused on the sound, often staring at their shoes as they do so.

slam dancing: seriously aggressive pushing, shoving, bumping, and banging, all in the name of "alternative rock."

stage diving: literally diving off a stage into a crowd of spectators. The precursor of "crowd surfing," where the stage dive-ee is passed around the mosh pit.

stiff: when a show does poorly. Aka "bomb."

straight edge: a vegan offshoot of the D.C. hardcore punk scene that espoused no drinkin', druggin', or animal products. Known for the X tattoo emblazoned on the backs of their hands. On either side of the X would appear the letters for the city they were from. Aka "sXe."

swag: free product or tickets that people weasel out of record companies. For example, two people at competing labels might "exchange swag," which isn't necessarily the kosher thing to do.

the talent: an artist. As opposed to "the act," which actually makes money.

techno: repetitive mind-numbing electronic dance music that makes punk seem like Vivaldi. Though only somewhat popular in the U.S., it's the rage in Europe.

that f**ng b**ch:** almost every promoter's term for Courtney Love, lead singer for Hole and a big-time movie star. As one insider put it, "She's very smart, entertaining, and likable, if you don't have to do business with her."

ticket to the doughboy's concert: a meal ticket to the backstage grub. Allows people to talk about the food discreetly without directly insulting the caterer. Example: "How was the doughboy's concert?" "The music was great" (i.e., the food was tasty). Also used in the film business.

tracks: there are no songs anymore, only tracks.

with a bullet: a song or album that's rising rapidly in "the charts." "The Spice Girls are number one with a bullet."

New York City

"New Yorkers seem to think the best thing two people can do is talk. Silence is okay when you're watching a movie (though it might be better if punctuated by clever asides) or when you're asleep (collecting dreams to tell when you're awake). Talking is a New Yorker's way of showing friendship, especially to strangers."

—DEBORAH TANNEN, AUTHOR OF YOU JUST DON'T UNDERSTAND: WOMEN AND MEN IN CONVERSATION

"To start with, there's the alien accent. 'Tree' is the number between two and four. 'Jeintz' is the name of a New York professional football team. A 'fit' is a bottle measuring seven ounces less than a quart. This exotic tongue has no relationship to any of the approved languages at the United Nations, and is only slightly less difficult to master than Urdu."   —FLETCHER KNEBEL

"Speak fast, sharp, and rudely, and take it from there."

—BARRY RITHOLTZ, A NATIVE NEW YORKER

SOME NINETY LANGUAGES ARE SPOKEN IN Manhattan alone, so it's kind of hard to talk about a uniform New Yorkese. There's never really been one language or dialect that encompassed the city's diverse people and cultures. In recent years, the influx of California digital geeks, Eurotrash, and Pakistani cabbies has only made the waters muddier. Has there ever been a New York speech? If so, is there still or is it dying, to be replaced by mallspeak? My informal, not-exactly-scientific survey indicates that there's something still here—a cross between an old Jewish storekeeper and an Italian dockworker with a bit of South Bronx rapper thrown in.

Standard Rules and Procedures

How to listen: Don't. New Yorkers show they are listening by interrupting what you are saying and commenting on it. A New Yorker's version of co-counseling: I'll talk about *your* problems.

Sound: THE LOUDER THE BETTER.

Speed: You can never talk fast enough. Remember, true New Yorkers (not the southern and West Coast transplants) have a lot of important things to say and never enough time to say them all. Hence the ubiquitous machine-gun question, thrown in at any point during a reply to a previous machine-gun question. When using the machine-gun question, the key is to interrupt someone's reply, answer questions for them, and punctuate their answer with asides, all to create the effect that "we're answering my question together."

What to talk about: Anything negative. New Yorkers, unlike Californians, are not holistically minded. It's good old-fashioned dualism out here in the East. Us versus Them. New Yorkers are quite happy to make small talk when there's someone or something to bitch about (e.g., the garbage, weather, traffic, the Jets). Through this persistent cathartic whining, New Yorkers create their own *esprit de corps*, "a sense of community against the common foe—THEM" (aka "the Fuck-Ups"). Whining is not a sign of poor health or unhappiness. It's as essential to a New Yorker's well-being as steam rising through manholes is to the underground's.

Pronunciation:

→ Substitute *K* for *P*: "He bunked into a car."

→ Drop words at will. Don't "play the piano." Simply "play piano."

→ *D* is often unnecessary. "She dint come over for dinner."

→ *R* is a free agent. On the one hand, it appears everywhere. "My wife's a lawryuh. Lovely Riter meter maid. Linder Ronstadt. Atlanter Braves. Bar, bar, black sheep, have you any wool? He's drawring pikshuhs of pigeons in the park. Gimme a slica pizzer anna soder." Then it suddenly disappears when you most need it: "Will you get us some cawfee down on toidy-toid street?" Or the unforgettable Brooklyn sportscaster's line, "Oh, no—Hoyt is hoit!" But then, just when you've figured out to pronounce every "er" word like "oi," suddenly you've got a bunch of "oy" and "oi" words that are pronounced "er" (as in "erster" for oyster and "berl" for boil).

→ Liberally season sentences with the all-purpose "fuck." Only in New York and parts of New Joisey, which is really a white trash suburb of New York, is "fuck" not taboo. It is taboo on stretches of Park Avenue, but that's New England, not New York, so don't sweat it.

Silence = death. In the Zenlike West the dictum would be a coarse and uncouth sign of spiritual depravity. But in "the throat chakra of the world" people put this slogan on billboards, badges, and bumper stickers. Ostensibly the rallying cry of an AIDS activist organization, "silence = death" speaks to a deeper affirmation of New Yorkers' primal need to BLAB.

A Basic Noo Yawk Vocabulary (aka "Brooklynese")

absofuckinglutely: absolutely.

alright, already: "Calm down, I get your point."

boids: our feathered friends.

brothuh: brother. "I got a 7-year-old brothuh who has no accent whatsoevuh." Aka "brudda."

cahd: a funny guy. "That Jerry, he's quite a cahd."

cockamamie: completely irrational, harebrained. "Mike, that's just another one of your cockamamie ideas."

da Bronx: the Bronx.

dallah: dollar. Canal Street pronunciation.

fegedaboutit: forget about it. All-purpose expression with positive and negative connotations.

finstins: for instance.

fuck: used at any time in front of any word. The courage to regularly use "the *f* word" is the litmus test of a true New Yorker. "Fuckin' A, we got fucked up on that fuckin' shit. Fuck it maaaan, whadda fuckin' mess. What da fuck, ho-lee fuckin' shit, that fuck-off really fucked up. Fuck that! Don't fuck wid me, you fuckface." A midwestern mother might have trouble with this particular linguistic trait.

gedoutahea: please leave now or, more congenially, you're not serious. "Gedoutahea, you're pullin' my leg."

go to business: go to work.

gwan: go on, come on. In other words, gimme a break. "Gwan, gedoutahea before I call the cops." Alternately, "awgwan."

hah-rubble: altogether unpleasant.

hey, do you think I'm crazy?: an expression of frustration with New York, New Yorkers, or people in general, leading into a plan to somehow leave New York, New Yorkers, or life in general. Or it can simply mean "You don't believe me?"

hey, I'm talkin' to you (said while grabbing one's testicles): you better listen to this person. Made famous by Robert De Niro in the film *Taxi Driver*.

How-ston: Houston Street.

I got news for you, bud: you are about to be informed by a knowledgeable male New Yorker that what you thought was true is no longer the case. To achieve the effect of greater condescension, replace "bud" with one of the following: "sport," "chump," "pal," or "boss."

I'm going down: going outside. Used by apartment dwellers.

jalettum: "Did you let them?"

juhhimee: "Do you hear me?"

k: okay.

knish: dough filled with meat and/or vegetables. A New York Jewish favorite. Pronounce the *k*.

lenths: lengths. "He went to heroic lenths to clean up after himself."

Long-Giland: Long Island.

Lunk Guylin: Long Island.

no problem: "You're welcome."

Noo Yawkah: a New Yorker.

noodge: a pest or nag. "Don't be a noodge."

on line: in line. For the rest of America, online means logging on to AOL or the Web. In New York it means standing and waiting, often at the post office. New Yorkers wait *on* lines, not *in* them.

ongana: "I'm going to."

or what?: put at end of accusing question. "Are you blind, or what?"

pisser: either a real bummer or a truly great person or thing. "My job's a real pisser" (I love it).

please: said in a subdued, understated huff. "Oh, please." Not to be confused with "puhleeez."

poppy wit a schmeer: a poppyseed bagel with cream cheese.

riz: risen. "Da grass is riz."

schlemiels: Yiddish for those who bring on their own misfortune in life. As opposed to "schlimazels," who are born losers and simply cannot help themselves. At one time both were used frequently, when Yiddish words were more commonly spoken by all New Yorkers. Words like "kvetch" (complain), "mensch" (a good guy), and "schnoz" (nose), memorable expressions like "I should have such luck" or "I need it like I need a hole in the head," and unusual word combinations like "an actor he's not," "monk schmonk," and the all-time favorite, "my son, the doctor!"

schlepp: cart or drag around, including oneself.

schmeer: (1) the cream cheese spread on a roll or bagel; (2) the sum total of things. "Look, I don't just want a little bit outta life, I want the whole schmeer."

schmooze: stand around and chat, though it's used in the broader goy culture to mean to push for something, to network or persuade. The penultimate New York Yiddish word, now popular throughout the country.

smatter wid you?: "Hey, don't you know better?"

sneak-us: athletic shoes.

soder: pop, soda.

soupa: super. "We had a soupa time at da fights."

Stat'n Oi-land: Staten Island.

take: have. "Take a haircut."

vanella: vanilla.

whaddaya: what do you want me to do? According to Tom Wolfe (*Bonfire of the Vanities*), "It's an age-old New York cry for mercy, unanswerable and undeniable."

what are ya, some kinda nut?: said by retailers to people like myself, as I sip on a carton of soymilk.

A Basic New York Vocabulary

Alphabet City: Avenues A–D on the eastern edge of the East Village. Aka "the Alphabets." Newly gentrified 'hood for yups and bups looking for what was once a fairly sketchy stretch of the city.

attaché cases: big portable radios. Aka "boom boxes," "ghetto blasters," or "Third World briefcases."

the Avenue of the Americas: exists only for tourists and corporate letterheads. To true New Yorkers, it's 6th Avenue.

the average New Yorker: a fallacy.

Bed-Sty: Bedford-Stuyvesant, an African-American neighborhood in Brooklyn. Made famous by Spike Lee and other black filmmakers. Aka "Deadsty," from the Flatlinerz' song.

the Big Apple: the ultimate cliché for NYC, used now only by first-time tourists from Iowa or Australia. One of many theories

is that it came from the slang of black jazz musicians: a booking at a New York club was "the big apple," while bookings at clubs in smaller cities were known as "the branches."

Black Rock: the monolithic black building that houses the CBS television network. On 6th Avenue between 52nd and 53rd.

Bloomie's: a term of endearment for Bloomingdale's, an Upper East Side department store.

the Borough of Homes: Queens. It's true. Unlike Manhattan, there's plenty of houses here.

the BQE: the Brooklyn-Queens Expressway.

the bridge and tunnel people: a breed of mutants who work or party in Manhattan but live elsewhere. Seen on weekends at all the "hot spots" and avoided by true New Yorkers like the plague.

Brits: Limeys who've magically persuaded gullible New York executives that they have something intelligent to offer simply because of their accent. Either they are recruited to rescue legendary American magazines (e.g., *Spy, Details,* and *The New Yorker*) or they are asked to serve as receptionists, which they do annoyingly well.

the Bronx Bombers: the New York Yankees.

brownie: meter maid.

brownstone: originally a 19th-century terraced house with a facade of brownstone (a type of sandstone). Now, any row or town house.

the Bullwinkle District: the racially gerrymandered 12th Congressional District of the state of New York, presided over by Nydia Velasquez. So named because it's shaped like Bullwinkle.

The Donald

I AM CERTAIN I SHARE AT LEAST ONE THING IN common with Don "the Donald" Trump. And that is a birthday: we were both born on June 14. So, of course, were Burl Ives, Ché Guevara, and Steffi Graf, so I am not sure that there is much more to draw from it than a date. However, there is a lot to draw from "the Donald" in regard to New York. In so many

ways he represents a very real, very much alive level of New York consciousness that will always be summed up in one word, "Queens."

Donald Trump is the original "bridge and tunnel" guy. A big part of his legacy is stories of the teenage Donald driving around in one of his dad's expensive cars, picking up chicks and bragging about his exploits. His disciples carry on the tradition today in big Jeep Cherokees, with loudspeakers blaring rap. The Outer Borough guy wanting to be a New York "bigwig"—that is the Donald Trump legacy.

Canyon of Heroes: lower Broadway in the Wall Street area, where parades in honor of returning war heroes, visiting dignitaries (Nelson Mandela), or champion sports teams (the Yankees) are held. Workers in the office buildings toss ticker tape on the throngs below.

canyons: the long narrow spaces spanning several blocks formed by an endless colonnade of skyscrapers.

cave cop: a transit police officer.

CBGB & OMFUG: the legendary punk club that gave birth to such national acts as the Talking Heads, Blondie, and the Ramones. Its mysterious acronym stands for Country, Bluegrass, Blues and Other Music for Uplifting Gourmandisers.

the City: New York City. Or, more precisely, Manhattan. True natives will also say "New York," but never "New York City." Interestingly, when you take the subway from the borough of

Brooklyn to the borough of Manhattan, you say you're going to "New York." As far as most Manhattanites are concerned, there is no other borough.

Club Condé: the restaurant in the lobby of the Royalton Hotel, on West 44th Street, a popular lunch spot for Condé Nast employees.

co-op: by no means unique to New York but worth noting as the most popular form of apartment ownership in the city. With a co-op, you buy shares in the building in which the apartment is located rather than the apartment itself.

Coney: a hot dog.

the Copa: the Copacabana, a legendary New York nightclub made famous by the Mob and the Rat Pack in the '40s and '50s.

the Cube: Bernard Rosenthal's giant black rotating sculpture, officially called the Alamo. A major landmark of the East Village in the heart of Astor Place. "Meet me at the Cube" is a frequent refrain. (By the way, if you push it hard enough, the Cube will rotate).

CUNY: the City University of New York. Originally the Harvard of the poor. Now a stronghold for bigoted professors and a dumbed-down student body.

the Dapper Don: the big-time Mafia godfather John Gotti, once known for his fine tailored suits, now spending the rest of his days in a prison uniform.

the de-flower district: New York's new red-light district, on Northern Boulevard in Queens. The queen of the street is Katherine, whose brothel caters to rich Manhattan types.

Donny Baseball: long-time hard-driving Yankee baseball star Don Mattingly.

DUMBO: Down Under the Manhattan Bridge Overpass. An area of Brooklyn where there are, apparently, a number of struggling artists.

egg cream: a seltzer, milk, and chocolate soda.

El Barrio: a section of Manhattan, above 96th Street on the Upper East Side, where many Dominicans and Puerto Ricans live. "The neighborhood" in Spanish.

ESSO: east of SoHo. Another annoying New York real estate designation.

Euro-snots: formerly called Eurotrash, they now have a far more specific description of their essential nature. New York is being remade both for them and the tourists from the 'burbs and hinterlands. Nothing pisses off a true blue Manhattanite quite like a Gucci-clad Frenchman or an Italian art girl. Watch for slacker "wilding" expeditions down West Broadway to stomp out these vermin before they take over.

the farm: JFK Airport in cabbie parlance.

flyover country: that vast hinterland between "the City" and Los Angeles.

Ginsboys: teenage lovers of the late Beat Industry poet laureate and alleged NAMBLA member Allen Ginsberg.

Gotham: the old name for the city, now back in vogue as a kind of retro thing.

greengrocer: a 24-hour grocery store owned by Koreans, with an incredible selection of natural foods, no-nonsense help, and an extensive if somewhat suspicious food buffet.

gridlock: a horrific traffic snafu, with an intersection completely jammed with vehicles going in all directions.

hero: a submarine sandwich or grinder.

heroin alley: the area from East 2nd to 5th streets and Avenues B and C in the East Village. Popular with people looking for a fix. Given the rapid gentrification all around, it might soon be the last seedy place in lower Manhattan.

the House That Ruth Built: Yankee Stadium. Refers to the all-time great Yankee baseball slugger George Herman "Babe" Ruth.

insulation: staying respectfully removed from the teeming masses. Requires lots of money, honey.

Island of Tears: old nickname for Ellis Island. Tears for all those grateful to have arrived in the New World and tears for the 2 million who were turned away.

the JAF: the James A. Farley post office building at 34th and 8th. Open 24 hours.

Jets Moments: the sadly absurd and preposterous mishaps that seem to plague the New York Jets football team both on and off the field.

the Jewel of Brooklyn: Prospect Park.

JoHo: just off Houston. Hot bar, club, and restaurant area on the Lower East Side, featuring slackers, club kids, and the "post-college Jägermeister set."

keh: the Koreans' revolving credit system, the linchpin of their success in "the City."

Kews: how Korean Americans describe themselves because their diligent work ethic approximates that of the early Jewish immigrants to the city.

How to Spot Eurotrash

"Americanism means the virtues of courage, honor, justice, truth, sincerity and hardihood—the things that made America. The things that will destroy America are prosperity at any price, peace at any price, safety-first instead of duty-first, the love of soft living and the get-rich theory of life."

—THEODORE ROOSEVELT, DIEHARD NEW YORKER

THEY'VE COME HERE FROM ITALY, FRANCE, SPAIN, and Germany. Because of the cheap dollar. Because of the glamour of being in the trendoid capital of a dying empire. Because of the cocaine.

They've come to pursue "art." To bask in the post-Warhol, post-Colacello, retro-Studio 54 glow. To ride their Harleys. They're Eurotrash, and as more and more Europeans descend on these shores, they've become omnipresent. Here's how to spot them.

1. They are well-tanned southern Europeans with gold chain purses, open shirts, pocketless pants, and expensive Italian loafers with tassels, or northern Europeans with arty glasses, black boots, and tight black Ts.

2. They express a definite interest in "art," especially visual art, but usually no solid understanding of anything spiritual, political, or digital.

3. They rave about SoHo and TriBeCa as if these were the hippest places on earth, unaware they are now pricey Eurotrash boutiques.

4. They invariably find a place on the Upper East Side or in one of the midtown Trump towers. The heir to Simca, Jean Pigozzi, did have a spread on Central Park West, but he was always way ahead of the curve for most Eurotrash.

5. They call other expatriates "Eurotrash" but have a pronounced inability to see themselves as same.

6. They use pickup lines like "You are the most beautiful woman I have ever seen."

7. They make a determined and highly practiced attempt to seem "cool" and distant.

$\rightarrow$

8. They are ridiculously arrogant yet simultaneously insecure.

9. They talk endlessly about their burgeoning "film career."

10. They don't have jobs, just "appointments." Though John Agnelli (king, avatar, and patron saint of Eurotrash) is an exception to this rule; he actually ran Fiat.

11. They prefer '80s-style drugs. As one astute observer put it, "Eurotrash have single-handedly kept the New York cocaine industry alive."

12. They are eyeware-intensive. LA Eyeworks is a favorite, or any other brand in the $500–$2,000 range.

13. They have an inability to be genuinely friendly, open-hearted, and enthusiastic. In other words, American.

14. They routinely trash America but exclaim, "I like New York because it's not like the rest of America."

15. They have seen very little of the rest of America, except maybe L.A. or Miami.

16. The men hanker after tall, thin American women, preferably black or blond models.

17. The women have a fetish for classic American tough guys (De Niro, Keitel, or anyone out of a Scorsese or Tarantino flick).

18. In deciding between a coldhearted asshole and a compassionate mensch, Eurotrash will choose the asshole every time.

19. Their favorite vocations are fashion, design, and anything involving film. Eurotrash like the "image" and opportunity of New York but don't want to get down and dirty with the true blue heart of the city.

If you own a New York store, club, or café, you will want to consider several ways to prevent the intrusion of Eurotrash:

A. post a large No Smoking sign in the window. This will severely decrease the numbers.

B. Confiscate all sunglasses at the door. They'll have a pair, even if it's the dead of winter.

C. Have a bevy of serious, text-heavy American magazines scattered about. *The New Republic*, *The Nation*, and *The Atlantic Monthly* will do. Nothing too image-oriented, like *Interview*, which might pique their interest.

Good luck!

Famous and Infamous New Yorkers Every American Should Know

the Dink: the low-key, nattily dressed former mayor David Dinkins, once described by local radio host Bob Grant as a "washroom attendant."

the Donald: the tacky, cheesy billionaire real estate tycoon Donald Trump. So named by his former wife, Ivana.

Holly Woodlawn: Harold Ajezenberg, a Warhol groupie and legendary icon of downtown nightlife.

the Oddfather: Vincente Gigante, the alleged head of the Genovese crime family (the nation's #1 crime family, taking over from John Gotti's Gambinos), known for strolling the streets of Little Italy in bathrobe and pajamas and allegedly feigning mental illness to avoid prosecution.

the Queen of Mean: Leona Helmsley, the tax-evading dominatrix of the Helmsley Hotel.

the Son of Sam: serial killer David Berkowitz, found guilty of murdering several couples (he signed his letters "Son of Sam"). In the minds of New Yorkers, he's up there with the self-proclaimed East Village messiah Daniel Rakowitz, who murdered his Swiss roommate, boiled her remains in a large pot, and then served them to the homeless of Tompkins Square Park.

the Subway Vigilante: Bernhard Goetz. The man in the aviator glasses who'd had just about enough of those street toughs making fun of his looks.

the Two Annes: Anne Getty and Anne Bass, two of New York's leading power socialites in the early '80s before the takeover decade kicked in.

La Mama: Ellen Stewart, the founder of La Mama, a leading independent theater in the East Village.

the Ladies' Mile: a fabled stretch of opulent department stores in Manhattan catering to women. 6th Avenue between 14th and 23rd streets.

landlord's halo: a bare lightbulb hanging in a tenement hallway.

Lex: Lexington Avenue.

Locust Valley Lockjaw: the halting, stiff, molar-crunching speech of the "vanishing species" of Long Island WASP. Example: "lawn gawn" or "obsuhd." Think Thurston Howell III. From *The Preppie Handbook*: the longer the driveway, the more severe the case of LVL.

Losaida: a Puerto Rican bastardization of "Lower East Side." Though Puerto Ricans tend to be more Americanized than other Latin American groups (they've been in New York longer), there are still hard-core areas of pure Puerto Rican energy. Losaida is clearly one.

Manahatta: the Native American name for Manhattan, which means "hilly island." Go to Broadway and 160th to see what they meant. Caveat: most stories of how the Algonquin Manhattan Indians sold Manahatta Island to the Dutch suggest that the Indians got swindled. But this might not be true. As the writer Robert Hendrickson notes, "If the Indians had invested their $24 at the prevailing interest rates, they would now have some $13 billion, $4 billion more than all the real estate in Manhattan is worth."

Mayor Cop: the former city prosecutor and current mayor, Rudy Giuliani. Thought by some to be overzealous in his commitment to law enforcement.

Meat Street: West 14th Street, in the Meatpacking District. At night transvestite prostitutes come here to ply their wares.

mother-daughter houses: solid brick houses with a separate upstairs unit, where Mom could live when son-in-law was away at war. Pioneered by Donald Trump's father, there are 50,000–60,000 of them all over Brooklyn and Queens.

MSG: Madison Square Garden, where the Rangers win championships and the Knicks blow them.

MTA: the Metropolitan Transit Authority. Now improved, with

radically reduced crime and panhandling, the MTA runs New York's bus and subway lines, including the BMT (Brooklyn-Manhattan Transit), the IND (Independent), and the IRT (Interborough Rapid Transit).

mugger's money: the extra $20 New Yorkers carry in their pocket so they don't have to endure the life-threatening nastiness of a disappointed mugger.

NoHo: north of Houston.

Nolita: another silly real estate acronym for a newly trendified area of Manhattan, northern Little Italy.

Noo Jork Ricans: New York Puerto Ricans. Has evolved into "Nuyorican."

off-off-Broadway: small, independent theaters far off Broadway, usually in Greenwich Village.

the Orient Express: the #7 subway line to Flushing, Queens, so called because of the many Asian Americans who ride it.

otaku: a Japanese expatriate in New York, usually in the East Village, usually on East 10th Street.

the Outer Boroughs: Queens, Brooklyn, the Bronx, and Staten Island. Every one but Manhattan. And therein lies the difference between the Brahmin and the Untouchables.

the Paper of Record: the *New York Times.* Known for its commanding, semiobjective voice of authority on all matters great and small.

PATH: Port Authority Trans Hudson, the commuter train line that connects Manhattan with New Jersey. A service that no halfway hip New Yorker would be caught dead on.

plaza: ostensibly a humane pedestrian space at the base of a giant skyscraper. In fact, a linguistic device used by cocky developers to put some extra cachet on the addresses of their prized buildings. Example: 1 Worldwide Plaza.

the principal owner: the *New York Times'* hilariously sardonic term for George Steinbrenner, the monomaniacal owner of the Yankees.

the radiant child: graffiti artist Keith Haring's signature image, seen throughout the city.

railroad apartment: unit in which all the rooms are in a row off a long hallway.

regular: a cup of "cawfee" with milk, no sugar. Forget that espresso crap.

RTR: the Russian Tea Room, a ridiculously overpriced and gaudy gathering place for the hip and "very now" entertainment

crowd (e.g., Harry Bela-
fonte).

the Shuberts: Bernie Jacobs
and Gerry Schoenfeld, al-
legedly the most powerful
landlords currently on
Broadway.

social x-ray: ridiculously
thin, overexercised New
York socialite. Popularized
by Tom Wolfe in *Bonfire of
the Vanities.*

SoHo: south of Houston.

Southside Triangle: the con-
fluence of Hasidic Jews and
Latinos in South Williams-
burg, Brooklyn.

the Squeegee People: street
people who dirty up your

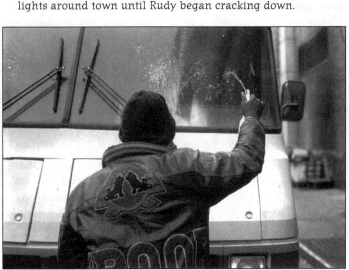

windshield with old dirty rags dunked in grimy old water and
who expect to be tipped for the favor. Ubiquitous at traffic
lights around town until Rudy began cracking down.

stoop: the small porch, platform, or staircase leading to the en-
trance of many houses or buildings. A favorite place to sit,
chat, or play stoopball, especially on long summer evenings.

stroller gridlock: in the late '80s and early '90s, as yuppies discovered that kids made a nice accessory, strollers became ubiquitous throughout TriBeCa and the Upper West Side as well as on Brooklyn's Park Slope.

Sty Town: Stuyvesant Town, a complex of 8,755 moderately priced apartments between East 14th and 20th streets and 1st Avenue and FDR Drive.

the tabs: the tabloids. The large-format, giant-fonted, bolder-than-bold-faced dailies that scream the day's headlines of sleaze, crime, and fiasco. The *Post* and the *Daily News* are the two primary "tabs," with the slightly more understated *Newsday* covering the same territory in Queens.

the Tombs: the New York Criminal Courts Building, downtown.

the Triangle of Tolerance: where Bedford Street meets 7th Avenue. There's a lesbian bar on one point, a gay restaurant on another, and a straight one on the third.

TriBeCa: the Triangle Below Canal Street. SoHo Jr. Still has the old empty, dark warehouse vibe that made SoHo great.

Triburbia: another name for "TriBeCa," now that the artsy-fartsy couples have decided to raise kids there.

WeChe: West Chelsea. The art galleries are said to be moving here, now that they can't afford SoHo.

Welfare Island: Roosevelt Island.

the West Side Kids: the white, liberal political cabal that came out of Stuyvesant High in the mid to late '60s and centered around Clinton's former political consultant Dick Morris.

whirlpooling: when a gang of boys circle around a girl and molest her in a public swimming pool. Aquatic "wilding."

wilding: an urban safari hosted by black ghetto youth.

Yuppieville: the Upper West Side.

Odds and Ends

THESE AMAZING WORDS DON'T FIT ANY particular category in this book, but they represent some of the newest and choicest slices of the American idiom.

add-on: an addition to a mobile home, making it truly immobile. Caveat: a mobile home is *not* a motor home, though it can be called a "trailer."

ADHD: Attention Deficit Hyperactivity Disorder. In other words, your sweet lovable little Johnny is banging off the wall, setting your tax return on fire, breaking and entering the neighbor's liquor cabinet, all by the age of 7.

Afro-Saxon: an African American who has adopted the behaviors and attitudes of the prevailing white culture. Aka "Oreo Tom."

amands: what almond growers call almonds.

ape-shit: very enthusiastic, excited. "He just went ape-shit over that Jim Jarmusch movie."

apple: a Native American who acts white.

arabbers: Baltimore's street vendors, who peddle vegetables, fruits, and other foods from horse-drawn carts. The subject of many animal rights protests. Comes from "arab," a 19th-century word for people who earned their income on the streets.

arachibutyrophobia (pron. "ar-uh-ki-byoo-ti-ro-fo-bee-uh"): the fear of peanut butter sticking to the roof of one's mouth. Completely fabricated by teenagers and still makes the rounds as a joke. Derivation: arach (peanut oil), butyrin (a fatty acid), phobia (an irrational fear).

art towns: towns under 50,000 population (though often smaller) that exhibit a high cultural consciousness, an aesthetically beautiful setting, and high property values conducive to developers selling the art town concept. Example: Santa Fe.

artist: a creature who adds cachet to a decaying neighborhood, paving the way for real estate speculation.

attack bard: in the vernacular of the SCA (the Society for Creative Anachronism, those medieval freaks), someone who comes to your campsite offering unwanted, unsolicited, and generally annoying entertainment. A "bard in a box" is a cassette tape player.

the Aztec two-step: diarrhea.

baby busters: kids born after the postwar baby boom, from the mid-'60s to the present.

balls to the wall: a command performance under intense pressure.

banana: an Asian who acts white.

banzai runner: an illegal alien who races through the U.S. border checkpoint in the hope of escaping arrest.

bastard pearl: a type of abalone found on the California coast.

Bawlmer, Murlin: Baltimore, Maryland, not only the birthplace of John Waters and Lila Purinton but the home of a fascinating American dialect known as "Bawlmerese." I once went to a Natural "Feuds" Trade Show in "Bawlmer," where I enjoyed a "cole race beef sanwich" (made of tofu, of course) and didn't think "nothink" of it. Besides "excaping" off to an "Oryuls" game, the thing I remember most was meeting a tall smart saleswoman in a "drucksterer" while shopping for "arspern." She was working for some "plug-ugly" vitamin outfit and wanted to spend time away from her cohorts. Unfortunately, we got split up in the "mezzaline" and I ended up on the "payment" with a blond "turst" "farner" in a red "x-raided" dress who was visiting "Mairka" and was, unfortunately, leaving "Bawlmer" "tuhmar." Though we had us a "sneet" old time, she probably didn't see much future in it, since I was running around all night in a white skirt and work boots, and she no doubt had a boyfriend at the lingonberry capsule booth she was modeling for. So I said "slong" for now and promised to "doll" her sometime down the road. I wonder where she is now. "Drooslin?" "Arlin?" "Yerp?" "Warshin?" Still in the "baffroon"? I wish someone would let me know.

been there, done that: widely overused way to say you've been down that road before. "Lived on the road for eleven years, selling ads from pay phones, surviving hand to mouth. Been there, done that."

the Beer City: Milwaukee. Aka "Beertown." Home of "Mold Style," "Old M'wacky," and "the Brew Crew" (the Milwaukee Brewers baseball franchise).

behind the Zion curtain: you're in Utah.

the Bland Belt: Wyoming and the Dakotas.

bliss ninny: a person overjoyed to the point of idiocy.

blurb: a short article about a client in the print media. "How about a little blurb announcing our release party?" Jim Monk's twist on the idea: "blurb-o-matic."

booboisie: the TV-watching middle-class mainstream.

boom!: exclamation for complete shock or outrageous coincidence. "I was talking about her, and when I turned the corner—boom!, there she was, walking out of a camera store with some ponytailed dude."

bummin': upset, disappointed. "Dude, I'm bummin', the Blue Devils ate it, *and* the U-2 concert was canceled."

bunny: a nonexistent street or piece of false information slipped into a map or book in order to detect plagiarism.

burl: tacky, expensive wood carvings found throughout the redwood country of northern California.

the Cereal City: Grand Rapids, Michigan.

channel surfing: randomly flicking the TV's remote control in an endless and often futile search for captivating entertainment.

the cold war university: an institution of higher learning inordinately dependent on research money from the Pentagon. Textbook example: Stanford.

couch surfing: moving from one person's couch to another every few days. Done by everyone from Seattle smackheads to Santa Cruz surfers to yours truly.

coyote: a person who helps sneak illegal aliens across the border.

crummy: an oversize van and bus that carries loggers from the parking lot to the logging site. Sometimes passed on to school districts for transporting athletes.

crunch: do something with great fervor and intensity. It has become one of the modern slanguistic all-stars, with several meanings at once: to "crunch numbers" (sophisticated accounting or math), "crunching" (trying to meet a deadline), or "crunches" (situps). For a society in a perpetual "time crunch," it's an apt metaphor.

curtain climber: a small child or baby, especially one who is just learning to walk. Aka "crumb crusher" or "rug ape."

the Dalai Lama of the United States: what the millionaire wrestling buff (and murderer of Olympic wrestler John Schultz) John du Pont required his friends to call him.

Deadbeat Dad: a father who "skips out" on his child support payments, often fleeing to another state. The new bogeyman on both sides of Congress.

deboning: removing all subscription cards and cardstock ads from a magazine to make it easier to read.

Del Martian: a resident of the Del Mar suburb of San Diego.

devival: the Church of the Subgenius' idea of a revival. All to encourage slack and, of course, to praise Bob.

die-in: a method of protest where demonstrators lie immobile on the ground, feigning death. Made popular by ACT-UP, then used in various antiwar protests.

dilberted: to be exploited or abused by your boss. Inspired by the popular comic strip "Dilbert."

Disneyland daddy: a quasi–"Deadbeat Dad," who rarely sees his children.

ditto: I totally agree.

dittoheads: (1) people who are in perfect alignment on an issue, an idea, or a belief system; (2) disciples of the unabashedly right-wing radio talk show host Rush Limbaugh, whose grossly imbalanced and often erroneous remarks send his followers into fits of ecstasy.

DIY: Do It Yourself. A seriously misguided mid-'80s notion, fostered by the illusory promise of desktop publishing and indie music, and pioneered by the likes of Bruce Pavitt and the Monks. It's been bastardized into a hellacious trend that dumps gazillions of worthless records, 'zines, and books onto the market every week that nobody cares about and few actually consume. Spawned "DDIY" (Don't Do It Yourself), a healthy rebellion led by former *Nose* editor Jack Boulware. Trust me: DIY will leave you broke.

donor fatigue: when gifts to humanitarian or religious organizations significantly decrease due to the donors' feeling of hopelessness or because donors are overburdened by requests. Aka "compassion fatigue."

door knockers: huge hoop earrings.

Ebonics: ebony plus phonics, or "Black English." Can be viewed in two ways. (1) A laughably misguided attempt by school districts to legitimize the slang of black students as a second language, on a par with standard English. (2) A welcome addition to our children's curriculum that could revolutionize educational speech. Think about it. An Ebonics national anthem written by Tim Dog? Bathroom doors changed from "Boys" to "G's" and "Girls" to "Ho's"? Used as in the following: "I swear this chick in the computer room at Kinko's was speaking Ebonics. I couldn't understand a word she said."

eight o'clock: a person who turns up at the library reference desk just before closing with an insanely difficult question. "I couldn't believe it. This eight o'clock shows up and wants to know the names of all the Soto Zen patriarchs since Dogen."

elevator surfing: riding on top of or hanging from below elevators for sport or entertainment. Aka "elevator action" or "helicopter" (which specifically refers to hanging from the electric cable at the base of the elevator).

Energizer bunny: high energy, full of pep. As in, "Marci went, like, all Energizer bunny the entire weekend." Just one of many examples of what *Blender Magazine* calls "popspeak," the use of pop culture icons as adjectives. Other examples: "That camerawork is so MTV"; "My grandma is looking more and more Yoda every day"; "Dan Rather, Connie Chung? That was too Wilson Phillips from the get-go."

Evianistas: the grinchlike purists who scowl at anyone ordering a stiff drink. Coined by the columnist Rob Morse.

family replacement meals: store-bought, store-made, full-course meals. Example: buying a whole Thanksgiving dinner for eight, including all the fixin's, at your A&P.

fat tooth: an insatiable appetite for fatty foods. Like "sweet tooth."

flack: a publicist for celebrity clients. To be "flacked" is to be pestered by a publicist. Aka a "praiser."

flacks fatales: female publicists who really push it.

flammy: flamboyant.

foodies: culinary connoisseurs who are a bit too anal about it all. "I created this restaurant for those who love great food, not for the foodies."

Fortress Hub: the home city for an American airline carrier. Pittsburgh for U.S. Airways, St. Louis for TWA, Atlanta for Delta.

freak the mundanes: an SCA term for traveling into town to freak out regular 1990s townfolk with your outlandish medieval getup and persona.

Fresno Indian: Armenian. Because they allegedly look like Cherokees.

fright mail: junk mail envelopes that appear to contain vitally important documents to encourage you to open them.

Garmento: someone who's sold their soul to the fashion industry.

gassed: very excited.

gate-crasher: one who weasels into concerts, games, and other public events without paying. Next to "Professor" Scott Kerman

Words and Expressions That Jim "the Mad Monk" Invented and/or Regularly Uses

boutique cities: smaller cities known for their creativity, livability, and beauty (Seattle, Portland, San Francisco—the queen of boutique cities), not for their power, money, and classism. Opposite of "power cities" (New York, L.A., and Washington, D.C.).

Cliff Notes: an abbreviated version of a story. "Let me give you the Cliff Notes version of how I met her." From Cliffs (with an "s") Notes, those insightful publishers of literary synopses so helpful in passing through college.

dashboard publishing: publishing from a moving vehicle (RV, car, truck, etc.). An extension of "desktop publishing."

mallification: the growing mono culture sweeping through America's cities, featuring major national chains and a slew of urban malls.

mallified: my disgust with the growing trend toward mallification.

Rouseification: the marriage of cuteness, commerce, and historic preservation. Characterized by mimes, jugglers, ice cream shops, and suburban-style stores filled with high-end cute, low-end cute, and horrifically cute merchandise. Any self-respecting city's worst paint-by-numbers nightmare. From the Rouse Development Company, which brought you Faneuil Hall, South Street Seaport, Baltimore's Inner Harbor, and other painfully quaint tourist meccas.

(author of *No Ticket? No Problem!*), I am probably one of the world's most notorious gate-crashers (something I'm no longer proud of, by the way). I once finagled Elke and me into the final home game of the 1995 American League Wild Card Playoffs between the New York Yankees and the Seattle Mariners *without a ticket*. Elke tried to leave in the 10th, then the 12th, then the 14th inning because she had to get up for a "shoot" in the morning. I said, "Shoot schmoot, this is the playoffs, this is Yankee Stadium, the House That Ruth Built, and we're in extra innings and no one else is leaving. Are you kidding me?" Elke tried to catch a cab but was talked out of it by security. She came storming back in the 15th inning and demanded that I take her home on the subway. I delayed as long as possible, backing ever so slowly up the stairs, trying to catch one final glimpse. Just as I was almost beyond the exit, I peeked around the corner and saw Jim Leyritz hit the game-winning home run over the right field wall. The place went ballistic. Elke smiled.

geeking out: *expressing extreme sympathy.*

get a grip: "Control yourself, you're really 'losing it.'" "You've gone 'nutso,' 'bonkers.'" "You need help." "You need to deal with that."

glazing: spacing out; dozing with your eyes open. "By the third week on the road, both Mike and I were *glazing.*"

golden hour: the window of opportunity following a major accident when the victim's life can be saved.

the Gooch: Bob Guccione, Sr., that swingin', hairy, overtanned founder of the *Penthouse* empire.

gut: an easy academic course. "I'm taking a gut."

haole (pron. "*how-lee*"): native Hawaiian for the white Christians who came and basically ruined their island paradise. Now applied to all white people.

happy camper: all is right in my world. The opposite of "unhappy camper" (a malcontent).

hitting the rails: going to holy communion in Roman Catholic vernacular.

HOMES: the mnemonic device for naming the Great Lakes: Huron, Ontario, Michigan, Erie, and Superior.

hoof it: forced to walk. "Luke's car got towed, so we had to hoof it to the show."

Hoosier: a permutation of "Who's there?" according to one popular theory. It has become the nickname for residents of Indiana, even though these days, it is largely applied to the Indiana Hoosiers basketball team, which, like the state, features all manner of hardworking, by-the-book white kids who get a masochistic thrill from being the brunt of Coach Knight's out-of-control bravura.

Houston, we have a problem: used whenever something has gone horribly wrong. From the film *Apollo 13*.

I Love You Maaaaaaaan: like so much of the funniest patter of the last decade, this expression of a guy high on ecstasy was made popular by the movie *Wayne's World*. It is now used regularly and sardonically anytime a man wants to express feelings without seeming too sincere or vulnerable, as in the recent Bud Lite commercials.

I'll go with that: I agree. Aka "You gotta go with that." Some claim this comes from Portland, Oregon, but I've heard it all over the country.

ink: a tattoo. Aka "tat," "piece."

it's a girl thing: annoying, overused breeder slang to keep boys at bay. "Go away, Ted, and let me read my *Inquirer*. It's a girl thing." Alternately, "It's a guy thing." For people who are living out some lame TV sitcom or for those who buy into the simplistic boundaries of *Men Are from Mars, Women Are from Venus*.

izzat: is that so? Really? Used when you've just caught up on some news. Popular on the Navajo "rez" (reservation).

janky: horrible, deceptive.

Jumbotron: a huge video screen, between 550 and 4,000 square feet, seen in large public areas, such as Times Square in New York.

just peachy: a slang term from the early 1900s for "cool," revived today to mean "everything's just fine" (with a strong cynical undertow).

lambada: a sexually provocative dance that started in the Bahia area of Brazil in the 1920s. It enjoyed a huge resurgence in popularity in Europe and then the U.S. in the 1990s, culminating in Vice-President Al Gore's offering to do his own version at the 1996 Democratic National Convention. A "lambaderia" is a place where the lambada is routinely danced.

Last Supper: a disastrous art gallery opening where around a dozen people show up.

leaf peepers: tourists who visit Vermont and New Hampshire in the fall to gawk at the changing foliage. Aka "flatlanders."

the Left Coast: the West Coast.

list lizard: an art gallery visitor who repeatedly asks for the price of works but never buys anything. Like a "be-back" in used car parlance.

Lloyd's Law: tourists destroy the thing they seek.

loin of fish: the prime or center cut of fish such as swordfish or tuna.

McPaper: your basic unoriginal, derivative, last-minute college term paper. A play on McDonald's.

memes: ideas, stories, jokes, and songs that appear to have a life of their own, spreading like wildfire through a subculture. Aka "urban legends."

the mile-a-minute plant: a fast-growing pesky thistle accidentally brought into the U.S. in the 1930s that is wreaking havoc on mid-Atlantic nurseries and orchards. Aka "Devil's tear thumb."

the million-dollar highway: U.S. 550.

modern primitives: persons deeply into scarification, branding, piercing, and tattoos. Made popular by an issue of *Re:Search*, which thoroughly documented the movement.

mother of all campaigns (or football games, love affairs, parties, etc.): made popular by Saddam Hussein's calling the Gulf War "the mother of all battles" (from the Arabic *umm al-ma'arik*). Because of this expression, Saddam is now known as "the Father of the Mother of All Clichés."

motivate: the ultimate dimwitted, corporate, "breeder yup" cheerleader term, used to rally the troops. "C'mon everybody, motivate!, or we'll miss the party."

motor voter law: the National Voter Registration Act, a federal statute that allows citizens to register to vote at nontraditional places like motor vehicle offices. Still, more registered voters watch the Super Bowl than vote.

mystery shopper: a quality control person who checks on prices at competing stores as well as customer service at a company's own store.

NIMBY: Not in My Backyard. Though it generally applies to homeowners opposed to the dumping of environmental waste in their neighborhood, in the nonprofit world it is sometimes used for a specific type of person: "They tried to put a parole office over there in North Portland, but a bunch of NIMBYs stopped them." NIMBYs usually have nothing to do with race; they are simply citizens overly concerned with government intervention in their neighborhood. Aka "GOOMBY" (Get Out of My Backyard) or "NIMEY" (Not in My Election Year), when used by politicians.

nuke 'n' puke: a meal cooked in a microwave.

1.5 generation: immigrants who come to the U.S. as adults and never quite lose their accents.

ooze ball: volleyball played in the mud.

out there: wholly unconventional, nutty, or cutting edge. "That fakir, he's out there."

outlanders: Pennsylvania Dutch for those who are not of their kind.

outta control: something that has gone beyond fun to become frightening or disorienting. "That Big Shot ride in Vegas is outta control."

owlie (North Dakota): out of sorts, crabby.

Patient Zero: a CDC term for the French airline attendant linked to most of the early AIDS fatalities.

peanuts: the name for those squishy little styrofoam things one uses in packaging.

pecker poles: tiny trees that loggers don't think should be cut, but sometimes inadvertently are.

Pennsylvania Dutch (from *Deutsch*): the dialect spoken by the hardworking German-Swiss "plain" people of southern Pennsylvania, who have successfully forced English words into German word order and syntax. Humorous examples abound: "Amos, come from the woodpile in; Mom's on the table and Poppa's et himself done already." "Lizzie, go in the house and smear Jakie all over with jam a piece of bread." "Cousin Sarah ain't good—she's been with the doctor all winter." "Don't dive there—come up here where the water is thicker." "Go out and tie the dog loose." "May your friends be many, your troubles few, and your sausages long." That about sums it up, don't you think?

the permanent establishment: old-money families who maintain a degree of noblesse oblige in a country overrun by vapid and self-centered nouveau riche. Examples: the Harrimans and Rockefellers.

perzines: magazines in which the editors are the prime

subjects. According to Mike Gunderloy (the founder of *Fact Sheet Five*, the bible of the 'zine revolution), *Monk, the Mobile Magazine* was "the king of the perzine," featuring the travels of two men and one cat in a 1986 Fleetwood motor home.

phreak: to procure phone services illegally.

PIB: People in Black. Found at an art school near you. "Yeah, RISD has a high PIB quotient." Distinct from MIB ("Men in Black").

plasma: caffeine.

poaching: when an agent tries to steal a major client from under the nose of another agent. Agents will usually appear with their clients at premieres and openings to ward off "poachers." Example: Bob Sugar trying to poach Rod Tidwell from Jerry McGuire in the film *Jerry McGuire*.

pod unit: an apartment in a large modern apartment complex.

power sludge: very strong coffee.

Protestantism: Christianity with all the fat, sugar, and taste removed.

pure dead brilliant: really, really, *really* good.

rock jock: a big-time rock climbing stud.

rug rats: children.

sagging: wearing pants so the waistline sags below the hips. Ubiquitous dress of '80s and '90s black and Hispanic teens and their wigger counterparts. From one perspective, an in-your-face statement of reckless nonconformity, but from a more obvious perspective, a ridiculous show of male cleavage that only makes the wearer look like a complete idiot. As Alicia Silverstone so eloquently puts it in the movie *Clueless*, "Okay, I don't want to be a traitor to my generation and all, but I don't get how guys dress today, I mean c'mon! It looks like they just fell out of bed and put on some baggy pants and take their greasy hair, OOOH!, and cover it up with a backwards cap, and, like, we're expected to swoon? I don't THINK so."

scratcher: an incompetent, poorly trained tattoo artist. "Spider's no scratcher, he's legit."

scrod: screwed over.

sensitivity training: if you're in the Navy, it means to reserve hazing females to sanctioned Navy situations; if you're a Dallas Cowboy, it means "Here's the rhetoric to toss around in case you get caught."

shadow dancers: people who obsessively stare at themselves in the mirror during an aerobics workout.

shithooks: fingers.

shock radio: in-your-face, often lurid radio programming. Notable examples are Howard Stern and Alex Bennett.

shoulder surfers: people who stand behind you at an ATM (automatic teller machine) to memorize your PIN (personal identification number).

sinead (pron. shin-*aid*): sabotage a great situation. From the Irish singer Sinead O'Connor. "I'm tellin' ya, you're pushin' it. If you don't sober up, you're going to sinead it."

skid marks: brown marks on your undies. Aka "brownie."

the Skinny: the widely popular cabbage diet in which you eat only cabbage soup for a solid week.

sky surfing: riding gusts of wind on a 5-foot "skyboard" attached to your feet for as long as possible before opening your parachute.

Smog Angeles: what San Diegans call Los Angeles.

soggie: what a Rhode Islander calls a greasy hot dog.

spreading: speaking as fast as humanly possible while delivering a mountain of information on a topic. Common practice in high school and college "policy" debate.

squat: nothing. "You ain't got squat."

squirrel: a highly esoteric affirmative debate case. During my senior year at Creighton Prep, we occasionally ran a squirrel called "detainers." And loved to torment out-of-state Nebraska teams with our "detainers" opening before switching to our standard (and "topical") "sentencing case." Debaters today also use "squirrel" to describe the judge who took "the minority position" on a three-judge panel.

stalkerazzi: photographers who go to absurd and aggressive lengths to get the shot. A step beyond "paparazzi."

stomping ground: one's favorite hangout. "And now we're approaching my old stomping ground, Printer's Row."

strapped: low on money. "Can I borrow a twenty?" "Sorry, man, I'm strapped. I've just got a ten to last me through the weekend."

the Superman Building: downtown Providence's Fleet National Bank, an Art Deco structure Superman scaled in the 1950s TV series.

swiped out: a credit or ATM card that has been used so much that its magnetic strip can no longer be read by the machine.

tall order: a difficult request. "Finding you cocaine, smack, and shrooms at this hour? Now, Courtney, that's a very tall order."

television: an electronic device which, when broken, stimulates conversation.

textbook: a representative example. "Nixon was a textbook pathological liar."

thingamabob: object you can't find the correct name for. "Give me that thingamabob you use to clean out the chimney."

third culture: Americans who straddle two or more cultures. Often children of military or government personnel stationed overseas, they don't identify strictly with their country of birth or their country(ies) of residence but the intersection of them all.

ticket spitter: a mechanical device that gives and receives your receipt at a large parking lot.

time-suck: a frivolous debate argument that an opponent must spend a huge amount of time refuting. Akin to a red herring. Now used in the world beyond debate (there is such a thing, you know). "I don't have TV in the house because it's a total time-suck."

toast: finished, destroyed, in deep trouble. "Dude, I flunked the biology midterm. I'm toast." Absolutely annoying surfer ripoff.

tomahawk chop: a mock Indian war dance gesture offensive to Native Americans, still used by Atlanta Braves baseball fans and the Florida State Seminoles. Political correctness aside, it shows how pretty damn stupid Americans can be. Aka "the chop."

town vs. gown: the often tumultuous relationship between colleges and the small towns they inhabit. Classic example: Yale vs. New Haven, Connecticut; Evergreen State College vs. Olympia, Washington.

trashed: extreme fatigue from too much work.

Trekker: a serious devotee of the popular TV series *Star Trek*. Only non-Trekkers use the term "Trekkie."

tri-state area: a news and weather report term used throughout the country. As Kurt Vonnegut put it, "Unless you live in Alaska or Hawaii, you are part of the tri-state area."

troll: a man who picks up male or female prostitutes. Aka "a John."

trophy wife: a woman who complements her husband's status by her incredible beauty, brains, or both. Jane Fonda to Ted Turner. A more déclassé example: Marla to Donald Trump.

tule fog: a low-lying fog that is far denser than regular fog. Found throughout the San Joaquin and Central valleys of California and elsewhere at least two to three weeks a year.

the 12-second tour: Arizonans' darkly humorous term for hikers who plunge to the bottom of the Grand Canyon.

U-lock: a superstrong bicycle lock, the only kind that deters thieves.

United States of Amnesia: Gore Vidal's poignant name for the United States.

up the ying-yang: a large quantity. "David Geffen's got boys up the ying-yang."

V-chip: a device installed in televisions that allows parents to "lock out" *Roadrunner*.

Vampire Time: a schedule where one sleeps all day and haunts clubs and coffeehouses at night. Followed by writers, artists, slackers, club kids, and other bohemian types.

waffle: equivocate.

wheatbacks: old pennies.

whirl-'n'-hurl: an older amusement ride that induces nausea and vomiting.

wig out: go crazy, lose one's focus or sanity. "Jill completely wigged out over the doo-doo scene in *Pink Flamingoes*."

willies: nervous, jumpy. As in, "That Jim Rose Circus act gives me the willies." Aka "heebie-jeebies."

wraps: hand-held, burrito-like flatbread sandwiches, considered the fast food trend of the '90s. Also refers to hair wraps: embroidered floss, woven and stitched around strands of hair, often beaded. Popular with Deadheads.

you're so ripe: you smell awful.

you're the man: you're the boss, you're number one. Made popular by sports radio wild man Scott Ferell: "How can I be the man when you're the man?" Now used regularly by white jocks everywhere.

zap zits: pop the dough bubbles in a pizza. A "moon crater" is a bubble that's been popped.

Pittsburgh

"So much of San Francisco is manufactured weirdness. Pittsburgh just has natural weirdness. People ask me, 'Is there a scene there?' I say no. They say, 'What do you do?' I say, 'I sit at home and watch TV.'" —ALYSON HOFF

I IDOLIZED MY OLDER BROTHER, RICK. Whatever he said, whatever he did, whomever he supported, I did too. My older sister, Julianna Fulcinari, called me "the shadow brother." And nowhere more so than when it came to sports. Because Rick was a Pittsburgh Pirates fan, I was too. One of the few in Omaha, which had as much in common with Pittsburgh as Mongolia does with Lichtenstein.

In my teens I expanded my love of the Pirates to all things Pittsburgh, including the other major sports franchises, such as the Steelers of football and the Penguins of hockey. As I grew older, I found that I liked Pittsburgh's teams because they all wore dark black uniforms. This greatly appealed to my noirish sensibility.

There is a distinct regional accent in Pittsburgh, aka "Picksburgh." But, more important, there is a distinct way of being. Let's call it "late industrial realness." Pittsburgh is one of the capitals of the Rust Belt, where they build suburban shopping centers on top of mounds of iron slag, where the football helmets carry the logo of a major steel manufacturing association, where nouvelle cuisine consists of an enormous platter of foods that end in *i* (haluski, pierogi, kielbasi, kluski, and golumpki, all of which go well with an Iron City brewski), where the locals are big, solid, and potbellied, where the local delicacy is pretzel Jell-O salad. That's right. Pretzels topped with strawberry Jell-O and a dollop of Cool Whip. Deeeelicious.

Here's Picksburgh.

Ahia: Ohio. "Yunz'll find d'Berg near Ahia" ("You'll find Pittsburgh near Ohio").

an' 'nat: and that. Ubiquitous Picksburgh expression, usually

tacked on the end of a sentence. "We went shopping an' 'nat."
Or, "You go out, you get a drink, you get a hot dog an' 'nat,
and you go in." Made famous by Scott Paulsen and Jimmy
Krenn, the town's top morning radio jocks, who put out a
comedy album titled *Hang'n Out an' 'Nat*.

the Black and Gold: the Steelers. Or any of the major sports
teams in town, since they all have black and gold uniforms.

the Blast Furnace: Three Rivers Stadium when the Steelers are
playing. A threatening taunt to the other team: "Welcome to
the Blast Furnace."

Bloom Filled: Bloomfield.

the Bucs: the Pittsburgh Pirates pro baseball team. From "buc-
caneers." Aka "the buccos." Though historically the Pirates
have fared very well, tough, big-shouldered Pittsburgh has
always struck me as more of a hockey and football town.
NBA basketball would never play here. Baseball barely does.
Caveat: contrary to popular belief, "Pirate" does not come from
any seafaring root but from the name of the club's first
owner, J. Palmer "Pirate" O'Neill, who earned his nickname by
pirating a player from another team.

chipped ham: "dirt cheap pressed ham" that is sliced so thin, it
can be used as luncheon meat. A "Pittsburgh barbecue sammitch" would be Isaly's chipped ham with Kraft barbecue
sauce and maybe a little relish.

city chicken: breaded veal or pork on a stick.

cross the Mon to the Sah Side: cross the Monongahela to the
South Side.

cuts: slices of pizza. "I'll have two cuts."

dahntahn (alternately "dauntaun" or "duntun"): downtown. One
word that inevitably trips up even the most eloquent "Picks-
burghers." They can't seem to drop it. Clear evidence of the
distinctive Pittsburgh tendency to change "ow" sounds to "ah."
For instance, if my last name was "Crowdy" it would still be
pronounced "Crotty." Believe it or not, you can hear this tendency in the voice of Mister Rogers, a native of Latrobe, Pennsylvania (along with Arnie Palmer and Rolling Rock Beer).

d'Berg: Pittsburgh, birthplace of Creighton University basketball player Bimbo Pietro (source of my family nickname,
Jimbo Pietro).

gummy bans (or "gumbands"): rubber bands. Never written,
only spoken. "Didja buy filum and gummy bans?" ("Did you
buy film and rubber bands?")

the Igloo: the Civic Arena, where the Penguins play. So called because of its shape and its connection to ice hockey.

the Iron City: Pittsburgh. Now that I think about it, there may have been an unconscious connection between my childhood nickname of "Iron" and my love of all things Pittsburgh. Aka "the Burgh."

jag-off: as a noun, jerk. As a verb, "jagging" ("stop jagging me"; i.e., stop doing what you're doing). "I knew to call people a jag-off before I knew what jack-off meant" (Rick Sebak).

Jaun's Tahn: Johnstown, the site of the great Johnstown Flood of 1889.

jeet yet?: did you eat yet?

jumbo: bologna. Contrary to fears, *not* an elephant "sammitch."

Jynt Iggle: Giant Eagle, a major grocery chain in Picksburgh. Its video department is actually called "the Iggle."

Kennywood's open: your zipper is down. Kennywood is the local amusement park.

lady locks: cream pastries. Known as "cream horns" elsewhere. Usually found on the "cookie table," a giant table with fancy cookies at ethnic weddings.

Mayor Smurphy: Mayor Murphy. Looks pale, meek, and drawn. Comes across as ineffectual but isn't.

Maz: Bill Mazerowski, the canonized Pittsburgh Pirate who hit the World Series–winning home run in the 9th inning against the Yankees in 1960.

Mean Joe Greene: a legendary defensive lineman for "the Stillers."

the Mon: the Monongahela River.

my house needs redd up: the textbook example of Pittsburgh's need to drop the verb "to be." "My car needs washed." One local posits that this tendency may be "a sign of a more advanced civilization." It's certainly more efficient.

Myron: the beloved "Stillers" announcer Myron Cope, who has had several distinct sayings attributed to him over the years. "Yoy!" is his signature exclamation. Followed by "the terrible tile," a little orange towel everyone in Three Rivers Stadium waves when the team scores. Cope has what might be called "a very distinctive voice," but most consider it "absolutely wretched" and grating.

nebby: nosy. "Don't be so nebby." Said when you're sticking your nose where it shouldn't be.

Penns Vein Yah: Pennsylvania.

Primanti: a local restaurant noted for its huge sandwich of fries, coleslaw, meat, and tomato all piled on thickly sliced Italian bread.

pump an' Eyern: drink Iron City Beer. Also connotes pumping iron. A band called Joe Grushecky and the House Rockers was once known as the Iron City Rockers. Bruce Springsteen performed with them on one of their recent songs, "Pumping Iron."

quit jaggin' dat jumbo!: kindly stop playing with your food.

redd up: clean up. "Get in there and redd up your room." Could come from "ready up."

the Sah Side: the South Side.

sammitches: sandwiches. As in a "Primanti sammitch."

skyscraper: a very tall, thin scoop of ice cream.

Sliberty: East Liberty.

slippy: slippery. "The roads are real slippy today."

Sophie: Sophie Masloff, the former "Jewish Grandmother" mayor of Pittsburgh, known for her big red laquered hair.

spicket: a water faucet.

sputzie: sparrow.

the still mill: the steel mill. The long *e* comes out as an *i* in "Picksburgh."

the Stillers: the Pittsburgh Steelers pro football team.

the Strip: the district (Italian groceries, Asian markets, wholesale produce) where the "still mills" started. Andrew Carnegie's first mill was here as well as George Westinghouse's railroad air brakes factory.

tile: towel.

the Tubes: the Liberty and Fort Pitt tunnels. Often used in traffic reports: "There's a backup in the Tubes." Loudon Wainwright has a song called "Ode to a Pittsburgh," where he swoons, "with your Tubes of Liberty."

what keller's yer high hills?: what color are your high heels?

the Yock: the Youghiogheny River.

yunz (sometimes pron. "yinz"): literally, you ones. Pittsburgh's version of "y'all." "Yunz goin' out?" "Yunz from d'Berg?" ("Are you all from Pittsburgh?"), "Yunz are very nize" ("You all are very nice"). You usually hear it from a waitress: "What are yunz having today?"

yunzer: singular form of "yunz." Used in speaking of someone who uses "yunz"; i.e., a working-class person ("That's a yunzer bar").

Portland, Oregon

In the 1600s, some greedy Spanish conquistadores allegedly reached the coast of Oregon and, on seeing a tribe of Salish Indians waiting there, shouted, "¡Orejon!" (What big ears!). What the Spaniards mistook for ears were, in fact, giant abalone earrings. Interestingly, strange flukes of language have characterized the state ever since. Not only is Oregon beset with town names like Drain, Boring, and Wankers Corner, it is said that the name of its major city was decided by a coin toss. Francis W. Pettygrove of Calais, Maine, wanted "Portland," the principal city of Maine, and A. L. Lovejoy of Massachusetts wanted "Boston," the main city of his state. Pettygrove won.

Portland, Oregon, may be the last true frontier in this country. Scratch that. Portland may be the last great place to buy a six-room, two-bathroom house for under forty grand. In fact, in its Albina neighborhood, you can still buy a well-built six-room house for under $30,000 (that is, if you can con that sweet little ole black lady out of it, as two developers did a while back). However, the property taxes are bound to get you in the end (there is no sales tax in Oregon): a real boon to propertyless monks like myself and a real headache to the Tectronix guys gentrifying their ghetto dream home on weekends.

Still, Portland is hot. But I bet most of you, pining away in Toad Suck and Traverse City, know nothing about how the natives talk and behave. Here's a break from the national hype about the Northwest, with the essential vocabulary, expressions, and factoids any real estate speculator or German transportation lobbyist needs to know to get by in Rip City.

ash report: L.A. has its smog alert, Portland has its volcanic ash report. This makes sense with the Mount Tabor volcano in the heart of Southeast Portland and the rather ferocious Mount Saint Helens over the river and through the woods in Washington. Factoid: when Saint Helens erupted, residents of Portland and eastern Washington took to wearing paper dust

masks to keep from inhaling the ash. When the stores ran out
of masks, thousands resorted to wet bandannas, which gave
the city the feeling of being overrun by armed banditos. An
added irony: Mount Saint Helens ash was allegedly selling for
$10 a vial on the streets of New York.

the Ban Roll-On Building: the Broadway Building (across
from "the Schnitz").

Beervana: Portland. This fine city, not Seattle, gave birth to the
national microbrew scene. Aka "Brewtopia" or "Munich on the
Willamette."

Benson bubblers: the handsome, bronze, four-pronged drinking fountains downtown, installed by lumberman Simon Benson in 1912 to divert thirsty employees from the evils of
whiskey. Benson proudly claimed that after his 20-odd bubblers were installed, "saloon sales" declined by 40%. Although
there are now 50 Benson bubblers in the city, alcohol con-
sumption continues to rise.

big pink: the U.S. Bancorp Tower, at 6th and West Burnside.
Aka "the Tower of Power."

the bins: the Goodwill As Is store, where used clothing is priced
by the pound. "Where did you get that blouse?" "I found it at
the bins."

Bridgetown: Portland. Created by Deborah Betron, a Realtor, in
honor of the eleven bridges that span the Willamette.

Burnside: the skateboard ramps beneath the Burnside Bridge.

Burnside bum: a homeless person with a substance-abuse problem, usually found hovering up and down Burnside, though
primarily around the Burnside Bridge in Northwest Portland.

Cadillac: a shopping cart in street lingo. Look for a line of elegantly parked Cadillacs in front of the "Nutwatch Headquarters" come winter.

California: the long-past-its-prime mecca for the disgruntled and dispossessed, who are perpetually on the prowl for untrammeled destinations on which to inflict their greed, utopianism, and all-encompassing angst.

Californian: the enemy.

Californicator: an enemy who's invaded. Factoid: only 47% of Oregon residents were born in the state.

the Clown Center: a FedEx driver's term for the Clackamas Town Center, where Tonya does her "practicing."

the Con: the Satyricon, an old-school punk and alternative club. Portland's answer to New York's CBGB's. Aka "Scary-con."

Portland Etiquette

IT TAKES A WHILE FOR TRANSPLANTS FROM L.A. or the Northeast to grasp the Portland vibe, the citywide edict against rudeness, conflict, or pain. What D-J Haanradts calls the culture of "aggravating friendliness." Here are some pointers.

→ Everybody knows everybody in Portland. So when there's a fallout, remember, you're going to eventually run into each other at Powell's City of Books.

→ When there is an argument, a true Portlander knows when to back off. Which is pretty much immediately. You do not win points by relentlessly attacking your opponent. MAKE NICE! is the prevailing mantra. After all, this is the land of "consensus building," not gangsta posing.

→ Irony is often in short supply here. Acerbic irony in particular. The average Portlander (Northwesterners in general, in fact) doesn't make jokes about recent tragedies and disasters. It was usually "outsiders" making the O.J. jokes a few years back.

→ Portland is sceneproof. To have a genuine "scene" one needs genuine elitism, which would cut directly against Portland's egalitarian spirit. You do have cliques of outsiders, who complain endlessly about the dorkiness of Portland and its lack of real "CULTURE," but they are relatively benign and easily ghettoized to a back corner at the Saucebox.

An Oregon Joke

A CALIFORNIAN, AN OREGONIAN, AND A TEXAN ARE sitting around the campfire. The Texan pulls out a full bottle of tequila, takes a swig, throws the bottle in the air, and shoots it to smithereens with a six-shooter. The Californian turns to him and asks, "Now why'd you go and do that?" The Texan replies, "Well, where I come from, we have plenty of that."

Not to be outdone, the Californian then takes out a bottle of vintage Napa Valley wine, uncorks it, takes a sip, tosses it in the air, draws his pistol, and shoots the bottle to pieces. The Texan turns to him and asks, "Now why'd you go and do that? That was a very expensive bottle of wine." And the Californian replies, "Well, where I come from, we have plenty of that."

Having seen all this, the Oregonian pulls out a cold bottle of Bridgeport Blue Heron ale, opens it up, sucks the whole bottle down, throws the bottle in the air, draws his gun, shoots the Californian, and catches the bottle. Horror-stricken, the Texan turns to him and shrieks, "Why'd you do that!?" The Oregonian replies, "Where I come from, we got plenty of those . . . but the bottle's worth a nickel."

couch (pron. "cooch"): Not a sofa but a street.

the Darth Vader Building: the 200 Southwest Market Street Building downtown. Aka "the Big Black Box" because of its '70s black glass exterior. Trivia: the building has no 13th floor. Superstition prevailed at the time of construction, so the 13th floor is called the 14th, and so on to the top.

Docs: Doc Marten shoes. Hipster and gutter punk footwear of choice. Those who sell them are "shoe dogs." Portland is the home of AirWare, the sole importer of Doc Martens to the U.S.

the Donut Street: Winchell.

Fake Oswego: Lake Oswego, a major yuppie suburb. Aka "Lake No Negro." Or "Lake Big Ego."

fake-n-Docs: fake Doc Martens. Aka "mock Docs."

fake-n-stocks: fake Birkenstocks, Portland's budget footwear of choice.

Fareless Square: a 300-block area downtown where public transit is free. Warning: ride a bus here and you risk meeting the nutty dregs of American civilization.

Fluff: Mike Cowan, a longtime caddy for pro golfer Peter Jacob-sen. Cowan recently defected to the hot PGA star and local kid made good, Tiger Woods.

4:20: a police term for smoking pot.

4:20 at Park Blocks: a teen street term for smoking pot. As a City Nightclub stripper, Malikyte, adroitly put it, at 4:20 p.m. in Portland, "If you have it, you smoke it."

Freaky Freddies: Fred Meyers' all-purpose shopping experi-ence. A favorite hangout of the paraplegic cartoonist John Callahan because of the range of bizarre and downright creepy characters found there. Invariably they are in the fruit section, stealing handfuls of grapes when no one is looking.

full on: cool.

Good Sam: Good Samaritan Hospital.

Grey-shum: Gresham. How an old resident of this suburb would pronounce it.

Grunt High: Grant High School after they "stole" the best ath-letes from Jefferson High, the city's perennial sports power-house.

hacky slackers: the all-time great approbation for Portland slackers. Taken from twentysomething stoner pastime of Hacky Sack® (aka "footbag").

Jailblazers: the Portland Trail Blazers basketball team. Coined by *Willamette Week* (aka *"Willie Week"*) because of the rash of new players with criminal records (Rasheed Wallace, Isaiah Rider, Jermaine O'Neal, Dontonio Wingfield) now playing on a heretofore very "clean team" (exemplified by former Blazers Buck Williams and Clyde Drexler).

Karma Corner: 37th and Hawthorne, where you will inevitably run into anyone you know. Along with Powell's City of Books, it's one of the vortexes of the city.

the Mayberry Effect: the uncanny premonition that everyone you know in Portland is a scant two degrees of separation from almost every other person in your life and that your for-mer lover is probably dating your former employer's former high school sweetheart. Coined by local writer Karen Steen. For a city of half a million, this place is very, very small. As Steen explains, "Suddenly it will become crystal clear why everyone here is so damned nice: no one wants to risk making an enemy in a town the size of a postage stamp."

Milie story (pron. "mi-lee"): named after its originator in which the conclusion is oddly anticlimactic. "Last night I was alone

Marketing Expressions Any True Local Has Heard and Uses

A PORTLANDER'S GOOD-NATURED USE OF THESE expressions indicates another local trait—the love of native sons.

"Free is a very good price." Courtesy of Tom Peterson, local furniture salesman, who's known for his hilarious marketing gimmicks, from Tom Peterson watches and alarm clocks ("Wake up! Hey, wake up!") to the inimitable free Tom Peterson flattop haircut, offered every Sunday in Tom's parking lot. Tom has made cameo appearances in most Gus Van Sant films. Caveat: to indicate the degree of Tom's influence, not only did Kurt Cobain wear a Tom Peterson watch, but Portlander Jennifer Scott, a spokesperson for her hubby's car company, has started touting wristwatches with her visage on them too.

"If you don't come see me today, I can't save you any money." There are many variations on this slogan of car dealer Scott Thomason. For instance, "If you don't leave a message, I can't call you back" or "If you don't come see me today, come see me tomorrow."

"You'll find it at Freddy's." Often used ironically when something is not found at Fred Meyers' or when you find something you weren't expecting, such as the loquacious psychotic behind you in the checkout line.

Portland vs. Seattle

THERE'S A FUNNY STORY THAT PERFECTLY DEMONstrates the difference between Portland and Seattle residents. If you tell a Seattleite that *Monk, the Mobile Magazine* is featuring it in its next issue, you will hear, "Wow! That's great! When's the issue coming out?!" If you tell Portlanders their city is being featured, the response will be, "Why would anyone want to feature Portland?"

Portland is like Seattle in several ways—rain, microbrews, heroin addiction, lattes, "Californicators"—but when it comes to glamour, celebrity, and cachet, "the Rose City" not only doesn't grasp it, it decidedly eschews it. Portland's reaction, for reasons both enlightened and downright hick, is "What's the big deal?"

This ornery mind-set does not necessarily find its way into a particular local accent but it definitely affects how locals talk. How you say something is very important in these parts. It must include the proper quota of low-key, beard-scratchin' self-abnegation as well as a high level of "just folks" everydayness. You go struttin' around your specialness, your arrogance, your East Coast better-than-thou-ness, and Portlanders won't give you the time of day, let alone directions to "Clown Center."

---

in the house when I heard what sounded like someone trying to break into the back bedroom. So I grabbed a flashlight and slipped out the side door. Entering the backyard, I stopped to watch the moon and then I went back into the house, ate a bowl of vanilla ice cream, and fell asleep on the sofa."

mock Docs: fake Doc Martens. See "fake-n-Docs."

Murphy and Finnigans: 1940s and '50s nickname for Meier and Franks, a major department store.

navigational tips: (1) Highway 26 is sometimes called "26," but west of the Willamette (Will-*am*-it) it's more often "the Sunset"; (2) I-84 is "the Banfield"; (3) Highway 10 is known as "the TV Highway" (the Tualatin Valley Highway); (4) Highway 8 is "Canyon Road"; (5) Terwilliger Boulevard is known as "Terwiggler" because of its wiggly nature; (6) "the Curves" refers to that section of I-5 under the Terwilliger Overpass—supposedly the most dangerous set of curves in the entire length of I-5; (7)

it's important to know the names of all ten bridges across the Willamette and to state whenever possible which bridge you intend to take (Sellwood, Ross Island, Marquam, Hawthorne, Morrison, Burnside, Steel Bridge, Broadway, Fremont, St. John). Some add an eleventh, the Burlington Northern railroad bridge; (8) it's "Sauvie Island," not Sauvie's. Those who've lived there for years and knew the original family are adamant about it; (9) the Lloyd Center mall is known simply as "Lloyd." If you are going to a movie there, specify "inside" or "outside" because there are two theater complexes, one in the mall proper and one outside it.

the Next Seattle: Portland. A complete myth, but a line heard quite frequently, though never by a true Portlander and rarely by the local press. It's always visitors who make this comparison, which is completely negated if you live here anytime at all.

OCA: Oregon Citizens Alliance to some, Oregon's Christian Assholes to others. Its founder, Lon Mabon, is a former mescaline freak who morphed into a powerful right-wing activist. He launched several dreaded ballot initiatives, including the infamous "Measure 9," which sought to limit the basic civil rights of homosexuals and other "sexual minorities." Lon got a bit power-mad in the end, alienating his core Republican base, but his legacy refuses to die. Factoid: Mabon's OCA is responsible for catapulting such ideologically loaded and rhetorically misleading terms as "minority status" (a benign legal term signifying equal protection for all regardless of race, creed, or sexual orientation transformed into a loaded buzzword to deny equal protection to gays and bisexuals) and "special rights" (aka "equal rights") into the national public policy arena, inspiring similar ballot measures from Colorado to Maine.

Old Dykes Tales: Old Wives Tales, a mostly veggie restaurant in near Southeast popular with lesbians.

Brave Nike World

IT'S ALL ABOUT SPORTS, WHICH IS "THE CULTURE OF the U.S." and the language of the world!

air: the gaseous substance in Nikes that cushions the foot as it lands. The shoes are named to match the particular athlete endorsing it and/or the particular use of the shoe. For example, the Air Jordan basketball shoe has what Nike terms "full length zoom air" (air bubbles the entire length of the shoe), which gives big leapers like myself that extra spring in the step when I go in for the slam dunk.

Air Hebrews: sandals by Nike. Aka "Air Nazareth."

behind the berm: insider term for the Nike World Headquarters because of the fortress-like berm surrounding the entire property. If one leaves the campus for lunch, one chooses to go "beyond the berm." Some regard the berm as a symbolic wedge between arrogant Nike and John Q. Public.

burn the berm: the mantra of a very small but growing band of disaffected Nike workers, who will be rooted out and dismissed once word of this reaches Bob Falcone's desk.

Code of Conduct: the rules on how workers should be mistreated in overseas factories.

communication is the detonator, product is the bomb: the marketing department's way of ingratiating itself with design. *Theory Z* meets *In Search of Excellence*.

consultants: Nike-babble for the highly paid superstars who endorse its products. At $20 million a year, Michael Jordan is unquestionably the highest paid "consultant" of any stripe in the world. So far as we know, Nike has not yet created a suitable nickname for the Indonesian ladies who actually make the shoes for around $2 a day.

Ekins: people who have been at Nike from the beginning. Look for the swoosh tattoo.

fashionable: a dirty 11-letter word.

Just Do It: a thousand-year-old Korean Zen principle brought to the U.S. by Zen Master Dae Seung Sa Nim. Later incorporated into Nike ads. But go easy, since even Portland cabbies claim they invented it.

→

Just Pay 'Em: the highly annoying slogan of extremist organizations trying to get Nike to pay its Asian workers a "livable" wage. Okay, so Michael Jordan and Andre Agassi both earn more money in a year for wearing their Nikes than 12,000 workers in Asia earn for actually making them. And, all right, Phil has over $5.2 billion in stock options. But is that any reason to disrupt a shareholders' meeting?

Factoid: a 1% reduction in Nike's annual $280 million ad budget would raise the income of all the workers in its six Indonesian factories above the poverty line. Then again, if Nike employees stayed at Motel 6 on business trips, it would produce the same result.

Nike: a fashion company. No, no, excuse me—a shoe company. No, no, sorry—a shoe and clothes company. No, no, oh God, of course—a "total brand" company. With tentacles stretching from Beaverton to China. Making the world safe for athleticism.

the Nike attitude: merge EST, bastardized Rinzai Zen, and *Jerry McGuire* and you've got it. A Nike operator elucidates: "Here at Nike, you don't just do the job, you try to make it better, man. 'Just Do It' isn't just for you out there, for marketing. It's for US! When I first came here, they told me to forget everything. Everything that I had ever been taught, man. Cuz here, you gotta understand, we have no guidelines. We have no hierarchy, man! Here, you are your own destiny. What do you want to do? Do you want to work →

outlet? You take outlet! You want to work the phones? You take those phones, and hold on tight, man!"

Nike Town: a tourist attraction that sells shoes.

Phil: Phillip H. Knight, chairman of the board and chief executive officer of Nike. Phil is good. Phil knows best. If Phil says the Indonesian workers are well paid, then they are well paid. If Phil says we are taking steps to monitor child labor and workplace conditions, then we are doing that too. Thank you for your investment. Aka "Bucky."

the R company: Reebok.

swooshtika: a pejorative name for the corporate symbol of Nike. Refers to the cultlike atmosphere engendered by the company and its occasional indulgence in militaristic symbols and metaphors. Used by locals who've yet to see the light.

Uncle Phil: Phil Knight, Nike's CEO. According to one insider, the customary line said after a big meal on a Nike business trip is "Thank you, Uncle Phil." Knight has accrued over 90 speeding tickets. Clearly he is not a "role model." Mitigating factor: he contributed $25,000 to the Tonya Harding Legal Defense Fund.

WHQ: employee term for Nike World Headquarters in Beaverton. Aka "the campus."

Oral-Groanian: the *Oregonian,* a daily newspaper (aka "the Borigonian"). As the joke goes, "If it matters to Oregonians, it's in the *Washington Post,*" recalling that the *Post* scooped the *Oregonian* on the Packwood sexual harassment scandal. Ironically, the *Oregonian* knew "firsthand" about Packwood's sexual proclivities two years before the *Post* story broke. Just ask its reporter Roberta Ulrich. Other major Oregon papers are "the Red Guard" (Eugene) and "the Statesman-Urinal" (Salem).

Paranoia Park: gutter punk term for O'Bryant Park, where many used to hang out before the police moved in nearby.

PDX: Portland International Airport, or Portland in general.

Po Hop: Portland hip-hop music.

Popo: street teen term for the Portland police. Usually shouted when you're smoking some weed and the cops are spotted.

Puddle-stomp: Portland rock 'n' roll.

Puddletown: Portland. Aka "Stumptown."

Queen Kong: *Portlandia,* the nation's second largest copper sculpture (after the Statue of Liberty) and the first hammered sculpture to be commissioned since Lady Liberty. Sometimes students from Portland State will dangle a giant yo-yo from her outstretched finger. Caveat: an inflatable King Kong jettisoned off the back of the Portland Building the day *Portlandia* was unveiled.

Quicksand River: the Sandy River, which gets silty in the summer.

Reedies: students, graduates, or dropouts of Reed College, a cross between Swarthmore and Evergreen State College. The stereotypical Reedy is an earnest intellectual leftist male or a radical feminist female who is probably from the East Coast, probably wears glasses, and has probably experimented broadly with drugs—depending on the context, either a disparaging insult or a term of endearment. Someone can be "like a Reedy" without having attended the college. Past students have included Beatniks Gary Snyder and Lew Welch, Zen Master Philip Whalen, pop culture icon Dr. Dimento (Barry Hansen), as well as gun nut William "Caligula" Abernathy (Reed's most infamous "scrounger").

Rip City!: said by legendary Trail Blazer announcer Bill "Holy Backboard!" Schonely (aka "the Schonz") every time the team makes a basket. There has been controversy over Schonely's claim to a term that may actually have originated on the drug-crazed streets of San Francisco when folks used to talk about getting "ripped."

the Schnitz: the Arlene Schnitzer Concert Hall, home of the Oregon Symphony Orchestra.

Silicon Forest: aka "Silicon Clear Cut," overhyped locus of Portland's digerati. Primarily Beaverton, Hillsboro, and the vicinity, where high-tech companies like Intel now make most of

Oregon in General

Ash-ram: Ashland. Aka "Hashland." Ashland is the site of renowned Shakespeare productions as well as Lithia Park, which ostensibly has a very high concentration of lithium in the drinking fountain water, possibly explaining why most Hashlanders have a balanced, mentally stable aura around them. Note: a lot of the settlers in Ashland from the early '60s on were hippie dropouts, and most likely many were into Eastern religions, hence "Ash-ram."

Bachelor Butte: the original name for Mount Bachelor, in central Oregon. The name changed when it became a ski area. Aka "the Bachelor."

Bag a Bagwan: the ubiquitous bumper sticker in the Wasco County area during the height of the conflict between residents and "the Rajneesh."

Bag Babbitt, Bailey, and Kerr: a bumper sticker common in rural eastern Oregon encouraging people to shoot Secretary of the Interior Bruce Babbitt and environmentalists Ric Bailey and Andy Kerr. Many there believe that these three men are the biggest threat to their God-given right to do anything they damn well please with "their" land. See "Ecobabble."

the Bay Area: Coos Bay, Charleston, and North Bend.

buckaroo: cowboy. From the Spanish *vaquero*.

Coho condos: Coho salmon nesting grounds.

Cow College: Oregon State Agricultural College before it added "arts and letters" classes and became Oregon State University.

Dreadford: Medford.

the Dulls: the Dalles. The seat of Wasco County, which a power-mad Rajneeshee, Sheila Silverstein (aka "Ma Anand Sheila"), unsuccessfully tried to take over through voter manipulation and the salmonella poisoning of hostile politicos. A statuary tribute to the "brave citizens of Antelope" who resisted Sheila and her posse can be found on the steps of the county courthouse. Sheila herself moved to Switzerland to escape extradition; several of her underlings have been convicted and are now in jail. Sheila allegedly runs a nursing home in Basel.

eastern Oregon: where the men are men, the women are men, and the sheep are nervous.

→

the environment: the holy grail. In Oregon, next to godliness. You simply do not understand environmentalism until you come here. Everywhere else the environment is a cause. Here it's a way of life.

go to the coast: where you go to see the big waves in Oregon. You do not go to "the beach" (that's California) or "the ocean" (that's Washington) or "the shore" (that's "Joisey").

got your buck?: what folks in central Oregon ask each other in the fall during hunting season.

Grass Pants: Grants Pass.

the Graveyard of the Pacific: the mouth of the Columbia River, due to the many maritime deaths that have occurred there.

the Great Migration: the beginning of major traffic on the Oregon Trail, ca. 1843.

greenways: ecologically sensitive areas protected by law from development. Pioneered by the late "green" governor, Tom McCall, who pioneered a philosophy of environmentalism now known as "McCallism."

Kitz and Katz Show: the state government when Portland's mayor, Vera Katz, was the speaker of the Oregon house and John Kitzhaber, Oregon's governor, was president of the senate.

Lon: as in Mabon, founder of the Oregon Citizens Alliance. As in Mabonic Plague. As in "Ding dong, Mabon calling." See "OCA."

my wife is pickup broke: she sits quietly in the truck while I'm inside drinking or doing business with the boys. Wives in eastern Oregon are used to waiting for hours while their husbands buy or sell cattle.

Oregon: a home away from home for "Californicators." The litmus test of true locals is whether they can pronounce "Oregon" properly. Most agree that it is pronounced "*or-ih-gun*," not "or-ih-*gahn*," though some, like Gary Fee, say it's "or-a-*gone*," not "or-e-*gun*," and refer to the U. of O. song ("'Or-e-*gone*,' my alma mater").

Rajneeshees: red-clad disciples of the Indian guru Bagwan Shree Rajneesh, aka "the Dogwan," who founded the colorful, outrageous, yet infamous community of Rajneeshpuram on the Big Muddy Ranch, about 27 miles outside Antelope. They still talk about "them Rajneeshees" at the

→

Antelope Café (known as Zorba the Buddha in the mid-
'80s). Don't be surprised if the patrons start looking at ya
kinda funny, though. They probably had a "Bag a Bagwan"
bumper sticker back in the heyday of the commune.

range maggots: historically, Oregon cattlemen have not
been big fans of sheep, especially at the turn of the century.
In fact in Prineville, in central Oregon, cattlemen were
happy to proclaim that they'd killed 10,000 sheep, calling
them "woolly monsters," "hooved locusts," and (my favorite)
"range maggots."

Sheila: Ma Anand Sheila, the closest Rajneesh aide and mas-
termind of the plot to poison Wasco County officials for
their refusal to abide her scheme to control county politics.

shlong haircut: short in front, long in back. Heavy metal
guys wear it. Aka "the Coos cut" (from Coos Bay area cartoonist Ward Sutton).

shoot the butte: when Spencer's Butte is covered in snow,
the bravest hikers often "shoot the butte." These "snow
shoots" introduce new trails covered in snow and
old-growth fir.

tree-hugger: an outsider's term for Oregonians. Also applied to environmentalists in general.

webfoot: gently derogatory term for an Oregonian.

wet-siders vs. dry-siders: the coastal areas of Oregon are
fairly wet, while the
eastern parts are dry
and almost desert-like.
The wet-siders look on
the dry-siders as yokels;
the dry-siders see the
wet ones as yuppies.
Caveat: those on the
western side of Mount
Hood are also known as
"valley people."

wind Johnnies: avid
windsurfers. Typically
found in Hood River,
one of the most popular
windsurfing meccas in
the world.

their chips. The Bay Area has Silicon Valley, New York, Silicon Alley, and Fargo, the Silicon Prairie. L.A. has silicone breast implants.

slug-snuck: the slimy trail that slugs leave behind.

Smashed Can store: a discount grocery outlet. "Why do you have a whole case of moon pies?" "I got them at Smashed Cans."

South Park Blocks: a long, tree-lined parkway and serious teen hangout, representing the vast spectrum of the Portland youth scene—from dopers to punks to slackers to skaters to baggers.

spendy: expensive.

squat rot: street kid term for the caked-on dirt that develops on one's body from sleeping outdoors.

the Stumble Zone: Hawthorne Street between 46th and 50th avenues. Several bars are within a short walking distance of one another, including Bar of the Gods and Space Room.

Stumptown: Portland. At the turn of the century, new lots were cleared of everything but the stumps. Because they were scattered over the downtown area, the stumps were painted white so folks wouldn't bump into them. In the 1920s and '30s, the name was strongly discouraged in the interest of a more hospitable image for the city. But it returned with a vengeance in the '80s as environmentalist rhetoric decrying the loss of ancient forests.

Theftway: Thriftway supermarket. Known for its high prices in an otherwise moderately priced food town.

Eugene

EUGENE WAS ONCE A NATURAL FOOD LOVER'S PAR-adise. The words "fresh," "homegrown," and "organic" were spoken frequently, and meat and poultry were sure to be rabbinically pure. In fact, two of the nation's largest producers of granola have their headquarters here. For years Eugene was also one of the last remaining strongholds of radical '60s consciousness and a major stop on the Deadhead trail. However, like many other '60s hotbeds (Ann Arbor, Berkeley, and Madison), Eugene has become increasingly gentrified in the last decade. Today you are as likely to find a gourmet yuppie restaurant as a whole foods co-op.

beer-thirty: 2:30 a.m. In some bars, if you call out, "Hey, it's almost beer-thirty," you better get the hell out of the way of the door because you're likely to cause a stampede. In Eugene, the 7-Elevens are required to stop selling alcohol at 2:30 a.m., so if you're in a drunken daze, the only reason you need to know the time is to know whether it's too late to buy more.

Civil War: the annual football game between the University of Oregon Ducks and the Oregon State Beavers.

Gang Green: the University of Oregon Ducks football team, particularly the defense. Also applied to Duck fans.

Icky's: punk, peace punk, gutter punk, anarchist, skinhead hangout. One of the last glimpses of authentic alternative culture in Eugene, where you're not required to be "a consumer" in order to hang out.

it's Willamette, damn it!: expression used on any Eugene newcomer who mispronounces the name of the Willamette River. Crucial for North Chicago transplants, who invariably confuse Willamette with Wilmette.

Kesey: the noted author and Merry Prankster Ken Kesey. No need for the first name; everyone in town knows who you mean.

the Pit: the University of Oregon's Mac Court, the oldest college fieldhouse in the nation.

Pre: the legendary hard-drivin', hard-drinkin', and seriously attitudinal University of Oregon runner Steve Prefontaine, the unofficial mascot of Nike.

→

Quacker Backers: diehard fans of the University of Oregon football team, the Ducks.

the sweep: three days of mass arrests commandeered by Eugene's "RDU" (Rapid Deployment Unit) on September 23–25, 1996. Some 120 people were arrested on 13th Street, the main drag at the University of Oregon. Most were for "status offenses," such as loitering, "cop watching," or lolly-gagging around looking scruffy. Essentially Eugene's attempt to test the widely popular criminological theory that if you cut down on skateboarding you'll make a huge dent in crime. In a town that still loves a good radical protest, "the sweep" failed.

Tracktown, USA: Eugene. Thanks to the renowned U. of O. track program, which launched the careers of Steve Prefontaine, Phil Knight, and Bill Bowerman, the holy trinity of Nike.

trustafarian: a wealthy white kid trying to be Rastafarian, the indigenous religion of Jamaican blacks, centered on the ritual celebration of good ganja, reggae music, and dreadlocks, mon. "Trustafarians" typically put chemicals in their hair to make it nap up Rasta style.

tits up!: the signature remark of former mayor Bud Clark when he foists back a brew. Ironically, what made the expression famous was the time when Clark fired the country's first woman police chief of a major city, Penny Harrington; leaving her house he said, "Tits up!" This is the same man who remarked after being challenged on his administration's sorry record on affirmative action, "Maybe I'll just get a suntan." Interestingly, Clark was well liked by all factions, precisely because of what one black community activist calls his honest and "unpolitical" demeanor.

the Tongue: former senator Bob Packwood, known not only for his failed advances on more than 19 female co-workers but for chronicling his amorous exploits in his diaries. The nickname comes from his alleged habit of forcibly sticking his tongue in women's mouths.

Trendy-3rd: 23rd Avenue, Northwest Portland. Increasingly gentrified, overpriced yuppie-cutesy-antiquey-touristy-schlocky-tile-and-trendy-boutique thoroughfare, with a gourmet coffee joint on almost every block. Symbolic of the

gradual desecration of the fundamentally grungy and deliberately unfashionable Portland aesthetic, which pioneering
'zines like *Snipehunt* are striving so hard to preserve.

true Urban Leaguer: a zealous staff member of the Urban
League of Portland.

Vaseline Alley: Stark Street. A major gay thoroughfare. There is
so much exploratory traffic in the neighboring Powell's men's
room, the store had to take the doors off the stalls.

West Winnebago: generic term for a suburb.

whoop whoop!!: the signature greeting of onetime mayor Bud
Clark. Says he learned it from a guinea pig as a child. Factoid:
Bud not only posed naked for the famous "Expose Yourself to
Art" poster, but during the 1960 Cuban Missile Crisis he put a
Cuban flag in the window of his tavern, known then as the
Spaten Haus.

Psychobabble

"We don't really change. We just go in bigger circles."

—RON ATHEY

YOU'VE HEARD 'EM—WELL-MEANING FOLKS WHO put big stock in deep, long, loving looks, who like to "call you on your stuff," who demand "integrity" and "space" in their "primary relationships." These are the bedrock—excuse me, the crystal rock—of the human potential industry: workshop junkies, "process queens," spiritual shoppers, psychobabblers. In certain areas of the country, like Marin County, Sedona, and even classier Santa Fe, they are omnipresent. But their vocabulary, which is an amalgam of speech codes from humanistic psychology to religious science to the 12 Steps, has entered the mainstream, particularly AM talk radio. A lot of people you know say they need "their space." It's something they wouldn't have said thirty years ago, when the only "space" Americans knew about had something to do with Sputnik.

You don't need to know this particular brand of speech to get by as an American, but if you want to get "deep" and "meaning-ful" in your "experience," espe-cially on the West Coast, or if you want to get a date with a particu-larly nice-looking Lynn Andrews look-alike, knowing your psycho-babble can only help. It'll plug you into a fascinating network of "facilitators," "seminars," "train-ings," and "multilevel pyramid schemes," all with a stated purpose of bringing you closer to: (a) your "hidden child" (sometimes re-ferred to as an "inner child" or "hidden kid"); (b) your "true self" (as opposed to your "false self," which pays the rent); (c) your "truth" (which coincidentally must correspond to the facilitator's set of "truths"); or (d) your "soul purpose" (definitely not what you are currently doing). It's up to you to sort out the charlatans from the sweethearts, the honest from the disingenuous. Just remember to act earnest, take everything at face value (including that airplane overhead everyone swears is "the mother ship"), and keep your wallet close at hand, because in "psychobabble land" you will be asked quite frequently to display your "prosperity consciousness."

actualize: manifest one's infinite potential.

affirmations: lies you tell yourself until you believe them. "I am smart. I am smart. I am smart."

are you okay with that?: does that mesh with your higher purpose and the rantings of your inner child?

Ariel: a common New Age name, most famously attributed to the late, great Ruth Norman, a wacky heiress who founded the even wackier Unarius Foundation in El Cajon, California, and who was best described as "Agnes Moorhead come back to life."

baggage: your accumulated "issues" and dysfunctions. Easily lightened by "becoming your own best friend" (aka "getting out of your own way").

be in integrity: acting from your higher purpose. Still confused? How about aligning with your "true calling"? Okay, let's make it simple: not consciously breaking the law.

boundaries: the capacity to give a firm resolute "NO!" to a hyped-up EST graduate.

channeling: (1) wisdom from people with incredible imaginations and a penchant for Elizabethan theatrics; (2) the New Age answer to speaking in tongues.

a Course in Miracles: Christianity with a New Age spin. Big with the Marianne Williamson (*Return to Love*) set.

don't let money stop you: what I've always said to potential ad buyers.

ESTies: annoyingly fervent EST graduates.

external validation: a source outside yourself affirms you are coming from integrity.

focus!: pay attention. Used anytime a workshop facilitator feels the attendees have forgotten who's the real star in this show.

follow your bliss: do what you love and the money won't flow.

functional: the triumph of the Protestant social prison over individual creative expression. There's something about the word that Michel Foucault would have found extremely distasteful. The current raging popularity of "functional" and "the functional mind-set" in America confirms Foucault's greatest observation—that modern society has finally succeeded in neutralizing our most "dangerous states." See "The 7 Habits of Highly Dysfunctional People."

the hidden kid: a marketing concept.

the higher self: your in-tune, in-touch, spiritually together self just waiting to be accessed if you only buy the speaker's book.

I have problems with that: your action or point of view violates a carefully worked out, ironclad, and rather PC view I have of the world.

I hear you: my hunch is that this staple started out as an anguished scream from an irate mother of ten—I HEAR YOU!—as one little rug rat screamed in holy terror. After several human potential seminars, she learned to modulate her response to a treacly sincere monotone: "I hear you." A new babble was born.

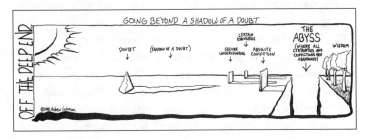

I honor that: I respect what you're saying. Probably the most annoying phrase of all psychobabble. Its roots are probably Native American by way of EST. The key here, as with most psychobabble, is to have an air of hushed earnest authenticity and seriousness about your delivery. Otherwise you won't "be in integrity."

I need my space: I need room to think, breathe, or cheat on my spouse.

I'm feeling resistance: how dare you disagree with me, MOFO!

integrity: the all-time, flat-out, most noxious concept of psychobabble. People have integrity when they are acting in accordance with someone else's moral and social code. They have no integrity when they step outside the other person's code. A word often used by people who have absolutely no integrity in some buried part of their life. When your lover starts tossing this word around, start heading for the exit.

intuit: voodoo intuition. "I intuit you're holding on to something."

EST

PERHAPS YOU KNOW SOMEONE WHO'S DONE EST.
Perhaps you've been asked by a "sponsor" to join about 500
other smiling people in some hotel banquet room who are all
genuinely eager for you to "get it"—if you first fork over a sizable wad of cash. Perhaps this experience reminded you of
some cheesy born-again Christian revival with overtones of a
high school pep rally or, worse, a corporate sales conference.
Perhaps you've experienced none of this but want to learn
more. Well, read on.

acknowledge: contrived ESTian verb to convey recognition
of another's point of view. Used in lieu of "I understand" or
"that's cool, dude." Example: "I acknowledge what you are
saying, Joan."

assholes: those who've yet to "get it"; i.e., drop their "social
act" and buy into the ESTian party line.

EST: Erhard Seminar Training, a ridiculously overpriced
human potential process named after a former used car
salesman, Werner Erhard (aka Jack Rosenberg). It amounts
to psychological boot camp for the masses. The popular
"training," as "ESTies" call it, features potty deprivation,
long-winded lectures, and a major league sales spiel. The
name (and its founder) came to carry so much "bag-

→

irony: one of the seven deadly New Age sins.

issues: (1) deep psychological difficulties best resolved through
hugely overpriced workshops or therapy (e.g., "It appears you
have issues with your mother"); (2) a very effective come-on
used by facilitators and therapists across America.

male bonding: homoerotic drumming for straight men.

newage: pseudospiritual garbage. Rhymes with "sewage."

past life regression: you and 10,000 other people were Cleopa-
tra in a past life.

a place of: really annoying phrase used in myriad ways: "she's
coming from a place of strength," "a place of balance," "a
place of serenity." Help!

poverty consciousness: I think I'm poor, I know I'm poor, I am
poor, damnit! A mental hang-up easily alleviated by taking an
even more expensive workshop.

gage" of its own, it's been changed to "the Forum." The perfect path for yuppies and spiritual kindergarteners so shut down they need something this crass.

est: how ESTians want you to spell EST. I clearly don't get "it."

the Forum: EST stripped of any pretense of spirituality.

got it: understood the teaching. "She got it."

the Hunger Project: ESTian version of social action that can be summed up in one principle: if we just change our thinking about scarcity, there will be plenty of food to feed the hungry by the year 2000. There's three years left, and last time I checked, several million people were still starving.

I-statements: I acknowledge. I take responsibility. I am coming from integrity. I do. I don't. Is it any wonder that Tom Wolfe opened his seminal essay on the "Me Generation" with a scene from EST?

it: the understanding that you and only you are the architect of your own destiny. Drives Christians nuts.

the Source: Werner Erhard.

take responsibility: Mom, Dad, and God can't help you now, buddy.

try: never ever use this word around an ESTie. You either "do" or you "don't." Understood?

the Weekend: what graduates affectionately call EST. Ready to sign up?

---

process: a mildly annoying verb that means to work out one's mental and emotional "stuff." Usually takes two or more people and a whole lot of deep, earnest yakking. Also a noun: "I respect your process," your schtick, the way you "do life."

reality check: are we getting a bit too woo-woo here?

rebirthing: pricey hyperventilation.

safe space: one of those really yucko terms psychic facilitators use that makes your skin crawl. Something to do with a workshop situation where you are free to explore "who you really are."

service: a word psychobabblers use to draw attention to themselves while appearing completely selfless. "I provide a necessary service to clients going through major spiritual transitions."

share: how a psychobabbler speaks. "I'd like to share something

The 7 Habits of Highly Dysfunctional People

MY HOMAGE TO STEPHEN COVEY, AUTHOR OF *THE 7 Habits of Highly Effective People* and father of nine children (it makes you wonder—on a planet that's grossly overpopulated, how can having nine kids be considered "effective"?).

One of the most popular (and overused) terms of the last decade is "dysfunctional." I don't know any Americans who have not characterized their families, their relationships, their lives, as somehow dysfunctional. As the joke goes, they held a convention for functional people, and both of them showed up. Interestingly, European families do not even use the concept. They've been around long enough to realize that "dysfunction" and "family" go together quite naturally, like wine and pasta. Why bother trying to change it. After years of trying to fit a definition of "functionality" I was never actually given, I've decided to throw out this hopeless quest for Protestant social conformity and embrace my dysfunctionality in all its wondrous, creative complexity in the hope that you too will see the light—and just give up. Here's how:

1. **Always be late.** If you really want to show that you are dysfunctional, be late. I have practiced this principle for years with great success (that is, if you define "success" as a complete "sabotage" of one's goals in life). Here's an easy way to remember it: "Reverse Vince Lombardi." Lombardi, the legendary coach of the Green Bay Packers during their heyday in the late '60s, demanded that all personnel report to any meeting 15 minutes early. This became known as "Vince Lombardi Time." "Reverse Vince Lombardi" simply says you must be at least 15 minutes *late*. You are then sure to consistently piss everyone off. A second way to ensure that you are always late is to leave at the time you are supposed to arrive. That way the appointment time has some real meaning for you. This is a favorite tactic of Geminis like myself, who assume they can magically transport themselves clear across town to an appointment, neglecting the real-world time-bound logistics involved. In the future, when we really will be able to transport ourselves telepathically, this argument will no longer be valid. For now, simply repeat my sacred motto: "Listen for whom the bell tolls; it tolls for them."

→

2. **Harbor major regrets.** Since life is really a series of losses and failures (rather than "lessons," as the psychobabblers would have you believe), it is important to continually work over in our heads where we really screwed up. This constant replaying of painful memories has a very important function for dysfunctionals: we never forget what losers we are. Remember: guilt is a great motivator. If you really really regret something, it will motivate you to do it again.

3. **Blame is the game.** Contrary to what you have been told, most foul-ups in life are caused by other people. As any basketball player knows, forgiveness is for chumps. And since life is nothing but a great big scoreboard, marking achievements and failures, it is absolutely critical to determine who screwed up so you can blame them. This way, you don't get points taken away from your own score when time runs out.

4. **Express your rage.** Rage is good. Repeat: rage is good. Therapists, human potential people, and the Prozac National Front all seem to have a thing against this rather useful emotion, but not we dysfunctionals. Rage is an incredible catharsis, and if you've grown up with a lot of craziness, it brings back all those exciting, adrenaline-pumping moments of yore. Plus, it allows you to act out your favorite Hollywood movie. I prefer Bette Davis scenes, but the choice is limitless.

5. **Fear and loathing.** The great thing about fear and loathing (especially self-loathing) is that it immediately puts you on the wavelength of most of your fellow humans. And, just as important, it puts you in the proper frame of mind for reading Kafka.

6. **Vengefulness.** Forget that useless rhetoric about how "love (or success) is the ultimate revenge." There is nothing like good old "getting back." I mean, how are they to know that they really did a number on you? Do you think the perpetrators of ill will really care that you have now lost 100 pounds? Do you think they will apologize for calling you "FAT"? Or a "loser." Or a "user." Or an "underachiever." Or "ugly." Or for thinking you weren't up to their standards. You need to teach these people a lesson. Otherwise, how will they know?

7. **Victimization.** Life has been very unfair. People expect so much of you, but you just aren't up to it, right? They just don't understand. But I do. Once you have mastered the →

previous six habits, the last one will fall naturally into place. As naturally as applying for food stamps, or SSI, or workers' comp. You have been seriously harmed. It's time to get paid for it.

That Was Zen, This Is Tao

IN THE BROADER SPIRITUAL LIFE OF AMERICA DURING the last three decades, no two words have enjoyed greater notoriety and concomitant misrepresentation than "Zen" and "Tao." Americans who have absolutely no concept of even the simplest elements of Zen meditation claim to grasp what Zen means. Maybe they've read *Zen and the Art of Motorcycle Maintenance*. Or *Zen and the Art of Writing*. Or *The Zen of Cooking*. Or maybe they've described something as "Zen." "Oh, that painting is so Zen." Or, "She's so Zen, you know." The true, ineffable meaning of the term, which in its highest form is understood best in the very act of zazen (sitting meditation), is lost. The same applies to Tao. Do you believe in a particular religion? "Oh, I'm a Taoist." I see. What's that? "Oh, you know, I really believe in going with the flow." Beautiful. Can you describe it further? Silence. Perhaps a fitting answer, but it's not going to help the uninitiated understand your point of view. And neither will *The Tao of Pooh*.

with the group. I was processing with my birth vehicle today when I realized I was projecting a lot of hidden anger from a lot of unresolved emotional baggage around fear of rejection from Father."

soulmate: (1) the best available partner with whom to share life's roller-coaster ride; (2) the projection of your perfectionist, hopelessly idealistic dreams.

stuff: the accumulated "baggage" of hang-ups, resentments, and neuroses. Aka "issues."

surrounded by light: the universe loves you just the way you are. Now rise up and give someone a hug.

thank you for sharing: how a facilitator gets in the last word after someone's share.

touchy-feely: (1) any group that expects you to gladly receive hugs from people you dislike. (2) a pejorative term for psy-

How to Talk American

chobabblers and their processes. Now used to describe every-thing from workplace sensitivity training to the 12 Steps. Origins? Imagine Fritz Perls and Abraham Maslow sitting in a hot tub at Michael Murphy's Esalen back in the '60s.

use your words: particularly effective with wife abusers.

victim: usually refers to what your parents did to you way back when. All psychobabblers have been victims at one time or another but are now "workin' it out."

what are you holding back?: you've got some excess "baggage" you want to let go of. Or, I want some of your money.

what I hear you saying: I don't really hear what *you* are saying. I hear how *I* think you ought to say it. A device to get the questioner to speed along so the facilitator can speak some more. Common on psychobabble talk radio.

woo-woo: an outsider's term for any kind of unconventional spiritual belief. Now embraced by New Agers as a self-deprecating preface to a statement. "This will sound kind of woo-woo, but I have this strong feeling we met in a past life."

you deserve it!: cloying, false-sounding encouragement from facilitators, who are usually talking to themselves.

Rainbow Nation

EVERY SUMMER, AROUND THE FOURTH OF July, thousands of slackers, Deadheads, aging hippies, and otherwise "normal" folk head to some part of the American wilderness and partake of the yearly Rainbow Gathering, a community built loosely around drugs, nudity, lots of dysentery, and a gross perversion of Native American spirituality. Since its beginning in the early '70s, "the Gathering" has created its own lexicon and rituals. Here's what I discovered on a recent visit.

A-camp: a checkpoint outside camp where all alcohol is officially confiscated and then unofficially consumed by righteous, rowdy, and gnarly men of the woods.

bliss cup: a makeshift homemade cup or bowl to eat, drink, or mooch from.

Bus Village: where buses, RVs, campers, and the people who choose to live in them are kept.

CALM: the Center for Alternative Living Medicine. The first aid tent. Yes, they also have a Western M.D.

crestfallen chickie poo: a chickie poo who has been used and abused by a High Holy brother. She eventually evolves into a "Truly High Sister with a Bad Attitude."

Deadheads: one of the many nomadic tribes that fall under the Rainbow Nation umbrella.

dose me: give me some acid. "It's my birthday, dose me."

Drainbows: the supreme slackers of the Rainbow Nation. They take, take, take, and give nothing back.

the feather: a talisman giving you the right to speak. The Rainbow equivalent of the Native American talking stick.

fix my pipe: give me some pot.

the Gathering: an insider's term for the Rainbow Gathering. "You going to the Gathering?" In addition to the yearly event, there are actually small, regional gatherings around the country throughout the year.

granola fuck: very far off the beaten track.

the Great Spirit: God. Literally, "the union of father and mother." No baptism or holy communion required.

green energy: moola, cash, money.

the High Holies: the elders of the Rainbow Nation. Often used sarcastically.

International Rainbow Hippie Circuit Theory (IRHCT): a very heterosexual theory of highly evolved Rainbow Brothers and Sisters which postulates that the International Rainbow Circuit is based on the migratory patterns of the "chickie poo" (the young,

A Rainbow Brother

beautiful, teenage girl who is the hope of the world). The IRHCT argues that the entire Rainbow Circuit rests on "the hope of the chickie poo." Entire rituals are built around her. For example, come spring, at some of the early regional "gatherings," highly evolved Rainbow people start looking for the "reigning chickie poo" for the year. There is only one. And she gets elevated to the center circle at the Gathering (qualifications can include, but are not limited to, how many "truly high brothers" she's rejected). According to Heather Wakefield, associate professor of the IRHCT and director of the Rumor Control Bureau (i.e., she is a sentry watching for chickie poos in the Bay Area), the theory is based on the "development of a young woman from 'chickie poo' to 'blond twirler' to 'truly high sister' to 'the mother of all tribes.'"

kiddie village: where children live, play, and eat while Mommy and Daddy go out tripping.

Madame Frogs: one of the most popular tents at the Rainbow Gathering, where you can get mushroom tea day or night.

the magic hat: the Rainbow collection box.

the Main Circle: the town hall of the Rainbow Nation. And a great place to cut loose after popping a dose.

medicine: drugs.

om: Rainbow's equivalent of the Lord's Prayer, said before and after meals.

plug in: help out. "We need everyone to plug in."

Rainbow Brother: someone who is automatically supposed to be your best friend in the world because you have something he wants to scrounge—pot, acid, or a Snickers bar.

seed camp: an advance team that secures the water and the site and sets up the kitchen.

Shanti Sena: a plea for help and peace when someone gets out of hand. The running Rainbow joke goes: "Who is Shanti Sena?" Answer: "Anyone with a belly button." In other words, we are all peacekeepers.

6 up!: the rangers are coming. From the police practice of waking up bums on city benches at 6:00 a.m.

truly high brother: not your average Rainbow Brother. A mover and shaker of the Rainbow Circuit. A key quality is moral integrity; in other words, not taking advantage of "chickie poos." Interestingly, the path of your average Rainbow Brother to that of "truly high brother" mirrors that of the "chickie poo." Most brothers actually start out as chickie poos (they want to be cool and cute), but as their commitment to earth and community deepens (evidenced by their owning land, hooking up with a woman in her blond twirler or truly high sister stage for a long-term relationship of five years or more, a garden, beautiful kids), then they get to be a "truly high brother." Some men can become honorary "truly high sisters" (where they get initiated into "the wise fat woman's ways"). And some men can break the bonds with women altogether and become creatively sexual (i.e., gay), but there is generally little room for the latter option in the Rainbow system.

truly high brother wannabes: Rainbow Brothers who just don't have the moral fiber to cut it as a "truly high brother."

umbalaga: "the earth is our home." In practice, this means I can piss upstream and you won't complain, plus any food you brought along is automatically mine since it came from the earth, and, like, the earth is our home.

we love you!: the oft-heard Rainbow mantra, usually shouted when someone's acid starts kicking in and quickly forgotten once it wears off.

welcome home!: the banner that greets you on entering the Rainbow camp. Since most Rainbow children come from dysfunctional homes, the saying is quite apt.

San Francisco

IF I HAD TO DESCRIBE HELL ON EARTH, I'D POINT to San Francisco. "WHAT?" you shriek. "It's the most breathtaking city in America." True. "It's the most cosmopolitan city in America." True. "It's extremely progressive, gay-friendly, tolerant." True. "The weather is ideal; it never snows." True. "So what's the problem?" You just named it, kid.

San Francisco is so precious, so refined, so enlightened, it makes me queasy. It's so totally bourgeois, so totally wine-and-cheese, so totally unreal, it should be grouped with those other un-American places (Hawaii and Santa Fe come to mind) and declared an independent state, to be leased as time-shares to those motivational seminar people.

It should really be named St. François. Because San "François-cans" secretly yearn to be French. I mean, people here have their eggs and ham on *croissants*. They have Folies-Bergère knockoffs with names like Chez Paree and stores like La Parisienne selling French jewelry and gifts. No wonder French tourists love it.

This is the city that gave birth to imitation Left Bank Beatniks wearing berets and today's neo-Beatniks, still wearing berets. "Da mayor," his sartorial highness Willie Brown, thinks of himself as some erudite Francophile. In fact, he recently went to France to make Paris a sister city. This town even has French public toilets!

Despite its pretentions of class (Brasserie Savoy, anyone?), San Francisco does have plenty of characters (Jerome Caja, anyone?). From Survival Research to San Francisco Cacophony, it can occasionally tip the scale into genuine, full-tilt, Dada high weirdness (a sensibility that is also quasi-Parisian in origin).

Yet even bona fide San Francisco characters can be a bit unreal. It's as if the city needs a slap in the face from an old New York cabbie or a lecture from a South Chicago steelworker. Or maybe a few other seasons besides permanent spring. Think about it—only people who are completely out of touch with reality would plan their lives and their children's around the vagaries of the most active earthquake fault in this hemisphere.

Of course, San Francisco has the highest urban attitude quotient outside Paris, so it doesn't care if it's real or not or if it's

American or not. San Franciscans just want to make sure they receive the highest possible rates on their rental property on Potrero Hill.

Here is the language of "the good life." Here is a snapshot of bourgeois hell. Here is my beloved spiritual home.

Adolph Sutro: the city's first great populist mayor and builder of the Sutro Baths who successfully ran against the Central Pacific "Octopus" in the 1890s. The forces of compassionate public service and self-serving greed have battled here ever since.

the Avenues: where all the people who voted for former mayor Frank Jordan live. Conventionally known as "the Sunset."

Bad Boys Beach: cruisey gay nude beach near the Golden Gate Bridge.

the Banker's Heart: a hideous black granite sculpture in the plaza of the Bank of America building.

the Barbary Coast: legendary name for the Marina and Embarcadero areas of turn-of-the-century San Francisco, when it really was raunchy and bawdy.

Berserkeley: Berkeley, home of the University of California at Berkeley. Because of its legendary history of radical student protest, crazed hippies, and even weirder shenanigans since the '60s, the decade that made it famous.

the Big Four: Collis P. Huntington, Mark Hopkins, Charles Crocker, and Leland Stanford—four robber barons who made their fortune building the Central Pacific Railroad in the late 1800s and whose names live on in major city landmarks (the former Crocker Bank, the Mark Hopkins Hotel, the Huntington Hotel, and Stanford University in Palo Alto).

the Big Game: annually, Stanford vs. Cal in college football. Held the Saturday before Thanksgiving.

the Big One: the inevitable earthquake that will one day level the city and kill us all.

BMW: Basic Marin Wheels. Marin County houses the nouveau riche who escaped the city two decades ago and now wish they hadn't. At least they have an expensive car when making their time-consuming commute over the Golden Gate Bridge.

the Bonnie Baker: the Bay to Breakers. San Francisco's "Aren't we wacky? Aren't we zany? Aren't we multi-culti?" road race held every May.

breeders: heterosexuals. In general, this city's are the best behaved in North America, owing to the mistaken notion that they are in a distinct minority (even though they represent 75% of the population). The gay ethos is so pervasive here that some straight men unconsciously strive to look and act gay just to fit in. Then again, there are those "breeder" males who seem intent on being as boorishly obnoxious as possible in order to signal to "breeder" females that they are not, in fact, "fags." Like all such ploys throughout history, this really turns the "ladies" on.

the bridge and tunnel crowd: the kids from the East Bay 'burbs who swarm all the "cool" clubs on Saturday night. Lifted from New York.

the Brie to Bakers: held in Berkeley the same day as the Bay to Breakers. The difference is that you eat and walk slowly.

Bruno: the San Francisco County Jail at San Bruno. "He's cool, he did Bruno with me." Aka "County." Caveat: Neil Cassady spent two years here, 1958–60, for trafficking dope in North Beach.

buds, doses: how to greet someone on Haight Street. Alternatively, "bugs and roses."

buyers club: the Marijuana Buyers Club, where a terminally ill person in this pot-crazed town can buy weed "for medicinal purposes only." A state initiative now makes this practice legal. But, as Jay Leno observes, "If marijuana was truly medicinal, Jerry Garcia would still be alive today."

Café Hairdo: Café Fleurs. Owing to a late '80s article shot at Fleurs called "Hairdos of Castro Street."

Cal: the University of California at Berkeley. For the rest of the UC system, the town in which the branch is located is cited (e.g., UC Santa Cruz), but not here.

the Cardinal: nickname for Stanford University's sports teams. Once called the Indians, before political correctness changed all that. Ironically, the Native American who served as the mascot

was very disappointed to lose his job because he performed real Indian war dances during games. Caveat: one of the names suggested by the student body was the Robber Barons (recalling founder Leland Stanford). It was, of course, rejected by the administration.

the Castro: a Madame Tussaud's of '70s gay life. Take your straight husband for a stroll here, and watch how suddenly affectionate he becomes.

Castro clones: Gay look-alikes in denim jeans, work boots, and flannel shirts who prowl the Castro Street bars.

the Charmed Corner: office building at 2nd and South Park where many semisuccessful magazines once resided, including the "yupscale" cyber mag *Wired* and niche mags like *Cups, Boing Boing, Might,* and *Just Go!*

Chinatown express: Muni's #38 Geary bus, which heads from Chinatown to "the new Chinatown," the Richmond District. So named because of the large infusion of Asian residents into the Richmond in the early '80s.

the City: San Francisco—the cyber-gay-hippie-yuppie mecca that is dead set on looking fabulous at all costs. Well, you are, dahling, YOU ARE! However, its image as a tolerant haven for good-natured creative genius is being seriously challenged by the growing ranks of outright mean and abrupt real estate jerks capitalizing on the tightest rental market in the world. Aka "San Fran." Never ever *ever* "Frisco."

Coitus Tower: Coit Tower. Shaped like a fire hose nozzle. Financed by a woman with a big-time fireman fetish. Or so the story goes.

connectedness: a holdover New Age phrase still used by the city's Ecstasy Heads.

Critical Mass: a monthly gathering of the San Francisco bicycle tribe, which clogs Market Street in defiance of the prevailing car culture. Attendees are churchlike in their devotion to two-wheeled and otherwise non-fossil-fueled transport.

Di-Fi: Dianne Feinstein, the former mayor and current senator, known for shepherding through the ban on automatic assault weapons.

diggedy dank: really good.

850: 850 Bryant Street, the main San Francisco County Jail. Aka "Bryant."

the Emperor: Mayor Willie Brown, who defines "debonair" in a 1980s *Ebony* magazine sort of way. Or, rather, in a provincial, imitating-old-money sort of way. The man rides in a limo and wears a ring on his pinkie, after all. In contrast to the other prominent "new wave" mayor, Rudy Giuliani of New York, it is not clear what, in fact, Brown has done for the city except for promoting his sartorial splendor. It is clear that for a town completely lost in a bourgeois time warp, Brown is the perfect figurehead.

fascist: anyone to the right of the *San Francisco Bay Guardian.*

Five & Tens: East Bay residents (area code 510).

the Fog Belt: the area west of Twin Peaks.

the Forty-Niners: (1) the early settlers of San Francisco, who came west in 1849 in search of gold in the nearby Sierra Nevada foothills. (2) the local pro football franchise.

the Freakway: Brad Weiners's term for the Safeway at Church and Market, the most eclectic and culturally diverse supermarket in America. If you want a snapshot of what San Francisco is really all about, linger at the checkout stand here at any hour.

full on: quite, extremely.

fully: totally.

the Giros: the San Francisco Giants baseball team.

glamour slammer: the spanking new jail adjoining 850 Bryant.

the Glass Coffin: Twin Peaks, an over-50s gay bar on Castro near Market, surrounded by windows.

Goatee Gulch: columnist Jack Boulware's nickname for South Park, where the young, beat, and invariably goateed assistants to the assistant webmasters hang out and utter profundities such as "We did this and we did that and then whoaaaaaaa!" Also generally applied to the faux Beat thing sweeping the city. Aka "Info Gulch."

gourmet gulch: that part of Berkeley's Shattuck Avenue that includes among its pricey shops and restaurants Peet's Coffee and Tea, the Cheese Board Collective, and the restaurant that revolutionized California cuisine, Alice Waters' world-renowned Chez Panisse. Aka "gourmet ghetto."

the Granite Lady: the Old Mint Building on 5th and Mission.

grubbin': as a verb, to eat. As an adjective, delicious.

Haightball: a particularly intense brand of pickup basketball found in the Panhandle near Haight Street.

Harbin: Harbin Hot Springs, the quintessential hippie hot springs up in Middleton, where the Bay Area counterculture goes to chill out amid beautiful mountains, excellent trails, and flabby New Age couples floating each other in the hot pool. Aka "Watsu World," home of the "Watsu People."

HayWired: sardonic new name for Wired Ventures, the über-hip cyber company that brought you *Wired* magazine, the Hot Wired web site, and Hard Wired books, due to their unfavorable reception on Wall Street in 1996 and the concomitant media backlash.

hella: very, really, excellent, extreme. "I got hella food, you

hungry?" "I went hella fast to get here." The signature San
Francisco term.

hella sketchy: really weird or scary.

Herb: the late *San Francisco Comical* columnist Herb Caen, whose
bad puns and provincial observations entertained locals for
decades.

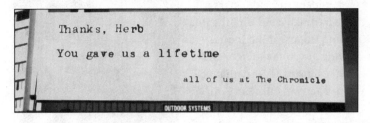

Thanks, Herb

You gave us a lifetime

all of us at The Chronicle

OUTDOOR SYSTEMS

the Herpes Triangle: the Golden Gate Grill, the Balboa Café,
and the Baja Cantina—three "breeder" pickup bars in Cow
Hollow. The only places in town where it's acceptable to order
a Coors Light.

the hills and the flats: two distinct socioeconomic and geographical areas of the East Bay.

Hippie Hill: a popular sunbathing spot in Golden Gate Park.

the 'Hood: the Lower Haight, where the crack- and smackheads
hang. Not to be confused with the lily white hippie and Euro
tourist scene on Upper Haight.

it's nice, but it's not San Francisco: the late Herb Caen's signature line about "the city beautiful," which perfectly sums up
an Old World mind-set of nights out at the opera, five-star
restaurants, and copious quantities of "Vitamin V."

Jerry's kids: grungy, nomadic, perennially broke creatures who
clutter Haight Street when the Dead are in town.

Joe: Joe Montana, former quarterback for the '49ers. Still deified
in these parts as well as in the town of Joe, Montana.

Jordie: Frank Jordan, the misfit former mayor of Baghdad by the
Bay, who looks as if he was plucked from a Kiwanis board
meeting.

the Jukebox: the Marriott on Mission. Aka "the Wurlitzer."

KGB: Killer Green Bud. A San Francisco, by way of Humboldt
County, word for "pot."

the King of Torts: the legendary San Francisco pugilist Melvin
Belli, whose main claim to fame (besides his many wives) was
defending Jack Ruby, the killer of Lee Harvey Oswald.

L.U.G.: Lesbian Until Graduation. Very East Bay.

the Lexus Freeway: Highway 280 on the Peninsula, a scenic cruise strip for the super-rich of Silicon Valley. Aka "the Mensa Freeway."

Louis and Jane: Louis Rossetto and Jane Metcalfe, the founders and publishers of *Wired* magazine, and the Bill and Hillary of the Digital Age. If you mention to anyone outside the city that you are active in the San Francisco cyberscene, the outsider will invariably ask, "Do you know Louis and Jane?" It's become such a de rigueur bit of bum-kissing that I regularly say that I "know" Louis Rossetto, even though my face-to-face contact with the man lasted no more than 60 seconds before Jane pulled him away with the line, "C'mon, Louis, we have to keep moving."

Lower Baja: the area between Noe Valley and the Mission; considered a real estate bonanza.

the Marina: the heterosexual flip side of the Castro. Aka "Breederville."

the Mayor of Castro Street: Harvey Milk, San Francisco's first openly gay supervisor and charismatic pioneer for gay rights. Along with Mayor George Moscone, he was felled by assassin Dan White.

the Mayor of Haight Street: Bernie Romano, the owner of Pacific Pharmacy, who's been a model of bodhisattva compassion and community support for over 30 years.

the Mish: the Mission District, the last true melting pot of the city. First an Irish neighborhood, it became Hispanic and in recent years has added Asian, black, poor white hipster, and Randy and Melissa Daar. Soon to be completely gentrified.

Mojo: *Mother Jones* magazine. Hard-hitting yet perennially broke leftie rag that secretly yearns to be *San Francisco Focus*.

Mondo: *Mondo 2000*, a drug cult that masquerades as a cyberzine.

Mount Tam: Mount Tamalpais, just across the Golden Gate Bridge in Marin County.

San Francisco Attitude

S AN FRANCISCO ATTITUDE COMES FROM A SINGLE source: the absence of four seasons. The city is like any gorgeous woman—never forced to face real hardship (major earthquakes notwithstanding). In equally cosmopolitan though less cosmetically beautiful cities like New York, the harsh winters, oppressive summers, and general abrasive edge of the metropolis make even gorgeous and rich locals a lot more humble. Nobody escapes some hardship in New York, but in San Francisco almost anybody can.

Multimedia Gulch: the South Park area south of Market, thought to contain the best and brightest in the burgeoning, if overhyped, field of multimedia. See "Goatee Gulch."

MUNI: the San Francisco Municipal Railway. Where "service" is a dirty seven-letter word.

Muniserable Railway: MUNI, because of the nasty, almost sadistic, tone of some of its drivers.

Nellie: Don Nelson, formerly an NBA star with the Boston Celtics, a troubled coach of the Golden State Warriors, and a pathetically troubled coach of the New York Knicks, now general manager of the lowly Dallas Mavericks. The blond Herman Munster made national waves with his incredibly sensitive treatment of Chris Webber, which sent the young basketball stud packing far away from the sight and liquored smell of "Coach Nelson." Though long gone, Nellie is not forgotten. Like Boston's Curse of the Bambino, the Warriors have self-destructed since the Webber fiasco, carrying on "Trader Don's" tradition of trading away major talent who soar to great heights elsewhere, most recently Tim Hardaway (leading scorer for the Miami Heat), Chris Gatling (leading scorer for the Dallas Mavericks), Tom Gugliotta (leading scorer for the Minnesota Timberwolves), Mitch Richmond (leading scorer for the Sacramento Kings), and, of course, Chris Webber (leading scorer for the Washington Bullets).

NEMO: bike messenger lingo for New Montgomery Street.

Nerd Hill: San Carlos, where many rich Silicon Valley geeks reside.

nickel-dime: the East Bay's 510 area code.

Berserkeley

Y OU'D THINK THIS NICKNAME WAS JUST SOME QUAINT neologism thought up to describe those crazy hippie kids trying to take over Sproul Hall. Oh, no. This town really does specialize in high weirdness. Over the last 30 years, Berserkeley brought us a homeless person committing hara-kiri in front of stunned spectators, routine suicides off the Campanile clock tower, a gunman who held an entire bar hostage, forcing men to sexually abuse women with carrots, a stressed-out physics grad student who clubbed his girlfriend to death and then set her body aflame, and, of course, the grisly affair of Brad Page and Bibi Lee. Bibi disappeared while jogging in a park. Brad was a major help in finding the body, but I guess he couldn't hold in his remorse, so he confessed not only to killing Bibi but to digging up her body a few hours later for one final in-and-out. And that's only the tip of the ice pick. According to John Marr of *Murder Can Be Fun,* who has an uncanny knack for chronicling this stuff, "The most bizarre" Berserkeley incident "happened in the unlikely locale of Stern Hall, the university's only remaining all-female dorm. Late one night . . . a freshman got up and went to the bathroom down the hall. In a stall, she quietly gave birth. Casually, she opened a window, tossed the baby out, and went back to bed. A woman returning from a late date heard cries and found the baby, still alive, beside the dorm a few hours later. . . . The reluctant mother was quickly caught, even though she'd managed to conceal her pregnancy from everyone including, quite possibly, herself."

Let there be no doubt how Berserkeley got its moniker.

the Niners: pro football's San Francisco '49ers. The only sports team San Franciscans are truly religious about.

no doubt: a way of agreeing without really listening. It beats "uh-huh."

Nowhere Valley: the Noe Valley neighborhood. *Leave It to Beaver* meets the Isle of Lesbos. So named from its moms-and-strollers Presbyterian provinciality.

the O.J. Projects: what white residents of Potrero Hill call the neighboring projects, where O.J. made his start into a life of violence, deception, and crime.

Pacific Graft and Extortion: PG&E, the local power company. Aka "Pigs, Ghosts, and Elephants."

the Painted Ladies: the row of pastel Victorian homes that line the east side of Alamo Square on Hayes Street Hill. The ultimate San Francisco "photo op," experienced by busloads of European visitors daily.

the Park: Golden Gate Park.

the Pink Palace: the city's most notorious low-income housing project (on Hayes), which was recently razed.

Polk: a gay hustler sleazoid mecca. Where the married queers from the Castro go to cheat on their husbands.

practice random kindness and senseless acts of beauty: like so many cultural innovations of the last four decades, this movement started in the Bay Area—Sausalito, in fact. Anne Herbert wrote these words on a restaurant placemat. They have since become a mantra for do-gooders around the country and the cornerstone of a growing movement known as "guerrilla goodness."

the Pyramid: the Transamerica Building. The most striking visual landmark downtown.

Rainbow: Rainbow Grocery, one of the last great natural food cooperatives in America now that corporations dominate the health food industry. Along with Zen Center and "the Freakway," one of the vortexes of city life.

riding academies: old Tenderloin term for brothels.

right on: you know what it means, and it's back in style in the city, but with a distinctly understated slacker pronunciation and delivery.

ring toss: any of the many predominantly male nude beaches in town.

Sacto: Sacramento, the comparatively conservative and low-key state capital to the north.

Sadcore: a new style of somber, lopey music now popular in the Bay Area. Alternately, "mope-rock."

San Francisco: nonconfrontational, nonintrusive, cyber-gay-hippie-yuppie mecca that is dead set on looking fabulous at all costs. Well, you are, dahling, you are! However, its image as a tolerant haven for good-natured creative people is being challenged by the growing ranks of outright mean and abrupt real estate assholes, capitalizing on the tightest rental market in the world.

the San Francisco Comical: the *San Francisco Chronicle*, the biggest joke in town. And, ironically, the one paper everyone reads—cover to cover. Frankly, I love it.

Sandalistas: an East Bay term for activists in search of a righteous cause. Named after southern Mexico's Zapatista National Liberation Army, whose insurgence reinvigorated an international network of human rights activists who'd been shopping for a cause since the civil wars ended in Nicaragua and El Salvador.

snivel: to bum or leach.

sniveler: a San Francisco slacker.

Snob Hill: Nob Hill.

soft drink: "soda" or "pop" in other parts of America.

SOMA: south of Market Street. Also known as "south of the Slot," for the cable car track that used to divide Market Street. Or "Little L.A." because it's flat, car-friendly, and gets more sunshine.

SOMA clone: gay, leather boy look-alikes south of Market.

Specific Whites: Pacific Heights, the upscale yuppie part of town.

Spree: Laetrelle Sprewell, the star shooting guard of the Golden State Warriors.

St. Maytag: St. Mary's Church, on Geary and Gough. Resembles a washing machine agitator (aka "Our Lady of the Spin Cycle").

the Stick: Candlestick Park, a windy, cold, yet beautiful stadium where the '49ers and Giants play. Now called 3Com Park at Candlestick Point after Silicon Valley's 3Com Corporation, part and parcel of the trend away from ballpark names that actually have some emotional resonance with the public. Others: Coors Field in Denver, FleetCenter in Boston, MCI Center in D.C., and RCA Dome in Indianapolis. In fact, there's been a rash of centers named after air carriers: United Center in Chicago, Delta Center in Salt Lake City, Continental Airlines Arena in East Rutherford, New Jersey, USAir Arena in Landover, Maryland, and the Air Canada Arena in Toronto.

supe: supervisor. San Francisco's version of a city council member.

the Swish Alps: a predominantly gay neighborhood in the hills above the Castro.

the Tenderloin: a neighborhood near Union Square that mixes opulence and squalor in equal portions. Named from the fine way the cops were treated by area madams and gambling operators.

the Terrific Triangle: Jones, O'Farrell, and Market streets in the old Tenderloin, where most of the heavy betting and petting traditionally went down.

tour de faux pas: Willie Brown's fabled yet ill-fated trip to Paris in November 1996, during which da mayor signed a sister city act with Paris, expanded trade and tourist opportunities, convinced leading AIDS researcher Luc Montagnier to locate a new AIDS research and treatment center in San Francisco, and called '49ers quarterback Elvis Grbek "an embarrassment to humankind" after the team's loss to Dallas (unbeknownst to Brown, Grbek's baby had undergone surgery for spina bifida the day before the game).

the Twelve Tombs: a '60s nickname for the Berkeley dorms.

the Twinkie Defense: the macroneurotic defense plea ("the harmful additives in my junk food diet made me do it") first used by supervisor and policeman Dan White, the assassin of Mayor George Moscone and gay supervisor Harvey Milk. It worked. White got only five years for manslaughter, spawning the largest gay riot in San Francisco's history. He later committed suicide, spawning decades of seriously dysfunctional behavior under the pretext of bad food choices.

the Twins: Vivian and Marian Brown, San Francisco's delightfully campy identical twosome who've come to represent the spirit of carefree consumerism that has now become this city's hallmark.

Upper Safeway: the no-man's-land between the Castro and the Haight. If you can see the enormous Safeway sign from your home, then you live here.

the Wall: the strip of cement on Sansome where bike messengers congregate between jobs.

wiggin': stressing or freaking out. Heard mostly in the Haight.

William Hurts: men who try to get laid by being pitiful, sympathy-inducing wrecks.

the Wine and Cheese Heads: the San Francisco '49ers. As opposed to the Cheeseheads, the Green Bay Packers.

the Wine Country: Mission Street between 5th and 8th, a prominent hangout for winos. A play off the real Wine Country, populated by gourmands and wine connoisseurs, in the Napa Valley.

the Zam: the *San Francisco Examiner,* an afternoon and Sunday paper. Tends to have more hard news than "the Comical" but is less beloved.

Santa Fe

While its raging popularity has died somewhat (along with the New Age mysticism and loose money that fueled its explosion), this charming town of adobes, opera, Native American art, and expensive restaurants still draws in the turquoise-jeweled Texan and Euro tourists seeking that slice of authentic Southwest *culture*. And Santa Fe—"the city different"—is all too happy to fulfill the fantasy. The following guide will help you navigate the treacherous terrain of Santa Fe style.

adobes: mud huts with big logs sticking through them.
Aspenization: the marriage of ostentatious wealth, bad taste, and skiing.
blue corn: sacred food sold as chips.
the Budge: Yogi Bhajan (pron. "Budgin"), whose towelhead

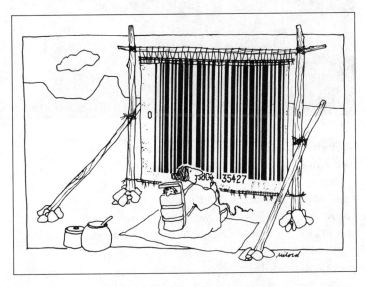

Sikh disciples live out in Espanola, in the heart of low rider country, but who are seen cruising around in their white Mercedes-Benzes.
canyon road: an artist-free zone. Great restaurants.

Georgia O'Keeffe: a famous bone collector.

haciendas: extra-big mud huts with even bigger logs sticking through.

the Indian Market: a photo opportunity.

Los Alamos: a '50s suburb where bombs were made.

the Plaza: the ultimate Native American theme park town square.

posole: overrated white corn.

pueblos: mud hut suburbs with barking dogs.

ristras: well-hung chiles.

Sanbusco: an underused marketplace noted for its pay phone.

Santa Fe: a marketing concept.

turquoise: a '70s fashion statement.

Seattle

B<small>ACK IN THE</small> 1980<small>S</small>, *E<small>SQUIRE</small>* <small>DESCRIBED</small>
Seattle as "a place so remote, so utterly far away from
everything, that your private demons will get lost trying to find
you." According to *Newsweek,* in the '90s everyone is "swimming to
Seattle," America's "most livable city."

And I say, good luck. It's over, baby!

But since many of you will persist, here's a handy guide to
Seattle-speak. While there is no distinct accent here, there are
unique expressions. If you drop a few, you will blend in like the
locals, of whom there are precious few these days, with the on-
slaught of Californicators.

Alki: by and by. Seattle was originally named "New York Alki." A
Statue of Liberty marks the spot on Alki Beach.

Aurora Ave.: Route 99, the fabled "highway to Alaska."

the Ave.: University Way in the U-District.

the B&J: Bruce Pavitt and Jonathan Poneman, former partners
in the pioneering Seattle music label Sub Pop (aka "Sub Plop").

Ballard: the old Scandie seafaring part of town.

Bucky: send a package by messenger. Named for Seattle's
Bucky's Courier Systems.

Bumbershoot: the English term for "umbrella" and the name of
a popular arts and music festival held every September. If you
carry a bumbershoot, you're not from Seattle.

Calvinists: disciples of the indie label pioneer and Beat Happening front man Calvin Johnson, of K Records in nearby
Olympia. Coined by the late Kurt Cobain.

Capitol Hill: where you live if you're young and hip and want
to be where "the action" is. Great bands. Lots of chicks.

carpetbaggers: an old Ballard term for yuppie families moving
into their traditional working-class community.

the CD: the Central District, Seattle's traditional African-American community. Near "the ID," the International District,
which has a mostly Asian population.

copcycles: cops on bikes. This unique Seattle innovation produces five times the arrest rate as cops in cars.

the Dawgs: the University of Washington Huskies.

the Diaper Run: the 10:10 a.m. ferry run from Bainbridge Island. Filled with mothers and babies on their way to Seattle pediatricians.

Dick's: a legendary Seattle drive-in burger joint. Made famous by the rapper Sir Mix-A-Lot in "My Posse on Broadway." Also known as a great place to spare change if you are one of Capitol Hill's omnipresent smackheads. Caveat: if you say "Get me a deluxe," anyone remotely near Capitol Hill will know you mean a Dick's Deluxe hamburger.

Dick's fries: any skinny, greasy, floppy fries are Dick's fries, no matter where they come from. "You gotta try some of these, they're total Dick's fries."

do the Puyallup: go to the State Fair in Puyallup. The ability to pronounce Puyallup ("pew-al-up") and another area town, Sequim ("squim"), is a telltale sign you've finally arrived.

the Emerald City: Seattle. It's rather appropriate; compared to gnarlier Portland, Seattle is prissy, clean, and good.

Evergreen: Evergreen State College in Olympia, where everyone says they knew Kurt Cobain. Most of the creative Northwest talent spent time attending or hanging out here, including Lynda Barry, Matt Groening, Bruce Pavitt, and, yes, Kurt Cobain. Students are known as "Greeners." Its mascot is the "geoduck." Unaffectionately known as "that damn hippie school" by locals.

Fauntleroy: the peninsula of Seattle.

Chief Sealth

THE MAJOR CITY OF THE GREAT NORTHWEST WAS named after Chief Sealth, whom Dr. Henry Smith described as "the largest Indian I ever saw, and by far the noblest looking."

Smith translated a speech given by Sealth to Isaac Stevens, the territorial governor, and a multitude of Indians and white settlers in December 1854. It was one of the most stirring statements ever delivered to the peoples of America. At one point Sealth is alleged to have said, "And when the last red man shall have perished from the earth and his memory among white men shall have become a myth, these shores shall swarm with the invisible dead of my tribe, and when your children's children shall think themselves alone in the field, the store, the shop, upon the highway, or in the silence of the woods, they will not be alone."

Over time Sealth evolved into Seattle. Ironically, in the town that took his name, most of Sealth's other prophecies have come or will come true (including the one about the Mariners' winning the 1997 World Series).

The Great "Grunge" Hoax of November '92

THE *NEW YORK TIMES* ACCOMPANIED A NOVEMBER 15, 1992, "Styles of the Times" article on "grunge" with a sidebar, "Lexicon of Grunge: Breaking the Code," defining the hip new "grunge speak, coming soon to a high school or mall near you." The piece translated groovy new terms for ripped jeans ("wack slacks"), an uncool person ("lame stain"), and hanging out ("swingin' on the flippity-flop") as well as other terms like "cob nobbler" and "harsh realm." The only problem was that the glossary turned out to be a prank. As first reported in the *Baffler*, the Great "Grunge" Hoax was perpetrated by Megan Jasper, at the time a receptionist at Sub Pop Records in Seattle, who had similarly duped the British magazine *Sky*. Understandably sensitive about being taken for yet another ride, journalists have treated any so-called Seattle vernacular with great circumspection ever since.

full city: the third rung up from the darkest coffee roast. Supposedly Starbucks is full city, though espresso scholars beg to differ.

Garlic Gulch: the neighborhood surrounding Our Lady of Mount Virgin Church in Rainier Valley. At one point many Italians lived here.

geoduck ("gooey duck"): a West Coast clam with an edible neck that has been compared to a "big giant horse cock." It's actually more like an elephant trunk. A local specialty.

the Giant Orange Juice Squeezer: the Kingdome. Also, "the concrete umbrella." And, most recently, the "Condome," thanks to an aborted plan to stretch a giant rubber sheet over the top to stop the leaking. When there's a large quantity of moss growing on top, it's known as "the world's largest Chia Pet."

going formal: wearing a clean flannel shirt.

the graveyard shift: coined when Seattle's early merchants voted to remove, in the middle of the night, graves buried under the original cobblestone streets. In New York City a variant evolved, "the lobster shift," for those who worked from midnight to 7:00 a.m., the same hours as lobstermen.

Green Lake: a residential area featuring a fine lake but surrounded by boring "breeder" yups and their requisite selection of pizza joints, brew pubs, and schlock shops. The place actually gets me depressed. Like San Francisco's Marina.

grunge: a marketing concept.

half-rack: a half-case of beer—12 bottles or cans. In Canada, a "half-rack" is what we call a sixpack.

haze: smog. Seattleites deflect questions about air pollution by calling it "haze," which is attributed to that convenient scapegoat, "moisture."

Hellvue: Bellevue. The Dead Zone. Residents parallel New York's "bridge and tunnel people." Symbolizes what many Seattleites most fear becoming—the Suburban "Scream."

the Herpes Triangle: three prime "breeder" pickup joints in the Lake Union area—Latitude 47, Triples, and Cucina Cucina.

Herschel: the first of many sea lions to start gorging on the easy pickin's of steelhead salmon trying to make their way through the Ballard Locks. Over the years, more than $1 million has been spent trying to dissuade the pesky sea lions, including blaring country music underwater, but nothing seems to work. Most recently, the National Marine Fisheries Service brought in "Fake Willy," a giant orca, to guard the area. It didn't work either. According to the Ballard Lock master, the most effective strategy has been to remove the most trouble-some sea lions and "ship 'em to Timbuktu."

it rains here all the time: Seattle mantra to ensure population control.

the Jet City: Seattle. So named because it is the headquarters of Boeing, which directly or indirectly employs 10% of all the people in the Puget Sound region.

the Kid: Ken Griffey, Jr., the outstanding power slugger and out-fielder for the Seattle Mariners. The son of baseball great Ken Griffey, Sr.

kinder-whore: slut-meets-baby-doll fashion style made famous by Courtney Love of the band Hole. Possibly originated with Carroll Baker in the movie *Baby Doll*.

the Lazy B: Boeing. Because the jobs pay well and the atmosphere is allegedly easygoing and cushy. Comes from a time when Boeing was flush.

the Lid Watch: when the police hang out on the west side of the Mercer Island Lid (tunnel).

loser: a badge of honor and term of endearment in slacker-infested Seattle. Marketed to great effect by Sub Pop Records.

lumber surf: a kind of "grunge" look—baggy shorts, hiking boots, and, of course, a lumberjack shirt. Like most grunge terms, this is used only by outsiders. In fact, no one ever makes a grunge or flannel reference in Seattle unless it is pierced tongue firmly in tattooed cheek.

the Magic Carpet: the free Metro bus zone downtown.

Meganisms: cheeky "grunge" terms Megan Jasper used to "prank" the *New York Times* (see "The Great 'Grunge' Hoax of November '92") that ended up becoming part of real Seattle vernacular. Example: "swingin' on the flippity-flop."

microserfs: the bastions of second-generation computer geeks

How to Talk Latte

Y OU'RE NOT OFFICIALLY AWAKE IN SEATTLE UNTIL you've had at least one double tall. And if you don't know what a double tall is, then, honey, you need one. From push-carts, to drive-throughs, to cafés, to McDonald's, espresso is on every corner in this town. For the uninitiated, ordering can be a journey through latte hell. Here's a short guide. And don't settle for Starbucks!

Cher sugar: Equal artificial sugar.

double no fun: double decaf latte.

no fun: decaf.

quad: quadruple.

skinny: nonfat.

speed ball, red eye: regular coffee with shots of espresso.

thunder thighs: double tall mocha made with whole milk and topped with extra whipped cream.

unleaded: decaf.

a Yankee dog with white hat on a leash: an Americano with foam, to go-go.

⚒ **Amount** (depends on your condition)

single (1 shot): you got laid through a *Stranger* ad and need a mild pickup.

double (2 shots): you woke up late, got ticketed for jaywalking, and need the basic gray-day maintenance plan.

triple (3 shots): you woke up under an ironing board in a necrophiliac's closet and need a jolt to bring you back.

quadruple (4 shots): your mother is coming for a week and you're opting for cardiac arrest.

⚒ **Strength** (depends on what's left of your stomach lining)

ristretto (with less water): your stomach's coated with iron and you gargle with battery acid.

→

lungo (with more water): you have ulcers and carry Tums in your pocket.

decaf or half caf: why bother. Drink herbal tea.

⚒ **Blends** (some places have an assortment. Get real, only anal retentives know their blends)

⚒ **Flavors** (dangerously close to ordering a hot milk shake; we don't advise): almond, mint, raspberry, orange, hazelnut, vanilla . . .

⚒ **Types** (depends on your personality)

Americano (espresso mixed with hot water approximating a real cup of coffee): for pretentious poets who write computer software.

espresso (hot pressurized water forced through ground coffee beans; "rapid" in Italian): for type As with tiny fingers.

cappuccino (one third espresso, one third steamed milk, and one third milk foam): for East Coast transplants with dreams of owning West Coast real estate.

latte (espresso with steamed milk, topped with milk foam): for bottle-fed baby boomers who've never been to Italy.

macchiato (shot marked with milk foam): for serious voyeurs with an eye for minimalism.

mocha (latte with chocolate): for lapsed 12-Step cocoa fiends with no sense of restraint.

⚒ **Moo Cow** (depends on how your jeans fit)

nonfat: you pop zippers and rip seams when you sit down.

2%: your pants roll up your thighs when you walk.

breve (half-and-half): your jeans are split and there's nothing left to lose.

soymilk: why are you drinking coffee?

whole: you wear baggy Levi's and don't give a shit.

⚒ **Toppings** (a clever way to imagine you're getting a full meal in a cup of java): nutmeg, cinnamon . . .

who slave for low pay and little recognition in service to the grand digital dream of Mr. Bill. So named by author Douglas Coupland (*Generation X*).

Moneydina: Medina.

Moo U: Washington State University, in Pullman. An agricultural college and Gary Larson's alma mater.

the mountain: 14,410-foot Mount Rainier. "The mountain is out today" is a standard refrain on a clear day.

Nice: Seattle is the Nice capital of America. Its motto: Be Nice. Seattleites are fundamentally scared that "people won't like us." As part of this culture of politeness, citizens bend over backward not to offend. Caveat: the smiley face was invented in Seattle.

Norwegian gasoline: coffee.

old growth: next to godliness.

Oly: Olympia. Where it's the bong water and a lot more.

Oregon mist: Washington rain that never quite made it to Oregon.

partly sunny: partly cloudy.

Pill Hill: First Hill, where the hospitals are.

potlatch: a Northwest Native American custom of lavishing gifts on guests. The source of today's "potluck," which means to lavish Jell-O and relish trays on unsuspecting visitors.

quarterback U: the University of Washington, which counts Warren Moon, Steve Pelleur, Mark Brunell, and Sonny Sixkiller among its former standouts.

rain: drizzle.

Red Square: the hub of radical student activity in front of Suzzallo Library, "U Dub."

the Roll-On Deodorant Building: the Second and Seneca Building, downtown.

Roslyn: the outdoor set for the TV series *Northern Exposure*. An influx of tourist schlock turned it into Northern Overexposure.

Sasquatch: the Northwest Native American name for Bigfoot.

scam: making out. Usually at a party, and usually when completely drunk.

scene: Seattle is the last "scene" of this millennium; i.e., "the place to be" for whatever reason the national media decide is important. The whole concept of a "scene" usually predates the consciousness of its existence. And the massive overhype given to the alleged "Seattle scene" killed the usefulness of the word for quite some time.

Seadawgs: the pro football Seattle Seahawks.

seamstresses: prostitutes in early Seattle.

Seattle: named after Chief Sealth, who saved some white folks from Chicago one winter on Alki Point. Over time they took all his land but honored him with some nice statues scattered hither and yon.

Seattle tuxedo: a clean flannel shirt.

Seattleite: a resident of Seattle. It is not spelled "Seattlite."

Skeletor: Washington's humorless senator, Slade Gordon.

Skid Row: derived from the practice of skidding cut logs down Yesler Street to Henry Yesler's sawmill on Elliott Bay. Caveat: the hill used to be so steep they finally pushed it into the bay, forming what is now Harbor Island, the second largest man-made island in America.

the Slugs: the Seattle Seahawks football team when they lose.

SNAG: a Sensitive New Age Guy. There are lots in the Nice Guy capital.

Space Noodle: a tall tourist attraction.

Starbucks: the McDonald's of lattes.

Tahoma: the Native American name for Mount Rainier.

thrifting: bargain hunting in thrift stores. This has been hyped as a unique Seattle phenomenon; in fact, it's a '60s and '70s trend that caught up to Seattle a few decades later.

U Dub: short for UW, aka "the University of Washington: Where Learning and Capitalism Hump."

vog: the combination of volcanic ash and fog. Until recently Washington's answer to smog.

yeah: the most important and tricky piece of Seattle vernacular. It's almost *Fargo*-esque but different (not as dorky, almost surfer-like) and best understood by example. "So you got mugged in New York?" "Yeah I did." "She is a total fox." "Yeah she is."

The South

With a bona fide, if educated, Bubba in the White House, the world has become quite fascinated with that netherworld known as the rural South, where, even since the advent of Wal-Mart and satellite TV, some folks still brew moonshine and eat possum. Here are some of the more colorful words your true blue Southerner might use if "ferners" like you weren't standing around trying to catch "the driff."

Warning: you will not hear many of these expressions at Juanita's in Little Rock or at some frat party in College Station. But many are still in use, often in the small, untrammeled backwaters of the South. Others are dated, but they reappear frequently enough to earn at least a cameo here.

about half-preacher: superficially pious. "Don't take a drink around Jim, he's about half-preacher."

Ad Lanna: home of the Braves. Aka "Hot Lanta."

an air: 60 minutes.

all: an important fossil fuel.

ammonia: a nasty kind of sickness.

another white belly up: another job finished. From the way a snake croaks.

Arkansas credit card: a hose for siphoning gasoline. Can substitute Oklahoma or any other southern state.

Arsh: a native of "Arlen" (Ireland).

ass cream: a milk-based frozen dessert. "Only two thangs I don't lack is yaller waddermillon and cawfee ass cream."

'Bama: Alabama. Often refers to the University of Alabama football team, "the Crimson Tide."

bird nest on the ground: a cushy job.

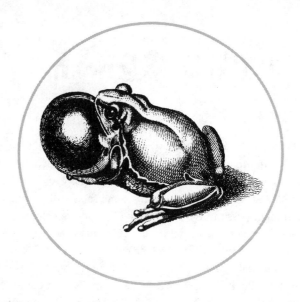

bligernt: quarrelsome.

bloodynoun: bullfrog. Heard in Charleston, South Carolina.

bookoo: a large quantity. From the French *beaucoup.* "He's got bookoo bucks" (he's wealthy).

Bubba: a white southern male. According to stereotype, often a redneck. Aka "good ole boy" or "cracker." Though "Beyill" Clinton is not the stereotypical Bubba (some say he's a "faux Bubba" or a "counterfeit cracker" due to his Ivy League education), since he entered the White House the term has become mighty popular. Examples: "Bubba factor," "the Bubba vote," "Bubba loves Rush."

buggies: shopping carts.

bumfuzzled: bewildered.

calf slobber: meringue on a pie or foam on a head of beer.

calm as a hog on ice: not calm at all.

chalk air center: where parents leave the kids when they go to work.

Chat Noogy: a Tennessee town.

cheerwine: cherry cola. Goes with mello Jell-O.

chiggers: tiny little insects that burrow into skin and *bite.* As opposed to "ticks" (which suck).

church: the focal point of religion, social life, and homophobia in southern small towns.

clean his plow: punch somebody hard. Akin to "clean his clock."

colder than a mother-in-law's kiss: very cold.

commonist: Communist. To be anything "common" is rarely a source of egalitarian pride in the historically elitist South.

cooter: a large water turtle. From the Carolinas.

couldn't stop a hog in a ditch: extremely bowlegged.

cracker: poor white redneck. See "Bubba."

crick: a small stream. "Uncle Coy twisted his neck when he fell in the crick."

cumanup: approaching. "Looks lack there's a storm cumanup around the bend."

dadgumit: a polite substitute for an unholy cussword. Don't ever get caught saying the original in the South.

the Death Belt: Arkansas, Alabama, Mississippi, and Texas—the states with the highest execution rates in the country.

the Deep South: Alabama, Mississippi, and Georgia. As opposed to the South as a whole, which includes everything from Texas to Tennessee to North Carolina.

Dew: Mountain Dew. Southern white trash soft drink of choice.

disappear like a blue jay on Friday: vanish.

Dixie: the area below the fabled Mason-Dixon Line, which historically has made up "the South." Literally speaking, it refers solely to the boundary between Pennsylvania and Maryland,

---

Southern Put-Downs

THE SOUTH HAS THE MOST ENTERTAINING WAYS of putting people down. In the tight-lipped Yankee North the speech has less of a rococo quality, less of the storyteller, more brute direct force. As in "Bug off!" Here are some classic ways Southerners describe someone they deem a complete idiot:

acts like his bread ain't done

a bubble off plumb

don't know which end of the fork to scratch his head with

et up with the dumb ass

a few ants shy of a picnic

he could fuck up a wet dream

he's a few barrels shy

he's [sic] don't have but one oar in the water

his belt don't go through all the loops

his elevator don't go all the way to the top

---

as established in the 1760s by two English astronomers, Charles Mason and Jeremiah Dixon. During the Civil War it took on a symbolic importance as the dividing line between the free and slaveholding states and thus between the North and the South. "Dixie" comes from this period.

doohickey: anything you don't know the proper name for. "Hand me that doohickey and hold still, Monk. I get chiggers off myself this way all the time."

dreckly: soon. "We'll be to the store dreckly."

easy as driving a swarm of bees through a snowstorm with a switch: completely useless or futile. Very hard.

enough to make a buzzard puke: offensive or distasteful.

eye deer: a thought or notion. "Do yawl have any eye deer where the spar tar is on this veehickel?"

eye-talian: a native of Italy.

a face so long he could eat oats out of a churn: dejected, downcast.

fade barn: where farmers keep their food for livestock.

far works: you light them on the Fourth of July.

fard: when your employment is no longer deemed necessary.

fern: not domestic. "Why, Aunt June's been to New Mexico and a whole bunch of other fern countries."

fill ya up?: after you eat dinner in the South, you're likely to be asked not whether the food tasted good or whether you're satisfied but, "Fill ya up?"

fishin': a ruse used by men to escape from the wife and kids.

fixin': getting ready to do something. "I'm fixin' to cook supper." A catchall term used frequently.

freaknik: the annual spring break pilgrimage of thousands of African-American college students to Atlanta.

gee-haw: connect with. "'The National Democratic Party just does not gee-haw with the main street voter in the South anymore,' said Mr. Coverdell, who ousted Wyche Fowler, Jr., a Democrat, in 1992" (*New York Times,* 10/8/95).

gimme a dope: give me a Coca-Cola. From the origins of the soft drink, when it contained trace amounts of cocaine.

gimme a holler: give me a phone call. Or "holler back at me."

goober: peanut. Aka "paynut."

good ole boy: polite form of "redneck." So popular that good ole boys now refer to themselves as such. "Yeah, that Fred, he's a good ole boy." Aka "cracker."

got a hitch in my get-along: saddled with a minor ailment.

🦆

grab a holt: get a grip, or hold, on an object or concept. A variation is "get a holt." As in, "I kept calling, but I never could get a holt of him."

grinning like a fox eating yellow jackets: a smile caused by inconvenient circumstances.

gubment: the machinery through which a political unit exercises authority.

Gullah: the remnant of the "Plantation Creole" spoken by the black residents of the Sea Islands off the coast of Georgia and South Carolina. This was the language spoken by African Americans during their first two centuries in this country. The Gullah word *njam* gave birth to the American "yam."

hard: recently employed.

Hartsfield Intergalactic: the Atlanta airport.

hayul: the opposite of heaven.

he can't walk and chew gum at the same time: awkward, uncoordinated.

he daddied that child: he's the illegitimate father.

he learned to whisper in a sawmill: he is easily overheard.

he lives so far out in the country, he has to walk toward town to hunt: a "genu-wine" backwoodsman.

he won't lie, but he'll bend the hell out of the truth: your standard southern politico.

he'd argue with a milepost: a very quarrelsome individual.

he's as tight as a bark on a hickory log: he's real cheap.

hey y'all: an Atlanta greeting. AKA "Hi due."

hidy: hello.

the higher a squirrel climbs the tree, the more rifles that can be aimed at its backside: a word of wisdom to aspiring Bill Clintons.

hipbilly: a hillbilly who smokes pot and may also be into "alternative music."

his eyes popped out like a stomped-on toad frog: aghast.

hoecake: cornbread. Aka "batter bread," "egg bread," or "corn pone."

hogmatism: the genuine belief in the supremacy of southern bar-be-cue.

hominy: a question of quantity. "Hominy deer yawl ketch?"

hot as a June bride in a feather bed: real hot weather.

I was driving one of those old drunk cars: Said after getting out of jail for DWI. Alternately, "I got a DWI last week for not having enough blood in my alcohol stream."

**if I ordered a trainload of sons of bitches and they just
sent him, I'd accept the shipment:** the man in question is
a major league jerk.

in high cotton: I'm in heaven. I'm a happy camper.

it's as easy as shoofly pie: very easy. The southern version of
an expression heard all over the U.S. Just change the object to
fit the region. In a northern state you might say, "It's as easy
as loganberry pie."

it's getting drunk outside: one is totally wasted, as if what
changes about one's perspective while drunk is exterior, not
interior. A favorite of hard-core southern inebriates.

Jew-lie: July.

juke joint: dance club.

lack: (1) similar to. "We used to have a satellite dish just lack
yawls only different." (2) be fond of. "I lack Ack, and Tina too."

Loosyana: the state just south of Arkansas.

lyberry: where books are kept.

Mackdonnell's: the home of the golden arches.

Manassas: what Northerners call "the Battle of Bull Run." Understanding how Southerners label the key battles of "the
War" will help avoid any serious friction while in southern
company. Other battles: "Sharpsburg" ("Antietam" in the
North) and "Murfreesboro" ("Stone River").

mash: push or press. "Mash that button."

mess: a quantity of something. "Mike made a whole mess of collard greens for supper."

might could do something: essentially the southern safety
net at work. Roughly, more likely than not, but I don't want to
commit. See "North Carolina."

minner paws: the change of life. "Bobby says her mama's mustache is caused by minner paws, but that sounds fishy to me."

Miss Sippy: the biggest river in the South.

moxican: a moccasin snake.

Murkin: a U.S. citizen.

naff: an instrument for cutting. "I got me a pocket naff and, for
special occasions, a sneaky ole boot naff."

negra: a negro, black person. Aka "colored."

Nogs Vull: another Tennessee town.

Northerner: anyone from Illinois.

okra: manhood. As in, "Look at ole Clyde, struttin' around his
okra for the ladies."

Ole Miss: the state of Mississippi.

par: a source of energy. "You think 800 horsepar is too much for a 12-foot bass boat?"

piece: a short, unspecified distance. As in, "You jist head down the road a piece, and yewl hit it."

poach: an open room attached to a house. "Do you want this warshing machine on the front poach or the back poach?"

poke: a sack. Like "a pig in a poke."

pot likker: the water used to cook collard or other hearty greens. The custom is to dunk one's cornbread into it. Good eatin'.

rarer than a hen's tooth: truly unique. Especially since hens have beaks, not teeth.

RC and a moonpie: wine and dine southern style.

right as rain: it's natural, so it must be right.

rivrin: a holy man.

roll Tide: an expression heard at 'Bama football games.

S.O.L.: Shit Outta Luck. "Boy, it looks like yer S.O.L." "You got that right."

sacka ass: a bag of ice cubes.

sane: a proverb. "My uncle Raford told me that ever time he loses a fish or misses a shot he just remembers that old sane, 'Never counts your chickens before they cross the road.'"

scoot: slide over while seated.

seeing double and feeling single: inebriated and incautiously carefree.

sexist: a superlative term southern women use to describe attractive southern men. "Load, Tammy, ain't that Bubba just the sexist thang you ever did see?"

shar: a shower.

she swallered a waddermillon seed: "the wife" is pregnant.

skeer: an unsettling experience. "That old moxican sure gave me a skeer."

skeert: frightened.

Slitz: Schlitz.

snake doctor: a dragonfly. Used in Tennessee.

sombitch: son of a bitch.

Soo-boo-roo: the type of Japanese car I drive. To my surprise, gaining in popularity in the backwaters of the South. "Charlie's got three of them Soo-boo-roos. Swears by 'em."

sorry: inferior quality.

spar tar: an extra wheel, used when you have a flat or to hold flowers in the front yard. Planters should be painted white unless you have fake flamingos, in which case either hot pink or chartreuse is acceptable.

spoor: a condition associated with a lack of funds. "I'd get me one of them new pocket fisherman if I wasn't spoor."

squealing like a stuck pig: bitching or moaning, or really yelling and "hollerin'." "Shut up, Junior, you're squealing like a stuck pig."

srimp: shrimp.

stars: how one walks to the second floor.

surp: the sweet stuff you pour on pancakes.

tamar: the day after today.

that dog'll hunt: that will work.

they are just latherin' you up for a shave: don't think the favorable publicity will last.

thianks: thanks.

thiankyou: thank you.

tire: tower.

toe up: extremely upset, overwrought.

tommytoe: a juicy red nightshade.

tump over: turn over and dump.

UPPS: in the South, UPS is not pronounced like an acronym but like a regular word. "Honey, there's an UPPS truck out front. Are you spectin' anythang?"

visitin': visiting. The true test of a Southerner. See "The Fine Art of Visitin'."

wacky-backy: marijuana. Aka "left-handed cigarette."

waddermillon: a large, juicy summer fruit that grows throughout the South.

the War: the Civil War. The only war that really matters to a Southerner. Aka "the War for States' Rights," "the Great Rebellion," "the War for Southern Freedom," "the War Between the States," or simply "Mr. Lincoln's War."

Watt House: the Oval Office.

well, if that don't beat all: isn't that something.

who's ya up to?: what are you doing? What's going on?

whup: spank or defeat (as in sports). "Vandy's gonna whup Memphis come Saturday."

yawl: second-person plural pronoun. Possessive: yawls. There is no singular. "I'll keel yawl if I ever ketch yawl messing with mah bass boat agin."

youngens: children.

yup: this all-purpose word is the same as "yes" but must be said with head hanging down, hat in hand, possibly kicking at some dirt, shooting out a spit now and then. Just a way of saying that nothing is going to phase this good ole boy, no matter how excited everyone else is. "Well, that nuklar bomb they dropped over at Toad Suck made a purty big noise." Your reply? "Yup."

Yurp: the continent where you'll find France, Germany, and Spain.

"Modern" Arkansas

"We're a contankerous, ingenious, mule-headed, generous, forgiving people (except when it comes to Texas)."
—DIANN SUTHERLIN SMITH, AUTHOR OF THE ARKANSAS HANDBOOK

Arkansawyer: the correct name for someone from "the Natural State." "Arkansan" is fine if you're a "ferner." And don't let any city newspaperman tell you any different.

Arkie: a pejorative form of "Arkansawyer," though sometimes embraced by natives as a term of endearment among themselves. "He's an old Arkie, he's okay."

been to Memphis: I've seen it all.

bunking party: a slumber party.

Chicken Man: Don Tyson, the wealthy, well-connected, coke-lovin', Clinton-backing, and recently convicted Frank Perdue clone, who lobbies hard for less stringent regulation of his massive chicken, pork, and fish processing industries.

doin' alright?: a frequent Arkansas greeting. It does not mean "My, you look awful, is something wrong?" It's more like "How's it going?"

Fayettenam: Fayetteville, home of the University of Arkansas, where the students party so hard that surviving socially and academically is as taxing and precarious as fighting a war.

fish: a species of aquatic craniate vertebrates whose sole purpose on the planet is to be caught by Arkansas fishermen and later frozen. Rarely eaten.

forty minutes of hell: Nolan Richardson's term for the intense
  pressure defense used by his Razorback basketball teams.

the giant killer: congressman Dale Bumpers, who in his political career has knocked off legendary Arkansas governor Orval
  Faubus (instigator of the "Crisis at Central High"), the ever-
  popular Winthrop Rockefeller, and the formidable J. William
  Fulbright.

hawg wallow: pigpen.

the Hogs: the University of Arkansas Razorback sports teams,
  which Arkansawyers are positively
  fanatical about. As the sayir
  goes, "If you ain't a
  Razorbacker, you
  ain't shit."

I'd borrow ye some: I'd
  loan you something.

little but loud: the way Arkan-
  sawyers describe the Texarkana native Ross Perot, who called
  Arkansans "Chicken Pluckers" in one of his infamous "infomercials."

the Little Rock Nine: the nine black students who tried to
  enter Little Rock's Central High School in 1957, when it had to
  desegregate under court order.

Nolan: no need to mention the last name because everybody in
  the state knows him—Nolan Richardson, coach of the Razor-
  backs basketball team.

out of pocket: hard to reach.

Puke: a resident of the neighboring state of Missouri.

Roger: Roger Clinton, Bill's younger brother, who's a recovering
  drug abuser and lovable if mediocre crooner. Roger is invariably trotted out at campaign time to show how serious Bill is
  about tackling drug abuse.

Slick Willie: Bill Clinton. They called him that for years back
  home before the national press caught on.

the Sugar Shack: a state building used for wild parties during
  the Clinton years by Secretary of State Bill McCuen, who was
  known for riding a Harley and employing a bevy of rather
  sexy female assistants.

tempo: a Little Rock term for the combination of marijuana and
  crack cocaine. Known as "primo" in nearby Alabama.

thank God for Mississippi: Arkansas is invariably ranked
  among the worst states in the country in several categories,

including teacher education, poverty, and environmental protection. But Arkansawyers laugh because they can always point to Mississippi, which invariably ranks worse.

t'ninecyest (pron. "t-nine-see-ist"): the tiniest, nicest. Often used by country men to describe female body parts.

Tyson: Tyson Foods, the humungous chicken empire that employs half of Arkansas. The other half works at Wal-Mart. "Yeah, Steve, he's workin' over at Tyson now."

University at Last Resort: U.A.L.R., the University of Arkansas at Little Rock, a commuter school with a high percentage of students who couldn't make it elsewhere.

woo pig suuuuuueeeeeee!!: the ubiquitous pig call heard at Razorback games.

Kentucky

TECHNICALLY SPEAKING, KENTUCKY IS NOT PART OF the South; it was neutral during "the War." Still, its colorful vocabulary, sensibility, and, yes, accent, put Kentucky squarely in the heart of Dixie.

Dick Miller: all-purpose interjection. "Oh, Dick Miller!" The same as "what the heck."

George: good.

Hey Nicky: happy greeting from one Kentuckian to another.

Luv-vull: Louisville. Aka "Lousy Ville," though the town is pretty okay.

monkey time: let's roll. Let's go with it.

oilheads: people who drink a lot of whiskey.

the Run for the Roses: the Kentucky Derby.

that's monkey: don't give me that garbage.

Tom: bad. The opposite of "George."

the U. of L.: the University of La Grange, where the prison is.

Wally World: Wallace Wilkerson, a corrupt former governor.

Louisiana

LOUISIANA IS NOT A STATE. IT'S NOT ANOTHER COUNtry. It's another planet. In fact, it's its own solar system. You do things here you simply do not and cannot do anywhere else in America. The 24-hour bars, drive-up daiquiri stands, the outrageous excesses of Mardi Gras, and a history of colorful politicians and rampant corruption have given Louisiana the image of a decadent and lawless land. It's not far from the truth.

A combination of Cajun, Creole, black, and "Yat," the language that is spoken here is as colorful and lawless as the people who live here.

Americans: old Cajun term for folks who are not Cajun. If you ask anybody in Louisiana what their nationality is, they will never say "American." That is citizenship. One's nationality is French or Italian or Spanish, etc.

banquette (pron. "bonk-ette"): sidewalk.

bodacious: a marriage of "boldly" and "audacious."

boudin: dirty rice in a sausage casing.

Cajun: a slang form of "Acadian." Cajuns are also known as "coon asses," which was once a pejorative term but is now widely accepted.

Cancer Alley: the stretch between New Orleans and Baton Rouge because of all the chemical companies there.

catch: have. Especially in sickness. You don't just "catch" colds in these parts, you "catch a stroke," "catch a heart attack," even "catch cancer."

chank-a-chank: the music of South Louisiana, which is either zydeco (a black form, which uses items like washboards, and is better for dancing) or Cajun (a white folk form, using more accordion and fiddle). "We went chank-a-chank." Means we went dancing. Nobody "bar-hops" here.

chitlins: hog intestines.

crawdads: crayfish. Aka "mud bugs."

the crawfish circuit: the group of clubs, bars, and festivals that Cajun musicians travel from New Orleans to Houston.

cush-cush (pron. "coosh-coosh"): fried couscous. Served hot with syrup. A high school rallying cry in Acadia makes fine use of it: "Hot boudin, cold cush-cush, c'mon team, poosh poosh poosh."

earbobs: earrings.

foreigner: anyone north of I-10. What Cajuns used to call "Americans."

gallery: a porch.

get down: come on in, or get out of the car. This can be quite confusing to Northerners new to town. For example, if a pile of friends and I drive up to your house, and you're sitting out front, you'd say, "Why don't y'all get down." Or, "Y'all want to

TWO CAJUN GENTLEMEN, MILTON AND FAUNTLEROY,
are watching the ten o'clock news when they see footage of
a man standing on the edge of the roof of the tallest building
in Lafayette. "A tense situation downtown!" the announcer
says. "Stay tuned for details."

Milton turns to Fauntleroy and says, "I'll bet you $100 that
fella doesn't jump." Fauntleroy says "okay." Then the news
comes back on and the man jumps and is splattered all over
Jefferson Street.

Milton says, "Well, okay, you won the bet." But Fauntleroy
tells him, "Milton, I cheated. I seen all this already on the six
o'clock news."

To which Milton replies, "Well, I saw it too, Faunt, but I did-
n't think that fella was gonna jump again!"

---

get down?" That is, get out and take a break. A direct translation from the French *descend de la voiture*.

gumbo: the traditional Cajun soup of meat and vegetables,
thickened with okra pods.

hose pipe: a water hose.

King Rex: the king of Mardi Gras.

the Kingfisher: Huey P. Long, a famous governor and U.S. senator who dominated Louisiana politics in the 1920s and '30s.

lagniappe (pron. "lan-yap"): a small present or restaurant tip.

make: you don't "do" things in South Louisiana, you "make"
them. For instance. . .

→ **make the block:** go around the block. To someone trying
to find a parking place, you'd say, "Go make the block, then
get down and come in."

→ **make groceries:** shop for groceries.

→ **make a miscarriage:** have a miscarriage. Or if women are
talking in front of children, they might whisper, "She made
a miss."

→ **make a supper:** eat dinner.

Mardi Gras: the day before Ash Wednesday, the start of Lent in
heavily Catholic New Orleans. Aka "Fat Tuesday" in French or
"Tuesday of the Feast." Though it's redundant, N'awlins residents actually say "Mardi Gras Day."

the Masquees (pron. "mask-ay"): what black people in New Orleans call the frightening characters wearing masques come
Mardi Gras.

Old South Louisiana Expressions

With a dubba thanks to Jennifer and Ed Martin, authors of *Speaking Louisiana*.

alice tration: illustration. As Bev McClain can attest, "Jean Jacques Audubon drew good alice trations of dem birds."

all: petroleum. "Man, you betta fix dat leak in yo modor, you gonna leak all on de bye."

allo: hello. "Allo, Cher, you der?"

arryting: everything. "T-Monk, arryting you touch, you break!"

bad dare: in the rear. "Bad dare is where we seen dem neckin'."

ball: boil. "We gonna ball dem crawdads, so y'all come on over."

bat: clean oneself in water. "Boy, you betta take a bat before we pass by de church house."

bonjour y'all: New Orleans greeting.

bye: the bayou. "She live just across the bye from me."

cher: dear. From the French *chérie*.

chirren: offspring. "De chirren is gone to school in de fall to learnt to make dere names."

coil: summon. "Supper's on de table; coil dem chirren in here."

Crease Moose: the celebration of the birth of Christ. "At Crease Moose Papa Noel make a pass de ohms of de good boys and girls."

don: do not. "Don drop dat bebe."

donna buy ya: down at the bayou.

dubba: double. "Ahm gonna bet dubba or nutin."

dumata: a juicy red nightshade. "You put too much dumata in dat swimp creole."

erster poboy: an oyster sandwich with lettuce, tomato, and mayonnaise.

fo true?: seriously?

four michael: a laminated plastic covering. "Ahm gonna cover mah counta top wit some four michael."

gaga: a nosy person. "Ah tole dat ole gaga to shoo befor ah git mah shootgun."

guff: the Gulf of Mexico. "Ahm takin mah Lafitte Skiff down →

to de guff dis week."

hairline: the Airline Highway, a major thoroughfare through South Louisiana. "You jest take de hairline straight down to N'awlins."

halo, statue: a telephone greeting. "Halo, statue?"

harry: hurry. "Harry up wit dat gombo, ahm starvin' to det."

ion: press clothes. "Ah got to ion yo clothes."

jaws: jars. "Bring one of dose jaws of hot sauce to de table."

launch: the noon meal. "Beulah make me de swimp poboy fo launch."

loopey long: the Huey P. Long Bridge, the most dangerous bridge in America.

may-may!: but or well, from the French *mais*. Used as an interjection.

moe betta: a definite improvement.

muffalotta: Italian sandwich.

opital: a building for sick people.

paunch: poke. "Paunch de button harder if de Coke want come ut at de bottom."

peeve: to asphalt the road.

pleece: law enforcement personnel. "De pleece gon to make a pass by here if yo don't cam down."

pleet: a plate. "You can't have no pralines til you clean you pleet."

pooyie: expletive showing offense or distaste. "Dat was a skunk in de road, pooyie!"

roday: rodeo.

slug ranch: a tool used to change a car tire.

smot: smart. "You too smot boy, you betta learn!"

swimps: edible crustaceans. "Jimmy is en de guff to catch us some swimps."

teet: teeth. "If you eat all dat sugah, you gonna lose yo teet."

tied: exhausted.

tink: cogitate.

tole: past tense of "tell." "Ah tole you about dat already."

trimper: one who catches "swimp."

trow: propel through the air. "Trow me dat footbahl!"

true: through. "Ahm true wit you."

tunda: the loud noise that follows a flash of lightning.

udder: other. "It was in de udder year."

very close: dilated. "She got very close veins."

→

violet: raging. "He got violet when he saw his belle wit dem."

vote: a unit of electricity. "Dass a hunred-ten-vote socket."

who dat!?: the quintessential Cajun expression. Most frequently mimicked by foreigners. Also referred to as the "battle cry" of the N'awlins Saints pro football team. "Who dat say dey gonna beat dem Saints, say who dat!?"

wit: with. "Ah gonna take Maclin wit me to de sto."

year: organ that detects sensory vibrations. "Ah hafta scream in Donny's year for him to hear."

yestitty: the day before.

zinc: a cleaning receptacle. "Wash dem clothes in de zink."

N'awlins: New Orleans, "the City That Care Forgot."

Needle Nose: a local politician (he actually puts this name on the ballot).

neutral ground: the median strip. Or the grassy area between the sidewalk and the street.

oo yi yi: said when something is good or when it hurts.

parish: what the rest of us call "county." The Catholic influence is strong down here.

pass by: visit someone or to stop and go into. You also may hear "to make a pass." "We're planning to pass by this afternoon. Will yawl be home?"

poboy: a submarine sandwich.

put the gris on someone: put the evil spell on them.

save: put away. Applied to any situation that might require "putting away." I.e., when you're done drying dishes in Louisiana, you "save the dishes." When you're done mowing the lawn, you "save the lawnmower." You fold and "save" the clothes. As one New Iberian, Donald Akers, puts it, "I would never say 'put away the dishes,' it's a foreign language to me."

shivaree: a noisy celebration, traditionally to mock a newly married couple.

sleeping water: a bayou.

soyabeans: soybeans.

T (from *petite*): Louisianans put T in front of a name to indicate that the person is the junior or is shorter. Example: "T-Mout," state senator and candidate for governor Edgar Mouton.

Tweety Bird: Governor Edwin Edwards' nickname, given to him by the late Poogie Moity, a New Iberia city councilman.

Uncle Earl: the former Louisiana governor Earl Long.

the vapors: a cold or congestion. Also, a fainting spell.

Vic and Nat'lie: New Orleans TV characters who are known for their "yat" expressions.

where y'at?: how are you? Common in the 9th Ward of New Orleans and the Irish Channel.

who dats: Saints fans.

yats: pejorative nickname for the folks who live along the Irish Channel because of their fondness for "where y'at?" Akin to Pittsburgh's "yonzers."

your momma works offshore: common insult in South Louisiana, where many men work on oil rigs in the "guff."

North Carolina

THE GOOD FOLKS OF NORTH CAROLINA HAVE AN interesting way of talking—what a linguistic scholar might call "multiple modal combinations."

Here are some examples, which I encourage you to sprinkle into your already colorful southern speech.

affirmative word combinations: might could, might would, might should, might can, might will, might ought to, might better, might did, may can, may will, may shall, may could, may would, may should, may might, may did, could might, would might, ought to, should might better, may might can, might should better. "I wonder if we 'might could' get some candy?"

The Fine Art of Visitin'

VISITIN' IS SHORT FOR "VISITING," AND IT'S A national pastime in the South. Those of us from the urban North take our visits in short bites, usually on the phone, at a restaurant, maybe in the car on the way to an event. In the rural South there's no pressing agenda. The only thing you must do is go to work and make an occasional appearance at the local Church of Christ.

But visitin'? Now that's another matter. It's part and parcel of living in these parts. You can spot a local from a Northerner by the degree of visitin' in which they engage. A Northerner, mind you, is anybody who wasn't born in the South, even if they've lived here since they were three years old.

Northerners are easy to spot. They are usually looking at their watches or occupying themselves with other things besides visitin'. They'll invariably be in a hurry, talk fast, use your phone, pace the floor, light two cigarettes, and leave early. They'll do anything to distract themselves from the undulating rhythms of visitin'.

What Northerners can't seem to get is that you've got to ease into visitin'. It's like entering a hot tub. You slide in like there is nothing else to do in the world. You've got to slooow down. Slow waaay down.

If I was to create a map of the great visitin' capitals of America, the late Ethel Lane's house in Gamaliel, Arkansas, would rate in the top 10. Right here you have all the accoutrements that make for all-star visitin'. First, you have a porch, with a rocking seat built for two and a couple of chairs (one rocks, one doesn't). This is a great place to watch the promenade of cars and trucks that careen down Highway 101 between Bakersfield, Missouri, and Mountain Home, Arkansas. Yet this is but a prelude to what awaits you.

Once inside you have Ethel's living room, with several chairs (some rock, some don't), two couches facing each other, a rarely used TV, and, most important, hundreds and hundreds of photos and scrapbooks (great entry points for prolonged visitin'). The living room is a get-to-know-you visitin' place. You want folks to feel comfortable and provided for, but close enough to the front door to make a quick exit.

After the living room you have the kitchen table, with six →

vinyl chairs, a frequently used visitin' stop in the past but today used only on Sundays and holidays, when the relatives come by for a great big visitin' jamboree. It's basically a middle ground between the centers of serious visitin'. A place to stand up, nibble on some brownies or pecan pie, and get some coffee, milk, water, or pop to wet your whistle.

By now you've warmed up. Those who are privileged will be led to the real stuff, the sanctuary where the hard-core aerobic visitin' marathons commence: Ethel's back porch.

It's the old back porch, where the concrete still shows and the spiders still crawl out of the woodstack, that holds the magic. No fancy furniture. No paintings of nature. Only an old wood stove and five chairs (some rock, some don't). This is where you sort it all out. Ethel says she spends most of her time back here, a true sign of a visitin' veteran.

This gal's a pro. Even at her age she'll stay up late with the best of 'em. Outvisitin' the champions of visitin'. Ethel can wait because she long ago embraced a fundamental truth: There's Nowhere to Go and There's Nothing to Do. The hallmark of a Visitin' Buddha.

While visitin' seems like a harmless art, it does have its pitfalls. Sometimes you get caught in a visitin' vortex, unable to pull away or, even worse, totally lost with nothing to say. Visitin' has this way of casting a spell over the visitors, and they begin to feel there are no other priorities in life but staying $\rightarrow$

right where they are. This can be hazardous to businessmen who risk a little visitin' during noontime. It's like heading through a drive-up daiquiri bar. You're not sure how you'll perform the rest of the afternoon, let alone whether you'll make it back at all.

And there are some visitin' horror stories. For example, one time my friend Michael Lane was so engaged in visitin', he lost track of time and took a month to get out of the rocker. Another memorable episode involves two sisters over in White County who neglected to notice the fire in the kitchen while partaking of some serious midafternoon visitin'. "Mabel, do you smell something burning?" "Well, Irma, you know I can't smell a thang." "Since when can't you smell?" "Since last spring when I got that allergy." "Why, I didn't know that!" "Why, I thought I told you." "No, you didn't." "Yes I did!" "Now I know better." Burn, burn, burn.

Visitin', mind you, is not to be confused with gossip. These are two separate animals. Gossip is reserved for the telephone and sessions at the beauty parlor. Gossiping tells it all in a low tone, with a hushed-up, frantic speed to it, like you have to say it all before someone else walks in. But with visitin' you leave a lot unsaid. You have to read between the lines.

Visitin' is the southern answer to Zen meditation, except you're allowed to talk now and then and you don't have to sit on strange black cushions or eat with chopsticks. Just pull up a chair, settle into a long vacant gaze, and start to rock.

Visitin' Checklist
You must absolutely, positively, have these items:
rocking chairs and plenty of 'em
reclining chairs (in lieu of rockers)
ten-foot couches or longer (so you can really cram 'em in)
lots of pop, coffee, and Kool-Aid
an old spit can for Grandpa
peanut brittle, peanuts, or popcorn
your Bible within arm's reach
a flyswatter (if summer)
plenty of wood (if winter)
a map of the United States (will settle many disputes)
a dictionary (settles even more disputes)
lots of picture scrapbooks of the whole family

$\rightarrow$

a flashlight (the men will inevitably need to take a look at: a.
the Chevy; b. the broken fridge; c. the washer and hot
water heater; d. the new siding on the back of the house)
a Betty Crocker cookbook (for recipe disputes)
plenty of toilet paper (a roll per dozen visitors)
a wet sponge mop (ready to wipe up the first spill)
a bottle of aspirin (one in ten will get a headache)
Band-Aids (one in three kids will bleed)
room deodorizer (spray before and after)

Familiarize Yourself with These Terms

ticks	**preacher**
sermon	**the ole schoolhouse**
the square	**an ole sow**
switch	**britches**
cemetery	**puttin' up (canning)**
canes	**holler (hollow)**

Visitin' Icebreakers

How's that ole heffer doin'? (substitute "man" or "woman" for
"heffer" or leave same)
What it's like over yonder? (refers to weather)
How'd you come? (keep the map handy)
Where've you been? (usually refers to church attendance)
Been fishin'? (for men)
You see that sale? (for women)
How tall are you now? (for kids)

Things to Hide

the unmade bed you were just about to climb in
your cheap, dirty detective novels (word could spread)
your box of chocolate cherries
the shutoff notice from the phone company (could prove embarrassing)
the ten pounds of pistachios you got for your birthday
your new VCR (they'll be coming back for videos)

Now, firmly planted in the rocker with your peanuts, Bible,
map, and deodorizer, you're ready for the visitin' to begin.

negative word combinations: might not could, might would-
n't, might shouldn't, might should not, might not should,
might not can, might will can't, may can't, may not can, may
won't, may couldn't, may shouldn't, may didn't, must didn't,
can't never would. Example: "It's a long way and he 'might
will can't' come, but I'm going to ask."

Texas

THERE'S A SUPERMARKET CHAIN IN TEXAS CALLED
H.E.B., which I always thought stood for Here Everything's
Big. Because that is the clearly stated ethos of this wonderfully big
and bodacious state, perhaps my favorite in all of the Union.

Texas is grouped with the South, but, as the cliché goes, it's really a whole other country. Folks either love Texans or hate 'em,
but they'll never forget 'em. The bighearted Texas mind-set comes
the closest to my own: if it can be dreamt, it can be built; if it's
broke, let's fix it; if you say no, I'll say yes. Now get out of the way,
and let me show you how it's done.

With a tip o' the ten-gallon hat to Ken Weaver, author of *Texas
Crude.*

Handy Texas Expressions to Get You Started

**"Better to have a man inside the tent pissin' out than a
man outside the tent pissin' in."**

If you're going to have to deal with an awnry troublemaker,
best to have him on your team, where he can cause trouble for
the enemy. Attributed to President Lyndon Baines Johnson,
who allegedly used this metaphor to justify why he kept J.
Edgar Hoover on as head of the FBI.

"Chief Nasty-Ass of the No-Wipe-um tribe."

An unclean person. "Here comes Chief Nasty-Ass of the No-
Wipe-um tribe. I bet a buzzard wouldn't eat him without takin'
a tetanus shot first."

"Get off the table, Mabel. The quarter's for the beer."

Sit down and behave yourself. Or get your elbows off the table.

"He's read a book."

He's got no real-world experience or common sense, though he
pretends like he knows what he's doing.

"I love you, but cut the cards."

You really are a good friend, but I'm smart enough to know I can't completely trust you.

"If he tells you that rooster can pull a railroad train, you better buy yourself a ticket."

The fella in question knows what he is talking about.

"It's raining pitchforks and bull yearlings."

It's raining very hard.

"I've enjoyed just about all of this I can stand."

I'm repulsed or bored, and I'm leaving.

"Might as well. Can't dance and it's too wet to plow."

I'll go along with that.

"People in hell want ice water too."

We simply don't have what you're asking for, or I'm not going to get it for you, so get used to it. "I'd like to get me one of those high-speed T-1 lines." "People in hell want ice water too."

"Put the big britches on 'em."

To better someone in a deal or competition.

"Put it where Grandpa put it: in Grandma."

Put it in the lowest gear (which is "Grandma" in Texas truck vernacular).

"Put a rattlesnake in his pocket and ask him for a match."

A good ole Texas way to get even.

"She was so ugly, she had to tie a pork chop around her neck to get her own dog to come to her."

An extremely ugly woman.

"That'd gag a maggot."

Something that is seriously foul and repulsive.

"Tough as a Mexican family."

Extremely tough. As any Texan knows, when you fight a Mexican, you take on the entire extended family, right down to the fourth cousin thrice removed.

"We're waitin' on you like one hog waits on another."

We ain't waitin'.

"You buy 'em books and you buy 'em books and they just chew on the covers."

Some people do not listen to wisdom. They just refuse to learn.

The Texas Accent

ass-steer: harsh or somber.

aw riot: managing quite well, thank you.

bob wahr: cattle fencing.

cyst paypal out: aid your fellow man.

do wut?: pardon me?

drouth: a prolonged lack of water.

forced: a dense growth of trees and underbrush.

free TOE pa: a meal made by pouring chili on Freetos.

hank rin: an urge to do something.

hatty: a popular Houston greeting.

jogger fee: the study of the earth's surface.

kin I carry you home?: need a lift?

Lowered Barn: a handsome and daring English poet of the early 19th century.

marge: a union of man and wife.

markin: a U.S. citizen.

moll: 5,280 feet.

prayed: a large procession. "In New Yawk we saw da Macy's Prayed."

rule: not urban.

San Tone: home of the Alamo.

tarred: a state of exhaustion. "Dahlin, I'm tarred."

Tex-sis: Texas. Aka "Take-sis," "Tex-siz," "Tex-suhs," "Tih-xas," or, most accurately, "Teax-isss."

toad: past tense of "tell." "I toad you to quit playin' with dose moxicans."

violet: not peaceful.

whore show: the horror show.

whored: difficult.

Yewst'un: the home of the Rockets.

Texicon

"Liquor in front, poker in back."

—SIGN ON THE WALL IN A TEXAS BEER JOINT

beantime: lunchtime.

beeshit: honey.

the Big D: Dallas. As Texans say, "Dallas is the pretty sister with the bad personality, and Houston is the ugly sister with the nice personality."

the Bird: Austin Nichols Wild Turkey Whiskey, a drink beloved by Texans.

cash money: greenbacks.

catacombing: cruising.

central distressway: what Dallas residents call the 75 central expressway.

Chicken Pluckers: Ross Perot's term for Arkansans. Used in one of his last infomercials during the 1992 presidential campaign.

Colorado Kool-Aid: Coors beer.

Cowboy Cadillac: an American pickup truck.

cowboy cool: room temperature beer.

the Crock from Little Rock: Jerry Jones, proud and arrogant owner of the Dallas Cowboys. So named by Dallas residents when he took over their NFL franchise.

foo-foo: perfume or other female accessories. "You don't need all that foo-foo, darlin'."

Fourteen Feathers: Thunderbird wine. There are 14 feathers on the wings of the thunderbird on the label. According to Ivan Stang of the Church of the Subgenius, Thunderbird is the veritable "blood of Bob."

head gaskets: condoms.

innertainment: entertainment. "Buford's workin' in the innertainment industry now."

jump-start: light one cigarette with another.

a roping rope: a lariat.

see-through buildings: the humorous name for the tall and empty skyscrapers in downtown Houston after the bottom fell out of the Texas oil boom.

she gave him the gate: she divorced him.

six flags: one reason Texas is seen as another country: it has actually been part of six different countries. Spain, 1519; France, 1685–90; Mexico, 1821–36; the Republic of Texas, 1836–45; the Confederacy, 1861–65; the USA, 1845–61 and 1865 to the present.

sixer: a sixpack of beer.

skeeter hawks: dragonflies. "That's just a skeeter hawk, that ain't gone hurt ya none."

snotnose: arrogance, or an arrogant, precocious young one.

soppin's: the gravy or liquid from beef served au jus. The liquid is "sopped up" with a piece of bread.

Spanglish: the mixture of Spanish and English words in a single conversation. Heard throughout the Southwest. Examples: truck + *camion* = trucko. Or battery + *acumaladora* = bateria. Aka "Tex-Mex."

a tall boy: a 16-ounce can of beer.

tarminated road: blacktop or paved road.

tenny runners: any pair of athletic shoes. What are called "tennises" in northern Florida.

Texas Cadillac: a pickup truck.

Texas tea: crude oil. Also called "payola," "black gold," "El Producto."

that'll drill: oil field expression for "that's fine" or "that'll work." It meets the criteria for success.

this won't hurt, did it?: Texas foreplay.

tow sacks: burlap bags. Aka "grass sacks."

tump it over: turn it over.

wet: a Mexican illegal alien. Aka "wetback."

whiskey dents: bumps in the side of a vehicle from too much "drunkin' driving."

Winsdy: Wednesday.

worm: a new, inexperienced oil field hand.

Wow Boys: the Dallas Cowboys football team.

Yankee: anyone north of the causeway in Dallas.

Sports

"Only in sports is it <u>dee</u>-fense, not d-<u>fense</u>."
— DANIEL SCHORR, NATIONAL PUBLIC RADIO

"Let's be honest. A proper definition of an amateur today is one who accepts cash, not checks."
— JACK KELLY, JR., FORMER VICE-PRESIDENT
OF THE U.S. OLYMPIC COMMITTEE

SPORTS IS MY WEAKNESS. SORT OF LIKE THE *National Enquirer* is for others. Whether I'm perusing Homer or Adorno, if the Bulls and Rockets are playing, I'm right there, baby. Here are the sports terms and nicknames, both new and old, any full-blooded American should know.

Air: Michael Jordan, due to his magnificent and awesome leaping ability. Aka "Michael."

the Ali shuffle: the fancy footwork of boxing champion Muhammad Ali that left opponents mesmerized, confused, and, ultimately, on the mat.

America's Team: the Dallas Cowboys. There is a definite irony in this appellation, given the recent criminal track history of the franchise.

the Ancient Mariner: what pitcher Gaylord Perry was called when he joined the Seattle Mariners late in his career.

Arnie's Army: the fans of the immortal golfer Arnold Palmer.

the assassin: Jack Tatum. A defensive star of the Oakland Raiders in the '70s, their heyday as the bad boys of pro football. Tatum's job was to crush the opposing team's receivers. He paralyzed one for life.

baseball Annies: baseball player groupies.

Big Dog: Glenn Robinson, a forward for the Milwaukee Bucks.

the Big Red Machine: the Cincinnati Reds during the '70s, which included Pete "Charlie Hustle" Rose, Johnny Bench, and Orlando "the Baby Bull" Cepeda.

the Big Train: Walter "Barney" Johnson, a star pitcher for the Washington Senators.

the Big Tuna: Bill Parcells, coach of the New York Jets. Led both the New England Patriots and the New York Giants (twice) to the Super Bowl.

the Big Unit: Randy Johnson, 6-foot-10 Seattle Mariner strikeout king.

bikini wax: in golf, a very short cropping of the greens. Aka "fast."

blue: a generic name for a baseball umpire. "Aw, c'mon, blue, that pitch was a foot over my head."

Boog Powell: a slugger for the Baltimore Orioles.

Broadway Joe Namath: the New York Jets quarterback who led them to the 1967 Super Bowl upset of the Baltimore Colts.

bubble team: a college basketball team that has an outside chance of being selected for the 64-team NCAA tournament. Aka "on the bubble."

the Cadavers: a nickname for the Cleveland Cavaliers basketball franchise before its winning ways in the early '90s.

the Cameron crazies: creatively exuberant fans of the Duke Blue Devils basketball team.

Captain Comeback: John Elway, a quarterback for the Denver Broncos.

Charlie O: Charles O. Finley, the late owner of the Oakland Athletics, who brought colorful uniforms and "the DH" (designated hitter) to baseball.

the Cheeseheads: the Green Bay Packers. As opposed to "the Wine and Cheese Heads," the more aesthetic San Francisco 49ers.

the Chief: Robert Parrish, long-time star of the Boston Celtics, who is the oldest person to ever play the game. Interestingly, another Boston player was also called "the Chief"—Johnny Bucyk, forward for the Boston Bruins.

Chief Wahoo: the mascot of the Cleveland Indians, who were named in honor of the first Native American to play major league baseball, Chief Louis M. Sockalexis.

Chris Neal "and Pray": the president of San Francisco's Zap Courier, who knows how to use the Buddha Belly to get an open shot. Chris is a graduate of my Jump Shot 12-Step program. Once he accepted its central tenet—"I am powerless over my J and my game has become unmanageable"—his shot radically improved.

Clank-Foo: commentator Jim Rome's nickname for Shaquille O'Neal. Because of his abysmal free-throw shooting.

Clyde the Glide: Clyde Drexler, a star guard for the Houston Cougars in college, then the Portland Trail Blazers and Houston Rockets as a pro.

Coach K: Duke's basketball coach, Mike Krzyzewski.

come out: leave college before graduation to play in the pros. Example: Allen Iverson "came out" after his sophomore year at Georgetown and now plays for the Philadelphia '76ers. Many of those who "come out" are not sufficiently mature or skilled for the demands of the pros. A model of a player who graduated and still went on to great financial and playing success is Grant Hill of the Detroit Pistons.

the Cubs Factor: the team with the most ex–Chicago Cubs will lose the World Series. The theory has held up pretty well, including the 1986 World Series, when ex-Cub Bill Buckner committed the crucial error that allowed the Red Sox to lose again.

a cup of coffee: a short stint in the major leagues. "He played several years in Triple A and a cup of coffee with the Kansas City Royals."

Dennis "Oil Can" Boyd: a former Red Sox pitcher, now with the Bangor Blue Ox.

desert swarm: the University of Arizona football defense.

Doctor K: Dwight Gooden, star pitcher for the New York Yankees.

Dr. J: Julius Irving, one of the most colorful and inspired players in NBA history.

the Dream: Hakeem Olajuwon of the Houston Rockets.

the Dunkin' Dutchman: 7-foot-4 Rick Smits of the Indiana Pacers.

Earl "the Pearl" Monroe: a star guard for the Baltimore Bullets and the New York Knicks in the '60s and '70s.

Enos "Country" Slaughter: outstanding baseball outfielder from 1939 to 1959. Aka "the Old Warhorse."

feeding the ponies: racetrack betting.

the Fly: Randy Vataha, a split end for the Stanford Cardinals and the favorite target of quarterback Jim Plunkett. Trivia: Plunkett was unique, not only because he was Native American, but because both his parents were blind.

the Flying Dutchman: John "Honus" Wagner, a turn-of-the-century shortstop for the Pittsburgh Pirates. Most famous for the "Wagner Card," an extremely rare baseball card of Wagner that fetches $25,000 in mint condition.

the Forty-Whiners: the San Francisco '49ers. So named after their loss to the Green Bay Packers in the 1996 NFL playoffs. Which so unnerved owner Eddie DeBartolo, he physically assaulted some of the Packer faithful.

Freddie "Downtown" Brown: Freddie Brown, a star basketball guard at the University of Iowa, who played on the only Seattle Supersonics team to win the NBA title.

fried egg: in golf, a ball in the sand trap.

the frozen tundra: Green Bay's storied Lambeau Field, home of "the Lambeau Leap" (when players leap into the stands after a touchdown) and "the Packarena."

Fun and Gun: Steve Spurrier's high-octane pass offense that can run up points quicker than Dennis Rodman can run up suspensions.

the Fun Devils: the 1996 Arizona State Sun Devils football team. So named because of the high-scoring, pass-oriented offense led by Jake "the Snake" Plummer.

garbage time: toward the end of a lopsided basketball game when the reserves are allowed to play.

the Gashouse Gang: the 1934 St. Louis Cardinals, which included Pepper Martin, Dizzy Dean, Leo "the Lip" Durocher, Hammering Hank Greenberg, and Wild Bill Hallahan.

Gentleman Jim: James J. Corbett, the 1892 heavyweight champion, one of the first in the gloved era.

George "Ice Man" Gervin: a star shooting forward for the San Antonio Spurs and four-time NBA scoring champion.

the Georgia Peach: the baseball legend Ty Cobb. Aka "the Georgia Ghost."

the Glove: Michael Jordan. Though the Bulls star is known to the public primarily for his scoring and jumping prowess, he is known throughout the NBA as a defensive master. Gary Payton of the Seattle Supersonics, probably the second best defensive player in the NBA, is also called "the Glove."

go-to guy: a player the team turns to when it needs to pull out a victory. Often used in basketball.

golden sombrero: when a batter strikes out three times in a game.

Grandma: pro basketball's Larry Johnson. Because he dresses as a slam-dunkin' grandma in his Reebok ads. Aka "LJ."

the Great Bambino: George Herman "Babe" Ruth. Aka "the Sultan of Swat." His famous quote: "I swing big, with everything I've got. I hit big or I miss big. I like to live as big as I can."

the Great One: Wayne Gretsky, a star pro hockey player for the Edmonton Oilers, Los Angeles Kings, St. Louis Blues, and New York Rangers. Aka "the Great Gretsky."

the Great Pumpkin: Dee Andros, a football coach of the Oregon State University Beavers during the '60s and '70s.

the Greatest: Muhammad Ali. Aka "Champ" (given to him by the late sports announcer and commentator Howard Cosell).

the Human Highlight Film: Dominique Wilkins, the longtime NBA scoring sensation. If the highlights were only offense. Aka "Nique."

human rain delay: a player who does a lot of scratching and fooling around before he settles into the batter's box.

the Intimidator: Dale Earnhardt, a NASCAR auto racer.

the Iron Horse: Lou Gehrig. Aka "the Durable Dutchman."

the I-70 Series: the 1985 World Series between the St. Louis Cardinals and the Kansas City Royals. Missouri's two main cities are connected by Interstate 70.

James "Bone Crusher" Smith: a WBC boxing champ from the 1980s.

Jimmy the Greek: Jimmy Snyder, the oddsmaker who earned a slot as a sports analyst before some ill-chosen racial slurs ended his career. Aka "the Greek."

Joltin' Joe: Joe DiMaggio, the Hall of Fame outfielder for the New York Yankees. Aka "the Yankee Clipper."

keystone: second base.

the Kid: Ted Williams, before Griffey Jr. made the scene.

the Killer Bees: the 1987 Boston Red Sox batting order: Burks, Barrett, Boggs, and Baylor, with "Billy" Buckner batting seventh.

the Kissing Bandit: Morganna Cottrell, the ample-cleavaged publicity hound who would run onto the field during televised baseball games and give the players a smooch.

Larry Legend: Larry Bird, one of the 50 greatest players ever to play the game of basketball.

Li'l Penny: the doll figure that represents star Orlando Magic basketball guard Penny Hardaway in popular Nike commercials.

a Linda Ronstadt fastball: it blew by you.

Magic: Earvin Johnson, basketball wizard for the Michigan State Spartans and Los Angeles Lakers, who has a hard time retiring.

the Meal Ticket: "King" Carl Hubbell, a Hall of Fame pitcher. Aka "the Meek Man from Meeker."

Mein Boy: Alex Levinsky, a Jewish player for the Toronto Maple Leafs in the 1930s.

moat: the gutter in bowling. Aka "in the ditch."

Monster Mash: Jamal Mashburn, the former University of Kentucky standout and now underachieving forward for the Miami Heat.

Mordecai "Three-Finger" Brown: a Hall of Fame pitcher for the Chicago Cubs. Aka "Miner."

Mount Mutombo: Dikembe Mutombo, Nigerian-born center for the Atlanta Hawks.

Mr. October: Reggie Jackson, a baseball all-star who consistently shone during the playoffs and World Series.

Mr. Sunshine: Ernie Banks, a Hall of Fame shortstop for the Chicago Cubs. Aka "Mr. Cub."

Murder's Row: the heart of the 1927 New York Yankee batting order, including Lazzeri, Gehrig, Ruth, Combs, and Meusel.

Nate the Skate: Nate "Tiny" Archibald, an outstanding pro basketball guard.

Negadelphia: Philadelphia, because of the harsh way the fans treat their sports teams and players, going as far as death threats against Mitch "Wild Thing" Williams after he gave up the World Series–ending home run to Toronto's Joe Carter in 1993.

on the dance floor: in golf, when your ball is on the green.

Pistol Pete: Peter Maravich, the sharpshooting All-American guard for LSU (his dad was the coach), who went on to fame in the NBA.

poodle: bowl a gutter ball. Aka "trench it." "Oh man, I got too excited and trenched it."

the Professor: Greg Maddux of the Atlanta Braves, perhaps the greatest pitcher in Major League Baseball. Known for his smart and consistent approach to the game.

the Purple People Eaters: the fearsome front defensive line of the Minnesota Vikings in the '70s, which included defensive end Jim Marshall.

Quack attack: the Oregon Ducks.

redshirting: benching a player for an entire season in order to keep him or her eligible for another year. Used in college sports.

the Rocket: Roger Clemens, a star pitcher for the Boston Red Sox who became a Toronto Blue Jay in 1997.

Rotisserie League baseball: fantasy baseball. The game was invented at the now defunct Rotisserie Restaurant in New York City.

sellin' the call: an extremely animated call by a baseball umpire. "YOU'RRRRRRRRE OUT!!!"

the Senator: Burleigh "Ol' Stubble Beard" Grimes, the last of the "spitball" pitchers.

Shaq: Shaquille O'Neal, the massively powerful and nearly unstoppable product endorser for Reebok, Taco Bell, and Pepsi, who also finds time to play center for the Los Angeles Lakers. Known as "Shaq Who?" by fans of the Orlando Magic.

Shoeless Joe: Joe Jackson, the baseball legend who was at the heart of the Black Sox Scandal of 1919. "Say it ain't so, Joe."

Slash: Kordell Stewart, the most versatile player in pro football. He has played wide receiver, running back, and quarterback for the Pittsburgh Steelers.

snowman: in golf, a score of 8 on a hole.

stunt: in football, a sudden shift of the players on the line of scrimmage to distract the offensive line.

Super Mario: Mario Lemieux, a star player and team captain for the Pittsburgh Penguins. From the Nintendo game "Super Mario Brothers."

Teddy Ballgame: Ted Williams, the legendary slugger for the Boston Red Sox.

Texas Leaguer: a short pop fly that lands between the infield and outfield in baseball. Its roots date from 1886.

Titletown USA: Green Bay, Wisconsin, home of the Packers, who have won 11 championships, the most in NFL history. It joins other North American "title towns"—Boston (Celtics) in basketball, New York (Yankees) in baseball, and Montreal (Canadiens) in hockey.

the Toeless Wonder: Ben "Automatic" Agajanian, a famous football place-kicker.

Touchdown Jesus: the 13-story mural of Jesus Christ on the side of the library seen through the uprights of Notre Dame's football stadium.

the Tribe: the Cleveland Indians of baseball.

Uncle Charlie: a curveball.

the Wacky WAC: the Western Athletic Football Conference. Known for its large and colorful assortment of teams (Hawaii, Wyoming, BYU), its predilection for the pass, and its high-scoring games.

wake-up call: some painful or disappointing event that prompts a team to get back on track. Also applied to many nonsports situations, such as politics.

the White House: the Dallas Cowboys' house of ill repute, where lots of wild women, wild drinkin', and wild druggin' went down. Just ask Leon Lett.

Wiggly Field: San Francisco's Candlestick (now 3Com) Park after the 1989 World Series earthquake.

William Anthony "Refrigerator" Perry: a former defensive lineman for the Chicago Bears. Near the goal, he also played short-yardage running back.

The Top Team Nicknames
in the Country

the Cal State Irvine Anteaters
the Campbell Fighting Camels
the Centenary Gentlemen
the Christ the King Crusaders
the Evergreen State College Geoducks
the Everly Cattle Feeders
the Gettysburg Bullets
the Hardware City Rock Cats
the Huntsville Channel Cats
the Hutto, Texas, Hippos
the Itaska, Texas, Wampus Cats
the Mallard Ducks
the Marshall Thundering Herd
the Ohio Wesleyan Battling Bishops
the Pace Setters
the Pittsburgh State Gorillas
the Pomona Sage Hens
the Providence College Lady Friars
the Toledo Mud Hens
the UC Santa Cruz Banana Slugs
the Washburn Ichabods
the West Wheeling Whalers
the Winston-Salem Warthogs

And how can you leave out the Terrible Swedes of Bethany College in Kansas and the Fighting Artichokes of Scottsdale Community College in Arizona.

the Worm: Dennis Rodman, the cross-dressing rebounding madman of the Chicago Bulls. Name comes from the way he maniacally worms to get the ball. The primary reason the Bulls regained the NBA championship in 1996.

Zo: Alonzo Mourning, star center for the Miami Heat. "Zo was huge last night."

Street Slang

WHETHER IN NEW YORK'S HELL'S KITCHEN, Boston's Combat Zone, San Francisco's Tenderloin, or on L.A.'s Santa Monica Boulevard, the denizens of street culture have their own curbside chatter. It's an amalgamation of everything poor—bus stations, soup kitchens, hotels that rent by the hour. College graduates are rarely found. This language is rooted in drug culture, a bedmate of black culture, a cousin to gang culture, but a distinct, "honky-tonk" rhetoric all its own, updated for the millennium by a whole new generation of "street people" rolling into town.

ain't wrapped too tight: mentally incompetent. "Watch out for the dude with the coat hanger 'round his neck. He ain't wrapped too tight!"

bone: lame, false. "Don't give me one of your bone excuses."

boosting: shoplifting. "Yeah, we's boosting Walkmans down at Macy's and selling them to that old Korean on Broadway for twenty each." Aka "pinch," "snake."

cap: bullet. "I took a cap in the arm, but it went clean through and hit my homey." To "bust a cap" is to shoot someone with a gun.

Carl Lewis (verb): flee the scene of a crime. From Olympic gold medal sprinter Carl Lewis.

cashed: used, spent, gone. "Got any milk?" "Nah, it's cashed."

committee of one: alone, a group of one. "Why are you sitting on the curb, the party's inside. You running a committee of one?"

crash: sleep. "My dog just had seven puppies and we need a place to crash. How 'bout it?"

crib: a place of residence. Aka "pad." "I got a crib down on Sunset with 20 friends, but there's always space on the floor."

custies: drug buyers. From "customers."

fed-ex: an ex-con.

five-o: a police officer. From the hit TV show *Hawaii Five-O*.

flip your gut: cause sadness, despair. "She's all crying 'cuz her mom's going to die. It really flip your gut."

flow: money. "Hey bro, can't party. I need to get me some flow."

get up outta here: you've got to be kidding. "The dog ate my pipe." "Get up outta here."

J-cat: a crazy person. "That J-cat keeps spraying baby oil all over his head."

jack: steal. "I'm standing at the window when that dude was smooth jacking me right behind my back."

loaded with lead: shot by a gun. "My homey was limping down the street loaded with lead, leaving a trail."

packin': carrying a gun.

paper: stealing checks from mailboxes. "Yeah, I was doing paper Upper East Side and got caught." Aka "papering."

peel a cap: shoot a gun. "That dude with the angel tattoo, he peel a cap at me when I come through the door." Aka "pop a cop" or "bust a cap."

product: stolen merchandise. "That electronic store on Broadway will buy all the product you can haul in."

roller: a slow cop car.

same page: thinking along the same line. "I said it cost you 20, not 10. Are we on the same page?"

shot out: messed up, out of sorts. "She's completely shot out from a four-week binge."

sketch: on the edge, questionable, flaky. "That's sketch, dude: five of them and only us two!"

straight up: completely honest. "Straight up, did you take my car or didn't you?"

that's real: the bottom line, a hard cold fact. "If I don't get a job soon, I'm gonna have to start selling again, and that's real."

tight: extremely close. "He'd never say that about me. We're tight, man."

toe up (tore up): so high on drugs, the person is completely discombobulated. "She be toe up coming home ten in the morning with her shoes on her head."

took out: hit or beat up. Aka "pounded." "Yeah, I took out all five of them. Didn't even get pounded."

twenty-four-seven: 24 hours a day, 7 days a week. "My old man, he's working it twenty-four-seven."

Surfing

I'VE BODY WOMPED. OR, RATHER, BODYSURFED. But never really surf surfed. I hope I never have to—with my luck I would be upended by a serious macker, molested inside the vaunted Green Room, chewed up in wave after succeeding wave, then the board would find me with its built-in "Kill Jim Monk" sonar, knocking out all memory of happy times. I would be a miserable pathetic wreck, muttering on and on about bennies, gremlins, and ankle slappers to anyone who would listen, which wouldn't be many.

As Tom Dalzell (*Flappers to Rappers*) carefully acknowledges, most of the vernacular of the extreme sports so popular in recent years owes a huge, gnarly, and bodacious debt to the awesome and stylin' sport of surfing.

Though you won't catch me beefin', biffin', and bombin' out in the sparkle factor anytime soon, here are some of the most killer terms unique to surfing, with insets dedicated to surfing's most popular "dude sport" offspring, snowboarding and skateboarding.

With bounteous good vibes to my man Trevor "Coconut" Cralle, author of *Surfin'ary*, the definitive all-time epic look at surfing vernacular and a genuine way rad credit to his sport.

aerial: a move where the surfer and board are briefly airborne.
ankle slappers: tiny waves that aren't worth surfing.
aqua boot: barf in the ocean.
axe: the lip of a wave. To be "axed" is to be flipped off your board by an "axe."
"bail, roach": "get outta here, kook."
bareback: surfing without a wetsuit.
barney cuts: the sharp cuts surfers get from barnacles.
barrel: the hollow area inside a curling wave. Aka "tube."
beach anxiety: feeling uncomfortable at the beach. Something says this is not a good day to surf.
beached: so stuffed with grunts (food), you are unable to surf.
beard: a veteran surfer.
benny: a surfing poseur.
big mama: the ocean.

boardhead: an ardent surfer.

body womp: riding waves on your stomach. Aka "body board-ing," "bodysurfing."

boneyard: the area of the water where the waves are breaking. Aka "the graveyard" or "impact zone."

bootie juice: according to Trevor Cralle, "seawater that accumu-lates in neoprene booties during a session, mixes with stinky feet, possibly urine, and empties out smelly and lukewarm."

borg: make a big mistake. Can refer to anyone from a total ama-teur to a full pro. Usage: "Borg!"

bountious: bountiful. One might use it to end a letter: "sending you bountious good vibes."

bro time: time spent away from your wife or girlfriend. "Hey, aren't we gonna have a little bro time?"

brotherhood wave: a wave you share with another surfer. "Brotherhood wave—share it?"

burly: very cold outside.

Casper: a person without a suntan. From the children's TV show *Casper the Friendly Ghost.*

clean peeler: the ideal wave.

Clinton wave: white water.

death: the perfect wave or surfing conditions. Aka "filthy."

debbie: a dumb beach chick who's afraid to get wet. Aka a "sand flea."

decoy: a nonsurfer.

dismo: talks surfing, lives surfing, dreams surfing, but never re-ally surfs. A poseur.

double stoked: serious stokage.

egg roll: a novice surfer.

evening glass: the calm surface of the ocean after the wind has died down.

formula 1: a hammerhead shark.

free ballin': surfing in the nude.

gator mini: a shriveled-up penis after a cold surfing session.

gel: calm down. Similar to "chill." Also refers to a complete loser or jerk. "That dude's a total gel."

gnarly: intense or extreme. A surfer's all-time stereotypical term. Alternates include "drastic" and "radical." Some suggest that the word comes from the gnarly roots of the Monterey cypress, which is found on several California beaches.

greased: a wipeout. You fell off your board. "Slater just got greased."

Dudes

SURFING VERNACULAR IS ONE OF THE MOST INFLUENTIAL modern American linguistic subcultures, giving birth to the dude in all his manifestations—slacker, stoner, skateboarder, snowboarder, grunge rocker, latte puller, footbagger, gutter punk, Bill and Ted, Garth and Wayne, even all the way north to Homer, Alaska, and south to Austin, Texas. The dude is the defining attitude of every white male born after 1965. Look around you, study the cues, observe the speech. You will concur.

In keeping with the antiestablishment, antiboomer, and antistress ethic of the postmodern dude, keep in mind the following stylistic considerations when analyzing his speech:

1. Given the preference for what Trevor Cralle calls "the laid-back, unhurried life," you will find dudes speaking in lazy monotones, using "minimal effort" expressions like "later" (instead of "see you later") or "nuch" for "not much" or "S'up?" for "What's up?"

2. The sound of the dude is often low and smoky. For good reason—dudes, as a rule, love to partake of the sacramental herb.

3. Dudes are intrinsically unhypeable. Their very stance is a rebellion against the modern American hard sell (their motto: I refuse to be part of your "target market"). In fact, one of the hallmarks of a true dude is the pronounced ability to be wholly unimpressed. And when impressed, not to show it. The gee-whiz adolescent excitement of *Leave It to Beaver* is long gone. The only way to know if a dude is truly interested is if he's still hanging around listening to you "go off."

Here is the lingo common to many dude sports and pastimes.

aggro: intense, aggressive, fast. An Australian slang word that has enjoyed enormous popularity with West Coast dudes in the '80s and '90s. Very big in skateboarding circles. See also "raging."

all over: really excited. "I'm all over that Beat Happening gig, dude."

bail: prematurely exit a trick, ride, or "maneuver." Aka "crash."

Barney: a loser. If you "Barneyed," you did something stupid. Aka "nine ball." Interestingly, in windsurfing vernacular a

"Fred" is any guy who can't surf but tries to look like he can.

believe that, dude: I totally agree with you.

Betty: a female. In surfing, an attractive female. In skateboarding, a "chick" who hangs around skaters, though not necessarily one herself.

big air: getting high above the water or ground. In snowboarding, air is big when the rider has the time to contemplate exactly how high up he or she is.

catching air: getting high off the ground during a trick.

cheesy: lame.

easy: chill out.

face plant: when your face meets snow, water, or pavement. Painful and not pretty. Opposite of a "butt plant."

fully: complete, solid, true.

grunts: food. "Let's grab some grunts."

late, lato, lates, laters, later ons: later. "Let's lates" (let's leave, "bail"). "Lates, bro" (saying good-bye to a buddy). "He totally lates it" (he wiped out).

latronic: see ya later. "Latronic, dude."

most excellent: truly great. Made popular by *Bill and Ted's Excellent Adventure*. So overused in the '80s, it's now heard mostly as parody.

nuch: not much. "Hey, wussup?" "Nuch."

rager: a great skater, surfer, boarder, biker, etc. Aka "ripper."

raging: doing crazy cool-ass tricks or maneuvers.

shred: do something quite proficiently or aggressively (surf, snowboard, whatever). "That Monk dude can totally shred." Aka "raging."

shredder: an '80s term for snowboarder, skateboarder, surfer, etc.

sick: awesome. "That was a sick move."

skank: a really foul, ugly person or situation.

sketchy: a borderline person or situation. Aka "sketch." In snowboarding, can also mean a "near wipeout."

tweaked: edgy, burned out. In mountain biking, being struck by a rock. Also used in cyberspeech.

vege: sit around and do nothing. Alternately, "vege out," which means to feast on food. "I don't want to go out tonight. I'm going to sit home and vege out instead." Unfortunately, "vege" is now popular with the college crowd, who overuse it.

Skateboarding

THOUGH IT'S GONE THROUGH SEVERAL UP-AND-down cycles since its founding in the 1960s, skateboarding still manages to retain its immense popularity with the young, urban dude contingent. You're about to get a better idea of why raging over a concrete barricade is the closest these people get to satori.

back side: a back-first trick.

blunt slide: a trick where the board is perpendicular to an edge, with the wheels and one end of the board dragging along.

cobbin': southern word for "raging" (i.e., great).

coping: the rounded edge or lip of a ramp. Usually made of PVC or steel.

dork: a cool person. Unlike the more macho world of surfing (where a dork or "dweeb" is clearly uncool), in the antimacho world of skateboarding there's a complete reversal of what is normally considered cool. To be a "dork" or a "geek" is to be "in."

fakie: coming out of a trick or transition backward.

50-50 grind: sliding with both trucks on an edge and the board running parallel to the direction of movement.

flip tricker: someone who flips the board. Also does "shifties" (shifts on the board in the air) and "slappies" (a trick on a curb or an object).

focus your board: intentionally break it. Especially after it's already cracked. Mundanely, it can refer to focusing on the trick.

front side: a face-forward trick.

goofy foot: skating with the left foot forward. Aka "regular foot." Crucial to "switch-dancing" (skateboarding opposite one's customary stance).

grab air: grabbing the board in midflight. There are various kinds of air, including "indie air," "method air," "slob air," and "stale fish." It is nearly impossible to define them specifically, and any skateboarder will give you the cold shoulder if you try to press him for an answer. Suffice it to say the range of air is as limitless as the imagination of the boarder.

grind: a slide on the trucks of the board along an edge (coping, swimming pools, half pipes). Types of grind include:

→ nose grind (grinding on the front truck only).

→ 5-0 (grinding on the back truck only).

→ 50-50 (sliding with both trucks on an edge and the board running parallel to the direction of movement).

→ crooked (a simultaneous nose grind and nose slide).

hair spray air: getting so high off the ground, you can punch a hole in the ozone.

half pipe: a concave surface for skating.

huck: (1) To get some "big air" off a jump or cliff. (2) To fling oneself into the air.

kick flip: spinning the board $360°$ in midair by kicking the outside edge of the board with the rear foot.

Kodak courage: an extra dose of courage. From the tendency to go beyond your usual physical limits when being filmed or photographed (also used in other "action sports," such as extreme skiing).

lip slide: sliding either the nose or tail of a board along an edge.

making lines: performing as many tricks in a row as possible.

manual: rolling on only one set of wheels, either front or back.

McTwist: a $540°$ spin on a ramp. Other tricks include the "backside 180" and the "heel flip."

→

mongo foot: pushing with the front foot, with the back foot still on the board. Aka "wrong-footed."

New School: most up-to-date anything. In the skateboard world it's the newest clothes, board, and attitude. The New School aesthetic is currently toward a clean-cut, jock image—tighter pants, not oversize. Likewise, with New School skating, one finds consistent and clean tricks. You look the way you ride.

nose blunt: when the nose and front wheels drag perpendicularly along an edge, tail up.

Old School: the roots of skateboarding. Someone or some trick that goes back awhile (at best 20 years in the young world of skateboarding).

Ollie: not grabbing the board while airborne. The trick that revolutionized the sport, now the foundation of all other maneuvers. From Alan Ollie Gelfand, its creator.

Ollie McTwist: a 540° twist without grabbing the board.

pop: slamming down hard on the back of a board. Crucial to launching an "Ollie."

punk: a girl who skates. Considered a pretty "hard-core" thing to do.

ride: skate.

shifty: a trick where you shift the board in the air.

shove it: flipping the board lengthwise 360°, end over end, by kicking with your rear foot.

sidewalk surfer: a '60s term for a skateboarder. The sport was started by surfers who wanted to surf when there weren't any waves. The first boards were made by nailing the base of a roller skate to a plank of wood.

Smith grind: a grind on the back truck, nose hanging over the edge.

stylie: stylish. Also, a type of skateboard maneuver.

switch dance: going the opposite way one normally goes on a board.

tail: the back end of a skateboard.

tail blunt: when the tail and rear trucks drag perpendicularly along the edge, nose up.

trucks: the wheel assembly mounted under the skateboard.

True School: a perennial. Possessing all the elements of New and Old School yet somehow transcending them both.

vert: any 90° surface you can ride. Aka "vertical."

the Green Room: inside the tube.

grommet: a disciple of a soul surfer. A surfing novice (aka "gremlin") or surf groupie.

gyro-spaz: a surfer who really messes up a wave by slashing it up into tiny bits.

hair: the courage to tackle monster waves.

hair ball: a big wave that can be surfed. Aka "grinder."

hang ten: riding so far to the front (or "nose") of the board that one's toes hang over the edge. AKA "ten over."

hollow wave: a wave with a steep face and a small barrel.

hondo: anyone from outside the immediate area, usually a tourist.

IGOM (pron. "eye-gom"): Immediate Go Out Material. Said when the surfing looks great.

junk: choppy, difficult waves created by local winds. Aka "junk surf."

kneebangers: the long baggy shorts worn by surfers.

kook: an annoying beginner who gets in the way of more accomplished surfers.

leash: the elastic cord attached to your ankle and the board to keep the board near you when you wipe out.

macker: a huge wave that is often too big to handle. From Mack truck. Aka "green monster."

manson: a psychotic surfer.

Maytag: wipe out. "We got Maytaged, bra."

meat wave: a vehicle filled with surfers.

night chargers: full moon surfers.

the nip factor: how cold it is.

nipple: very cold water.

nipple rash: when body boarding or surfing rubs your nipples raw.

the oval office: inside a barrel.

pearling: when the nose of the board momentarily buries into the water.

pet the cat: surfing low on the board while moving your arms for balance.

quakers: very large waves.

Queen Mary: a board that is too big for the rider.

quimby: a jerk, loser.

quiver: a collection of different boards to accommodate varying surf conditions.

raw: excellent. "Hey, you've got some raw moves, man."

Snowboarding

Anything that reclaims the ski slopes from the coke-snortin', nouveau riche Gucci set is fine by me. And snowboarders, bless their gnarly hearts, are set to do just that. I challenge you to embrace these dudes and their speech as a direct "bonk" in the face to all things overpriced and exceedingly bourgeois. Here are some terms unique to snowboarding, not used in any of the other dude sports, including surfing, which "snurfing" (snow + surf) is directly patterned after.

biff: wipe out.

boarder-cross: the Rollerball of boarding. A rather physical race that involves aggressive jockeying for position between several boarders to see who can cross the finish line first.

bone out: when you straighten your leg to its fullest while airborne.

butt-checking: letting your rear end touch the snow after a jump, to maintain balance and continue down the slope.

butter the muffin: do a spin on the nose of the snowboard.

Canadian bacon: grabbing the board between one's legs during a jump.

carving: making very smooth, excellent turns.

chowder: thick, deep, newly fallen snow.

corduroy: excellent, well-conditioned snow.

corn snow: a granular snow that is ideal for boarding. Created when the snow is melted by the sun during the day, then refrozen at night. Common during the warmth of spring.

dad: a boarder form of address, usually at the end of a name. "Mike-dad," "Jeremy-dad," "Kevin-dad."

death cookies: chunks of avalanche debris that are to be avoided at all costs.

dialed: in the zone. At a level of unconscious perfection. Aka "dialed in."

fakie: riding backward. "I was riding fakie when I ran into that Peter dude."

firn snow: snow that hasn't melted during the summer.

freshies: the first tracks down a virgin slope. Whoever rides the ridge first gets "the freshies."

→

fun box: any object planted in the snow used by riders to bonk off.

going through the car wash: boarding through tight trees.

goofy-footed: riding with the right foot forward. Aka "goofy." Borrowed from surfing.

gorby: an inexperienced snowboarder.

hit: a jump.

jib: jump or do tricks.

jibber: a compulsive boarder. Derogatory for a boarder who spends his or her life on a short board practicing maneuvers in the snowboard park.

kicker: a jump with a sharp lip that launches a boarder into the air.

kook: a derogatory label for someone who pays more attention to the people on the mountain than to the mountain itself.

lawn chair air: get high off the ground, then land like a lawn chair.

lift-op, liftie: a lift operator. Many times the "lift-op" is a snowboarder who might share local knowledge of the mountain if you ask politely.

line: the path you take down a pitch or run. The best lines maximize the terrain's potential, thereby showcasing a boarder's skill and creativity.

oatmeal: warm Pacific Northwest snow.

pat the dog: touch the snow with one's hand while heading down a run.

pow-pow: powder.

pump speed: first compress, then decompress the legs coming out of a turn in order to accelerate.

rider: snowboarder. Aka "boarder."

riding goofy: putting your right foot forward on the board. Putting your left foot forward is "regular."

rolling down the window: losing your balance coming off a jump, so that you have to rotate your arms in a backward motion to keep from crashing.

Shred Betty: a female snowboarder. "Check out that Shred Betty stylin' down the slopes."

slurpee: slushy snow conditions.

the Snowboarder look, elements of: (1) clothes: any-

thing will do, but be sure to don some colorful headwear
(bandanna, beret, backward baseball cap, a goofy stocking
cap—preferably Dr. Seuss–style); (2) when your gloves rip,
patch them with duct tape (in fact, patch them with duct
tape whether or not they've ripped); (3) cover your board
with stickers (the equivalent of an Indy 500 racer); (4)
transportation: any beat-up old Cadillac, a VW hippie bus,
or hitchhiking—forget those yuppie Jeeps; (5) music—
Beastie Boys, Snoop, Gas Huffer, White Zombie.

starfish: crash and roll down a slope at high speed, with
outstretched arms and legs in a painful ballet that conjures
up images of the sea creature.

steeps: the steep sections of a mountain.

stick it: execute a trick successfully.

tail: the rear of the snowboard.

tip: the front of the snowboard.

toeside: front side.

turn: ride. "It was good turning with you, man."

wired: get a trick down right.

yard sale: lose control and crash, scattering your gear all
over the slope.

rhino: a giant wave.

sandruff: a head full of sand.

schmeg: the dregs of the world.

scrut: eat maximum quantities of food. Aka "haken," "pig out."

sharking: surfing.

shoulder hopper: a surfer who cuts in front of another surfer
during crowded conditions.

skank: a raunchy girl.

skegging: way fun.

skin cancer ward: a tanning center.

smog monster: a nonsurfer, or someone who doesn't live near
the beach. Aka "inland squids," "flatlanders," or "chalk people."

soul surfer: one who surfs for the feel, not the look. He would-
n't explain to a nonsurfer why he surfs because he knows the
nonsurfer wouldn't have a clue.

sponge: body boarding.

sponger: a body boarder.

stoked: the totally intense feeling you did something awesome,
such as when you ran out of a barrel. Or simply when you are

very happy or excited with anticipation. "We're going to that party tonight, dude. I'm stoked."

styling: surfing really well. Aka "killing it."

talking to the seals: vomiting.

taste: gorgeous, appealing. "That road babe is taste."

tonar: totally gnarly. "I went to this party, man. It was tonar."

tube chip: a tortilla chip that's shaped like a curling wave.

tube ride: when a surfer is enveloped in a barreling wave. According to Trevor Cralle, it's "the ultimate surfing experience," with serious religious overtones, as evidenced by other terms for the event, including "whirling cathedral," "going to church," and being in "the pope's living room."

tubular: literally surfing in a tube. Alternately, anything that is most excellent.

underboarded: using a surfboard that is too small for the waves at hand.

wag: an idiotic male personage. Aka a "Gilligan" (from the TV show *Gilligan's Island*) or a "Barney" (from Barney Rubble on *The Flintstones*).

wall: when the entire wave breaks at the same time. You can't ride walls without getting "worked."

weeded: crushed by a wave. Aka "worked," "biffed," "toaded," "lunched," "pounded," or "prosecuted."

Wilma: a dumb babe. Wilma was Fred's wife in *The Flintstones*.

windmill: paddling real hard to catch a wave.

woofy: polluted water.

yabba-dabba-doo!: all-purpose surfer greeting, borrowed from *The Flintstones*. The signature line of Fred Flintstone.

yar!: way cool. "Yar! Excellent ride, dude."

yowza!: said by a happy surfer, usually after an excellent ride.

zipper: a fast-breaking wave.

Truckers

Truckers own the American highway. When you squeeze in with your little Honda Civic, you are just renting space on their turf. Please keep that in mind next time you forget to yield to an oncoming rig.

Most of these terms are used by truckers in conversations over CB radio. The CB is like a communal force field, a highly imaginary universe that allows truckers to live in a colorful virtual reality populated by bears, beavers, and other creatures as they navigate the cold hard reality of the superslab.

alligator: any piece of tire on the road. Truckers do a lot with alligators. For instance, "Mile Marker 171, alligator trying to cross the road." The next trucker will then pad the description: "Looks like a mean alligator." And the next: "Watch out for this alligator. He tried to jump up and bite me." And a long retread with a bunch of small chunks around is called "a family of alligators." Originated with southern truckers, who from afar thought the pieces of tire on the side of the road looked like alligators crawling out of a ditch.

back out of it: slow down.

backing off: traffic is going real slow.

bad shoe: a flat tire.

beaver: a good-looking gal one sees in passing.

bed bug hauler: a long-distance household mover. Aka "bed bugger."

big trucks: what truckers call trucks, no matter what size. "Rig" has gone somewhat out of fashion.

bird dog: radar detector. If you have "heavy contact," the "bird dog" is "jumping on the dash."

brake check: traffic is stopping ahead.

breakdown lane: the shoulder of the road.

"breaker, breaker": said when you want to break into a CB conversation. Breaking in is not as common as it used to be. Aka "Break 1-9."

burnt coffee with fluffy milk: a trucker's idea of cappuccino.

Buster Brown: a UPS truck.

cannonballers: high-speed truckers. Aka "triple-digit truck"—because it's exceeding 100 mph.

cashbox: a toll plaza.

cat scales: the yellow and black scales at truck stops used to weigh a load. If a trucker is found surpassing his weight limit, he will be fined.

CB channels:
- → "In the Basement" (Channel 1).
- → "Double Harley" (Channel 11).
- → "Baskin-Robbins" (Channel 31). Aka "the ice cream channel."

CB Rambo: a driver who talks big on the CB but usually can't back it up.

chase car: the cop who actually chases down a speeder after he's been clocked on the radar a mile back by another cop.

checking out the seat covers: noting the women in adjacent cars or trucks.

chicken coops: weigh stations. Aka "chicken house" or "hen house." One trucker might remind others to "have your ducks in a row" (paperwork together). Another might respond: "I got 'em lined up on the dash." Or, "There's four of them, but one is missing."

chicken lights: the same as "Christmas tree," but more commonly used.

chicken truck: a truck that carries frozen or live chickens. Tyson is the only manufacturer of chicken trucks, though there are several chicken haulers. When passing one, a trucker might say, "Cluck, cluck, chicken truck." Chicken haulers have a glowing reputation because they receive the highest

JB Hunt

Historically, this Arkansas trucking company had a reputation for the "slowest trucks and dumbest drivers," though that has changed in recent years as it has invested in better equipment and has dramatically increased its pay scale to lure better drivers. Though you might say the company is getting the last laugh, "JB" (as its drivers are collectively known) still bears the brunt of many trucker jokes. For example:

JB in the Hardware Store

JB Hunt spent three days in a hardware store and he never could find what he was looking for.

What was he looking for?

His CB handle.

or . . .

JB and the Monkey

JB is on his way to St. Louis and sees a monkey on the side of the road, so he stops and picks him up. Soon a state trooper comes in behind him and walks up to the cab and says, "JB, what are you doing with that monkey in your truck?"

"Well, he needed a ride, so I picked him up."

The cop says, "You take him right there to the zoo, okay?"

JB says "okay" and drives away.

Next day, here comes JB driving the same truck, but in the opposite direction, with the same monkey, who's now wearing a baseball cap.

The same cop pulls him over and says, "Hey, JB, what are you doing with that monkey in the truck? I thought I told you to take him to the zoo?"

"Well," JB replies, "we had so much fun at the zoo, now I'm taking him to the ball game."

pay, drive the fastest trucks, have the biggest CB radios, and have the most adventure (a chicken truck is more likely to head to inner-city meat markets). Chicken truckers are also mavericks and usually the trendsetters. As trucker Steve Lane put it, "If a chicken trucker has neon lights underneath the fuel tank, suddenly every trucker has to have neon lights underneath the fuel tank." Chicken truckers also lead the way in violating trucking rules, including the widespread practice of keeping several different logs.

Christmas tree: a truck with a lot of lights around it. Also called "chicken lights."

co-median: the grass strip in the middle of the roadway.

common carriers: long-distance trucking companies not affiliated with a union. Became ubiquitous after the 1970s trucking deregulation. Yellow Freight, CF, and Roadway are *not* common carriers.

condo: any two-story, two-bunk truck.

county mounties: sheriffs.

Know Your Bears

bear: a state trooper, cop, or any law enforcement personnel.

bear den: state trooper headquarters.

bear in the air: a cop in a plane.

bear in the dark: a cop with his lights off.

bear in the grass: a cop in the grassy median. Aka "bear in the middle." Also watch out for "bear in the bushes" or "bear behind a tree" (aka "bear in the tree").

diesel bears: DOT cops, who monitor weight limits and driver logs.

Evel Knievel: a motorcycle cop.

mama bear: a female highway cop.

she-bear: a female cop. Aka "city kitty."

You can also say a bear has got you on his speed radar, such as:

shooting you in the back (aka "shooting you in the gas hole").

shooting you in the face (aka "They're lookin' at ya," "They're taking your picture").

There are also ways to describe a "bear on the move":

advertising (lights and sirens going): aka "blue light special," "disco lights."

the bear did a flip: a U-turn.

the bear's got a customer: stopped someone for a ticket.

donut run: a bear driving fast with no lights or siren.

---

crackerheads: bad truckers. Or stupid truckers. Coined as inexperienced drivers started taking to the road.

diesel van: a DOT (U.S. Department of Transportation) inspection van.

doghouse: the engine cover inside a cab-over truck (in a cab-over, you're basically sitting on the engine—you have to climb over the "doghouse" to get to the sleeper).

doughnut: a truck tire. Which becomes "tall rubber" or "small rubber," depending on the "profile" of the tire. Tall rubber has more rubber on the tire. But if you need more clearance, say, when carrying tall equipment, you go with a low-profile tire, or small rubber.

Dr. Pepsi: any diet drink.

drivers: what truckers call one another.

fine night for trailer truckin': conditions are perfect—the sky is clear, the wind isn't blowing, and there's a full moon.

the fog line: the white divider line. The only thing a trucker can see when it's real foggy.

the fork lift: a trucker exercise program.

four-wheeler: a car. Almost never used in a positive sense. Right or wrong, most truckers consider all drivers of four-wheelers to be lousy drivers.

freight haulers: Teamsters, because they handle "general commodity freight" (no refrigeration, no special items). Many truckers see them as unable to keep up with the times in terms of technology, training, and benefits.

get-on ramp: the on ramp. The opposite of a "get-off ramp."

getting contact: trucker's "fuzz buster" shows that a cop has his radar on.

go-fast: the drug speed.

the granny lane: the slow lane.

groceries: a meal. "I'm going to stop and get some groceries."

hammer, hammer: pick up speed. Aka "mash your motor," "put gas on it," "blow your doors off," "getting on with the program," "not letting any grass grow under your wheels," "flames shooting out of stacks," "hammer down," "right foot buried in radiator," "both feet flat on the floor," "put it in the wind."

hammer lane: the fast lane.

handle: the name a trucker uses to communicate by CB radio. There have been some legendary trucker handles over the years. Most notable was Poppa Smurf, who was so famous and so well liked, when he died there was a procession of trucks at his funeral.

have you got your ears on?: is your CB on?

high-speed driving award: a speeding ticket.

JB: the collective term for JB Hunt drivers, the brunt of many trucker jokes. As in, "Look out, JB's backing up."

keep the left door nailed shut: don't stop.

kick a tire: take a leak. Aka "check a tire," "cool down a tire." For women, "cool down the driveshaft."

load: what one is hauling.

lot lizard: a truck-stop prostitute. Lot lizards will often advertise on the CB by asking truckers if they need any "commercial company." A male prostitute will invite truckers to turn to channel "BJ-17." In general, four-wheelers have no legitimate business hanging around a truck stop. Invariably, they are either selling drugs or "a hot load of meat."

Know Your Trucks

banana truck: a Chiquita brand truck.

bull wagon: a trailer carrying livestock. Aka "bull rack."

coal bucket: a dump truck. Aka "rock truck."

drop deck: in between a "flatbed" and a "lowboy."

dry box: any unrefrigerated trailer.

garbage hauler: a trailer carrying produce.

haulin' dispatcher brains: an empty trailer.

large car: a truck with an extended hood.

lowboy: a wide load truck. Aka a "permit hauler." Carrying large equipment or houses.

milkman: a tanker with milk in it. Or a dairy truck.

saltshaker: a sand or salt truck.

skateboard: a flatbed trailer.

stagecoach: a bus.

stick hauler: a lumber truck.

thermos bottle: a propane truck.

tin can: any container you'd set on a trailer.

wiggle wagon: a two- or three-trailer truck.

A Trucker's Guide to the U.S.

Akron: the Rubber. Aka "the Rubber City."

Alaska: Eskimo Pie Land.

Albuquerque: Balloon Town.

Amarillo: Armadillo.

Atlanta: the Big A.

Belchertown, Mass.: Burp.

Boise: the Big Potato.

Boston: Beantown.

Charleston, W. Va.: Charlie Town.

Charlotte, N.C.: the Queen City. Ditto for Cincy.

Chattanooga: Choo-Choo.

Chicago: the Windy City.

Council Bluffs: Sowtown.

Dallas: the Big D.

Denver: the Mile-High City.

Detroit: the Motor City.

Flagstaff: Flag.

Fort Worth: Cowtown.

Gary, Ind.: Soot City.

Houston: the Dome.

Illinois: Land of Lincoln.

Indiana: the Hoosier.

Indianapolis: the Circle.

Jacksonville: J-Ville.

Kansas City: Bright Lights.

Kentucky: Finger Lickin' Country.

Little Rock: the Rock.

Los Angeles: the Angel City. Aka "Shaky."

Louisiana: Lucy Anna.

Louisville: the Derby.

Memphis: Mud Island.

Miami: Little Cuba.

Milwaukee: Beertown.

Missouri: the Show-Me State.

Montgomery, Ala.: Monkey Town.

Nashville: the Music City. Aka "Guitar Town."

New Orleans: Mardi Gras.

North Platte: Flat Rock.

Oklahoma City: Okie City.

Omaha: O-Town.

Pennsylvania: the Keystone.

Phoenix: Sticker Patch.

Portland, Ore.: the Rose City.

Reno: the Divorce City.

Salt Lake City: Salty.

San Antonio: the Alamo.

San Clemente, Calif.: Tricky Dick's.

San Diego: Sailor Town. Aka "Dago."

San Francisco: Gay Bay.

Springdale, Ark.: Chickendale. The home of Tyson Foods.

St. Louis: the Gateway.

Toledo: the Glass City.

Topeka: Twister City.

Tulsa: T-Town.

Virginia: the Communist State. The cops are extra hard on truckers.

West Virginia: the Hillbilly State.

Winston-Salem: Smoke City.

Lucille: cocaine. "Has anybody seen Lucille?"

lumpers: people who unload trucks. Often waiting near a warehouse, they negotiate a price with the driver by CB as he arrives. Can make up to $100 per truck (all tax free). The money is so good, many truckers have gone into "lumping" full-time. Also, a male prostitute ("He's a different kind of lumper").

mama's house: where your wife ("mama") lives.

Mary: marijuana. "Has anybody seen my friend Mary?"

meat wagon: an ambulance.

movie stars: MS carriers. Its drivers always wear sunglasses and are so neatly dressed, they look like movie stars.

new shoe: a new tire.

ole smoky: a cop. Aka "Smoky the bear" or "bear."

one-finger salute: flipping a driver "the bird" (the middle finger).

the Orange Ball: a Union 76 truck stop.

Petercar: a Peterbilt. "What do you get when you combine a Peterbilt, a Kenworth, and a Freightshaker? A Peter worth shaking."

picture taker: radar. A "bear" who's got you on his radar is "taking pictures."

pumpkin: Schneider, because the trucks are orange. A Schneider terminal is known as a "pumpkin patch." Orange barrels in highway construction zones are called "Schneider rigs."

puppy dog: a Mack truck, because the hood ornament is a bulldog. "I'm going to have to twist the tail on this puppy dog and make it go faster." Aka "two-stack Mack with a window in the back" (a top-of-the-line Mack truck).

ratchet jaw: someone who talks too much.

Rip-Offs: Rip Griffin, a chain of pricey truck stops out West.

road conditions:
→ "dry and dusty" (light, blowing snow).
→ "greasy" (ice-covered or slick).
→ "hole in the wall" (a tunnel).
→ "lost the road" (a whiteout).
→ "run out of real estate" (lane closed due to construction).
→ "throwin' iron" (putting on chains).
→ "turn off the fan" (windy). "Will someone shut that fan off?"
→ "turn off the light" (driving into the sunset). "Will someone reach up and turn that light off?"

road dog: a hitchhiker or street person.

the road is rough as a cob: a very bumpy road. Alternately,

"That road will beat you to death." Or, "That road will make your hemorrhoids pop out of your ears."

run out of hours: a trucker has to stop for 8 hours for every 10 hours he is on the road. One (illegal) way around this is a separate log.

she had a kickstand: a transvestite. "She looked pretty good, but she had a kickstand" (a penis).

shiny hiney: the back doors of a trailer.

shiny pants: Teamsters. Because they allegedly never work. Aka "freight haulers."

skinny road: a two-lane highway. Aka "two-lane" or "going through the woods."

smoke: crack or pot. As in, "What's the twenty on the smoke?"

stinker: a Dick Simon truck. It has skunks painted on the side.

superslab: a freeway. Aka "big road," "concrete ribbon," "boulevard."

swig: a cup of coffee.

tarp your load: put a condom on. Graffiti found on condom machines at truck stops.

Teamsters: the fabled and preeminent union of truckers now considered long past its prime. The days when they could shut down the entire trucking industry are over. According to *Trucking News,* there are an estimated 10 million trucks on the roadways. Most truckers are not unionized, and since the deregulation of the trucking industry in the 1970s, many more are owner-operators. One trucker comments, "If the Teamsters called a strike tomorrow, it would have little impact on the movement of freight. However, if the entire trucking industry went on strike, even for a week, the nation would be devastated."

10-4: okay. Aka "4-10," "42," "Roger," "10 dash 4."

10-33: an accident.

10-36: what time is it?

Tits and Ass: Truckstops of America. Aka "TA."

Tonka toy: a big truck.

USA truck: an Army truck.

Wally World: Wal-Mart.

Weenie Wagon: a Werner. The ugly stepchild of trucks.

what's your handle?: what's your CB code name? Examples: Dragonslayer, Tittytwister, Pantychaser, Yosemite Sam, Bozo the Clown.

what's your twenty?: where are you? What's your location?

How to Talk American

white line fever: when you are so tired that straddling the white line is the best you can do.

you missed me: said by one trucker to a passing truck when it has safely passed him. Caveat: traditionally, at night, truckers have always dimmed their lights when it's okay to come back over to their lane. Lately, however, many truckers have been hitting the high beams in imitation of four-wheelers, much to the chagrin of long-term truckers.

12 Steps

I KNOW YOU ARE SUFFERING. LISTEN, I FEEL your pain. I know he's hitting the bottle again. And I know you're playing all those same games—hiding the liquor, giving him admonishing looks, pouring the booze down the drain. But before seeking "help" from a 12-Step program and sending him off to same, be prepared for what this may do to your daily discourse. You might end up preferring heavy drinking to all the babble about "stinking thinking." Just a thought—take what you like and burn the rest.

alcoholics: the evil, sick, out-of-control bad guys who have completely mucked up our lives and who basically run the world. In other words, the enemy. But you're not supposed to think that. No way.

all that you hear here, let it stay here: we will maintain one another's anonymity unless one of us is famous, in which case all's fair. I cannot tell you how many diehard 12-Steppers have revealed to me, completely unsolicited, the names of all the rock and film stars at "their meeting."

the Big Book: the bible of the 12 Steps. It's big, it's blue, and at $5.95, a pretty good deal.

cross-addicted: you smoke after sex.

disease: alcoholism is a disease, drug abuse is a disease, overeating is a disease, sex addiction is a disease, codependency is a disease, chain smoking is a disease. Okay? If you don't buy this concept, you need to "keep coming back" until you do.

don't stop before the miracle: what can I say, it's twooo, it's twoo.

don't take my inventory: in other words, "Judge not, lest ye be judged." From the 10th Step of AA: "Continued to take personal inventory and when we were wrong, promptly denied it."

Dr. Bob: along with William Wilson, one of the founders of AA. Proof that more than Devo and rubber tires have come out of Akron, Ohio. Praise Bob.

easy does it: you don't need to ram into your wife's car when she's upset you at a party.

fake it till you make it: I tried this on Elke once, and it didn't work.

get help: get in the program.

get up, suit up, and show up: get your lazy butt to a meeting.

HALT: Hungry, Angry, Lonely, Tired. Watch out for these signs—they can lead you to have a cigarette. My own version: Horny, Antsy, Loquacious, Television.

hit bottom: a really, really bad hangover. So bad you completely forget who you are and briefly join the other team.

I need to get to a meeting: I feel like shooting up.

keep coming back, it works: so does practically any self-help program, for that matter.

keep it simple: embrace this one concept and you will be immediately transported to the Land of Pure Thought.

let go, let God: proof of William James' belief that even if God did not exist, we would have to invent Her anyway.

macroneurotic: for various specious and sound reasons, you feel compelled to eat some kind of whole grain at every meal. Personally, I'm a cross-addicted macroneurotic—I prefer a little soymilk with my brown rice. But I'm way ahead of the curve on all of this, since macroneuroses won't be recognized as a valid 12-Step addiction until Michio Kushi's been pickled in the grave for at least a decade.

meetings: 12-Step meetings. In L.A., where everyone goes to network. In Omaha, where everyone goes to find their next spouse. In New York, where everyone goes to talk, talk, talk!

one day at a time: you don't have to worry now if you'll be sober for the New Year's Eve party at the Rainbow Room in the year 2000.

one step at a time: when you want to drink real bad, remember this adage.

a power greater than ourselves: where you turn when all else fails and you're ready to take that fatal sip of Sloe Gin

What's Your Program?

HERE IS A SELECTION OF PROGRAMS BASED ON the 12 Steps of Recovery as pioneered by AA. Take your pick. And remember: you don't have to choose just one.

Adult Children of Alcoholics (ACA or ACOA): baby boomers who've done hallucinogens and can talk about their "inner child" with a straight face.

Adult Children of Catholic Republicans (ACCR): my 12-Step program. I am powerless over Phyllis Schlafly and my life has been quite unmanageable.

AL-ANON: a support group for people with alcoholics in their lives. Prerequisite: the ability to break down and cry, intellectually explain your tears, and thank the group for the opportunity all in three minutes.

Alcoholics Anonymous (AA): doctors, lawyers, and teachers.

Co-dependents Anonymous (CODA): anyone who has ever been truly in love.

Debtors Anonymous (DA): entrepreneurs and publishers of small, niche-market travel magazines.

Gamblers Anonymous (GA): men with rings on their pinkies who will take bets on whether they can stay "clean."

Narcotics Anonymous (NA): rock stars and celebrities.

Nicotine Addicts Anonymous (NAA): Marlboro men.

Overeaters Anonymous (OA): divas, housewives, and lesbians.

Sex and Love Addicts Anonymous (SLA). Scorpios and Leos. Absolutely not related to the Symbionese Liberation Army.

Fizz. The 12 Steps are not strictly a Judeo-Christian program. But you do need to accept this fundamental Christian concept in order to "get help."

principles, not personalities: one of the central tenets of the egalitarian 12 Steps that is slavishly followed in all parts of the country except L.A.

the program: the 12 Steps. Not nearly as hard a sell as EST, not nearly as tacky as Pentecostalism, but Lutheran all the same.

sponsor: the person you confess all your sins to in the hope that you won't "slip" (take a drink, shoot up, call that lousy you-know-who).

stinking thinking: a brief revelation that you are, in fact, in control of your destiny that is quickly quashed by your "sponsor."

take what you like and leave the rest: you don't have to listen to that massively overweight and sanctimonious woman who's found God.

think, think, think: consider the consequences before taking that first snort.

triggers: those people and things that get you to use. Such as unresponsive girlfriends, reruns of *Dallas*, or disingenuous personnel consultants.

working the program: you are going to "meetings" and practicing "the Steps." Bully for you.

Wall Street

"There are only two places a 28-year-old can make half a million dollars—Wall Street and dealing dope."

—Ross Perot

It used to be that all the Ivy League hot-shots went to Wall Street until Ivan "the Terrible" Boesky and Mike "Friend of the Nation of Islam" Milken gave the sport a bad name. Still, there's a colorful idiom alive and well down there, even if Sherman McCoy's in jail and Biff has gone multimedia.

alligator spread: when commissions are larger than the profit made from the deal.

a bar: $1 million.

bear hug: when a larger company inadvertently squeezes the life out of a smaller company it has just acquired.

the Big Board: the New York Stock Exchange.

black book: an anticipatory strike against a hostile takeover.

blown out: refusing to "puke out," to the point where another broker from a clearing company comes down and liquidates your position.

blue chip: the dependable stock of an established corporation that can be counted on to maintain a high purchase price per share. Example: Mass. Mutual, Pepsico.

Bo Dereks: bonds due to mature in 2010. Based on the Bo Derek character in the movie 10.

boot: a cash incentive added to sweeten a deal.

the brass ring: partnership in the firm.

BSD (Big Swinging Dick): a bond trader who takes huge and risky positions. Aka "a junk bond daddy."

bulge bracket firm: the biggest brokerage houses on the Street, such as Merrill Lynch, Dean Witter, and PaineWebber. As opposed to a regional broker, such as Dain Bosworth.

carp: a slow-witted trader who merely repeats the prices shouted by quicker traders.

cats and dogs: stocks without a proven track record.

Chinese Wall: the biggest joke on Wall Street—a broker's written pledge he will not engage in insider trading.

chopped up: lose money in an erratic market. "I got chopped up."

churn: the rather sleazy practice of urging a client to buy and sell stocks for the sole purpose of generating commissions.

day traders: the large number of Type A traders trying to make a living with little capital who have to "square up" (balance out) their positions at the end of every trading day. In the words of Wall Street watcher John Dolphin, "2% of day traders make a fortune and 98% lose."

dead-cat bounce: a fleeting upsurge in the market that gives the illusion of a recovery.

distressed securities: financially troubled companies.

a do: a go-ahead. A yes. "That's a do." After a "do" has been ordered and completed, one might say, "Done on that."

the Fed: the Federal Reserve, whose control of interest rates can affect everything from housing construction to political careers. Forget Clinton, Gates, and Buffett. Any stock trader will tell you, the Fed runs the world.

the floor: the area where securities are traded.

FOK: Fill or Kill. When a customer instructs a broker to fill an order at a specific price or cancel the order.

friction costs: the costs incurred in trading securities (taxes, commissions, surcharges, etc.).

greenmail: paying a hostile investor to go away. Scenario: a hostile investor buys a portion of a company's stock at $20 a share; the company agrees to buy back those shares at $25 a pop if the investor doesn't buy any more stock. Wall Street's version of blackmail.

hickey: the loss incurred by a broker when a client fails to pay.

hit and run: make enough money in the morning to make you happy for the rest of the day. Popular strategy of "day traders."

hoover: gobbling up a stock or stocks. From the vacuum cleaner.

insider trading: trading securities based on knowledge not publicly available. The secret to success on Wall Street.

junk bonds: (1) high-risk, high-yield bonds; (2) phony money used to buy undervalued stock.

killer bees: support staff such as flacks and lawyers who help battle a takeover attempt.

kinds of markets:

→ **choppy:** volatile trading conditions, with not enough buyers or sellers. The opposite of a "smooth" or "fluid" market.

→ **fast:** a market so volatile that warnings are posted on the trading floor.

→ **grinding:** a market where prices are moving up or down very slowly.

→ **sleeping:** a market in which prices are not moving at all.

master of the universe: the self-referential term used by Sherman McCoy, a wealthy junk bond daddy whose fortunes turn sour, in Tom Wolfe's *Bonfire of the Vanities*.

mooch: a trader who makes money by taking advantage of others' trading errors.

poison pill: a last-ditch effort to make a company less attractive and thus foil a hostile takeover.

porcupine provision: a legal instrument used to deter sharks.

puke out: the point at which you decide to liquidate your trading position at a loss because the contracts have become such big losers.

red herring: a prospectus whose registration has not "gone final" with the SEC. Primarily a selling tool to woo investors. Origins: in red ink at the top of a prospectus are the words "This is not final." In logic, a red herring is a decoy argument, used to distract attention from the important argument.

road show: when company salespeople (aka "sell-siders") try to hawk the stock to potential investors (aka "buy-siders").

screen: the increasingly common practice of investing in companies that meet certain ethical criteria (e.g., gay rights programs, environmentally sensitive, affirmative action). Aka "social screening."

sexy: a stock or category of stocks that is attracting a lot of interest. "Digital stocks are looking sexy right now."

Business Nicknames

"**T**HE BUSINESS OF AMERICA IS BUSINESS," SAID Cal Coolidge back when people still debated the point. Today one might say the business of America is BIG BUSINESS, even though "small businesses" make up most of the businesses in the land. Along with Big Business comes a certain degree of familiarity and contempt. In fact, the former naturally breeds the latter, as evidenced by the following brand name jargon.

the B.K. Lounge: Burger King. I still can't see why people eat at McDonald's when the prices at B.K. are substantially lower (a 99¢ Rainforest Whopper is the best deal going, next to the Taco Bell seven-layer burrito).

Baby Bell: one of the seven regional phone companies (NYNEX, Bell Atlantic, Bell South, US West, Ameritech, Southwestern Bell, Pac Bell) formed by the breakup of AT&T ("Ma Bell").

Big Blue: IBM. Comes from the color of its logo.

the Brethren: Brooks Brothers. Since 1818, the standard-bearer of preppie male dress.

the Dirty Dog: Greyhound Bus Lines. Truckers call it "the grey dog."

Double Os: Kool cigarettes.

FedEx: Federal Express, an "absolutely positively overnight" courier service. Aka "Federal Distress" (if you're a driver) or "Federal Excess" (when you get the bill).

→

Grease in the Box: Jack in the Box, a hamburger chain known for a variety of sins, including undercooking its meat. Lately making a comeback due to the popularity of "Jack," whom I met outside a franchise in Techapie, California.

Jacques Penné: JC Penney, a low-priced department store chain.

Ma Bell: AT&T. Earned when AT&T was a federally protected monopoly and has stuck even after the breakup into "Baby Bells."

Mickey D's: McDonald's, your kinda corporate happy place.

Monkey Ward: Montgomery Ward.

Needless Markups: Neiman Marcus, a high-priced clothing store.

Sprawlmart: Wal-Mart, America's largest retail chain. It tends to set up shop on the periphery of towns, devouring open space, creating auto dependency, and putting smaller retailers out of business. Coined in Vermont, until recently the only state in the contiguous U.S. without a Wal-Mart.

Tar-zhay: a deliberately faux French pronunciation of the Target discount store chain.

Targetto: a Target store in the "bad" part of town.

Useless News and World Distort: *U.S. News & World Report,* a right-leaning newsweekly.

Then there are those business names that are funny enough on their own: the oxymoronic United Diversified and the poorly chosen Zero Corporation, Coffin Air Services, and Kiwi Air (not only a fruit, but a bird that cannot fly).

shark: an investor who engages in a hostile takeover. Aka "corporate raider" or "black knight." Classics from the shark-invested '80s: Carl Icahn and Saul Steinberg.

shark repellent: a move to fend off a hostile takeover. Example: an amendment to the company by-laws that says: "If any one investor buys more than *x* percent of stock, a provision is automatically triggered whereby existing shareholders get a huge number of options to buy additional shares."

sheet monkey: a Chicago options trader who just works from a sheet of paper given to him by his company and doesn't make his own decisions.

smoked: lose a lot of money. "I got smoked on the May soybean call options."

soft landing: essentially, the economy is slowing down without crashing. Aircraft terminology applied to the fiscal policies of "the Fed."

swooner: a stock that is hypersensitive to news of any kind. Example: Apple's fluctuations of recent years due to factors that include poor earnings and glamorous events like the return of Steve Jobs.

symbols for corporations on the major stock exchanges: the Boston Beer Company (SAM), Dr Pepper Co. (DOC), Nutrition World (NUTS), 1 Potato 2 Inc. (SPUD), and Anheuser-Busch (BUD).

ticks: an increment of price movement. When markets move by three or four ticks, that's a "gap market"—a scary market because the news can move the market faster than the market's ability to absorb.

value investing: buying stocks that are selling below their perceived market value. "Value investors" are contrarians who tend to look for stocks that are out of favor, or "oversold," such as IBM a few years back. By contrast, "momentum investors" tend to look for stocks whose price is rising fast, or "overbought," such as 3Com or U.S. Robotics.

vulture: an investor who buys shares in companies deep in debt in the hope of reaping a profit when they turn around. A classic vulture is Chicago real estate investor Sam Zell, who's considered a bit of a "magician" due to his knack for buying "distressed securities" and selling them at a handsome profit.

walking in tall corn: making big bucks.

war chest: a pool of money assembled from various institutional and private investors and used to hunt for acquisitions. Ivan Boesky was a pro at amassing a sizable "war chest."

white shoe: a WASPy old-money Wall Street brokerage firm. E.g., Morgan Stanley. As opposed to the new-money and decidedly un-WASPy firm of Goldman Sachs.

Washington, D.C.

"I'm proud that I am a politician. A politician is a man who understands government, and it takes a politician to run a government. A statesman is a politician who has been dead 10 or 15 years." —HARRY TRUMAN

WHEN I WATCH *THE NEWSHOUR WITH JIM LEHRER* on the East Coast, I take the stuffy intellectualism of the hosts and guests for granted. It's perfectly normal, even a bit stimulating. But when seen from the far more open and loose West Coast, these people seem comically nuts—uptight, denatured, in serious need of a cosmic hit of California kookiness. The same goes for the town's politicos. These are the people who ran for student congress back in high school. They always struck you as a little square—and you know what, they still are.

aardvark politics: a political movement with no history and no future. Originally applied to the 1992 Perot campaign, though less often now, given the tiny Texan's staying power.

Al Gore: the vice-president's Secret Service code name.

ayatollah: a political insider with a dictatorial personality and a great deal of power.

Barney Fag: Congressman Dick Armey's compassionate term for Barney Frank, a gay Massachusetts congressman.

Beltway: the area inside I-495/95, the heart of our nation's capital.

Beltway bandits: military consultants.

Big Tent: all-embracing. A brilliant piece of propaganda used during the Reagan and Bush terms to signify the GOP's willingness to allow blacks, Hispanics, and women (but not gays) to play larger roles in the party. Applied mostly to the abortion issue. The '92 convention, with Buchanan bashing women and lesbians, made a mockery of the concept.

bimbo eruptions: when former sexual partners of President Clinton go public. Best remembered is his long-term lust affair with Arkansas gold digger Gennifer Flowers. Aka "the Bimbo Factor."

blue dog: a right-leaning House Democrat who has finally made the switch to "the other side of the aisle." Two possible sources: (1) from the paintings of blue dogs many southern politicians have in their offices; (2) a play on "Yellow Dog Democrats," who would rather have voted for a yellow dog than a Republican. In the words of Congressman Mike Parker of Mississippi, a blue dog is "a yellow dog that's been squeezed until it turns blue. If you keep squeezing long enough, he becomes a Republican."

BobDole: Bob Dole's name for Bob Dole. As in the classic line made popular by the Capitol Steps: "Do you take Libby to be your lawful and wedded wife?" "BobDole do."

Boll Weevils: conservative southern Democrats. Aka "Dixiecrats." See "Reagan Democrats."

Borking: intense questioning of cabinet and Supreme Court nominees. From the highly partisan questioning of the Supreme Court nominee and nicotine freak Robert Bork. Supporters claimed he was picked on because of his conservative legal opinions, though more sensible observers concede that it was probably just his bad hair.

a bridge to the 21st century: Clinton's 1996 mantra, said at every single stop on the campaign trail. At one point I decided that if Bill didn't quit saying this, we'd all push him off.

bundling: giving candidates a lot of small donations rather than one large gift. How PACs circumvent campaign finance laws.

businesscrat: coined by *Business Week* to describe the new breed of Democrat who has significant experience in the private sector.

campaign finance reform: a running joke.

centrist: what everybody aspires to be in today's vanilla Washington.

character issue: what a candidate's personal behavior says about his or her suitability for public office.

the Chocolate City and her Vanilla Suburbs: George Clinton's telling description of Washington, D.C. (80% African

Politics

"A liberal sees a drowning man 50 feet from shore, throws a 100-foot line, and lets his end go. A conservative throws a 25-foot line and holds tight."

—J. Kenneth Blackwell, treasurer, state of Ohio, New York Times, October 8, 1995

AMERICA MAY BE THE MOST POLITICAL NATION on earth. It's the land where the struggle to win is more important than the ideologies at stake. More "ink" is devoted in America to how an issue will "play" with the public than to whether the idea is sound—or even whether the person holds the idea for any other than political reasons. Here are the main terms you will need to know in your quest to elevate process and power over point of view.

attack ads: political ads that directly criticize the opponent and his record, sometimes personally. Made popular and quite effective in the '80s by Republican "attack dog" Lee Atwater but in relative decline ever since.

attack fax: political news releases fiercely critical of the opposition faxed to media outlets in a "fax attack."

attackmeister: a specialist in negative politics, using such time-honored tools as attack faxes, attack videos, and, of course, attack ads.

bounce: when a candidate's standing in the polls makes a sudden upsurge due to an orchestrated act, some favorable publicity, or, in most cases, from the enthusiasm generated by a nominating convention.

bushlips: a disingenuous political statement. From George Bush's fatal 1992 campaign pledge "Read my lips: no new taxes."

chicken hawk: a politician who didn't serve in Vietnam but who supported the Gulf War.

communitarianism: the new political philosophy that argues that the rights of the community are as paramount as the rights of the individual and that America has gone too far in the protection of the latter.

comparative ads: euphemism for "attack ads." Aka "mud-slinging."

→

DLC: the Democratic Leadership Council. A group of centrist Democrats who were tired of losing to Republicans on issues of welfare, crime, and defense. Helped cement the thinking and election of William Jefferson Clinton.

dorm storming: rallying college students behind a political issue, then getting them to call or write their congressman on a crucial vote.

furlough issue: an emotionally loaded issue that could prove embarrassing to the opposition candidate (from Willie Horton, a convicted murderer who raped a woman while out on "furlough"). Example: Clinton's draft record in the 1992 election.

grassy knoll theory: a cock-eyed conspiratorial theory launched by a candidate. Example: Perot's completely wacky assertion that the GOP tried to sabotage his daughter's wedding. From the still popular theory that there were other gunmen shooting at JFK from the "grassy knoll" in Dallas. Aka "Perotnoia."

the happiest millionaire: Steve Forbes. The editor of *Forbes* magazine and a Republican primary presidential candidate, he spent $30 million of his own money to win the delegates of Arizona and Delaware. What that says about Arizona and Delaware is anybody's guess.

hardball: a baseball metaphor for a hard-fought negotiation. A beautiful story illustrates the point. Charlotte Daar was explaining to her son in San Francisco that her daughter-in-law Sheila wouldn't be back until at least 9:00 p.m. because, as Charlotte heard it, "Sheila was going up to Sacramento and from there was going to catch a baseball game." When Sheila arrived home at 6:00 p.m., both Charlotte and Sheila's husband were shocked. Her husband asked, "What happened?" Sheila replied, "Didn't Charlotte tell you? I was going up to Sacramento to play hardball with the big boys and then I'd be home."

hot button issue: an emotionally loaded political issue, such as flag burning or abortion. In general, any issue that a group of people will vote on at the expense of all other issues.

the L word: liberal. Absolutely the wrong political label to identify with in early '90s America. The new L word,

→

which is scaring the hell out of the traditional liberal media, is "libertarian," a heretofore fringe ideology that is steadily gaining proponents from statehouses to cyberspace.

Modem: a moderate Democrat (from *Primary Colors*).

neoconservative: a conservative who has smoked pot or whose lesbian daughter has.

opposition research: research team that digs up dirt on the opposing candidate, scanning all public documents for any possible malfeasance. Aka "oppo."

the permanent campaign: a governing strategy developed by Dick Morris, a Clinton campaign aide, that keeps the elected representative actively trumpeting his position on an issue through various campaign tactics, from TV spots to bus tours.

soft money: contributions made to a state or national party organization to use for "party-building activities." There are no restrictions on "soft money" (aka "sewer money"), as opposed to "hard money," which is direct contributions to specific candidates.

the sportsmen's lobby: a euphemism for the National Rifle Assocation (NRA).

stealth candidates: candidates of the religious right who win elections not by making public appearances but instead by promoting themselves through church newsletters, pew registrations, and other tactics that don't require confrontation with the public, the opposing candidate, or the press. These tactics are known as "the San Diego Model."

supervoter list: the names of people who routinely vote in elections. Used by savvy political campaign operatives to effectively target their door-to-door canvassing and advertising.

Willie Horton: play on unfounded racial fears in order to defeat a rival candidate. From the Republican advertising strategy against Michael Dukakis of Massachusetts in the 1988 presidential campaign. Willie Horton was a black convict who raped a woman while out on a Massachusetts furlough program.

you people: Ross Perot's fatal term for African Americans when he addressed the NAACP.

American), and the surrounding Maryland and Virginia towns that supply most of the federal work force and are overwhelmingly white.

Clinton: a complete policy reversal that is similar to waffling but far smoother. In the words of William Saletan, there are several varieties: (a) a half Clinton (simple reversal); (b) a full Clinton (a reversal with feeling); (c) a double Clinton (a reversal followed by a denial of the reversal).

cook the numbers: manipulate statistics so they don't look so politically embarrassing.

Deep Throat: Woodward and Bernstein's (*All the President's Men*) name for their chief source on Watergate misdeeds. The source is unknown to this day, though the award-winning journalists promise to release the name once Cord Meyer dies.

demosclerosis: Jonathan Rauch's term for "the gradual petrification of government, caused by Washington's inability to get rid of anything old"; i.e., so-called "temporary programs."

dittoheads: disciples of AM radio commentator Rush Limbaugh. Seen by his opponents as aiding and abetting the Republican politics of destruction, at several million bucks a year. Followers got the moniker from their tendency to nod in agreement with the man's opinions.

Doves: the "We Are the World" school of foreign policy. Doves aren't motivated to fight wars simply to protect "vital U.S. interests" (e.g., oil in the Gulf). They need something more altruistic, like wars to liberate oppressed peoples (e.g., Haiti).

entitlements: programs to help poor people, the disadvantaged, and the elderly. As opposed to programs to help rich people (called tax cuts).

executive privilege: the right to pardon one's allies or withhold information damaging to one's own credibility.

F.O.B.: a Friend of Bill's, everybody's favorite communitarian. Qualifications can include: a Yale degree, a direct link to Don Tyson, an awareness of Bill's sexcapades.

F.O.H.: a Friend of Hillary's, the intelligent voter's cookie baker. Qualifications can include: a Yale degree, a direct link to the Rose law firm, a feigned indifference to Bill's sexcapades.

Filegate: the Clinton staff's alleged perusal of over 400 FBI files on prominent Republicans.

freshman: a first-term congressperson.

fright mail: a type of direct mail solicitation that plays on the recipient's primal fears (e.g., an NRA solicitation playing on a gun nut's fear of greater government restrictions).

Fundies: fundamentalist Christians, a powerful contingent in the Republican Party who deep down believe that the separation of church and state is some horribly misguided mistake and not at all "what the Founding Fathers intended."

G-men: FBI agents.

G.O.P.: Gridlock Obviously Pays. Aka "the Grand Old Party" (the Republicans).

gergenize: quietly send an unpopular aide packing. What essentially happened to commentator David Gergen after one year in the Clinton White House. And what some believed actually happened to Dick Morris.

goat food: a symbolic move made by a lawmaker to look good in the public's eye.

good government: an oxymoron. Aka "political reform."

GOPAC: Newt's little propaganda arm.

gray ghost: a congressperson's top aide.

gridlock: the seeming inability of Congress to pass meaningful legislation due to its slavish devotion to partisan politics.

grinches: coined by Donella Meadows to describe Washington's current variety of coldhearted, obstructionist, bellicose Republicans, as distinct from the far more moderate and conciliatory old-line Republicans. From "Gingrich."

Groundhog Day: a Clinton White House insider term for a meeting they keep having over and over again (say, on bimbo eruptions, the budget, or the use of the Lincoln bedroom). From the Bill Murray movie, in which the main character relives the same day over and over again.

grown in office: said of any politician who entered the capital at a young age. Roughly translated: "I've learned how to properly kowtow to the powers that be and work the levers of government to ensure my reelection."

Gucci Gulch: the community of Beltway lobbyists.

Gypsy Moths: liberal to moderate Republicans. The Yankee answer to the Boll Weevil.

Hawks: the "nuke 'em and ask questions later" school of foreign policy. Hawks believe any war that places the U.S. against a godless enemy or is fought to preserve the basic corporate order (e.g., oil in the Gulf) is worth fighting. See "Doves."

the Hill: Capitol Hill, where Congress resides.

Hill rat: a congressional staff member.

The Pentagon

L EARN TO SPEAK LIKE A ROBOT. LEARN TO DISTANCE yourself emotionally from the horrid effects of war. Learn to fool politicians and the public through a smoke screen of "bureaucratese." Learn how to kill thousands of people and return home content to your sweetie at night. Learn to talk Pentagon.

accuracy in reporting: censorship.

across the river: the White House and Congress, cowering defense industry sugar daddies across the Potomac from the Pentagon.

antipersonnel: weapons designed specifically to destroy people, not buildings.

arms control: a contradiction.

the Ballistic Missile Defense Organization: Star Wars. The program formerly known as the Strategic Defense Initiative, or SDI. Programs don't die at the Pentagon, they just get renamed.

Beltway commando: a military bureaucrat.

blue top: a Pentagon press release.

broken arrow: a nuclear weapons accident. Aka an "event."

civilian casualties: people got killed.

Code 1: the president.

collateral damage: lots of people got killed.

defense: next to godliness.

defense spending: corporate welfare under the guise of national security.

delivery of ordnance: bomb 'em!

DoD: the Department of Defense.

Fort Fumble: the Pentagon.

heavy beads: allegedly the most important and definitely the most expensive items in the defense budget.

human remains pouch: a body bag.

inconvenience bombing: bombing civilian support "mechanisms," such as power plants, TV stations, and telephone lines, without directly bombing civilians.

Indians: support personnel to the Chiefs of Staff.

insult bombing: bombing statues and monuments dedicated to enemy leaders.

$\rightarrow$

intercept: two missiles passing in the night. Though in the Gulf War, the Pentagon no doubt wanted to convey the impression that it meant two missiles *colliding* in the night.

MAD: Mutually Assured Destruction, the prevailing theory of deterrence during the Cold War.

megadeth: lots and lots and lots of people got killed. Somewhere around a million.

milicrat: a military bureaucrat.

national defense: what most people want to spend lots of money on. As opposed to "military spending," which gets far less support.

neutralize: kill.

new dangers: buzzword to justify bloated defense budgets in the post–Cold War world.

new world order: the same old defense spending.

peace dividend: a large cut in unnecessary defense spending that can be used to pay for needed social services or to trim the debt, which never materializes because of the Pentagon's constant trumpeting of "new dangers." The end of the Cold War with Russia should have yielded the largest "peace dividend" in history but, instead, yielded little or no savings at all.

Peace Through Strength: a Zen koan.

pencil: a war correspondent.

reporting guidelines: censorship.

sanitize: delete or severely edit a public statement or portions of a document that might compromise the Pentagon's reputation with "Uncle Sugar" or "Joe Sixpack."

sea turkeys: Seawolf submarines. You'd never hear Pentagon brass say this, but any right-thinking citizen knows the function of each of these $2 billion boondoggles: to guarantee an election day victory in the Connecticut shipyards.

Star Wars: the Strategic Defense Initiative, the giant laser umbrella that was supposed to protect all of us late capitalist American consumers from Soviet attack. Popular folklore says that when Reagan whispered the idea in diplomatic circles, Gorby finally threw in the towel.

the Tank: the conference room used by the Joint Chiefs of Staff. Aka "the Gold Room."

the U.S. military: the largest public works program on the planet.

→

Uncle Sugar: the federal government.

weapons system: a boondoggle.

window: a great opportunity to bomb the heck out of the suckers.

"I could have stayed home and baked cookies": Hillary Clinton's peculiar way of ingratiating herself with fellow feminists. One of the most-remembered lines of the 1992 presidential campaign.

"I didn't inhale": when paired with Bill's other great line ("I tried it but didn't like it"), one is left with a question: how does Bill know he didn't like it if he never inhaled? Another enduring Clinton koan.

Jeff Mem: the Jefferson Memorial, according to D.C. traffic announcers.

Joe Sixpack: the average guy. "I don't think that gay rights measure is going to fly with Joe Sixpack."

Langley: the CIA, based in Langley, Virginia.

the liberal media: those members of the "cultural elite" who dominate most talk shows and skew the news toward a liberal or Democratic perspective. Names like G. Gordon Liddy, Caspar Weinberger, Edwin Meese, George Will, Richard Perle, Mona Charen, Pat Buchanan, David Gergen, Peggy Noonan, Ollie North, Linda Chavez, John Sununu, Kenneth Adelman, Rush Limbaugh, and Jeane Kirkpatrick.

Spookspeak: Inside the Lingo of the CIA

"I don't see why we need to stand by and watch a country go Communist due to the irresponsibility of its own people."
—HENRY KISSINGER,
JUSTIFYING THE NIXON ADMINISTRATION'S
COVERT POLICY TO "DESTABILIZE" ALLENDE'S CHILE

IN THE POST-WATERGATE, POST–CHURCH HEARINGS, post–Cold War era there is serious doubt whether our nation needs the services of the spook (CIA operative). In fact, the information-gathering capacity of many of our mass media (most notably CNN and sites on the Internet) is so vast that the CIA's own processes seem backward by comparison. Still, the CIA carries on. As Robert Michel said of all organizations nearly a century ago, it finds a way to perpetuate itself.

To do so, it must promulgate in the minds of Congress, the president, and the public the impression of a whole lot of dangerous stuff going on when, perhaps, there isn't. Indeed, the CIA is the most blatant example of deliberate "disinformation" and wanton disregard of civil liberties in the interest of national security. For this reason, its jargon is among the most intriguing I have found.

babbler: an electronic counterbugging device that emits gibberish in several languages at once.

backstopping: the complete and total outfitting of an agent: fake passport, driver's license, address, occupation, etc.

black propaganda: the source of the disinformation is deliberately concealed or misrepresented. Aka "gray propaganda."

blown back: false propaganda planted in a foreign country that gets "blown back" to U.S. media as "the truth." When false propaganda planted by "the other side" ends up in U.S. papers, it is called "playback."

clean: an agent, safe house, letter drop, etc., that has not been used before and thus is unknown to the opposition.

the Company: the CIA. To insiders, it's never *the* CIA. Aka "Langley" (from its headquarters in Langley, Virginia). Or, "the Agency."

→

the Custodial Detention List: former FBI chief J. Edgar Hoover's list of Americans who might be deemed grave security risks in the event of a major crisis or war. Term later changed to the "Security Index," "Reserve Index," and "Communist Index." In the late '60s, "the Rabble Rouser List" was developed to include Vietnam War protesters and civil rights organizations. Hoover even had his own "Not-to-Contact List" of persons from the press to be denied access to FBI information because they had written unfavorable stories about the Bureau or himself.

dry cleaning: the various methods a subject uses to avoid surveillance.

fix: a foreign agent the CIA can blackmail into cooperating (through photos of illicit sex or other embarrassing activities the "fix" may have engaged in).

flutter: the polygraph test the CIA routinely gives employees with access to highly classified information.

go private: leave the CIA and enter the civilian sector. For top agents this is often akin to going into the FBI Witness Protection Program—complicated indeed.

go to ground: when an agent "disappears" (goes into hiding) because he suspects surveillance of his activities. When he reappears, he has "surfaced."

the gray man: the ideal spy, so inconspicuous he doesn't even catch a waiter's attention in a restaurant.

honey trap: using sex to trap possible agents. Aka "sexpionage."

K: the KGB. Used by agents living in Russia. "I think K is tailing us." Aka "Uncle."

letter drop: a public place where a top-secret communication can be left. Example: under a certain rock in New York's Central Park.

MICE: an acronym for the most common reasons a Soviet spy would defect: Money, Ideology, Compromise, or Ego.

Never Say Anything: the National Security Agency.

noise: diverting enemy intelligence operatives through a smoke screen of information that proves to be completely useless. A red herring.

one-shot: one-time informants who try to get a large sum of cash for a vital piece of information. They usually don't succeed because intelligence agencies prefer steady, long-term informants.

→

Operation CHAOS: the CIA's notorious effort to destabilize and destroy the Vietnam antiwar movement.

the Pit: the basement room at Langley where documents are shredded or burned and then sent to a Virginia landfill.

plumbing: the complete support infrastructure an agent needs to complete a job (including safe houses, surveillance teams, soundmen, maps, train schedules, drop boxes). When it is being set up, it is called "putting in the plumbing." Ironically, the team Nixon hired to cover up White House "leaks" was called "the Plumbers."

PNUT (pron. "Peanut"): Possible Nuclear Test Site.

safe house: an ordinary house or apartment where agents can meet freely.

sleeper: an agent who poses as a normal civilian (sometimes for years) until he is needed. Aka "back marker."

soundman: an expert in bugging or wiretapping.

South Cafeteria: the CIA's "classified" or "covert" employee dining room. A "spook" can eat there knowing that no "outsiders" will be there. And the food is better than in the "overt" cafeteria.

spook: a CIA officer. Used derisively and affectionately by both outsiders and spooks themselves.

suitability files: the highly personal files the CIA keeps on its own staff and federal employees to determine if they may become security risks. Information can include sexual activities, financial difficulties, marital problems, and questionable friends and associates. Aka "soft files."

tank: a bugproof, windowless room found at major CIA centers around the world where top-secret conversations are held. It always reminds me of the "Cone of Silence" that never seemed to work in *Get Smart*.

turn: persuade an enemy agent to join one's own intelligence service. Probably from "turncoat."

wash: the recycling of a valid passport by theft or purchase for use by CIA operatives abroad.

Watch List: persons closely monitored by the CIA as possible spies or sources of information. John Steinbeck and Edward Albee were both on the list.

wetwork: espionage that involves a bit of murder.

white propaganda: information available openly through government agencies, country newspapers, and books.

→

> During the height of the Cold War, the Soviet Embassy in
> Washington received close to a ton of white propaganda a
> year.
>
> **witting:** a person who knowingly cooperates with an intelli-
> gence agency. Example, a CEO who provides corporate
> cover for a CIA operative.

majority maker: freshman G.O.P. congressman's term for the
elephantine radio commentator Rush Limbaugh.

the Mall: where the monuments and tourists are and where
most major political rallies are held.

Mediscare: a Republican code word for the alleged Clinton policy of "scaring seniors" about Republican cuts in Medicare. A
person who engages in Mediscare is a "Medagogue."

the MOD Squad: the Merchants of Death Squad. What lobbyists
for alcohol, tobacco, and firearms jokingly call themselves
when they periodically meet at their favorite Beltway water-
ing holes.

the Murder Board: the Senate Judiciary Committee, known for
its intense, sometimes vicious, questioning of prospective
Supreme Court justices.

nattering nabobs of negativism: the East Coast media establishment. VP Spiro Agnew's sole memorable contribution to
Beltway vernacular, which to this day gets cited by the Beltway punditocracy.

the NEA: the National Endowment for the Arts, a favorite whip-
ping boy of congressional homophobes.

the NEA 4: the artists Karen Finley, John Fleck, Holly Hughes,
and Tim Miller, who had their NEA funding revoked because
they produced "controversial" art. It was later restored by the
courts.

Newt: the humane, caring, hardworking Speaker of the House of
Representatives Newt Gingrich, who has confidently forged a
fair and honest moral vision of peace, liberty, and freedom for
all Americans. As opposed to his pathetically permissive and
radical Democratic opponents, who remain steadfastly anti-
family, anti-work, anti-flag, and traitorously corrupt, greedy,
and self-serving.

Newter: invoking the specter of the controversial and hugely
unpopular Speaker of the House Newt Gingrich to defeat Republicans in Senate and House races.

the October Surprise: the alleged plot concocted by presidential candidate Ronald Reagan and the leaders of Iran to delay the release of American hostages until after the 1980 election, thereby denying what would have been a decisive political coup for President Jimmy Carter. Reagan won the election.

OEOB: the Old Executive Office Building.

oilies: oil industry lobbyists.

the one-party state: Jerry "Moonbeam" Brown's famous term for the token differences between the Democratic and Republican parties. They're so similar they've really become one party. Aka "the Incumbent Party."

our nation's capital: Washington, D.C., the most messed-up city in America. So lacking in proper management, it has had its day-to-day affairs turned over to a congressional Finance Committee. So broke it has told employees to bring their own toilet paper and light bulbs because the city can't pay the contractors. So completely skewed it reelected a former crackhead mayor. Aka "Washington."

out of the loop: not privy to important inside information. George Bush's wonderfully creative justification for his alleged noninvolvement in Iran-contra.

PACs: Political Action Committees. The lifeblood of Washington.

peace dividend: government funds made available by the end of the Cold War, ostensibly for solving major internal problems, such as health care, the environment, and "decaying infrastructure."

Perot (pron. "puh-*row*"): to con. "He could Perot a Floridian into buying a heater in July."

Perotistas: slavishly devoted followers of the diminutive paranoid control freak H. Ross Perot, a candidate for president in 1992 and 1996. Aka "Perotbots," "Perotians," "Perotites," and "Perotniks."

policy difference: Iran-contra.

pork barrel: funding for ostensibly unnecessary pet projects, often in a legislator's state or district, to please the folks back home. Aka "pork."

power couple: a hetero twosome, both of whom have prestige jobs. Old School—Elizabeth and Bob Dole. New School—Bill and Hillary Clinton.

Pravda on the Potomac: old Republican phrase for the *Washington Post*, especially after Woodward and Bernstein helped bring down the Nixon presidency.

preserve, protect, and strengthen: a Republican rhetorical misnomer. Roughly translated, we are going to cut this program.

Primary Colors: the most talked-about political book of the mid-'90s. Ostensibly a fictional account of a few months in the life of a southern governor running for the presidency, the book was actually a tell-all about the inside workings of the Clinton campaign, including revealing looks at Hillary Clinton and James Carville as well as secondary characters like Harlem librarian Daria Carter-Clark, who is suing Joe Klein (the author known as "Anonymous" until a word analysis in several New York magazines forced his hand) for portraying her as "sexually promiscuous, immoral, unethical, and unprofessional."

punditocracy: the small coterie of Washington media pundits whose views are treated as gospel, even though they may be completely out of sync with public opinion. Aka "telepundits" (Safire).

read my lips: George Bush's fatal assertion that he would not raise taxes, which was turned against him in the 1992 presidential election. Now applied to any candidate's macho assertions that have the ring of falsehood.

Reagan Democrats: conservative Democrats who bolted from their party in the 1980 and 1984 general elections to vote for Reagan. Elected officials who represent the viewpoints of same.

Reaganomics: the trickle-down economic theory that gave us the Decade of Greed.

Legendary Washingtonians Any Full-Blooded, Flag-Waving American Should Know

B-1 Bob: the "dangerously unstable" ex-congressman from California, Bob Dornan, whose bellicose backing of all things military earned him the label.

Babs: former First Lady Barbara Bush.

the Bear: General Norman Schwarzkopf.

Bebe: Charles Gregory Rebozo, Nixon's pal. Aka "the Aerosol King."

Billary: the team of Bill and Hillary Clinton.

the Brush: H. R. "Bob" Haldeman, the chief White House aide to President Nixon and a convicted Watergate criminal. His haircut resembled the bristles on a hard brush.

Cap the Knife: Caspar Weinberger, secretary of defense under President Reagan.

Fiddle and **Faddle:** the Secret Service code names for the young pretties the married President John F. Kennedy had on call, ready to service their country (not to mention his libido).

George Herbert "Hoover" Bush: a career political insider who had the misfortune to be president when the economy took a significant downturn and who blindly believed it would naturally correct itself in time for his reelection (much like President Herbert Hoover). Gave birth to the slogan "It's the economy, stupid," because of his incessant trumpeting of his Gulf War victory when the public wanted to hear about "meat and potatoes" economic issues.

the Grim Reaper: David Stockman, budget director during Reagan's first term.

H: First Lady Hillary Rodham "I'm Investing as Fast as I Can" Clinton.

Hizzoner: D.C. mayor Marion Barry, the Democrats' answer to Ollie North—a lying criminal who's so popular with voters he's been dubbed "Mayor for Life."

the King of Pork: Democrat Tom Bevill of Alabama, who in his 15 years in the House became known for funneling millions of federal dollars to pet projects in his state.

Lady Bird: former First Lady Claudia Alta Taylor Johnson.

$\rightarrow$

Mr. Bill: President Clinton. From the children's TV character. Aka "Slick Willie."

Nancy: First Lady Nancy Reagan. The social x-ray wife of "Ron."

Ollie: Oliver North, the Republicans' answer to Marion Barry: a lying, cheating criminal who is popular with the public.

Pat: (1) Pat Buchanan, erstwhile presidential candidate, who lives in a delightfully inane Revolutionary War bubble ("Do not wait for orders from headquarters! Mount up! And ride to the sound of guns!"). (2) Pat Buckley, who marches to the tune of Oscar de la Renta.

Ronbo: President Ronald Reagan, for his simplistic, jingoistic, and, ultimately, quite effective foreign policy. From the Sylvester Stallone movie *Rambo*.

the senator from Boeing: the late Washington State senator Henry "Scoop" Jackson, owing to the tremendous political clout held by Boeing, the Seattle region's largest employer.

Tailgunner Joe: Joe McCarthy, the Red-baiting senator from Wisconsin in the 1950s, who was finally stymied by attorney Joseph Welch's unforgettable line: "Have you no sense of decency, sir, at long last? Have you no sense of decency?"

the Teflon president: Ronald Reagan. Because nothing stuck to him, including negative criticism and, some say, original thoughts. Aka "the Great Communicator," "the Gipper."

the Tidal Basin Bombshell: Fanne Foxe, the stripper who was found cavorting in a fountain with Wilbur Mills, a conservative congressman from Arkansas. Aka "the Argentine Firecracker" (her original name was Annabel Batistella).

Tip: Thomas P. O'Neill, the large, savvy Massachusetts congressman who was Speaker of the House for many years and who coined one of the most memorable lines in politics: "All politics is local."

the Unabomber: not Ted Kaczynski but Dick Morris, a vaunted insider political consultant to everyone from Jesse Helms to Howard Metzenbaum, who came to national prominence as the man who moved Bill Clinton to the "sensible center." Ironically, Morris' controlling nature earned him no helping hand when he met his own Waterloo at the hands of call girl Sherry Rowlands in the Jefferson Hotel.

redundancy of human resources: too many friggin' employees.

reg-neg: softening government regulations to please a certain powerful constituent. See "Chicken Man" under Arkansas.

Republicrats: term bandied about in the '90s for the one-party state in D.C. and the minor differences that now exist between Republicans and Democrats.

revenue enhancement: a tax increase.

revenue shortfall: the need for more taxes.

RFK: where the Washington Redskins play.

Rose Garden strategy: holding a press conference in the White House Rose Garden during a presidential campaign to make the incumbent look "in charge" and "presidential."

Rubbergate: the House banking scandal of the early '90s, involving several House members and their families who used the now defunct "House Bank." The chief feature of the scandal was the amazing number of legislators writing bad checks.

sagebrush rebels: western congressmen who keep a close eye on public land use issues.

Sallie Mae: Student Loan Marketing Association, a government-sponsored corporation that owns or manages $37.4 billion in student loans.

shadow senator: the senator from the District of Columbia. So named because the office has no voting power.

special interests: the real constituents. The main contributors to political campaigns; e.g., the NRA, AMA, and AFL-CIO.

spin: turn unfavorable news or publicity into something favorable or less damaging. "Put a positive spin on it." In political circles, the person in charge is the "spin doctor."

spin doctor: a "hired gun" for politicians and business who gives a favorable "spin" to any news that affects the client. Used to deflect criticism or redefine negative news positively. At their worst, spin doctors craft language to fool the public into believing that bad acts are actually good.

stopgap measure: a legislative bill or policy that is a short-term fix to a long-term problem.

subsidies: corporate welfare. Aka "tax incentives."

there you go again: Ronald Reagan's disarming no-brainer used to charm Middle America in his presidential debate with Jimmy Carter.

Uncle Whiskers: the U.S. or its government (used by former secretary of state James "Jim" Baker).

the veep: the vice-president of the U.S. A salutary position.

Victims of Bill (V.O.B.): the columnist Paul Greenberg's term for long-term F.O.B.'s deemed no longer useful. Example: Harold Ickes.

the Wall: Maya Lin's evocative black granite Vietnam Veterans' War Memorial. It symbolizes the generational and political wall around that conflict that is still with us today.

war chest: a politician's campaign coffers.

web issue: an issue that brings together unlikely bedfellows, such as right-wing gun owners and liberal African Americans against the crime bill.

wedge issue: an issue that divides a political party (abortion for the Republicans, welfare for the Democrats).

welfare queens: Republican for "poor black women."

wet deposition: an EPA euphemism for acid rain.

wiggle room: the safety net politicians create around their public utterances, giving them enough leeway to alter their opinion. Also "waffle."

wonk: a public policy nerd. Especially one who enjoys debating the more arcane and complicated aspects of public policy. E.g., Bill Clinton, aka "Willie Wonka."

WOPs: Wrinkly Old Parasites. See "AARP."

Zoed: to be politically hung out and left for dead with no protection from the opposition. For Clinton's attorney general nominee Zoe Baird. Aka "Borked."

The Workplace

As a man of the road who has basically run his own businesses for the last 11 years, I have secretly yearned for the comfort, discipline, and camaraderie of the corporate world. Reporting to work at a normal hour. Getting a regular paycheck. Having a boss who tells me right from wrong. Year-end company parties with more in attendance than Mike, me, and our cat, Dolly Lama. Perks. Pats on the back. Sexual Harassment in the Workplace workshops. Insurance!

Periodically I try to get jobs in the regular work world. And invariably the interviewer tries to communicate in so many words that I am not suited to corporate life. That I'm already doing the dream. That they secretly envy me! So I've finally given up.

Strangely, the more I seek the comfort and regularity of my fantasy corporate life, the more corporate life begins to resemble the lean, mobile, and free-form model of work I've been pioneering for over a decade. It all comes full circle, and once again I ain't got a paycheck or an invite to the annual Christmas party. (So I'm throwing one instead.)

alpha-geek: the person in the office who knows the most about technology. You have a problem with your e-mail? Printer won't work? Call the "alpha-geek."

the annual Christmas party: the big reward for another year of puttin' out for the Man (or the Woman, as the case may be). It's when all the inmates get to dress up in suits and gowns, get completely sloshed, dance on the tables, throw up, then go home and sleep with each other and talk about it till next year's party. One day we'll all wake up from our late-20th-century trance and laugh at the silly rituals of the Corporate Era (believe me, it is an era).

arrow shooters: "the visionaries in an organization who generate the brilliant ideas and trace their far-reaching trajectories" (*Wired*).

bells and whistles: the exciting, innovative stuff that grabs people's attention but isn't the substance of a project.

How to Talk American

bennies: employee benefits, such as health insurance and retirement funds.

the big picture: the large strategic situation as distinct from the little details. Includes the surrounding circumstances.

blame-storming: brainstorming to determine who is to blame when a deadline is missed or a project fails.

burn a copy: make a photocopy.

change management: getting used to being fired. Or consultants who specialize in this very up-and-coming field.

circling the drain: medical slang for a patient near death who refuses to "give up the ghost." Used about projects that have no more life in them but refuse to die. "That *Hillary Clinton Real Estate Tips* CD-ROM has been circling the drain for years."

the circular file: a wastebasket.

clustering: phenomenon described by Steve Kurland, the owner of Shakespeare and Company (a bookstore), in the *New York Times* (June 13, 1996): "It's a strategy the superstores use. They call it 'clustering': open a store north and south of the smaller store, and then just squeeze them out."

copreneurs: codependent couples who don't feel it's enough to sleep and have a home life together but must be business partners too.

cross-functionals: people who perform multiple tasks (i.e., "wear many hats") in an understaffed office. In my experience, "cross-functionals" become dysfunctionals pretty quickly.

cut steel: build a mold for a cast product. "The psilocybin paperweight design was okayed. Let's cut steel."

desk jockey: a run-of-the-mill corporate drone with no real authority. An office worker.

dipping your pen in the company ink: having sexual relations with a co-worker. Aka "getting your meat and your bread at the same store."

Don Quixote: a prospective employee with an inflated idea of his skills and worth. Used by headhunters.

drop paper: a firm purchasing agreement. "We're not ready to drop paper on it yet, but we have several likely prospects."

dupe: a duplicate copy, especially of a letter or another text. "Make a dupe" means to make a copy.

EuroYank: Americans, in cahoots with select European partners, who are successfully infiltrating and ultimately taking over major European entertainment industries.

fish off the company pier: date a co-worker. A big no-no.

fix it in post: video production lingo that means "We [or somebody else] will deal with this in post-production." Sometimes used as an excuse to get out of a sticky situation, postponing the agony of confronting a difficult problem. "C'mon, Mark, let's catch the last of the Dodgers game." "But what about Nick's monologue?" "We'll fix it in post."

going postal: a euphemism for being totally stressed out. Aka "losing it." Comes from the large number of postal workers who have snapped and gone on shooting rampages.

golden coffin: the benefits package given to an executive's heirs on his or her death.

golden handcuffs: the sizable perks and benefits used to keep an executive locked into a job for a given period of time.

golden parachute: a generous severance package given to an executive forced into retirement. Aka "golden handshake."

It All Started with the Yuppie

IN THE BEGINNING WAS THE "YUPPIE" (YOUNG upwardly mobile professional), which spawned an acronym boom the likes of which this country has never seen. We now have the **biddies** (baby boomers in debt), **buppies** (black upwardly mobile professionals), **dimps** (dual income, money problems), **dinks** (dual income, no kids), **dopies** (disgruntled older persons), **droppies** (disillusioned, relatively ordinary professionals preferring independent employment situations), **flyers** (fun-loving youth en route to success), **frumpies** (former radical upwardly mobile persons), **grumpies** (grown-up mature professionals), **guppies** (gay upwardly mobile professionals), **maddies** (middle-age debtors), **maffies** (middle-age affluent folks), **mossies** (middle-age overstressed semiaffluent suburbanites), **muppies** (Mennonite urban professionals), **nebbies** (negative equity baby boomers), **rubbies** (rich urban bikers), **rumpies** (rural upwardly mobile professionals), **sasc** (surprisingly alert and spry centenarians), **skippies** (school kids with income and purchasing power), **woopies** (well-off older persons), **yobs** (young obnoxious bores), **yuffies** (young urban failures), and **yummies** (young upwardly mobile mommies).

That about it covers it, don't you think?

How to Be a Corporate Drone

HERE IS THE JARGON YOU NEED AS YOUR JOB AND your life get restructured, reengineered, reorganized, and redeployed in the fascinating and compassionate world of corporate America.

business decision: a decision everyone below top management will find rather unpleasant. "We've had to lay off 1,000 people. You have to understand, it was purely a business decision."

campus: the corporate grounds. Used by giant modern corporations to keep everyone feeling collegial and permanently adolescent, all ready to go "Rah Rah!" for the home team. Akin to the classic corporate oxymoron "the industrial park."

decision-making at the lowest level: decisions so completely trivial, we may as well let the little people make them.

developmental position: we don't actually want to come right out and say this, but you've been promoted! Aka an "appointment."

diversity: a clear and accurate record of the total number of African Americans, Hispanic Americans, Native Americans, and women currently on the payroll.

get a life: an existence outside work that doesn't center around friends from work. A frequent refrain of today's corporate drone: "I need to get a life." It's often temporarily achieved by some radical form of character building (like a mountain climbing expedition), marriage, or both.

made redundant: you've been laid off.

managing diversity: keeping the minority workforce numbers high and placated enough to avoid drawing the ire of civil rights organizations.

market breakthrough: the magic bullet. But nobody knows what it is.

openness and trust: a beautiful idea.

performance management: finding innovative ways to downsize the workforce without getting sued.

reengineering: reduce, rename, recycle—people, not paper.

reorganization: letting go of workers who didn't fit into the "reengineering" plans.

→

resource planning: figuring out how we can accomplish more and spend less with far fewer people.

strategic planning: the voluminous charts, graphs, and pretty documents that prove there's a "market breakthrough."

systems approach: authoritative-sounding term intended to convince workers there is a brilliant master plan behind management decisions.

teamwork: a noble term used in expensive management workshops.

How You Know . . . YOU'RE FIRED!

constructive dismissal: you're fired.

decruitment: lots of you are fired.

downsizing: your services are no longer required by this company.

excess to requirements: you're fired.

excessed: you're fired.

focused reduction: you're fired.

involuntary severance: you're fired.

productive cessation: everyone's fired! Aka "elimination of positions."

reducing duplication: you're fired.

redundant: guess what? You're fired!

refocusing of the company's skills sets: lots and lots of you are fired. Aka "chemistry adjustment," "skill-mix adjustment," "operations improvement," "proactive downsizing," "employee empowerment."

release of resources: lots and lots and lots of you are fired.

repositioning: you're fired.

restructuring: lots of you are fired.

rightsizing: we are warning you ahead of time, so at least you have a choice: quit now and save some of your dignity or be fired when we close your division.

transitioned: you're fired.

unassigned: please don't return.

voluntary severance: you're fired, but we want to make it seem like this is your own personal decision.

Advertising Sales

ADVERTISING SALES IS A SACRED CALLING. AND, IN my humble opinion, the highest form of selling. Ad salespeople are sleazy and smooth in all the right ways. Besides, the rush of adrenaline is higher than in other areas of selling. Perfect for speed freaks.

I consider ad sales my one true calling. I don't have the training to do anything else. I mean, what else are you supposed to do with a degree in Communication Studies—great for grasping Michel's Theory of Oligarchy but useless for nailing a job that requires a real skill. Fortunately, asking for money comes quite naturally to me. The astrologer Elizabeth Feldman says it's because I have Sagittarius in the 8th House. I say it's because I have the Irish gift of blarney.

ad sales animal: a natural salesperson. People who read all the self-help books, take all the Dale Carnegie courses, and practice, practice, practice can come pretty close to the success rate of a true "ad sales animal." But, in the end, the subtle differences are as big as those between a Rembrandt and a Rembrandt knockoff—as infinite as space itself. "Ad sales animals" are born, not made.

advertorial: a special section designed to look like regular editorial but is actually one big plug for a sponsor or an industry.

art: the advertisement. "When do you need art?" is the most frequently asked question of media buyers.

barter: getting an ad in exchange for a product or service. Often used by broke start-ups.

book: a magazine. In Frank Strazzulla's treasured words, "You gotta good book." In other words, you have superb editorial, which really helps in selling ads, though it's by no means a prerequisite.

church and state: editorial is "church," advertising is "state." Oh, how often they get blurred. See "advertorial."

close: they love you, they want to get serious, now you've got to pop the big question.

closer: a sales rep who brings home the bacon.

cover 2: the inside front cover of the magazine.

cover 3: the inside back cover.

→

cover 4: the back cover.

CPM: cost per thousand circulation.

double truck: a two-page ad.

float: a third- or half-page fractional. What I call a "flotation device" (useful in case of a magazine crash landing).

fractional: any ad that is smaller than a full page.

hole: ad space available at the last minute. Usually sold at a "remnant" price. "Brad, gotta a hole to fill. Cover 3. Want it?"

lead: a potential ad buyer. Ad reps never talk of "prospects," though lowlier salespeople do.

lead list: a list of potential buyers. Usually kept in a database. The sacred treasure of any ad rep, given out on a quid pro quo basis to other reps or to lovers who are reps.

media buyers: the best-looking, most fun-loving, most exceptional people in the ad business, who get zero respect from their peers.

numbers: the circulation of the magazine. Also, other demographic information (household income, occupation, age, number of Asian transvestite readers in Columbus, Ohio).

our budget's been spent: the first lie a media buyer is trained to tell an ad rep. Lesson 1 in ad sales: there's always money in the budget . . . for the right "book" or the right "offer."

personality sell: selling based not on numbers or market research but on the sheer chutzpah of the publishers.

the plan: the media buying schedule for the year. When dealing with agencies, you are always trying to get into "the plan." Aka "the schedule." Caveat: convincing the agency you belong on "the schedule" is only the first hurdle. The "client" can then "drop" you (and you're not there to plead your case).

Reatha: the legendary Reatha Braxton, goddess of media buying at Chiat Day/TBWA. If you want Absolut vodka in your mag (and who doesn't), you have to go through her.

remnant: significantly discounted ad space.

send me your kit and we'll call you if we're interested: forget it.

Simmons: Simmons Market Research, a company that polls readers to determine what soap they use (among other vitally important consumer questions). Used by agencies in deciding whether to "go into" your "book."

→

skew: direction. "Our current ads skew to a younger, more drug-addicted audience than your book reaches." In other words, don't bother us ever again.

space: real estate in a magazine. Ad rep: "I've got a great space right near TOC."

talk to our agency: the line you will usually hear when trying to talk directly with "the client."

TOC: the table of contents, a premium ad position.

what can you do for us?: a 1990s media buyer's favorite question to get a rep to display a wealth of people-pleasing skills. In other words, we don't need to "go into" your sketchy, infrequent magazine, but we'll consider it if you throw in some goodies (e.g., promotional tie-ins, parties, T-shirts, a Polaroid snapshot with Annie Sprinkle). The party line is that media buyers live for goodies.

what's your circ?: how many people read this thing?

when do you have to know?: the second most frequently asked question of media buyers.

who's your target audience?: who reads this? In other words, do they smoke or drink?

---

headhunters: people who hire top talent away from a competitor. Or, in a more benign sense, an employment agency that links qualified professionals with the right jobs.

idea hamster: a person who is a virtual idea factory. "The man's a total idea hamster. Give him a concept and he'll turn it over 'til it becomes something great."

in the can: the project is complete. Originally a film industry term.

ink a deal: sign a contract.

interrupt-driven: a worker who moves reactively through the day, responding to a series of interruptions rather than defined goals.

Kevorking (for Dr. Jack Kevorkian, aka "Dr. Death"): killing something. "Look, Kevork that project and let's go out for a tofu burger."

kill your babies: used in any production situation in which your favorite pieces of work have to be deleted. "You've run out of disk space for this sales pitch, Monk. Time to kill some of your babies in the sound files."

life support: a business or product fighting for its life in the marketplace. "They're still in business, but definitely on full life support."

McJobs: the endless stream of low-pay, low-brain, no-future jobs available to overeducated slacker youth. First noted by Douglas Coupland in *Generation X*. Like most things about the defiantly undefinable twentysomething set, more likely to be used by boomer media writing about slackers.

the mommy track: women who pursue motherhood and a career at the same time.

mouse milking: expending a large effort for a disproportional small return.

nonemployees: the real "microserfs." Outside contractors who toil long hours on behalf of Bill's Microsoft dream without benefits, insurance, or even the right to attend "real employee" parties and classes, not to mention shopping at the company store.

open-collar worker: telecommuters or cottage industry types who can wear whatever they please.

out of the box: innovative thinking.

outsourcing: hiring cheaper people from outside the company. Otherwise known as freelancing. A great way to get out of paying "bennies."

permahold: purposely putting callers on indefinite hold so they will hang up. Receptionist's revenge.

plug-and-play: a new employee who doesn't require any training.

rainmaker: a salesman or executive who brings in lots of new business for the company.

road builders: the people in an organization who come in behind the "arrow shooters" and pave the way for profitable applications.

road warriors: mobile employees.

sandwich generation: women between 40 and 50 who are required to care for both their children and their parents. When working, they are said to be on the "granny track."

scenery: a board of directors chosen for their unblemished reputations in order to make a shaky company look good.

steel-collar worker: a robot.

telephone number salary: a seven-digit salary (or project budget).

Texas disease: massive savings-and-loan failures.

velvet: quick, painless profit.

voice jail system: a voice mail system with so many submenus you get lost and have to hang up and call back.

whistle blowers: employees who expose corruption and/or misdeeds inside the company. And who are now looking for new work.

win-win: a business and spiritual philosophy pioneered by Tom Crum back in the mid-'80s, now in common usage. Some regard it as a total oxymoron; how can there be two winners in a capitalist system? Others see it as honest-to-God enlightenment.

win-win-win: a policy where business, consumers, *and* the environment all come out ahead. Example: the rapidly growing "health food" industry.

your call is important to us: roughly, you are about to experience a long and unnecessary wait on the phone. Used by companies who really don't give a damn about customer service or there would be someone to answer your call. Another disingenuous piece of rhetoric to watch for: "Due to the high-volume response to our recent sales promotion, you may experience some delay." You got that right. Folks, heed the advice of Howard Beale and go to your window right now and shout, "I'm mad as hell and I'm not going to be treated like a 2-year-old brain fart anymore!" Good, that'll do it. "Please hold, a customer service rep will be right with you."

zero out: not paying taxes legally. You found all the loopholes. The secret to success in corporate America.

Advertising

How many advertising execs does it take to change a light bulb? Interesting question. What do you think?

I T'S A CLICHÉ, BUT WHEN I WATCH TV, I WATCH FOR the ads. This completely perplexes the average boob-tuber. But the fact is, the quality of the best ads far exceeds that of the programming. This has to do with the ridiculous extremes ad agencies go to "to get it right"—the long hours and endless rethinks, retakes, redrafts, all to please themselves and, in the end, the client. Here's a snapshot of a maligned and neglected industry that is one of the cornerstones of the American cultural superiority complex.

account: the client. "Margeottes just landed the Stoli account."

account side: the part of the agency that deals directly with the client, selling them, getting feedback, and basically ass-kissing all the way. High liquor tolerance is an absolute prerequisite. Completely separate from "creative."

acknowledgment: an ad on public broadcasting.

ad police: groups or individuals who judge political advertising for truth and fairness.

addy: when a person or a campaign idea just reeks of advertising culture. Ironically, "Addy" with a capital *A* is the name of a leading industry award (like the Oscar).

the agency: one's particular agency. Most agencies are like a scene from *Microserfs*—all work, with bouts of extreme play, and very incestuous. Each has its own special culture, with revered deities, slang, and expected behaviors. "There's an agency party tonight." Fraternity life meets *Friends*.

agency review: when a client decides to formally examine its relationship with an agency. Afterward, "the account" is sometimes put up for bid to other agencies, including the present one, which can "win" it back. Clients use reviews to keep agencies on their toes.

AOR: the Agency of Record.

astroturfing: an ad technique that puts a disarming little-guy face on corporate avarice, perfidy, and guile. Example: the insurance industry's "Harry and Louise" ads dissing Clinton's health plan.

BBDO: a major ad agency whose name was homogenized after repeated complaints that its original name, Batten, Barton, Durstine and Osborne, sounded like a trunk falling down a flight of stairs.

the Big Idea: the zinger idea underpinning an ad campaign. Examples: "It Just Keeps Going and Going" (the Energizer bunny) or "Absolutely Positively Overnight" (FedEx). From the David Oglivy dictum "Unless your campaign contains a Big Idea, it will pass like a ship in the night."

the book: one's compilation of "work" (i.e., past creative). "Creatives" will often talk about a potential employee's having a "good book" or a "weak book." Said determination comes down to: (a) the quality of the creative, (b) the prestige of the account, (c) the prestige of the agency, and (d) whether "the book" is presented in one of those big black portfolios.

boutique: a small agency, usually noted for its creative.

brief: a pithy statement of the goal of a given campaign that art directors use as a foundation for new creative.

the client: the business paying for all this hoopla. "I'm sorry you're going to commit suicide, but I can't talk, I have a meeting with the client in an hour." Way before friends, lovers, and family, in the ad world there is one ass you must kiss before all others, and that is the client's.

the creative: the actual advertisement.

creative team: two or more people assigned to a specific account or campaign. At the very least, an art director and a copywriter.

creatives: the people who dream up and design the ads. Visual creatives dream of making films. Copy creatives dream of writing the Great American Novel. And all "creatives" talk incessantly about getting "great work" into their "book." In addition, there is often a Maginot Line between "the creatives" and "the account people." In general, "the account people" drool over "the creatives," and "the creatives" are secretly dismissive of "the account people."

gang bang: several creative teams pitted against one another. Whoever has the best idea gets to work on "the creative." Progressive agencies eschew the "gang bang" because it creates too much friction. Also used in television to signify a "group writing session."

go out for a drink: as in, "Let's go out for a drink later." Nowhere is this cliché used more than in the ad business. Drinking heavily is a sine qua non to being in the game. In this way, American ad people come the closest to emulating the widespread Japanese business practice of getting completely shitfaced on a regular basis. It's as if the "12 Steps," "human potential," and "holistic health" movements passed this group by. Higher consciousness? Yeah, let's use that in the next Infiniti campaign. Mitigating factor: performing random acts of "Bushashita" will not cost you your job.

going outside: when a client uses a non-ad agency to produce the creative. Example: Coca-Cola's choice of Creative Artists (a talent agency) as its "worldwide media and communications consultant."

handholding: reassuring a nervous client that all the money he's spent on the dancing bear campaign is going to produce results.

M.O.S.: the Man on the Street. Getting a quote from an "M.O.S." lends authenticity to a product.

media: the department in charge of buying ad space for the client. Often relegated to a separate floor or building, completely removed from the creative process. The only consolation is that media people regularly receive mountains of useless knickknacks from visiting reps and never have to worry about paying for lunch.

overpitching: spending too much of an agency's time and resources seeking new business with little to show in return.

pitch: sell. In the ad world, you "pitch new business" (try to bring in a new client). Aka "bid" ("MCI just sent the business out for bid"). Woe to any agency whose main clients learn of the enormous amount of creative time and resources spent (some say wasted) "pitching" new business.

presentation: used by creatives in showing off new creative to either a superior (creative director) or the client. "I cannot go skiing this weekend, I have a major presentation on Monday."

Q: a celebrity's recognizability quotient, used to gauge the usefulness of the person "touting" a product. Helps a company find those magical celebrities so ridiculously popular with the public that their endorsement alone will boost sales of a product, despite the client's lousy environmental, labor, and customer service record.

resign: when an agency fires a client. "We resigned the account. They made airline food for people who are going nowhere."

review: when a client puts its "account" up for bid from other agencies. This is done when a client is dissatisfied with the current agency or wants to keep it on the ball. "Did you hear? Sprint just put the entire account up for review."

roadblock: the complete saturation of the airwaves with ads for the same product running at the same time on all the networks, to guarantee viewer awareness of the product. Aka "blitz."

shoot: a photo session for an ad campaign. "I'm off on a shoot, I'll get back to you next week." "Shoots" are no trifling affair, often costing more than $20,000 a day for the photographer, assistants, and the endless number of personnel from the client and the agency directly responsible for getting "the right shot."

shop: a small ad agency. Also a generic term for an agency of any size.

teaser: a brief, often provocative, glimpse of a product in order to pique people's interest.

trash cash: ads that look like currency. Handed out on urban street corners.

unbundle: when very large clients spread out various aspects of the business among several agencies. Example: Coca-Cola.

waste circulation: when your ad is not hitting its target audience.

work: in a precise sense, the actual "creative." Often refers to the efforts of the agency as a whole. "We were working incredibly long hours, doing great work—and there was nothing to show for it."

Conclusion

"My time is up. Thank you for yours."
—Former Omaha newscaster Meryl Workoven

IT IS SAID THAT AMERICANS SAY GOOD-BYE WITHOUT
ever leaving and that the British leave without ever saying
good-bye. As an American with real "issues" around "closure," I
feel compelled to leave you with an assortment of expressions that
say, well, good-bye. Of course, as an eternally optimistic, forward-
thinking, option-oriented midwestern American, I invite you to
understand that while I am *saying* good-bye, I am not really leaving. I hope to continue providing you with ever more fantastic
looks at our native tongues. And I ask you to help me in this quest
by writing to Jim Crotty, *Monk Magazine*, 175 Fifth Avenue, Suite
2322, New York, New York 10010. Or by calling 212-465-3231.
E-mail: monkmag@aol.com.

Okay, that's it. Nineteen ways we say "sayonara":

"Now, get out of here, and I mean it." "There you have it." Peace out. Adios, amigo. See ya! I'm Elvis. Aloha. Hasta la vista. Later, dude. Or, as we say in the Great Plains of Nebraska, Buh-bye. Ciao, baby. Stay black. So long. Happy trails. Ta-ta. I'm history. I'll give you a call. Awright den. Let's blow. Let's head 'em up and move 'em out. Let's head 'em up and move 'em out.